Perspectives on Justice
An Introduction
Second Edition

Doris Marie Provine
Reshawna Chapple
Kishonna Gray
Ophir Sefiha
Michael F. Walker

Kendall Hunt
publishing company

Kendall Hunt
publishing company

www.kendallhunt.com
Send all inquiries to:
4050 Westmark Drive
Dubuque, IA 52004-1840

Printed in the United States of America
10 9 8 7 6 5 4 3 2 1

CONTENTS

FIRST THINGS: GETTING ORIENTED

The purpose of this text is to introduce students to justice as a field of study and a matter of importance in every person's life. Justice is an elusive idea, hard to define and even harder to put into practice. Justice provides a rallying point for demanding change, but also a bulwark for defenders of the status quo. Debates about what justice entails have occurred throughout the history of civilization and can be found at every level—from families to international organizations. People explore justice issues on Web pages and in social media, clubs and organizations, political parties, government documents, campaign speeches, and, we hope, in your college or university classrooms.

We have designed these readings to introduce you to fundamental concepts of justice, such as equality of opportunity, fairness, and human rights, and to encourage critical thinking and debate about how to implement these ideals. By studying these readings and the commentary and questions that surround them, you will become familiar with some classic and contemporary concepts of justice as they exist in theory and in action. You will learn how to analyze arguments about justice and injustice in a social context. You will recognize implicit justice issues as well as those that are articulated by advocates. At Arizona State University, where this book was created, the faculty and students in Justice & Social Inquiry are committed to just this kind of effort. Some of the readings and commentary in this book have been written by our faculty and graduate students. And the idea for the overall layout of the book comes from the organization of our academic unit around themes of justice in society.

Learning about justice involves thinking about the proper roles of government and private power and being aware of informal, as well as formal, means of social control. It is important to consider why some issues, but not others, are deemed so important that they deserve a major commitment of public resources. Should the United States be engaged in a massive "war" on drugs, for example? Should military spending be nearly $1 trillion per year? It is also important for students of justice to be sensitive to the ways in which race, class, gender, disability, and other life-affecting factors create differences in perspective. Studying justice as a social phenomenon, fully embedded in social context but full of timeless ideas about the significance of human life, will help you understand why societies always fall short in their promises to provide justice for all. We hope that, as the course proceeds, you will resolve to do something about this shortfall.

The chapters in this book have been organized, for convenience, around five broad areas that raise justice concerns. After this introductory chapter, we begin with the individual level, considering readings and commentary on how we know who we are and how justice is implicated in identity and community (Chapter 1: Social Identities and Communities). This chapter sets the stage for thinking about communication at the mass level and its implications, the major focus of Chapter 2: Media, Technology, and Culture. From there we turn to the capacity of laws and policies to maintain the status quo or to provoke positive or negative changes (Chapter 3: Law, Policy, and Social Change). We continue this discussion of law and change on a broader scale in Chapter 4: Human Rights, Migration, and Citizenship. This chapter raises fundamental questions about what we owe to each other as human beings. The final chapter, Globalization, Sustainability, and Economic Justice (Chapter 5), focuses on economic and environmental justice concerns at an international level. A major issue in this chapter is the existence of so much poverty in the midst of great wealth.

Reading Justice in This Course

This book features important documents – articles, speeches, and excerpts from longer works. They should be read carefully and critically. You will find introductory material at the beginning of each chapter and at the beginning of each section. These prefatory paragraphs are designed to help you digest the documents that follow. At the end of each section are questions for class discussion. Along the way you will find key terms defined and footnotes that take you to additional sources.

Our goal is to help you develop a repertoire of key concepts associated with economic and social justice. We also hope that you will understand some of the key processes designed to produce justice. A third objective is to increase critical thinking skills that can help you apply ideas about justice to particular situations. We encourage you to practice these critical thinking skills in class discussion, display these skills in papers and exams in this course, and rely on them in daily living.

To illustrate the kinds of questions you should be asking in reading the documents in this volume, we offer an initial example drawn from a dramatic law enforcement event: a raid by nearly 900 Immigration and Customs Enforcement (ICE) agents of the Agriprocessors kosher meat-packing plant in Postville, Iowa. We begin with the observations of Dr. Erik

Camayd-Freixas, a professor of Spanish at Florida International University, but more relevantly for this reading, a certified Spanish interpreter. He broke the usual code of confidentiality among legal interpreters to comment on the May 12, 2008, immigration raid.

The raid, which rounded up nearly 400 mostly Guatemalan workers, led to criminal charges of aggravated identity theft for 270 of them. The defendants were hoping instead for a quick deportation so that they could begin looking for jobs again. But the federal government, perhaps to discourage repeated illegal entry into the country, opted for criminal charges instead. Hearings for all 270 defendants occurred within four days. The federal district court brought in the defendants in batches of ten, following a script provided by federal immigration authorities. All of the defendants pled guilty, despite serious questions about the appropriateness of the charges. Why? Because they did not have the resources to challenge the charges or the understanding of American law and the English language to fully evaluate their options. The appropriateness of deploying a charge of aggravated identity theft in these circumstances was later sharply criticized by a unanimous United States Supreme Court, which rejected the approach the government took in charging "knowing" theft. But by that time, the workers had served most of their six-month prison terms, and Postville had lost over half of its population.

What follows is an abbreviated version of the report Dr. Camayd-Freixas made public in the wake of this case. After reading his on-the-spot analysis, you will find five brief analyses. Each one represents a perspective on justice that will be developed in a later chapter of this book. Like many other real-world examples, the Postville raid raises a number of justice issues, each worthy of serious consideration. Seeing these perspectives raised in brief in the context of a single case will, we hope, make it easier to see the links in the chapters ahead. By noting the questions raised in these pieces and thinking about your own questions, you will be better prepared for the chapters that follow.

INTERPRETING AFTER THE LARGEST ICE RAID IN U.S. HISTORY: A PERSONAL ACCOUNT
BY ERIK CAMAYD-FREIXAS

On Monday, May 12, 2008, at 10:00 a.m., in an operation involving some 900 agents, Immigration and Customs Enforcement (ICE) executed a raid of Agriprocessors Inc., the nation's largest kosher slaughterhouse and meat packing plant located in the town of Postville, Iowa. The raid—officials boasted—was "the largest single-site operation of its kind in American history." . . . I arrived late that Monday night and missed the 8 p.m. interpreters briefing. I was instructed by phone to meet at 7 a.m. in the hotel lobby and carpool to the National Cattle

"Interpreting after the Largest ICE Raid in US History: A Personal Account" by Erik Camayd-Freixas, June 13, 2008. Palgrave Macmillan.

Congress (NCC) where we would begin our work. We arrived at the heavily guarded compound, went through security, and gathered inside the retro "Electric Park Ballroom" where a makeshift court had been set up. . . . The NCC is a 60-acre cattle fairground that had been transformed into a sort of concentration camp or detention center. Fenced in behind the ballroom/courtroom were 23 trailers from federal authorities, including two set up as sentencing courts; various Homeland Security buses and an "incident response" truck; scores of ICE agents and U.S. Marshals; and in the background two large buildings: a pavilion where agents and prosecutors had established a command center; and a gymnasium filled with tight rows of cots where some 300 male detainees were kept, the women being housed in county jails. . . .

Then began the saddest procession I have ever witnessed, which the public would never see, because cameras were not allowed past the perimeter of the compound (only a few journalists came to court the following days, notepad in hand). Driven single-file in groups of 10, shackled at the wrists, waist and ankles, chains dragging as they shuffled through, the slaughterhouse workers were brought in for arraignment, sat and listened through headsets to the interpreted initial appearance, before marching out again to be bused to different county jails, only to make room for the next row of 10. They appeared to be uniformly no more than 5 ft. tall, mostly illiterate Guatemalan peasants with Mayan last names, some being relatives (various Tajtaj, Xicay, Sajché, Sologüí . . .), some in tears; others with faces of worry, fear, and embarrassment. They all spoke Spanish, a few rather laboriously. It dawned on me that, aside from their Guatemalan or Mexican nationality, which was imposed on their people after Independence, they too were Native Americans, in shackles. They stood out in stark racial contrast with the rest of us as they started their slow penguin march across the makeshift court. "Sad spectacle" I heard a colleague say, reading my mind. They had all waived their right to be indicted by a grand jury and accepted instead an *information* or simple charging document by the U.S. Attorney, hoping to be quickly deported since they had families to support back home. But it was not to be. They were criminally charged with "aggravated identity theft" and "Social Security fraud" —charges they did not understand . . . and, frankly, neither could I. . . .

This was the immediate collateral damage. Postville, Iowa (pop. 2,273), where nearly half the people worked at Agriprocessors, had lost 1/3 of its population by Tuesday morning. Businesses were empty, amid looming concerns that if the plant closed it would become a ghost town. Beside those arrested, many had fled the town in fear. Several families had taken refuge at St. Bridget's Catholic Church, terrified, sleeping on pews and refusing to leave for days. Volunteers from the community served food and organized activities for the children. At the local high school, only three of the 15 Latino students came back on Tuesday, while at the elementary and middle school, 120 of the 363 children were absent. In the following days the principal went around town on the school bus and gathered 70 students after convincing the parents to let them come back to school; 50 remained unaccounted for. Some American parents complained that their children were traumatized by the sudden disappearance of so many of their school friends. The principal reported the same reaction in the classrooms, saying that for the children it was as if ten of their classmates had suddenly died. Counselors were brought in. American children were having nightmares that their parents too were being taken away. The superintendant said the school district's future was unclear: "This literally blew our town away." In some cases both parents were picked up and small children were left behind for up to 72 hours. Typically, the mother would be released "on humanitarian grounds" with an ankle GPS monitor, pending prosecution and deportation, while the husband took first turn in serving his prison sentence. Meanwhile the mother would have no income and could not work to provide for her children. Some of the children were born in the U.S. and are American citizens. Sometimes one parent was a deportable alien while the other was not. "Hundreds of families were torn apart by this raid," said a Catholic nun. "The humanitarian impact of this raid is obvious to anyone in Postville. The economic impact will soon be evident."

But this was only the surface damage. Alongside the many courageous actions and expressions of humanitarian concern in the true American spirit, the news blogs were filled with snide remarks of racial prejudice and bigotry, poorly disguised beneath an empty rhetoric of misguided patriotism, not to mention the insults to anyone who publicly showed compassion, safely hurled from behind a cowardly online nickname. One could feel the moral fabric of society coming apart beneath it all . . .

The interpreters were divided into two shifts, 8 a.m. to 3 p.m. and 3 p.m. to 10 p.m. I chose the latter. Through the day, the procession continued, ten by ten, hour after hour, the same charges, the same recitation from the magistrates, the same faces, chains and shackles on the defendants. There was little to remind us that they were actually 306 individuals, except that occasionally, as though to break the monotony, one would dare to speak for the others and beg to be deported quickly so that they could feed their families back home. . . . Thus far the work had oddly resembled a judicial assembly line where the meat packers were mass processed. But things were about to get a lot more personal as we prepared to interpret for individual attorney-client conferences . . . Each of the 18 court appointed attorneys represented 17 defendants on average. By now, the clients had been sent to several state and county prisons throughout eastern Iowa, so we had to interview them in jail. . . . The purpose was for the attorney to explain the uniform Plea Agreement that the government was offering. The explanation, which we repeated over and over to each client, went like this. There are three possibilities. If you plead guilty to the charge of "knowingly using a false Social Security number," the government will withdraw the heavier charge of "aggravated identity theft," and you will serve 5 months in jail, be deported without a hearing, and placed on supervised release for 3 years. If you plead not guilty, you could wait in jail 6 to 8 months for a trial (without right of bail since you are on an immigration detainer). Even if you win at trial, you will still be deported, and could end up waiting longer in jail than if you just pled guilty. You would also risk losing at trial and receiving a 2-year minimum sentence, before being deported. Some clients understood their "options" better than others.

That first interview, though, took three hours. The client, a Guatemalan peasant afraid for his family, spent most of that time weeping at our table, in a corner of the crowded jailhouse visiting room. How did he come here from Guatemala? *I walked.* What? *I walked for a month and ten days until I crossed the river.* We understood immediately how desperate his family's situation was. He crossed alone, met other immigrants, and hitched a truck ride to Dallas, then Postville, where he heard there was sure work. He slept in an apartment hallway with other immigrants until employed. He had scarcely been working a couple of months when he was arrested. Maybe he was lucky: another man who began that Monday had only been working for 20 minutes. "I just wanted to work a year or two, save, and then go back to my family, but it was not to be." His case and that of a million others could simply be solved by a temporary work permit as part of our much overdue immigration reform. . . . This man, like many others, was in fact not guilty. "Knowingly" and "intent" are necessary elements of the charges, but most of the clients we interviewed did not even know what a Social Security number was or what purpose it served. This worker simply had the papers filled out for him at the plant, since he could not read or write Spanish, let alone English. But the lawyer still had to advise him that pleading guilty was in his best interest. He was unable to make a decision. "You all do and undo," he said. "So you can do whatever you want with me." To him we were part of the system keeping him from being deported back to his country, where his children, wife, mother, and sister depended on him. He was their sole support and did not know how they were going to make it with him in jail for 5 months. None of the "options" really mattered to him. Caught between despair and hopelessness, he just wept. He had failed his family, and was devastated . . . We will never know how many of the 290 Guatemalans had legitimate asylum claims for fear of persecution, back in a country stigmatized by the worst human rights situation in the hemisphere, a by-product of the U.S.-backed Contra wars in Central America under the old domino theory of the 1980s. For three decades, anti-insurgent government death squads have ravaged the countryside, killing tens of thousands and displacing almost two million peasants. Even as we proceeded with the hearings during those two weeks in May, news coming out of Guatemala reported farm workers being assassinated for complaining publicly about their working conditions. Not only have we ignored the many root causes of illegal immigration, we also will never know which of these deportations will turn out to be a death sentence, or how many of these displaced workers are last survivors with no family or village to return to.

There were 17 cases for each attorney, and the Plea offer was only good for 7 days. . . . In addition, the prosecutors would not accept any changes to the Plea Agreement . . . Presumably if you gave different terms to one individual, the others will want the same. . . . At this point, it is worth remembering also that even real criminals have an 8th Amendment right to reasonable bail, but not illegal workers, because their immigration detainer makes bail a moot issue. We had already circumvented habeas corpus by doubling the court's business hours. What about the 6th Amendment right to a "speedy trial"? In many states "speedy" means 90 days, but in federal law it is vaguely defined, potentially exceeding the recommended sentence, given the backlog of *real* cases. This served as another loophole to force a guilty plea. Many of these workers were sole earners begging to be deported, desperate to feed their families, for whom every day counted. "If you want to see your children or don't want your family to starve, sign here"—that is what their deal amounted to. Their Plea Agreement was coerced. . . .

It works like this. By handing down the inflated charge of "aggravated identity theft," which carries a mandatory minimum sentence of 2 years in prison, the government forced the defendants into pleading guilty to the lesser charge and accepting 5 months in jail. Clearly, without the inflated charge, the government had no bargaining leverage, because the lesser charge by itself, using a false Social Security number, carries only a discretionary sentence of 0–6 months. The judges would be free to impose sentence within those guidelines, depending on the circumstances of each case and any prior record. Virtually all the defendants would have received only probation and been immediately deported. In fact, the government's offer at the higher end of the guidelines (one month shy of the maximum sentence) was indeed no bargain. What is worse, the inflated charge, via the binding 11(C)(1)(c) Plea Agreement, reduced the judges to mere bureaucrats, pronouncing the same litany over and over for the record in order to legalize the proceedings, but having absolutely no discretion or decision-making power. . . .

Created by Congress in an Act of 1998, the new federal offense of identity theft, as described by the DOJ (http://www.usdoj.gov/criminal/fraud/websites/idtheft.html), bears no relation to the Postville cases. It specifically states: "knowingly uses a means of identification of another person with *the intent to commit any unlawful activity or felony*" [18 USC §1028(a)]. The offense clearly refers to harmful, felonious acts, such as obtaining credit under another person's identity. Obtaining work, however, is not an "unlawful activity." No way would a grand jury find probable cause of identity theft here. But with the promise of faster deportation, their ignorance of the legal system, and the limited opportunity to consult with counsel before arraignment, all the workers, without exception, were led to waive their 5th Amendment right to grand jury indictment on felony charges. Waiting for a grand jury meant months in jail on an immigration detainer, without the possibility of bail. So the attorneys could not recommend it as a defense strategy.

Once the inflated charge was handed down, all the pieces fell into place like a row of dominoes. Even the court was banking on it when it agreed to participate, because if a good number of defendants asked for a grand jury or trial, the system would be overwhelmed. In short, "fast-tracking" had worked like a dream. . . No doubt, ICE fulfills an extremely important and noble duty. The question is why tarnish its stellar reputation by targeting harmless illegal workers. The answer is economics and politics. After 9/11 we had to create a massive force with readiness "to prevent, prepare for and respond to a wide range of catastrophic incidents, including terrorist attacks, natural disasters, pandemics and other such significant events that require large-scale government and law enforcement response" (23). The problem is that disasters, criminality, and terrorism do not provide enough daily business to maintain the readiness and muscle tone of this expensive force. . . . Yet, as of October 1, 2007, the "case backlog consisted of 594,756 ICE fugitive aliens" (5). So again, why focus on illegal workers who pose no threat? Elementary: they are easy pickings. True criminal and fugitive aliens have to be picked up one at a time, whereas raiding a slaughterhouse is like hitting a small jackpot: it beefs up the numbers. . . . Meanwhile, the underlying charge of "knowingly possessing or using false employment documents *with intent to deceive*" places the blame on the workers and holds corporate individuals harmless. . . .

This massive buildup for the New Era is the outward manifestation of an internal shift in the operational imperatives of the Long War, away from the "war on terror" (which has yielded lean statistics) and onto another front where we can claim success: the escalating undeclared war on illegal immigration. . . . According to its new paradigm, the agency fancies that it can conflate the diverse aspects of its operations and pretend that immigration enforcement is really part and parcel of the "war on terror." This way, statistics in the former translate as evidence of success in the latter. Thus, the Postville charges—document fraud and identity theft—treat every illegal alien as a potential terrorist, and with the same rigor. At sentencing, as I interpreted, there was one condition of probation that was entirely new to me: "You shall not be in possession of an explosive artifact." The Guatemalan peasants in shackles looked at each other, perplexed. . . .

A line was crossed at Postville. The day after in Des Moines, there was a citizens' protest featured in the evening news. With quiet anguish, a mature all-American woman, a mother, said something striking, as only the plain truth can be. "This is not humane," she said. "There has to be a better way."

The Postville Raid and the Challenges of Justice

The remainder of this chapter considers the Postville, Iowa, raid from five different perspectives, reflected in the five chapters that follow. Each of these brief sections gives you a taste of what is to come, and offers a chance to compare what you can expect to get from one vantage point when compared to another. Consider particularly the questions raised in each section.

Social Identities and Communities in Postville

Let's put this raid into the context of its time and place. How do people understand each other in a situation like this where foreign workers are at center stage in a small place isolated from major cities? In order to truly comprehend the Postville, Iowa, raid, one must consider how culture and identity are understood in Postville, and why these meanings are contested. What comes to mind when you think about a midwestern town like Postville? Maybe a small town, mostly white, where the main source of income is a local factory or Wal-Mart? Postville was not quite like that—it was a thriving economic community and a site of much cultural and ethnic diversity. Postville's diversity is an emerging trend in the United States and a real change from the earlier homogenous character[1] of many rural towns. All over the United States, immigrants from around the world are arriving in search of work and opportunity.

Aside from the workers of Mexican and Guatemalan descent, Postville contained a rather large population of Hasidic Jews who came in 1987 after purchasing an abandoned factory on the outskirts of town. They turned the old factory there into a kosher slaughterhouse and went into business. The arrival of these newcomers was a big change

---

[1]Douglas S. Massey (ed.), *New Faces in New Places: The Changing Geography of American Immigration.* NY: Sage, 2008.

for Postville, which had historically been predominantly German and Norwegian and of Lutheran faith.[2] The Jews were not welcomed in the community, but the factory kept the local economy afloat.[3] Old-time residents had to accept that the situation had changed and that the Jews were a powerful part of their community. This altered the political, religious, and ethnic climate of the town.

From the beginning, the Agriprocessors meat-packing plant was the site of controversy. The state of Iowa fined the company for occupational health and safety violations in 2005. In 2007, employees filed a class-action lawsuit against Agriprocessors, claiming that the company had failed to pay promised wages. In 2006, the federal Environmental Protection Agency sued the company for water pollution; in 2007, the Department of Agriculture investigated Agriprocessors for charges of animal cruelty and later issued a citation for elevated levels of salmonella in the company's poultry products.[4] The 2008 raid by the Department of Homeland Security, in other words, was the most recent in a long series of actions against the company's Postville plant.

This raid accomplished what some Postville residents thought they wanted—a return to a homogenous population. But this came at an almost unfathomable cost. Postville lost half of its population when its Hispanic workers left. Half of the students in the local schools were instantly gone. The local economy was devastated by the departure of so many people and by the closing of the Agriprocessors plant. Local churches and community groups sympathetic to the families torn apart by the raids have strained to provide support, spending up to $80,000 dollars a month to provide shelter, food, and other services. Meanwhile, Postville has become a name associated with harsh enforcement that yielded few benefits to anyone.

The foreign workers were not the only ones arrested in the wake of this raid. Corporate actors were also held accountable. Agriprocessor manager, Sholom Rubashkin, was arrested and charged with 89 counts of fraud. Many members of the Jewish community have been concerned that he is being treated harshly and possibly scapegoated as a religious minority. For the workers, the criminal sentences were imposed immediately, and then, after five months and a successful appeal, they were deported. So for everyone concerned, the raid was a life-changing event with implications that are far reaching and continue today.

How did the rhetoric of efficient, effective enforcement look in the context of a single local community? How can all of the consequences of an enforcement action, not just the ones officials might choose to think about, be factored into the decisions officials make? And why was being a foreign worker without legal authorization considered so important that it merited a major police action and criminal prosecution? Some observers note that we achieve our social identities—as outsiders, insiders, members of

------

[2]S. G. Bloom, Postville: A Clash of Cultures in Heartland America. New York: Harcourt, 2000.

[3]Ibid.

[4]P. R. Moyers, "Butchering Statutes: The Postville Raids and the Misinterpretation of Federal Criminal Law." 32 U. Seattle L. Rev. 651, 673–74 (2009).

trusted groups, or mistrusted groups—through the actions of others. We do not simply choose our identities; they are to a significant extent chosen for us. One's identity as a foreigner is certainly chosen by others, in this case, the legal system and the officials who administer it. In Postville, where some people knew these workers as parents, customers, neighbors, and friends, their legal status may have faded in significance. Every social category that we impose on each other, including perhaps "foreigner," should be up for critical scrutiny.

Media, Technology, and Culture in This Conflict

We often forget that the news does not come to us unfiltered. It arrives via our mass media system, which shapes and structures what we know about the world. As will be discussed in more detail later in this book, the mass media in the United States are mostly for-profit enterprises that rely on advertising to make money. News is a commodity. Stories must be interesting—and even entertaining—to attract consumers. One should never imagine that news stories are simply dry accounts of facts. Rather they are dramatic in their language and intent, emphasizing conflict, and often creating casts of heroes and villains. In covering the Postville raid, *The Des Moines Register* emphasized the size and complexity of the raid, describing it as "the largest workplace raid in Iowa history"[5] which took "months to plan" and involved the effort of "16 local, state, and federal agencies." This was not just any raid; this was a highly coordinated government operation that was history-making in its implications.

The Register highlighted the drama of the moment, suggesting that the arrests "reignited the debate over immigration." This metaphor implies that immigration is a "hot" topic which can cause smoldering emotions to flare up. Reinforcing this theme, the story described a group of protesters and a smaller group of counter-protesters who congregated outside the detention area and yelled slogans at each other. The theme of conflict also permeated the historical references. The paper noted, for example, that the meat-packing facility had earlier been taken over by Hasidic Jews, whose "arrival turned Postville, a community of 2,273 people on the Allamakee-Clayton county border in northeast Iowa, into one of Iowa's most ethnically diverse." Quoting Postville Mayor Robert Penrod, "There's people who hate the Hispanics, and there's people who don't like the Jews and would like to run them out of town."

Heroes and villains also emerge in this story. The heroes were the government officials who professionally planned and humanely carried out the raid. Iowa Governor Chet Culver is quoted as insisting that the workers' rights would not be violated, but that immigration law would have to be upheld. The article created villains by focusing on the "criminal acts" that prompted the raid, noting that the "feds allege rampant ID fraud," and that "as many as three-fourths of the company's workers last year were

---

[5]N. Duara, W. Petroski, and G. Schulte, "Claims of ID Fraud Lead to Largest Raid in State History." *The Des Moines Register,* May 12, 2008. Retrieved April 22, 2010, from http://www.desmoinesregister.com/article/20080512/NEWS/80512012/Claims-of-ID-fraud-lead-to-largest-raid-in-state-history/.

using fraudulent social security numbers." The article repeated the rumor asserting that some employees were running a methamphetamine lab and bringing guns to work. Management also emerged as villains as the story noted that workers were paid less than minimum wage, and that one manager allegedly physically abused a worker by covering his eyes with duct tape and striking him with a meat hook.

Although this article appears to give a great deal of information, media coverage is limited by time, space, and access and can leave out important details. Iowans do not learn from this story that many of those arrested were Mayans who constitute a significantly disadvantaged ethnic minority in their own countries. It was not made clear that many of the workers arrested did not speak English, that some spoke Spanish as a second language, and that many were illiterate. If readers had been aware of these facts, they would have been more likely to wonder if these defendants understood what the term Social Security number meant, or understood anything about the legal machinery that confronted them, or knew that they had rights and options in this situation.

Cameras were not allowed into the detention center, which meant that there was no one "'watching' the watchers," that is, the media covering the event and those preparing official accounts of what transpired. The only exception was Erik Camayd-Freixas, who was present because he was part of the process, assisting as a Spanish-language interpreter in various phases of the operation. As he explained, the procedures in place during the raid and its aftermath provided a veneer of fairness, but gave lip-service to due process and did not live up to the spirit of civil rights.

None of this is to claim that the *Des Moines Register* was prejudiced or biased for or against any party in this dispute. Rather the point is to demonstrate that the news is not "just the facts." The news is part of a larger media structure that imposes a set of norms on the information that news agencies convey. These norms create news as a "story" that is both a description of an event, but also part of a larger narrative that is always incomplete and always imperfect. We need to remember that Postville is not simply a massive raid on a plant in an isolated Iowa town. We need to look past the colorful cast of characters embroiled in a dramatic law-enforcement event to see the more enduring aspects of this situation. The raid suggests themes of work and immigration in corporate America, dangerous jobs and fragile ties of membership in a small American community, criminal justice and fairness in a transnational environment, and human rights and duties in this age of immigration.

Law, Policy, and Social Change in Postville

As the previous section notes, the mass media coverage of the Postville raid helps to frame how people think about justice in a situation like this. What are we to make of the boast of federal officials that this was the largest raid in American history and that it was done absolutely in accordance with law? How should we respond to people labeled as *illegals*, a term not generally used for other violations of law? Law was undoubtedly at the center of the Postville raid. There were many layers of law in this story—immigration law, criminal law, criminal procedure, contract law, and regulatory law. For the workers involved in this raid, contract law came first, starting with the purchase of a false social security card and its use in getting work with the Postville Agriprocessors kosher meat-packing plant. For their deception in contracting for employment, the Postville workers were charged with aggravated identity theft, which brought them into contact with the penal law that defines crimes and the federal code of criminal procedure that sets the standards for processing criminal cases. But against the backdrop of these activities stands federal immigration law, which forbids entry into the United States "without inspection" and imposes other important limits on the rights of noncitizens. A visitor's visa, for example, is limited in duration, and does not give its holder the right to work.

A critical reading of the Postville saga requires, at a minimum, that we consider the purposes of the laws involved, and whether these purposes were achieved by the actions that officials took in exercising their powers in this case. Starting with federal immigration legislation, we should ask whether officials acted efficiently and reasonably in their goal of deterring unauthorized immigration. Why did federal immigration officials opt to prosecute 300 workers rather than use the same amount of resources to prosecute employers? Going after employers, particularly large operations known to be looking for low-wage labor, would dry up jobs for unauthorized immigrants and thereby make unauthorized immigration less attractive. There would seem to be a lot more "bang for the buck" with this approach if the goal were to reduce the incentive to immigrate without permission. But maybe efficient use of scarce enforcement resources wasn't the most important goal of this operation. What did Dr. Camayd-Freixas think that the actual goals of the agency were in this case when he described the agency as "hitting a small jackpot"?

The ideals of the criminal law definitely took a beating in the Postville prosecution. Dr. Camayd-Freixas describes a rushed mass processing of cases in which the federal judge in charge of the proceedings seemed to be working from a prepared script and the accused were mute. Anyone accused of a crime has the right to be informed of the charges against him or her, the right to a lawyer, and the right to a timely hearing before a judge. The Constitution does not make distinctions among people in basic rights when there are criminal charges at issue, whether those accused are citizens or simply residents. Did these defendants understand their rights? Many of the workers were illiterate. They could not read English or Spanish and may not have understood either language very well. Dr. Camayd-Freixas was aware of these limitations, but it is not clear that everyone involved was. Should they have been? Is comprehension and freedom to participate part of the obligation of due process before penalties are imposed?

But the problem goes deeper. These workers were overcharged in order to induce a guilty plea to a lesser charge. This is a way to speed up the criminal process: make the prospect of trial, with the possibility of a conviction, so frightening that the person "willingly" pleads guilty. This is not uncommon in criminal prosecution, but this case involved a particularly vulnerable population. Not only were the defendants handicapped by language and cultural differences, they were also very poor and needed to work in order to survive. They could not afford to take the risk of a long prison term to vindicate their rights, even if they had understood that they were charged with something they did not do, that is, with knowingly stealing a particular person's identity for gain. Their goal was to use an identity document to get a job and nothing more. Should a prosecutor be held to a higher standard than this?

Looking at the matter from another perspective, how could it be that Agriprocessors was not aware of the fact that it was hiring unauthorized workers at bargain prices? How did they complete their job applications without arousing suspicion that they might not be U.S. citizens?

Now, looking at the whole operation and thinking about the basic goals of a legal system (e.g., fair and accurate procedures, "a day in court," public safety, security in our possessions and lives, equal justice for all), were any of these goals promoted by the Postville raid? After reading the story of the Postville raid, the question remains, how did the arrest and prosecution of 289 workers benefit society and keep the community safe?

What are the possibilities for social change here? One possibility lies with the capacity of human beings for empathy, despite the law. Many of the residents of Postville were appalled at what had happened. They reached out to the remains of the immigrant families left behind after the raid through their churches and organizations. A translator broke the normal code of silence in describing these events. Were these actions designed to promote social change? Whether that was the intention or not, some change has occurred as a result. Federal immigration control changed course after Postville. There is less emphasis now on raids and more on investigation of employers who hire workers with suspect papers. And the case provoked another kind of social change, from the U.S. Supreme Court, which reacted sharply to the charge of aggravated identity theft in this case, rejecting it as inconsistent with the facts. The Court's action sets a precedent for those involved in future prosecutions. The Court, in this sense "makes law" that can be applied to other cases.

And finally, what does this case teach Americans about the possibilities for social change? Do you feel empowered to right the wrongs you may have spotted in studying this case?

Citizenship, Migration, and Human Rights in the Raid

The Immigration and Customs Enforcement (ICE) raid on Agriprocessors and its workers was a drastic reaction to the long-standing U.S. practice of hiring foreign workers who accept low wages because they lack legal status. This is a saga in which citizenship and migration play leading roles; human rights, on the other hand, is notable by its absence. U. S. citizens would not have been attracted to these jobs, nor would they have been treated as these migrants were. Nor would this raid have taken the form that it did if the United States had a healthy respect for the human rights of its noncitizen residents.

The raid emblemizes bureaucratic rationality, in which efficiency is the predominant goal, not rights protections. No one could complain that this operation, which involved nearly 800 law-enforcement officials, was conducted inefficiently. But the insensitivity of those who planned the raid to the larger context in which it occurred is troubling. Of course, those who were "boots on the ground" were simply following orders, but what about those who conceived the idea of rounding up workers and prosecuting them for a crime that they did not commit? It was, in a sense, rational to overcharge these defendants to produce a negotiated plea. But is this the level playing field in which legal combat is supposed to occur? Not according to Dr. Camayd-Freixas. Whose job should it be to consider the circumstances of defendants, such as their inability to read or speak English? Should anyone be tasked with taking into account the oppression that led these Guatemalan peasants to seek these jobs?

Migration is, of course, a choice, but often a choice made among bleak alternatives. Guatemala, the nation from which many of these workers came, has one of the highest poverty rates in Latin America. In 2000, 56 percent of its population lived in poverty and nearly a third of the population was illiterate. The nation's 36-year civil war took a toll on its development, but long-standing discrimination against the indigenous population and rural isolation make the situation much worse. Over three-quarters of Guatemala's indigenous population live in poverty. Many people do not have enough food to eat; 44 percent of children under the age of five are stunted in their growth, and infant and maternal mortality are high, particularly for indigenous populations.[6]

Under these circumstances, it should not be surprising that people feel impelled to leave their homes to support themselves and their families. What is a rich country's obligation to help, if any? A wealthy nation cannot open its doors to everyone, but how should it respond to the presence of extreme poverty that is close by? People are people, regardless of nationality. If all people have some basic rights, do other people have an obligation to help them achieve those rights? Adequate food and access to education might be a starting point. Or maybe rich countries should open some jobs to people from nearby nations who are in desperate circumstances.

Does it seem ironic, given the circumstances of the workers, that they were selected for punishment? They accepted jobs offered to them by a company that profited by their labor, and that company had to know that it was violating the law in hiring them. What about the town of Postville that accepted these workers as customers and taxpayers? Their lack of legal status could not have been a complete surprise to anyone. And what about those more distant beneficiaries: the consumers of kosher meat products, the company's stockholders, the companies that supplied products and services for Agriprocessors? All benefitted from the cheap labor these workers provided and their steadfastness in their work. The law that made these people subject to deportation, in short, rewards other members of society.

We are all aware that citizenship provides certain privileges like the right to vote and hold political office. Citizenship also allows people to move freely to get work. Racism

---

[6]For details see *Poverty in Guatemala*, Report No. 24221-GU, February 20, 2003, a World Bank document, available from http://www.wds.worldbank.org/servlet/WDSContentServer/WDSP/IB/2003/04/05/000094946_03032104003172/Rendered/PDF/multi0page.pdf

and various forms of inequality exist, but citizenship at least gives people grounds for complaint and action. None of this holds for people who lack legal status, and often these people suffer terrible injustices. In a just world, would distinctions by legal status carry as much weight as they do in contemporary society? Why should the accident of where one is born determine one's chances to be healthy, to have a fair hearing, to enjoy economic opportunity, to go to school?

The guiding idea behind human rights is that one's nationality is not particularly important in its own right. Humans across the globe share a desire to have a dignified existence, with their basic needs met. This idea of human dignity provides a starting point for thinking about human rights. But to declare rights is not enough: How can they be made real? Here is where nations become important again. Nations are the only institutions with enough power and organization to potentially guarantee human rights. Yet the nation-state is often part of the human-rights problem. Consider those migrant workers arrested in Postville, for example. They left their homes, enduring the dangers of migration, and took these low-paying jobs because their governments offered them little hope of a decent life. Failed and failing states create pressure to migrate, especially among the most down-trodden parts of their population. The success of human rights as an ideal for a more just world thus depends on governments, even though the idea behind human rights looks beyond national membership to our common humanity.

Globalization, Sustainability, and Economic Justice . . . for All?

Now let's consider what nationhood means in an increasingly interconnected world. Postville encapsulates many of the fundamental tensions and contradictions of a globalized world. Globalization expands both markets and labor, allowing people to escape grinding poverty and sometimes violent homelands to find a more stable life for themselves and their families. At the same time, globalization tends to lower the price of goods and services. But globalization has a downside, and Postville illustrates some of these less attractive features, such as the bait and switch that U.S. companies use to lure immigrants with promises of jobs for them, and with promises of new industry and an expanded tax base to economically depressed towns. Places, like workers, are vulnerable under globalization. Postville is a case in point.

Massive technological changes have helped to facilitate globalization by speeding up transit and reducing labor costs. The decrease in transit times allows perishable goods like meat to be processed far from their places of origin, freeing industry from traditional geographic confines. The Postville plant would likely not have existed half a century ago because it would have been too isolated from population centers. Free movement of products offers new products to an international clientele, while at the same time allowing producers to find the locations that are most amenable to maximizing profit.

The benefits of and drawbacks of globalization are not evenly distributed. Indeed, many of globalization's disadvantages are shouldered primarily by poorer countries and their citizens in the form of environmental degradation, dangerous working conditions, and persistently low wages. Globalization facilitates economic inequality. Ninety-four percent of the world's income goes to 40 percent of the world's people, while the other 60 percent of the world's people live on just 6 percent of total income. What responsibilities, if any, do wealthy countries have toward the nations with which they conduct business? The United Nations Declaration of Human Rights states that meaningful work and the ability to form unions are fundamental human rights. Rich and poor nations have committed themselves to these goals, but the increasing mobility of capital and investment makes them difficult to achieve.

People frequently look to their government, and sometimes to international organizations, to create fair trade and labor policies. Yet multilateral institutions designed to reduce poverty and spur development, such as the World Bank and the International Monetary Fund, have had limited success, prompting many to question their usefulness in achieving economic justice and sustainable economies. Economist Muhammad Yunus criticizes these organizations for focusing too much on large-scale economic growth and increases in a nation's Gross Domestic Product (GDP) because these are indicators of economic well-being that tend to leave out the situation of the nation's poorest citizens. Poverty resists simple, one-size-fits-all solutions.

As the Postville story suggests, migration is one response to poverty. People move to where they can find work and send money to the family members they leave behind. The pressure to migrate is particularly strong in areas disrupted by development. Globalization is thus both part of the pull factor that brings people to new places and part of the push factor that induces people to travel long distances, risking their lives in some cases, to find work, including low-wage, dangerous work.

Postville also highlights another feature of our contemporary world—the fragility of economic development. Towns like Postville can become dependent for their survival on a single big employer and on the consumer and tax base that immigrant labor provides for the town's merchants, schools, and services. Nearly 40 percent of the town disappeared after the raids, taking with it much of Postville's tax base and devastating its municipal infrastructure. Like the "company towns" of old, Postville reminds us that dependence on a single employer or industry is neither stable nor sustainable. Yet the demand for cheap labor and cheaper goods, the regime of what Robert Reich has called "supercapitalism," offers small towns few choices for a sustainable economy. Sociologist Michele Devlin explains the current situation succinctly. "It's a triangle: Employers who want maximum profit, workers who need the work, and consumers who want cheap food." To this, one might add investors who want maximum returns and who will readily shift their investments to achieve them.

The raids at Postville exposed a web of connections that characterize our modern world. Yet the raids also brought into sharp relief many of the inequalities that exist within our current relationships. Where does justice lie in this scenario? Must we ask "Justice for whom?" Or, with the right arrangements, can economic justice and a sustainable economy be achieved for all?

Chapter 1

SOCIAL IDENTITIES AND COMMUNITIES

The concept of identity is a complex one, shaped by individual characteristics, family dynamics, historical factors, and social and political contexts. Who am I? The answer depends in large part on who the world around me says I am. Who do my parents say I am? Who do peers say I am? What message is reflected back to me in the faces and voices of my teachers, my neighbors, store clerks? What do I learn from the media about myself? How am I represented in the cultural images around me? Or am I missing from the picture altogether?[1]

Beverly Tatum's observation is a reminder of how much others contribute to our own sense of identity. This interdependent relationship between self and society raises important issues of justice. Discrimination, for example, can harm a person's sense of self and erode the confidence necessary to assert oneself in the world. But it is no easy task to figure out how to interpret the messages society gives us and to identify who we are as individuals and where we are in a collective sense. It is not simply a matter of answering, "I am smart. I am an athlete. I am male. I am bisexual." By using terms like these to describe ourselves, we are accepting predefined, predetermined, and preconstructed categories of meaning and belonging. Such categories come with a history, a politics, and an image in the media. So when one attempts to answer the question "who am I?", that individual must be prepared to address the

---

[1]Beverly Tatum, "The Complexity of Identity: 'Who Am I?,'" in *Readings for Diversity and Social Justice,* edited by Maurianne Adams (New York: Routledge, 2000), pp. 9–14.

rootedness of identity in facts and norms determined by society. We necessarily move from the individual to the collective in thinking about who we are.

People tend to identify with others who appear to share something important, forming groups within the collective we call a society. The sense of belonging is an important part of identity, shaping one's sense of place and giving life meaning. The group memberships that constitute one's identity are not necessarily chosen. Some are given. You are figuratively at least "thrown" into some groups by society at large. Iris Marion Young, whose ideas about group difference and democracy you will review in Chapter 4, developed this idea to suggest the imposition of identity upon us.

The readings in this chapter outline the conflicts that arise in defining ourselves as individuals and as communities. Many of us embody privilege and take for granted our advantaged place in the world. On the other hand, some of us are forced to address issues of identity because of the challenges posed by our physical bodies. Consider the example of Ronald Takaki, who, as a person of Japanese ancestry, reports how he felt obliged to defend his American identity. Takaki was visiting a small town in the United States when a cab driver asked him how long he had lived in the country. He responded "All my life," adding that he was born in the United States. The driver, assuming he was transporting a foreigner, had been surprised that his passenger's English was so perfect. Takaki used this occasion to explain to the cab driver that his family migrated from Japan in the 1880s, before many Eastern Europeans even arrived in the United States. But at the same time, the incident was a reminder to Takaki that since his eyes and complexion did not look "American," to some people he remained a perpetual foreigner in his own homeland.

In a nation as racially and ethnically diverse as the United States, it may seem surprising that people can appear "foreign" by skin color or appearance of one's eyes or nose alone. This example suggests that American identity itself remains an unresolved issue. The United States has a long and bloody history of debate and division over identity, most dramatically in the context of slavery and other forms of racial oppression that were once legitimated by law. The Civil War, of course, is unforgettable, as are its long-lasting consequences for the descendants of the former slaves. It is easy, however, to overlook the other ways in which identity has been used to exclude. And as Takaki's experience in the cab illustrates, it is also important to recognize the diversity that has always constituted the American identity.

Gender is another identity that is often taken for granted as a simple binary. Our gendered identities are constructed from the moment we are born. "Is it a boy or a girl?" As Judith Lorber explains, we take our gendered identities for granted, assuming it is a natural part of our lives. We don't realize that gender is one part of our identity that is "constantly created and re-created out of human interaction . . ."

> For the individual, gender construction starts with the assignment to a sex category on the basis of what the genitalia look like at birth. Then babies are dressed or adorned in a way that displays the category . . . As soon as they can talk, they start to refer to themselves as members of their gender. Sex doesn't

come into play again until puberty, but by that time, sexual feelings and desires and practices have been shaped by gendered norms and expectations . . . Parenting is gendered, with different expectations for mothers and for fathers . . . all of these processes constitute the social construction of gender.

In the above passage, Lorber employs an important sociological concept that permeates this book: social construction. The social construction of identities occurs, not so much as a conscious activity, like teaching or lecturing to kids, but rather as a habitual pattern in which we as humans engage with each other. Children learn by watching what adults do without much conscious thought:

All human activity is subject to habitualization. Any action that is repeated frequently becomes cast into a pattern, which can then be reproduced with an economy of effort and which . . . is apprehended by its performer as that pattern. Habitualization further implies that the action in question may be performed again in the future in the same manner . . .

For the most part, these patterns are taken for granted and never questioned. We simply accept them, ignoring their interconnections and overall influence. As Berger and Luckmann explain, "society is a human product," and "man is a social product." There is a reciprocal relationship here that is difficult to disturb without conscious and sustained effort, and even with that effort, deep-seated preconceptions are hard to shake. We tend to notice information that confirms our stereotypes and prejudices and reject information that is inconsistent with what we already believe.

Identities are not static, however. Changes in law, social organization, and the built environment can help shift attitudes. Whether schooling occurs in a racially or ethnically segregated environment, for example, will affect the friendships children make and the social knowledge they develop. How parents are taught to treat their children has an impact. At the same time, communities of people can come together to resist the dominant narrative of their identity. The women's movement is an example in its opposition to masculinist constructions of womanhood.

Popular culture shapes identity in various ways, suggesting that some aspects of our identities are more fluid than others and quite subject to change over time. Law and its administration also have an impact on identity. The 1980 census included the term "Hispanic" as a means to "count Hispanics without racializing them as non-Whites." In the process, some observers noted a kind of separate-but-equal whiteness being established. The issue of identities in the census remains unsettled and subject to controversy, suggesting a certain unease in the categories people use to describe themselves and each other.

As the chapter that follows this one reminds us, advances in information technology—computers, mobile devices, and Internet communities—are likely to have a significant effect on how we understand identity and community. Early Internet scholars assumed that in the virtual spaces that the Internet provides, physical bodies would not matter much: "On the Internet, nobody knows you're a dog." Edward Castronova, for example, suggests that online spaces are exempt from real-world problems such as racism, classism, sexism, and other types of social inequality. This appears to be incorrect.

Scholars have found that gender and ethnicity emerge in online spaces. Lisa Nakamura, for instance, found that although our bodies are hidden from public view, race still has a way of inserting itself into virtual space. This was true even though many online users employ an avatar to create a virtual representation of the physical body, often choosing the avatar precisely to bear no resemblance to the user's own body. In her research on racialization in the game "World of Warcraft," Nakamura found that Chinese and Korean players were often the subject of oppression by other players who surmised racial/ethnic differences based on language use, identity construction, and reliance on an avatar. Hegemonic culture, that is, the taken-for-granted superiority of things white, appears to maintain its dominance in virtual spaces, as in physical spaces, all the while denying that social inequalities exist. Research on the virtual gaming space of Xbox Live reinforces Nakamura's finding that linguistic profiling leads to oppressive behavior in virtual space. Ethnographic study reveals that black males using Xbox are subject to acts of racism solely based on how they sound. The process begins immediately with questioning from other players asking the individual to confirm his black identity. Then the questioning moves to instigation and provocation, then to outright racist remarks and hate speech. So, even in gaming spaces, identity is a major concern for many women and people of color; these sites tend to be occupied and dominated by white males who regularly assert their dominance.

As has been outlined, our social identity is linked to larger communities, both physical and virtual. Critical reflection on these connections is the goal of this chapter.

Social Identities

Racial identity has long been a hotly debated issue in the United States. The first reading will help to explain the continuing significance of race in a nation that many claim is a "post-racial" society. Those who believe that we are finally in a post-racial era often cite the election of President Barack Obama to argue that race no longer matters to Americans. It is true that attitudes have changed and that the prevailing view is that color-blindness is the best approach in dealing with fellow workers, fellow students, and people in general. But that is not to say that race is irrelevant. In fact, Eduardo Bonilla-Silva suggests that the ideology of color blindness, which argues that race differences should not matter in any context, leads to racial inequality in public policy. Color blindness, embraced as a description of contemporary reality, accepts racial inequality and removes responsibility for altering social structures that perpetuate differential opportunities depending upon the person's race.

How should we understand race? Many people assume that one's race is given—a known factor that is relatively easy to describe. But racial identity is not always clear. Think about the debate surrounding President Obama's racial identity. Racial identity has been an issue for a long time. For Susie Guillory Phipps, the issue was the conflict between how she viewed herself and how the law viewed her in racial terms. She sued the Louisiana Bureau of Vital Records, unsuccessfully, to change her racial classification from black to white. Her suit challenged a 1970 state law requiring that anyone with at least one-thirty-second of "Negro blood" be classified in state records as "Black." Although physically Susie Phipps appeared white, and she had always thought of herself (and been considered by friends and family) to be white, she could not change the law's definition of her race. This is an old case, but it suggests the problems associated with attempting to classify people by race.

Whiteness has also been a hotly debated subject, though this history tends to be forgotten. As immigrants from Eastern and Southern Europe poured into the United States in the early 20th century, for example, there was considerable disagreement about who was white, and how one could "become white." This is something to consider when you have the opportunity to classify yourself for the federal census.

THE POWER OF IMAGES
MARJORIE S. ZATZ AND CORAMAE RICHEY MANN

Race and Racism as Social Constructions

It is generally recognized today that race is a *social construction*. This means that (1) race is not a fixed identity—it is socially decided rather than biologically determined; (2) racial categories and the meanings attached to race make sense only in their historical contexts and in light of specific social relations (such as slave-master, maid-employer, and doctor-patient); and (3) racial dynamics are flexible, fluid, and *always* political. In some contexts, attributions of race can change overnight. Marvin Harris wrote in 1964 that Brazilians recognized 40 different racial types. In Brazil, and to a lesser extent in other parts of Latin America, one's 'color' is based more on one's wealth and social status than on skin hue. In Harris' words,

> In Brazil one can pass to another racial category regardless of how dark one may be without changing one's residence. The passing is accomplished by achieving economic success or high educational status. Brazilians say "Money whitens," meaning that the richer a dark man gets the lighter will be the racial category to which he will be assigned by his friends, relatives and business associates. Similarly, light-skinned individuals who rank extremely low in terms of educational and occupational criteria are frequently regarded as actually being darker in color than they really are. (1964, 59)

Although some members of racial or ethnic minorities in the United States can "pass" as white, it is not uncommon for light skinned African Americans to find that people who previously had acted friendly withdraw upon learning they are black.

Thus, recognition that race is socially constructed does not mean that it is without consequences; on the contrary, social constructions of race have very real consequences for people's life chances and for race relations in the United States. Also, education and wealth offer little protection from abuse by law enforcement agents. Physicians of color with M.D. emblems on their cars are pulled over routinely by police, as are minority lawyers, university professors, and other professionals. Sometimes they are stopped precisely because they are driving "fancy" cars (which could mean anything that is not ready for the junkyard), the implication being that they must have stolen them, because persons of color could not possibly afford nice cars unless they are drug dealers or pimps. The expression "Driving While Black" (and "Driving While Brown") refers' to the odious practice of racial profiling of African American (and often Latino/a) motorists by police officers. Such harassment has far-reaching consequences for police-citizen relations and for the civic order more generally.

Like race, racism is socially constructed. Whether we are talking about racist structures or racist ideologies, racism is all about power. Because conditions of dominance and subordination, and of control and resistance, differ across social and historical contexts, racism, too, must be multifaceted and flexible. That is, the ways in which racism displays itself—what we might call its form—change as social conditions change. For instance, it is hard to imagine a juvenile court judge today saying publicly what Judge Chargin of Santa Clara, California, told a Chicano boy in 1969:

> You ought to commit suicide. That's what I think of people of this kind. You are lower than animals and haven't the right to live in organized society—just miserable, lousy, rotten people. . . . Maybe Hitler was right, (cited in Hernández, Haug, and Wagner 1976, 62–63).

Although such overtly racist statements in courts of law are unusual today, stories of police beatings of young African American and Latino men are not. Rodney King's beating galvanized the nation because it was irrefutably visible on videotape, not because it was rare. The police departments of many major cities today face formal charges or citizen complaints of excessive force in subduing persons of color.

Race relations in our country are complex, however, and we cannot assume that the same stance will be taken by all social control agents. Perhaps one of the most striking aspects of Judge Chargin's tirade is that it came from a member of the judiciary. While it is undeniable that some judges operate on the basis of racial prejudices, such overtly racial statements are, as we stated, rare today. More common are judges who simply follow the law because that is their responsibility, regardless of any personal concern that the law's effects may be racially biased. And yet, several Euro-American state and federal judges and the U.S. Sentencing Commission have taken public stands against the harsher penalties for possession of crack than powder cocaine because they view these statutes as racially discriminatory in their impacts, whether or not that was the intent of the legislators. In addition, the Minnesota Supreme Court in 1991 formally ruled that differing sentences for possession of crack and powder cocaine are racially discriminatory.

Defining Racism

This brings us to a very important point the definition of racism. At its most general, racism can be defined as

> social practices which (explicitly or implicitly) attribute merits or allocate values to members of racially categorized groups solely because of their "race." (Omi and Winant 1986, 145)

Although our nation's history has many positive aspects, it is undeniable that our national economy was based initially on a system of slave labor, on the theft of land from American Indians, and on the conquest of massive territories from Mexico. As Cornel West said of "this democratic experiment we call America,"

> [it] began by taking for granted the ugly conquest of Amerindians and Mexicans, the exclusion of women, the subordination of European working-class men and the closeting of homosexuals. . . . What made America distinctly American for [European-Americans] was not simply the presence of unprecedented opportunities, but the struggle for seizing these opportunities in a new land in which black slavery and racial caste served as the floor upon which white class, ethnic, and gender struggles could be diffused and diverted. (1994, 156)

Accordingly, we must consider the ways in which economic, political, and social relations reinforce and perpetuate racial inequalities.

This perspective is in marked contrast to the view of those who would define racism simply as behavior that results from the prejudicial attitude of an individual. Like most social scientists, we think this narrow definition is seriously flawed. Everyone, regardless of skin color, has certain prejudices. However, not everyone has the *power* to act on the basis of those prejudices. As long as Euro-Americans continue to control the major political, economic, and social institutions in this country, including the criminal justice system, they have the institutional resources to discriminate, whereas people of color do not.

Racism has at least three guises: (1) *personal prejudice*, which, as we have discussed, is the most limiting view of racism and serves simply to disguise and defend racial privileges; (2) *ideological*, in which culture and biology are invoked to rationalize and justify the superior social, economic, and political position of Euro-Americans; and (3) *institutional*, in which the policies and practices of societal institutions operate in a way that produces systematic and persistent differences between racial groups. It is the *outcome* that matters most when we look at institutional racism. It does not matter whether those persons creating the policies and continuing the practices consciously intend to discriminate or not. As Daniel Georges-Abeyie has noted,

> the key issue is *result, not intent*. Institutional racism is often the legacy of overt racism, of *de facto* practices that often get codified by *de jure* mechanisms. (1990, 28).

Another aspect of institutionalized racism is what Georges-Abeyie has called "petit apartheid realities." These are the everyday activities that contribute to poor relations between the police and persons of color, such as routines stop-and-question or stop-and-frisk law enforcement practices.

African Americans have been the victims of a particularly virulent form of racism because of their early status as slaves and because their continued economic plight has resulted in substantial media attention to segregated urban communities characterized by poverty, single-parent families, poor schools, and visible street crimes. Nevertheless, American Indians, Asian Americans, and Latinos and Latinas have also suffered from arbitrary and legally sanctioned exclusion and from other forms of discrimination. Many of the red and brown people in this country were the only residents who did *not* immigrate here. "America" was their land initially.

One consequence of racism that echoes and exacerbates the deep schisms among American citizens is racial segregation in housing and jobs. The proliferation of African American rural and inner-city ghettos, Latino barrios and Chinatowns, and the shameful theft of land from Indians that left them on small isolated reservations, reflect the imposed segregation that is more entrenched in American cities today than ever imagined. This social isolation creates many deleterious effects, both structural (for example, systematic differences in opportunities to acquire disposable income and to generate wealth) and psychological, for example, being unable to understand what life is like for members of other groups).

As Peterson and Harrell (1992, 1) suggest, there are many ways to look at isolation:

> The concept of isolation has multiple dimensions. There is literal, physical separation such as the distancing of inner-city residents from the suburban locations where jobs are being created, and the racial isolation imposed by segregated housing patterns. There is social isolation resulting from class homogeneity of contacts, and according to some authors, weak participation of inner-city residents in social organizations. There is the isolation imposed by high rates of crime and drug activity, as well as the habits of inner-city street life, where acceptance of neighborhood behavioral norms can progressively cut off access to mainstream society. . . . These dimensions of isolation overlap with one another and profoundly affect opportunity patterns.

The renowned African American sociologist William Julius Wilson made us intensely aware of the social isolation of inner-city African Americans in his classic work, *The Truly Disadvantaged* (1987), in which he also introduced the controversial notion of the black "underclass." Wilson described this underclass as "socially isolated," or lacking contact or "sustained interaction with the individuals or institutions that represent mainstream society" (1987, 60). Mainstream society, in this instance, was epitomized by gainfully employed people who lived in stable areas free from blight, who were not on public welfare rolls, and who could provide conventional role models.

It is important to recognize, though, that while many impoverished communities are quite isolated socially, others retain residents who serve as *bridge people*, to borrow Regina Austin's (1992) term. Bridge people are typically well-educated and hold stable jobs in respected professions, often coming back to the neighborhoods in which they grew up after living elsewhere. As the term suggests, bridge people can cross social and economic borders fairly readily, with ties to both those who survive through the illegal or underground economy and those who are considered quite respectable by middle-class norms. They serve as social buffers and, in at least some cases, carry sufficient political, economic, and social clout to bring new resources to bear on the community's problems.

Recent theoretical work on *racialized space* offers promising possibilities for better understanding how fears of dangerous places are closely intertwined with economic restructuring and other manifestations of institutionalized racism, and how these are reinforced by the media and politicians and manifested daily in policing practices.

Racial Formation

Another term we must introduce here is "racial formation," the process by which people attach meaning and importance to racial categories. What it means to be African American in the United States at this time, for instance, is determined by social, economic, and political factors such as the globalization of the economy, the decline of the middle class, the political decision to wage a "war" on drugs and drug users, the assault on affirmative action policies, and so forth. The meaning and material consequences attached to being black are thus different now from what they were at the apex of the civil rights movement or under slavery.

At the individual level, racial formation is part of the process by which people formulate their identities; at the societal level, racial formation is structural, based on social relations between groups. When we think about racial formation this way, it becomes clear that race plays a central role in social relations and cannot be reduced to something else, such as socioeconomic class or nationality. Thus, although a poor Euro-American person and a poor African American person will both face some of the same difficulties, such as an inability to pay the necessary bail to get out of jail until his or her trial date, their situations will not be identical. To the extent that these differences are structured in such a way that most African Americans have one set of experiences and most Euro-Americans another, the differences can be said to be racialized. More formally, *racialization* is "the extension of racial meaning to a previously racially unclassified relationship, social practice, or group" (Omi and Winant 1986, 64). Racialization is an ideological process, and it is necessarily historically specific.

Race and Gender as Interlocking Systems of Oppression. Thus far, we have been speaking only in terms of race; however, people's relations with others and with societal institutions are simultaneously constructed along *gender* lines. Race, ethnicity, and gender intersect in multifaceted and interlocking ways. Sometimes, race or ethnicity is most salient; at other times, gender is most salient. But most of the time, race, ethnicity, and gender cannot be separated. To try to do so risks splitting a person in two, Kimberlé Crenshaw refers to this as the "intersectionality" of race and gender. An African American woman is never just black, she is also always a woman; and she is never just a woman, she is also always black.

Failure to recognize this intersectionality has been the bane of the women's movement and of movements based on ethnicity. Many women of color have described feeling subordinated and oppressed in these contexts by the Euro-American women who felt that they could speak for every woman and by the men of color who felt that they could speak for everyone of color. For instance, within the white women's movement a central concern has been the "public-private" split. This split reflects the invisibility and exclusion of Euro-American women from the public arena of the workplace and the state's reluctance to interfere in the private sphere of the home, where the women are to be found, because this is the jurisdiction, or "castle," of the man who lives there. Yet this split ignores the reality of many African American women's lives, which are spent not only in the paid labor force but also physically in the homes of wealthier Euro-American women, caring for their babies, scrubbing their floors, and cleaning their toilets. Viewing gender in context of the experiences of various groups shows how "gender is configured through cross-cutting forms of differences that carry deep social and economic consequences" (Baca Zinn, Hondagneu-Sotelo, and Messner 2005, 6).

The conflicts are not just between women, and they are not based solely on race, ethnicity, or class. There are also serious' conflicts between men and women of the same race or ethnicity, as well as between straight and gay, liberal and conservative, and rich and poor women or men of the same race. As Toni Morrison (1992, xxx) states in the book she edited, appropriately entitled *Race-ing Justice, En-gendering Power,*

> It is clear to the most reductionist intellect that black people think differently from one another; it is also clear that the time for undiscriminating racial unity, has passed. A conversation, a serious exchange between black men and women, has begun in a new arena, and the contestants defy the mold. Nor is it as easy as it used to be to split along racial lines, as the alliances and coalitions between white and black women, and the conflicts among black women, and among black men, during the intense debates regarding Anita Hill's testimony against Clarence Thomas's appointment prove.

If *intersectionality* describes how each person simultaneously experiences racial and gender oppression at the individual level, at the societal level we can speak of how race, gender, and class—the three fundamental and interrelated axes of our social structure—create interlocking, systems of domination and oppression. As Margaret Anderson and Patricia Hill Collins point out, the patterns of race, class, and gender relations that are formed and reformed from this matrix affect individual consciousness, interactions between and within social groups, and group access to institutional power and privileges (Anderson and Collins 1995, xi).

Racial and ethnic typifications are very much gendered. Consider, for example, the centrality of gender to stereotypes of African American welfare queens, drunken American Indian men, and Latino drug-dealing gangbangers. Consider, too, Aunt Jemima of pancake batter and syrup fame; the evil Fu Manchu and the sexy Susie Wong; and Pocahontas and her Mexican counterpart, La Malinche, who fell in love with white conquerors and are depicted alternatively as race traitors and mothers of "new" races. Gender is very much a part of each of these racist depictions.

These stereotypes reflect our *simultaneously racialized and gendered* social relations, institutions, and ideologies. Gender is not just about women and that race is not just about people of color. *Everyone's* experiences are shaped by the interrelationships among race, gender, class, culture, sexual orientation, and, in many parts of the world, religion.

The Faces of Oppression and the Power of Stereotypes. When we begin to think about social relations, and especially race or ethnicity, gender, and class simultaneously and as inextricably interwoven, what Iris Young (1990, 48–65) has called the "faces of oppression" become quite evident. Young identifies five such, faces: exploitation, marginalization, powerlessness, violence, and cultural imperialism.

Exploitation is the process whereby the work performed by one group benefits a different group. Slavery is the starkest example of this form of oppression, but exploitation can also be seen in other contexts, such as when garment workers in the Third World and in U.S. slums are paid very low wages for their work while the clothes they produce are sold for tremendous profits.

Young suggests that today *marginalization* is a more common form of social oppression than exploitation. "Marginals," she suggests, "are people the system of labor cannot or will not use" (1990, 53). Among other social categories, the marginalized may be old people, young African Americans and Latinos who are unable to secure jobs, single mothers, the physically disabled, or American Indians living on reservations.

Powerlessness refers to the daily situation of those who have little or no control over their working conditions. They can make few if any decisions in the workplace and are not allowed any creativity in designing the work product or even in deciding how best to do their work. No one reports to them, but they are constantly reporting to and being judged by others. Think of the clerk at a drugstore, a food server at McDonald's, or a factory worker on an assembly line and you will realize how little say any of these people have over their work conditions. They are powerless. Powerlessness is also evidenced by the inability of women and girls in patriarchal cultures to control their own destinies and to make their own decisions about their health, their sexuality, and how they will earn their livelihood.

Hate crimes exemplify yet another face of oppression—systemic *violence*. Random, unprovoked attacks on persons or their property that have no purpose other than to damage, humiliate, or destroy the person—and that occur *because* the person is a member of a given social group—are oppressive. Consider, for example, the string of church burnings throughout the South in recent years—31 incidents since 1989. These churches were set on fire solely because most members of their congregations were African American. Consider, too, the practice of "gay bashing," in which groups of straight young men go looking for gay men to beat up; the looting of Korean groceries in urban neighborhoods; the painting of swastikas on synagogues; and the old practice of giving "gifts" of smallpox-infested blankets to American Indians.

The senseless and blind bigotry associated with hate crimes are vividly underscored by reports of recent attacks on Arab Americans in this nation. Citizens who had lived peaceably in the United States for generations found themselves targets of racial hatred and violence following the September 11, 2001, terrorist attacks. One of the most insidious examples of race hate crimes was the slaughter of a Sikh gas station owner in Mesa, Arizona, in the aftermath of these attacks. Balbir Singh Sodhi was shot by an ignorant racist zealot because Sodhi had a beard and wore a turban, and thus was presumed to be Muslim. The attacks on Arab and Arab American students on college and university campuses, supposedly bastions of enlightened thought and liberalism, are also quite chilling.

The final face of oppression identified by Young is *cultural imperialism*. This occurs when members of one group, which has power over another group, assume that their way of doing something is the only way. The dominant group's experiences, values, goals, and achievements are taken as normal, as the way things are. And thus it becomes surprising when members of a subordinated group do things differently, whether we are speaking of styles of dress, religious practices, ways of conducting business, or any other category.

Stereotyping is an important part of cultural imperialism. Typically, stereotypes connect something about the "nature" of subordinated groups to an undeniable and often visible aspect of their bodies. Young (1990, 59) states:

> These stereotypes so permeate the society that they are not noticed as contestable. Just as everyone knows that the earth goes around the sun, so everyone knows that gay people are promiscuous, that Indians are alcoholics, and that women are good with children. White males, on the other hand, insofar as they escape group marking, can be individuals.

Ironically, it is the very invisibility of race when we are talking about Euro-Americans, and of gender when we are talking about men, that should signal that we are dealing with a social construction. Members of certain groups—Euro-Americans, men, heterosexuals, the able-bodied, and the wealthy—often do not even recognize their own privilege. They simply take it for granted as "normal." The danger, of course, is that anyone different becomes "not normal," or "the Other."

The media play very important roles in portraying members of some groups as normal and others as Other. In particular, films and television programs use the power of visual images to create and reinforce stereotypic images of Others as scary and different. As Michael Omi and Howard Winant suggest, these media

> have been notorious in disseminating images of racial minorities which establish for audiences what people from these groups look like, how they behave, and "who they are." The power of the media lies not in their ability to reflect the dominant racial ideology, but in their capacity to shape that ideology in the first place. (1986, 63)

They note further that efforts to reach a large and diverse television audience have led "to the perpetuation of racial caricatures, as racial stereotypes serve as shorthand for scriptwriters, directors and actors" (p. 63).

In the reading below, Howard Winant discusses the politics of racial identities and the controversies surrounding the creation of identities. So as you read, reflect on your ethnic and racial makeup, and consider ways in which this portion of your identity remains debatable.

RACIAL POLITICS IN THE TWENTY-FIRST CENTURY
HOWARD WINANT

Racial globalism, racial difference, and racial justice are among our most fundamental political challenges. The modern epoch was founded on European imperialism and African slavery. Both these systems were organized racially. The theft of labor and life, of land and resources, from millions of Africans and Native Americans, and from Asians and Pacific Islanders as well financed the rise of Europe and made possible both its subsequent mercantilism and its later industrialism. Conquest, imperial rule, and the chattelization of labor (principally but not entirely African labor) divided humanity into Europeans and "others." Ferocious and unending cultural and psychic energies were expended to sustain this schism, which was also constantly challenged and undermined in innumerable ways.

From *New Politics of Race: Globalism, Difference, Justice* by Howard Winant. University of Minnesota Press, 2004. Reprinted by permission of the University of Minnesota Press.

The central issue is racial politics. Democracy can be pragmatically measured by the degree and scope of racial inclusion and racial justice available in a given society. Since the origins of our modern world political system lie in racial dictatorship, it should not be surprising that where racial difference is concerned, democracy continues to be in short supply. Even though reform of state racial policies has occurred in several historical "breaks"—when the abolition of slavery, decolonization, and large-scale extensions of citizenship and civil rights took place—the contemporary world remains fully mired in the same racial history from which it originally sprung.

Colonial rule and slavocracy were systems whose fundamental political character was dictatorial. By seizure of territory, by kidnapping and theft, by coercive and authoritarian rule, Europe-based imperial regimes destroyed countless lives and sensibilities. No amount of rationalization, no invocation of themes of development and uplift, no efforts at historical relativization can justify these predations or deodorize their moral stink.

We live in history. We live in continuity with a past that includes conquest and slavery. Not far in our past are state-sponsored racial exclusion and segregation, apartheid, colonial occupation, genocide, peonage. Indeed, these phenomena are not really in the past at all! Ghettoization persists across the world from Rocinha in Rio de Janeiro to Bedford-Stuyvesant, from Soweto to the banlieues of suburban Paris and the disparagingly named "casbahs" of Marseilles and Frankfurt. Apartheid lives on in South Africa despite the efforts of the ANC-led government to undo its legacy. The West Bank is colonially occupied. U.S. military bases in the Horn of Africa, the Dominican Republic, the Philippines (yet again!), and now Iraq signal the onset of a twenty-first-century imperialism that is openly avowed by policy makers in the regime of Bush II. In the past few years genocide and "ethnic cleansing" have swept across East Timor, Central and West Africa, Colombia, and Gujarat (to name only a few recent and current locales); indeed, there are many survivors of genocide living among us: both victims and perpetrators. Peonage not too distinct from slavery persists on cocoa and rubber plantations, in rug, shoe, and apparel factories, on electronic components assembly lines, in urban informal economies around the world, and in the massive global sex trade of women and girls.

Yes, we live in history. We live in continuity with a past that includes not only conquest and slavery but also abolitionism, anticolonialism, and unending efforts, large and small, to secure racial freedom, justice, and equality. So we live in the shadows not only of the predatory and degrading practices that were carried out against colonial subjects and coerced laborers—past and present—by their putative "masters." We also live in the bright sunlight of the rejection of these practices by those same subjects. Reasserting freedom, refusing to surrender collective and individual autonomy, maintaining subjecthood by any means necessary—however imperfect or contradictory—have been the constant effort of the subordinated: this is the work of workers, of women, of prisoners, as well as that of the colonized and enslaved.

The limited but real democracy of the present is thus a product of a vast labor the herculean efforts of the enormous numbers of people who opposed and subverted slavery and empire, who organized labor and vindicated women's rights, who built and served and educated the communities and collectivities of the oppressed and exploited, who worked for reform, fomented rebellion, and made revolution. The achievement of labor rights, of the franchise, of popular sovereignty and freedom of expression, of national liberation from imperial rule, of reproductive rights and women's emancipation more generally, and of popular democracy in all its forms can be traced back to conflict over and about the racial divide, conflict fundamental to the modern world's gestation and development.

In U.S. racial history we may discern two historical moments or periods when large-scale shifts were effected in the system of racial domination, two breaks, when the fabric of the veil was torn, if not dissolved: during and after the Civil War, and during and after World War II. These upheavals were primarily political events, phenomena of crisis. They occurred—*as have all other racial breaks, both locally and globally*—when the instability of the old racial system became too great and popular opposition had acquired too much disruptive power to be successfully ignored or repressed. They occurred when the dialectic of the racial oppression/ resistance meant in practical terms that *the white supremacist system depended too comprensively and openly on the racially oppressed*. In this situation, the logic of racial domination, the very fabric of what Du Bois called "the veil," threatens to burst apart.

After Hegemony

So now what? Is democracy still possible? Have race consciousness and racial injustice been driven off the political stage? Is the world regressing to a situation like that of a century ago, when white supremacy was taken for granted by those in power? Is the United States enacting a simulacrum of those times, living in a kind of racial Disneyland where race is a thing of the past, where the happy pirates can at last frolic again, undisturbed, on the Caribbean beach?

Today the bombs rain down once again on impoverished countries of the global South (and global East). A quarter century after we thought that the age of imperialism was finally over, dreams of empire have been revived.

Meanwhile the opposite dream, Dr. King's dream, of an inclusive and peaceful U.S. society (and world society) seems to have gone up in smoke. In the United States, state policy is being made by corporate predators, religious fanatics, and militarists. Society's vulnerable groups—the chief inheritors of the legacies of conquest, slavery, and imperialism—are being left to their own devices. The welfare state has been effectively ended, for the politically vulnerable anyway (for those with resources and influence, the state's largesse is unprecedented). The poor, racial and sexual minorities, women and children, the aged and infirm: let them eat cake! And since the United States wields the biggest stick in the neighborhood, these rules are being imposed far and wide, well beyond the country's frontiers. For most of the planet's population, which lacks adequate shelter, education, nutrition, and health care, the message is the same: get used to it. Don't dare to oppose the big brother from the North (or the West). Don't assume your culture, your lands, your resources, or your media are truly yours. Empire rules.

And yet, and yet . . ., the horrors of the present are not the whole story. Social movements have emerged once again: different movements that strive to reinvent democratic politics. Opposition, noncompliance, critique, subversion, and, yes, service to those sacrificed on the altars of greed and the arrogance of power are flourishing as people in the United States and around the world explore new approaches to creating collectivity and cooperation, and as they experiment with new ideas about organizing. Where there is oppression, there is resistance. Empire falls.

But we are still a long way from that fall. The U.S. imperium retains a great deal of power, not only through its virtual monopolization of the means of destruction, but also through its unending quest to reinforce and justify its own, uniquely American greed.

Much of that power and a great deal of that greed are framed in racial terms. This is the problem of the twenty-first-century racial rule: not the problem of the color-line, but the problem of how the color-line can be both affirmed and denied, simultaneously reinforced and undermined. This is also the problem of twenty-first-centry movements for racial democracy: how to affirm racial identity/difference without reifying it; how to oppose racism without restricting racial autonomy.

Winning Is Losing

To understand movement politics under conditions of racial hegemony is to recognize that reforms won will usually be more "moderate" than what was demanded, that insurgent movements are generally split by their very achievements into accommodationist and radical fractions, and that gains thus achieved are purchased at the price of at least partial demobilization. The successful movement has undermined some of the conditions for its own existence. It falls back to a quiescent or marginalized phase of the political trajectory. Winning is losing.

But Losing Is Also Winning

If hegemony offers only temporary political equilibrium to the state and elites that achieve it, then it can only generate temporary quiescence for the movements that accept it. To achieve the incorporation of movement demands into state policies—winning the civil rights legislation, for example, that outlawed de jure segregation—is perforce to recognize the very limitations of any given set of movement demands. There is no dishonor in this, for the "horizon" of our demands is necessarily set by the terms of the injustice we face. Demanding desegregation was a logical thing to do when Jim Crow was the law of the land. Achieving it—however incompletely or imperfectly—was a great victory. Yet, after its achievement, the inadequacy of this moderate reform quickly became obvious. The "horizon" of racial democracy had moved. When no gains are possible and no movement exists (what I am describing as the phase of movement quiescence or marginalization), alternative possibilities become almost inconceivable. "That's just the way it is/Some things will never change": the "horizon" of possibility seems fixed. But as one advances toward the "horizon," it in turn recedes the criticisms of the movement radicals who had previously resisted incorporation and denounced the reforms achieved as inadequate now appear vindicated. Indeed, entirely new demands begin to take shape as the new situation of racial hegemony is consolidated. There are new stirrings in the jug. The incorporation of movement demands ceases to be a solution and begins to look like a problem. New strategies, new tactics, are developed as those marginalized and afflicted by the power and greed of the racial state and dominant elites rouse their anger and discontent yet again. A new movement trajectory begins.

Race is only part of the description of who we are. Gender, class, sexuality, religion, and other characteristics, like disability, height, and looks, also define us. Nationality and language are other, less personal defining characteristics. These different identities that make up who we are form intersecting realities that influence our lives. At times, this influence is positive, and at other times, not. Consider, for example, women who are indigenous to the United States. Understanding their experiences of struggle and survival suggests what is meant by intersecting realities:

> We survive war and conquest; we survive colonization, acculturation, assimilation; we survive beating, rape, starvation, mutilation, sterilization, abandonment, neglect, death of our children, our loved ones, destruction of our land, our homes, our past, and our future. We survive, and we do more than just survive. We bond, we care, we fight, we teach, we nurse, we bear, we feed, we earn, we laugh, we love, we hang in there, no matter what.[2]

The readings that follow provide a theoretical framework for understanding the inequalities inherent in ascribed categories of race, gender, and sexuality, and the oppression that arises in the intersections of these categories. As Patricia Hill-Collins explains, oppressions cannot be reduced to either one or the other; they work simultaneously in producing injustices.[3] Kimberlé Crenshaw is similar, noting that "because the intersectional experience is greater than the sum of racism and sexism," studying only one or the other fails to sufficiently address the ways in which women of color are subordinated.[4]

---

[2]Paula Gunn Allen, *The Sacred Hoop: Recovering the Feminism in American Indian Traditions* (Boston: Beacon Press, 1986), p. 190.

[3]Patricia Hill-Collins, From Black Power to Hip Hop:Racism, Nationalism, and Feminism (Philadelphia: Temple University Press, 2006).

[4]Kimberlé Crenshaw, "Demarginalizing the Intersection of Race and Sex: A Black Feminist Critique of Antidiscrimination Doctrine, Feminist Theory and Antiracist Politics," *The University of Chicago Legal Forum*, 139–67 (1989).

We turn now to the other side of the coin, to privileged identities that many of us take for granted:

> Whiteness is everywhere in U.S. culture, but it is very hard to see. As Richard Dyer suggests, "[W]hite power secures its dominance by seeming not to be anything in particular." As the unmarked category against which difference is constructed, whiteness never has to speak its name, never has to acknowledge its role as an organizing principle in social and cultural relations.[5]

Societies, not surprisingly, attempt to maintain the status quo, and Peggy McIntosh provides an example. She explains that although men are willing to admit that women are disadvantaged, they are not as willing to grant that they, as men, are over privileged.[6] White privilege operates in the same manner:

> I think whites are carefully taught not to recognize white privilege, as males are taught not to recognize male privilege. So I have begun in an untutored way to ask what it is like to have white privilege. I have come to see white privilege as an invisible package of unearned assets which I can count on cashing in each day, but about which I was 'meant' to remain oblivious. White privilege is like an invisible weightless knapsack of special provisions, maps, passports, codebooks, visas, clothes, tools and blank checks.[7]

The two readings below show how this occurs. The authors challenge those with privilege to acknowledge their good fortune and to work for a more egalitarian—and just—society. They suggest that one must actively fight the tendency to hold negative views of marginalized groups—the views that society uses to justify continued subordination.[8] The message is encouraging—you can become an ally for justice by looking more closely at the privileges you enjoy.

---

[5]George Lipsitz, *The Possessive Investment in Whiteness: How White People Profit from Identity Politics*, (Philadelphia: Temple University Press, 2006), p. 1.

[6]Peggy McIntosh, "White Privilege: Unpacking the Invisible Knapsack," Working paper. (Wellesley, MA: Wellesley College Center for Research on Women, 1988).

[7]Ibid., para. 5.

[8]Ana Guinote, Guillermo Willis, and Cristiana Martellotta, "Social Power Increases Implicit Prejudice," *Journal of Experimental Social Psychology*, vol. 46 (2): 299–307 (March 2010).

MEMBERSHIP HAS ITS PRIVILEGES: THOUGHTS ON ACKNOWLEDGING AND CHALLENGING WHITENESS

TIM WISE

Being white means never having to think about it. James Baldwin said that many years ago, and it's perhaps the truest thing ever said about race in America. That's why I get looks of bewilderment whenever I ask, as I do when lecturing to a mostly white audience: "what do you like about being white?"

Never having contemplated the question, folks take a while to come up with anything.

We're used to talking about race as a Black issue, or Latino, Asian, or Indian problem. We're used to books written about "them," but few that analyze what it means to be white in this culture. Statistics tell of the disadvantages of "blackness" or "brownness" but few examine the flipside: namely, the advantages whites receive as a result.

When we hear about things like racial profiling, we think of it in terms of what people of color go through, never contemplating what it means for whites and what we don't have to put up with. We might know that a book like *The Bell Curve* denigrates the intellect of blacks, but we ignore the fact that in so doing, it elevates the same in whites, much to our advantage in the job market and schools, where those in authority will likely view us as more competent than persons of color.

That which keeps people of color off-balance in a racist society is that which keeps whites in control: a truism that must be discussed if whites are to understand our responsibility to work for change. Each thing with which "they" have to contend as they navigate the waters of American life, is one less thing whites have to sweat: and that makes everything easier, from finding jobs, to getting loans, to attending college.

On a personal level, it has been made clear to me repeatedly:

Like the time I attended a party in a white suburb and one of the few black men there announced he had to leave before midnight, fearing his trip home—which required that he travel through all-white neighborhoods—would likely result in being pulled over by police, who would wonder what he was doing out so late in the "wrong" part of town.

"Membership Has Its Privileges: Thoughts on Acknowledging and Challenging Whiteness" by Tim Wise, reprinted courtesy of the author.

He would have to be cognizant—in a way I would not—of every lane change, every blinker he did or didn't remember to use, whether his lights were too bright, or too dim, and whether he was going even 5 miles an hour over the limit: as any of those could serve as pretexts for pulling one over, and those pretexts are used regularly for certain folks, and not others.

The virtual invisibility that whiteness affords those of us who have it is like psychological money in the bank, the proceeds of which we cash in every day while others are in a state of perpetual overdraft.

Yet, it isn't enough to see these things, or think about them, or come to appreciate what whiteness means: though important, this enlightenment is no end in itself. Rather, it is what we do with the knowledge and understanding that matters.

If we recognize our privileges, yet fail to challenge them, what good is our insight? If we intuit discrimination, yet fail to speak against it, what have we done to rectify the injustice?

And that's the hard part: because privilege tastes good and we're loath to relinquish it. Or even if wilting, we often wonder how to resist: how to attack unfairness and make a difference.

As to why we should want to end racial privilege—aside from the moral argument— the answer is straightforward: The price we pay to stay one step ahead of others is enormous. In the labor market, we benefit from racial discrimination in the relative sense, but in absolute terms this discrimination holds down most of our wages and living standards by keeping working people divided and creating a surplus labor pool of "others" to whom employers can turn when the labor market gets tight or workers demand too much in wages or benefits.

We benefit in relative terms from discrimination against people of color in education, by receiving, on average, better resources and class offerings. But in absolute terms, can anyone deny that the creation and perpetuation of miseducated persons of color harms us all?

And even disparate treatment in the justice system has its blowback on the white community. We may think little of the racist growth of the prison-industrial complex, as it snares far fewer of our children. But considering that the prisons warehousing black and brown bodies compete for the same dollars needed to build colleges for everyone, the impact is far from negligible.

In California, since 1980, nearly 30 new prisons have opened, compared to two four-year colleges, with the effect that the space available for people of color and whites to receive a good education has been curtailed. So folks fight over the pieces of a diminishing pie—as with Proposition 209 to end affirmative action— instead of uniting against their common problem: the mostly white lawmakers who prioritize jails and slashing taxes on the wealthy, over meeting the needs of most people.

As for how whites can challenge the system—other than by joining the occasional demonstration or voting for candidates with a decent record on race issues—this is where we'll need creativity.

Imagine, for example, that groups of whites and people of color started going to local department stores as discrimination "tester" teams. And imagine the whites spent a few hours, in shifts, observing how they were treated relative to the black and brown folks who came with them. And imagine what would happen if every white person on the team approached a different white clerk and returned just-purchased merchandise, if and when they observed disparate treatment, explaining they weren't going to shop in a store that profiled or otherwise racially discriminated. Imagine the faces of the clerks, confronted by other whites demanding equal treatment for persons of color.

Far from insignificant, if this happened often enough, it could have a serious effect on behavior, and the institutional mistreatment of people of color in at least this one setting: after all, white clerks could no longer be sure if the white shopper in lady's lingerie was an ally who would wink at unequal treatment, or whether they might be one of "those" whites: the kind that would call them out for doing what they always assumed was acceptable.

Or what about setting up "cop watch" programs like those already in place in a few cities? White folks, following police, filming officer's interactions with people of color, and making, their presence known, when and if they observe officers engaged in abusive behavior.

Or contingents of white parents, speaking out in a school board meeting against racial tracking in class assignments: a process through which kids of color are much more likely to be placed in basic classes, while whites are elevated to honors and advanced placement, irrespective of ability. Protesting this kind of privilege—especially when it might be working to the advantage of one's own children—is the sort of thing we'll need to do if we hope to alter the system we swear we're against.

We'll have to stop moving from neighborhoods when "too many" people of color move in.

We'll have to stop running to private schools, or suburban public ones, and instead fight to make the schools serving all children in our community better.

We'll need to consider taking advantage of the push for publicly funded charter schools by joining with parents of color to start institutions of our own, similar to the "Freedom Schools" established in Mississippi by the Student Non-Violent Coordinating Committee in 1964. These schools would teach not only traditional subject matter, but also the importance of critical thinking, and social and economic justice. If these are things we say we care about, yet we haven't at present the outlets to demonstrate our commitment, we'll have to create those institutions ourselves.

And we must protest the privileging of elite, white male perspectives in school textbooks. We have to demand that the stories of all who have struggled to radically transform society be told: and if the existing texts don't do that, we must dip into our own pockets and pay for supplemental materials that teachers could use to make the classes they teach meaningful.

And if we're in a position to make a hiring decision, we should go out of our way to recruit, identify and hire a person of color.

What these suggestions have in common—and they're hardly an exhaustive list—is that they require whites to leave the comfort zone to which we have grown accustomed. They require time, perhaps money, and above all else, courage; and they ask us to focus a little less on the relatively easy, though important, goal of "fixing" racism's victims (with a bit more money for this or that, or a little more affirmative action), and instead to pay attention to the need to challenge and change the perpetrators of and collaborators with the system of racial privilege. And those are the people we work with, live with, and wake up to every day. It's time to revoke the privileges of whiteness.

"Privileges" extend beyond whiteness. Heterosexuality is another privileged condition. Just think about the struggle to get official recognition of marriage outside of the heterosexual paradigm of one man and one woman. Other forms of discrimination, sometimes violently imposed, are also familiar ways of enforcing heterosexual norms. Kathleen P. Marvel addresses hetero-normativity through a personal story of her own experience "in the closet" and now outside of it. The costs of closeting oneself, she suggests, are borne, not just by the individual, but by the workplace and society.

A PERSONAL TESTIMONIAL: ENDURING LIFE IN THE SHADOWS AS A LESBIAN VS. THRIVING IN THE SPOTLIGHT
KETHLEEN P. MARVEL

When I retired from the Chubb Group of Insurance Companies in 2009, I had been working there for over 28 years. I began my career at Chubb as a programmer trainee in 1981, and ended it as the chief diversity officer in 2009. For the first 14 years, I remained in the closet, yet it was after I came out that my career really took off. My reasons for not coming out sooner were no different than many other people, I suspect.

The year before I started working at Chubb, I came out to my parents. Their reaction was to cut me out of family functions, and to take back all the furnishings they had given me to set up my new apartment. Their reaction impacted the way I viewed coming out to anyone else. Since the people who loved me responded so negatively, I was certainly loath to coming out to a new employer. It seemed far safer to remain closeted.

I loved programming at Chubb, and I excelled at it. I was promoted through the ranks, and soon I was supervising programmers. By the time I was promoted into management, I had told so many lies about who I was dating, and where I was going on vacation, that I had to focus very hard to keep the details of my stories straight. Mostly, I just refrained from talking about my personal life, but when pointedly asked about it, I would lie. In time, I had come out to very few other gay or lesbian employees, but not to anyone that I thought was straight. The deception, though, started to have an impact on me and my relationship with others. I didn't know it then, but people were beginning to trust me a little less because they felt that I was withholding information from them. They didn't know what I was holding back, but they felt I was being less than truthful with them. This impacted the people I was managing, as well as the people to whom I reported.

The Negative Impact of Being "In The Closet"

During this time in the closet, I observed how harshly we closeted employees treated the few out gay and lesbian employees. I recall one particular example very clearly. An out lesbian came to work in the Information Technology department as a programmer. She was very up front about her sexual orientation, and her openness scared the heck out of the closeted lesbians and gay men. We avoided eating, talking and even making eye contact with her. We ostracized her because she was out, and thought people would assume we were gay too if we had anything to do with her. Needless to say, she didn't stay with us for very long.

A major turning point in my life came when my father died. I had been working at Chubb for 13 years, and had many friends and acquaintances who very kindly came to my father's wake. They were there to support me, but I couldn't focus on their kindness, nor on my grief. All I could think about was how to avoid introducing them to my partner of 18 years. After making myself miserable, and my partner feel completely invisible and devalued, I realized that I needed to change something to reconcile my work and personal life.

It's not as if Chubb wasn't trying to create a welcoming place for gay and lesbian employees during all this time. (I purposely omit bisexual and transgender employees because they were not included in the company's earliest efforts.) There were a few gay individuals who were out, and when it came time to transfer them to different offices for career growth, the company actually relocated them and their partners, just as they would have done with a straight married couple. The company also granted domestic partner benefits in the early 1990s, with no prompting by any organized group of employees. They felt it was only fair, so they did it as soon as they realized the inequity that existed.

There were also some wonderful Human Resources managers who were pushing the envelope regarding accepting and welcoming diversity in the workplace. In the late 1980s we had company-wide diversity training, which regrettably didn't talk about sexual orientation. Then, in the early 1990s, we had diversity training for Information Technology employees that did address sexual orientation. It didn't do so well, but it did tackle the issue.

During this training, the facilitators conducted an exercise that was meant to illustrate how we may be different from others based on one dimension of diversity, but similar to them on another. They asked us to gather into clusters based on race, then religion, and then on a slew of other dimensions of diversity. When they asked us to cluster based on sexual orientation, they were forcing anyone who was closeted either to come out, or to lie.

I had heard that this was going to happen, so I spoke to one of the facilitators privately. This was after my father had died, so I knew I wanted to start coming out at work, but not this way. I pleaded with the facilitator to change the exercise so it didn't force me to make that choice in that manner. He refused, and, the following day, I lied to the class. It was a horrible experience. In other sessions, some closeted people came out to the group in that exercise, not in the way they would have preferred, but in a manner that forced their hand. The intention of the training was good, but the process was terribly flawed.

An Experience that Changes Lives

That experience stayed with me, and on Coming Out Day in 1995, I called one of the lesbians who had come out in a training session. "Today is Coming Out Day!" I said. "So, what are you going to do about it?" she replied.

That simple challenge was all it took to get me to take a major step, and to choose my first straight ally. The woman I picked was in Human Resources, and was the most supportive ally one could ask for. For the second time in my life, a reaction to my coming out changed the way I proceeded through the coming out process. She had heard some of what went on in the training sessions, and was interested in starting the dialogue in a more productive way. She encouraged a few of us who were out to her to start an employee resource group. We did so in early 1996. As a spokesperson for the group, I found that I had to come out to more and more people. Each time I did, I had thousands of butterflies in my stomach, but it always turned out okay, and a little easier.

What I then found the hardest to do was to go back and come out to all of those people to whom I had lied for so many years. It was very uncomfortable to admit that I had been less than truthful with colleagues I now considered friends. And figuring out how to bring it up was very challenging. I found, though, that the more

I did with the employee group, the more people heard I was involved. They just assumed I must be lesbian because I was working on gay and lesbian issues. This made the coming out process just a bit easier.

The Positive Impact of "Coming Out"

Once I was out, I found that I had far more energy to put into my work, rather than into worrying about what I would say if someone asked about my personal life. I also found that people seemed to trust me, and believe in me more. Now, my career really took off. I was given challenging and innovative projects to work on. I was promoted several more levels. Because of my involvement with the employee group, and my level of outness, I was given access to senior level managers to discuss gay and lesbian issues in the workplace.

The employee group was able to influence improvements to the workplace environment by including bisexual and transgender employees in the discussion, by equalizing benefits, by providing managers with education about managing gay and transgender issues, and by sponsoring legislation for the Employment Non-Discrimination Act (ENDA). I was invited to represent the employee group, and speak to the board of directors about issues we encountered in the workplace. In short, I was recognized for my leadership within Information Technology, and also for my leadership on gay and lesbian workplace issues.

I accepted the position of chief diversity officer in 1995. From the start, I realized that I needed to be as out as I could be because I had an opportunity to impact many, many people now. I made sure that I included my partner's name in conversations as frequently as my peers included their spouses' names. I created teachable moments out of every possible opportunity. I encouraged dialogue about gay and transgender issues with employees who still couldn't understand why they were workplace concerns.

At my retirement party in June of 2009, unlike at my father's funeral, my partner was a visible and vital presence. I cannot imagine how incomplete the closure of my career with Chubb would have been had she had not been present. I'm extremely grateful for the positive support I received at work when I first decided to come out. Living life in the spotlight was so much more rewarding and fulfilling than living it in the shadows.

The reading that concludes this first section considers what happens when past injustices and institutional discrimination are ignored. In this case, the issue is the lasting impact that colonization has had on a Native American community in the United States. Native Americans, ironically, are often left out in discussing national identity in the United States. The author argues that this is a failure of large and disturbing proportions.

ENVISIONING JUSTICE IN MINNESOTA

WAZIYATAWIN, PH.D.

*Until America begins to build a moral record in
her dealings with the Indian people she should
try not to fool the rest of the world about her
intentions on other continents. America has
always been a militantly imperialistic world
power eagerly grasping for economic control
over weaker nations. . . . There has not been a
time since the founding of the republic when the
motives of this country were innocent.*

—VINE DELORIA JR.

In 2008, the State of Minnesota is celebrating 150 years of statehood. Parades, fes-
tivities, and much whoopla are accompanying this important anniversary in
Minnesota history. The state government, institutions, and appointed
Sesquicentennial Commission are asking all of us to reflect on what Minnesotans
have *gained* in the last century and a half as well as what *progress* Minnesotans have
achieved. Minnesota's original inhabitants, the Dakota Oyate (Nation), have a different perspective on those 150 years. Rather than measuring the years by what we have
gained, Dakota people more often measure what we have *lost*. We ask ourselves such
questions as

- What does it mean that a settler society established the State of Minnesota at
  the expense of Indigenous Peoples?

- What does it mean that Minnesota's citizens advocated, supported, and perpetrated genocidal policies so they could obtain Dakota homeland?

- What does it mean that Dakota extermination and forced removal (as well as
  Ho-Chunk removal) were the price of Minnesota's statehood?

- And, what does it mean in the twenty-first century when Minnesotans celebrate the establishment of the state, despite its shameful historical legacy and
  the harmful consequences to whole nations of Indigenous Peoples?

"Envisioning Justice in Minnesota," from *What Does Justice Look Like: The Struggle for Liberation
in the Dakota Homeland* by Waziyatawin, (2008) pp. 3–6. Reprinted by permission of Living
Justice Press.

Addressing Harms Internationally

We pose these questions at a time when the international community is beginning to address both the historical harms perpetrated against Indigenous Peoples globally and the contemporary harms we suffer because of ongoing subjugation and oppression. On September 13, 2007, the General Assembly of the United Nations adopted the Declaration on the Rights of Indigenous Peoples with an overwhelming majority. This declaration affirms both the individual and collective rights of Indigenous people as a way to promote justice and peace for all human beings throughout the world without discrimination. Article 8 of the declaration is particularly relevant to the discussion of Minnesota history:

1. Indigenous peoples and individuals have the right not to be subjected to forced assimilation or destruction of their culture.

2. States shall provide effective mechanisms for prevention of, and redress for:

   (a) Any action which has the aim or effect of depriving them of their integrity as distinct peoples, or of their cultural values or ethnic identities;

   (b) Any action which has the aim or effect of dispossessing them of their lands, territories or resources;

   (c) Any form of forced population transfer which has the aim or effect of violating or undermining any of their rights;

   (d) Any form of forced assimilation or integration;

   (e) Any form of propaganda designed to promote or incite racial or ethnic discrimination directed against them.

Every one of these applies to the internationally recognized crimes perpetrated by Minnesota citizens and the United States government against the Dakota people of Minnesota to obtain Dakota lands and resources as well as eliminate our populations. By eliminating or severely debilitating the original owners of the land and its resources, White Minnesotans ensured that Dakota people could no longer threaten the genocidal and exploitative policies that would continue to enrich them and other U.S. citizens.

Article 8 of the declaration directly challenges Minnesota's right to establish itself at the expense of Indigenous Peoples. It dictates that the United States (as the State) and Minnesota have an obligation to acknowledge and ensure some kind of reparative justice for these harms. Furthermore, the declaration would certainly condemn the celebration of that which was gained at the expense of Indigenous populations such as the Dakota. In this context, Minnesota's decision to celebrate the sesquicentennial is completely out of sync with an international community committed to working toward peace and justice.

In fact, rather than celebrating, other world powers are apologizing for their treatment of Indigenous Peoples. On February 13, 2008, as the first item of business for Australia's new parliament, Prime Minister Kevin Rudd apologized to Aboriginal

Australians for the "laws and policies of successive parliaments and governments that have inflicted profound grief, suffering and loss on these our fellow Australians." He apologized especially to the stolen generations of Aboriginal children forcibly removed from their families because of federal policies that lasted through the late 1960s.

Like Indigenous Peoples in the United States, Australian Aborigines comprise only a small percentage of the population (2 percent), yet they suffer the highest rates of infant mortality, drug abuse, alcoholism, and unemployment. Many hope the apology will "allow Australia to re-commit to improving the lives of Indigenous people." In the best-case scenario, this apology would mark just the beginning of a long process toward creating Aboriginal justice in Australia. It remains to be seen, however, whether the country will act on the apology, or if they will remain just words. As the Aboriginal leader Noel Pearson put it, "Blackfellas will get the words, the Whitefellas keep the money." Still this event is now part of a worldwide discourse regarding truth telling, acknowledgement of harms, and reparative justice.

Frankly, it is more comfortable for White Minnesotans to consider what is happening to Indigenous Peoples in other parts of the world, rather than to investigate what is happening to Indigenous Peoples in their own backyard. Minnesota's restorative justice workers, for example, frequently empathize with suffering elsewhere and join in the global chorus of voices demanding justice for oppressed Peoples across the oceans. They help victims and offenders engage in transformative healing practices elsewhere while condemning violence and holding perpetrators of harms accountable for their actions. Meanwhile, the monumental harms perpetrated against Dakota people remain unacknowledged and unaddressed. Yet, all Minnesotans continue to benefit from Dakota dispossession and every day they continue to deny justice to Dakota people.

Discussion Questions

- Who am I?

- How would you describe American identity? Who created it? Who disputes it?

- Explain why, and how, some identities are privileged while others are not. What can be done to dismantle this system of privilege? What can you do about it?

- Explain the intersectional approach in studying women and people of color. Why is this approach necessary?

- Describe the politics associated with the construction of our racial identities. Has our understanding of race and ethnicity changed over time?

Communities

Injustice often comes to groups, not just individuals. Whole communities suffer. For purposes of this discussion, "community" refers to a social group or a "collective of persons differentiated from at least one other group by cultural forms, practices, or way of life."[9]

> Our ordinary discourse differentiates people according to social groups such as women and men, age groups, racial and ethnic groups, religious groups, and so on. Social groups of this sort are not simply collections of people, for they are more fundamentally intertwined with the identities of the people described as belonging to them.[10]

Many concerned individuals suggest that emerging digital technologies are negatively impacting our notion of community, but Internet scholars suggest that virtual communities operate similarly to physical communities.[11] In both cases, Pincus suggests, it is helpful to think about discrimination at three levels—individual, institutional, and structural—that sometimes operate simultaneously.[12] However, the level that permeates the following readings is structural discrimination which is defined below:

> . . . *structural discrimination* refers to the policies of dominant race/ethnic/ gender institutions and the behavior of the individuals who implement these policies and control these institutions, which are race/ethnic/gender neutral in intent but which have a differential and/or harmful effect on minority race/ethnic/gender groups.[13]

Although all three forms of discrimination are distinct from racial prejudice, which is an attitude, all are mostly hidden from public view and operate covertly. However, a recent example actually brought discrimination and racism to the surface and began a much needed public debate as the following reading demonstrates. Hurricane Katrina devastated the Gulf Coast of the United States, and the media were on hand to capture the images of sick, helpless, and dying Americans.

> The barrage of images in newspapers and on television tested the nation's collective sense of reality . . . Photo snaps and film shots captured legions of men and women . . . crying in wild-eyed desperation for help, for any help, from somebody, anybody, who would listen to their unanswered pleas. The filth and squalor of

---

[9]Iris Marion Young, *Justice and the Politics of Difference* (Princeton, NJ: Princeton University Press, 1990), p. 43.

[10]Ibid., p. 44.

[11]See Howard Rheingold, *The Virtual Community* (Reading, MA: Addison-Wesley, 1993).

[12]Fred Pincus, "Discrimination Comes in Many Forms: Individual, Institutional, and Structural," *American Behavioral Scientist*, vol. 40 (2): 186–87 (November/December 1996).

[13]Ibid., p. 186.

their confinement—defecating where they stood or sat, or more likely, dropped, bathed in a brutal wash of dredge and sickening pollutants that choked the air with ungodly stench—grieved the camera lenses that recorded their plight.[14]

The imagery associated with the unnatural disaster is forever burned into our minds. The power of images can have a positive or negative impact. In the case of these victims in the Gulf, the effect was both positive and negative. The country recognized its impoverished underbelly, but at the same time, failed to create meaningful solutions. The nation has grown accustomed to images of color being associated with poverty and crime and distrustful of the effectiveness of governmental intervention. So on the negative side, the desperate imagery associated with poor, black victims of Hurricane Katrina reinforced already potent negative stereotypes.

The readings that conclude this chapter provide further evidence of the power that images have in constructing identities and negatively impacting communities. The first focuses on negative imagery associated with Latina reproduction and the government's panicky response. Latinas have been framed as breeding machines that need to be controlled, illustrating the point that Zatz and Mann make connecting images and public-policy outcomes. Shades here of a moral panic, which occurs when the media portray a social phenomenon as a threat to fundamental societal interests and values. Immigration, or simply reproduction by an "other," can provoke a moral panic.

FERTILE MATTERS: THE POLITICS OF MEXICAN-ORIGIN WOMEN'S REPRODUCTION

ELENA R. GUTIÉRREZ

The Advent of Surgical Sterilization

Academics and others typically define sterilization abuse as "the misinformed, coerced, or unknowing termination of the reproductive capacity of women and men." The long and well-researched history of sterilization abuse in the United States has demonstrated that practitioners of coercive sterilization have targeted their subjects according to race, class, and gender. As historian Adelaida Del Castillo has noted, sterilization abuse of Mexican-origin peoples for eugenic reasons had occurred previously. Before sterilization was widely available, individual judges

---

[14]Michael Eric Dyson, *Come Hell or High Water: Hurricane Katrina and the Color of Disaster* (New York: Basic Civitas, 2006), pp. 1–2.

---

would make parole and other conditions of probation dependent upon sterilization. In 1966, for example, Nancy Hernández was sentenced to jail when she refused to agree to be sterilized for a misdemeanor conviction.

During the 1970s, several circumstances directly precipitated sterilization abuse nationwide. For one thing, medical regulations governing sterilization options for most women had become less restrictive. Earlier, sterilization was guided by an age-parity formula, whereby a doctor would only sterilize a woman if her age multiplied by the number of her children exceeded 120. In 1970 the American College of Obstetrics and Gynecology withdraw this standard, offering millions of women access to the procedure. The liberalization of medical guidelines for sterilization was coupled with increased availability of funding. Governmental grants to the poor increased substantially after 1965, most notably through passage of the Family Planning Services and Population Research Act in 1970. While in 1965 only $5 million of federal money was available for family planning services for the poor, in 1979 the government distributed $260 million for this purpose.

Government financing for sterilization procedures in particular was substantial. Prior to 1969 the government had prohibited federally supported family planning services from subsidizing sterilization and abortion services. Funds for sterilization became accessible officially in 1971, with Medicaid covering 90 percent of the cost. Most federal funds were offered through the Office of Economic Opportunity (OEO), which was established to fight the "war on poverty." The combination of technical advances in tubal ligation surgery, increased availability of federal funding, and relaxed requirements for the procedures led to sterilization becoming the most popular form of birth control in the United States.

California long held the highest rates of sterilization in the nation, and these developments increased those rates even more. Sterilizations at the Women's Hospital of LACMC exemplified the extraordinary surge in the numbers of women undergoing such procedures. During the two-year period between July 1968 and July 1970, elective hysterectomy increased by 742 percent, elective tubal ligation by 470 percent, and tubal ligation after delivery by 151 percent.

An "Epidemic" of Sterilization Abuse Revealed

Despite the dramatic increase in rates of sterilization through the 1970s, no medical community boards or governmental officials monitored these procedures. No safeguards to prevent widespread abuses were in effect during the first three years that publicly funded sterilization procedures were available, although OEO-funded family planning clinics were asked to refrain from performing the operation until a set of federal guidelines could be administered. Although guidelines were printed in 1972, the U.S. government did not distribute them to clinics until 1974. Within this unregulated environment, many coerced sterilizations occurred without much notice until the case of the Relf sisters captured public attention.

In June 1973, Mary Alice and Katie Relf, two African American sisters in their early teens, were sterilized in a Montgomery, Alabama hospital even though neither of the girls, nor their parents, gave permission for, or even knew about, the operations. The hospital paid for these operations using OEO funds. Although Mrs. Relf signed an "X" on a consent form she could not read, neither she nor her daughters were advised of the specific nature of the "shots" the nurse advised were necessary. Realizing later that their daughters had been unwittingly sterilized, the parents reported the incident to the Southern Poverty Law Center. National objection to the treatment of the Relf sisters forced the federal Department of Health, Education, and Welfare to suspend the availability of federal funds for the sterilization of minors and the "mentally incompetent" until the government enacted regulations. However, coercive sterilization of adults continued unchecked.

One major study in this era, conducted and coauthored by Drs. Bernard Rosenfeld and Sidney Wolfe, and later published by the Ralph Nader Health Research Group in 1973, exposed several reputable teaching institutions for coercively targeting poor women of color for sterilization. The report verified that doctors at some of the nation's most prestigious hospitals pressured women into consenting to sterilization.

Based on medical journal articles, observation, and interviews with medical students and doctors trained in hospitals across the nation, the report revealed an "epidemic of sterilization . . . in . . . almost every major American teaching hospital in the past two years." In most cases, women were not adequately informed of the range of birth control options available to them nor the permanence of the sterilization operation. Moreover, many were unaware that they had been sterilized. In almost every major medical teaching hospital in the country, the number of elective tubal ligations had at least doubled between the years of 1971 and 1973. On finding that most of the victimized women were low-income minorities, the authors of the report charged that doctors and other hospital personnel acted out of racist attitudes regarding "overpopulation" and "ideal family size." Studies also showed that of the many cases of coercive sterilization reported, none documented abuses against white women. In fact, doctors often tried to talk white middle-class women out of sterilization surgery.

While doctors and others targeted African American women in the South, Native American women suffered from rampant sterilization abuse at Indian Health Service (IHS) clinics. Dr. Connie Uri, who interviewed many native women sterilized while under duress or without complete information, became their advocate. The national attention that she brought to these abuses resulted in a study requested by Senator James Abourzek and conducted by the General Accounting Office (GAO). The report revealed that many women had felt coerced into sterilization by the IHS and under threat of losing their welfare benefits if they did not agree to the operation. In the four IHS areas examined in the GAO study, 3,406 sterilizations were performed between 1973 and 1976, an estimated one-quarter of all Native Americans sterilized during those three years. Many of these women were under the age of twenty-one, a violation of the moratorium called by the Department of Health, Education, and Welfare in 1974.

Elsewhere I have argued that although sterilization abuse of women of color was widespread across the nation at this time, institutions in different regions of the country coerced women in numerous ways, using a variety of justifications. The sterilization abuse of women of Mexican origin followed a pattern similar to that of other women of color, but several factors distinguish what occurred at LACMC from other cases. For example, abuses that have received widespread national attention, such as *Relf v. Weinberger* and *Walker v. Pierce,* occurred in the South and targeted African American women receiving public assistance. The case of *Madrigal v. Quilligan,* on the other hand, took place in Los Angeles and involved mostly poor Mexican immigrant women with limited English-speaking ability—none of whom were receiving public assistance. These differences raise unique issues of citizenship, regional racial politics, language, and culture. How these factors shaped the sterilization abuse of Mexican-origin women is best exemplified in the case of *Madrigal v. Quilligan.*

Forced Sterilization at Los Angeles County Medical Center

"Birth control" in this case included rampant sterilization abuse at LACMC, yet this was only one aspect of the systematic effort by the hospital staff to reduce the birthrate of their mostly minority clientele. Several other programs reflected the department's attempt to cut the birthrate of the Mexican and African American populations, who made up the majority of the hospital's patients. Bilingual family planning counselors actively visited each new mother prior to her discharge from the ward to ensure her commitment to practice some form of birth control; no woman was released until this was promised. Counselors aggressively recommended IUDs, a long-term method of birth control that women themselves cannot regulate.

Dr. Karen Benker recounted that "the drive to insert IUDs was so great that the women actually did not receive a postpartum check-up or have any of their questions about their baby or their health answered. They were merely placed on the table one after another and an IUD was popped into place. In her affidavit Benker stated that these facts demonstrate the great emphasis that the department did put on 'cutting the birth rate of the Mexican and Negro population.'"

Doctors implemented the most effective form of birth control during delivery when they terminated the childbearing capabilities of women of Mexican origin by tubal ligation. As was common in teaching hospitals across the nation, LACMC students were encouraged to conduct several surgical procedures to refine their skills. According to Dr. Bernard Rosenfeld, coauthor of the Health Research Group Report and a resident in the Obstetrics-Gynecology Department at LACMC during this period, staff doctors would often congratulate residents on the number of postpartum tubal ligations accomplished within a week's time. Similarly, residents reportedly encouraged interns to press women into agreeing to a sterilization procedure. In one instance, after a patient had refused a resident's solicitations for sterilization, the resident's supervisor remarked, "Talk her into it. You can always talk her into it." In June 1973 a resident told new interns, "I want you to ask every one of the girls if they want their tubes tied, regardless of how old they are. Remember everyone you get to get her tubes tied means two tubes [i.e., two procedures] for some resident or intern. Rosenfeld estimated that 10 to 20 percent of the physicians at LACMC "actively pushed sterilization on women who either did not understand what was happening to them or who had not been given all the facts regarding their options.

Physicians most often approached women for sterilization while they were in the last stages of labor, during their wait in the Active Labor Room, where they stayed until actual delivery. Here women in the most painful stages of labor were attached to fetal monitors and placed in beds side by side. Dr. Karen Benker recalled the scene as one of "crowding, screams of pain, bright lights, lack of sleep by patients and staff, and an assembly-line' approach so that many women were literally terrified of what was happening at the time they signed the consents. Of course, this was especially true of non-English-speaking mothers who were left with no explanation of what was happening. Dr. Benker's acknowledgment that non-English-speaking women were "of course" more likely to experience medical mistreatment speaks to the critical importance of language in the sterilization abuse cases that occurred at LACMC. Most residents and doctors were not bilingual; most knew only a few obstetrical-related words. There was "virtually no one available" to interpret for Spanish-speaking women. Often women were sterilized on the basis of one question, "¿Más niños?" (More babies?) While some nurses or translators tried to communicate with Spanish-speaking women, as illustrated below, the doctors apparently took advantage of the women's inability to understand English and manipulated them into consenting to sterilization.

Residents and nurses often approached women to sign consent forms immediately before childbirth. Medical personnel gave women in labor a shot of Valium or Demerol in preparation for the delivery, and they shoved consent forms into the hands of laboring women while they were too groggy to understand or notice that they were signing forms granting permission for their own sterilization. Dr. Benker described seeing this type of coercion "on almost a daily basis": "The doctor would hold a syringe in front of the mother who was in labor pain and ask her if she wanted a pain killer; while the woman was in the throes of a contraction the doctor would say, `Do you want the pain killer? Then sign the papers. Do you want the pain to stop? Do you want to have to go through this again? Sign the papers.'"

Moreover, hospital staff did not fully explain the irreversible nature of the sterilization procedure. Many women agreed to the surgery believing that their tubes were being tied temporarily and that they could be untied later and their fertility restored. A physician first asked Maria Figueroa if she wanted tubal ligation as she was being prepared for surgery. She specifically recalled that the doctor told her the procedure entailed the "tying of a woman's tubes" and she could later have them untied. She initially rejected the procedure, but tired from her labor and of the doctor's urgings, Mrs. Figueroa agreed to sterilization if she delivered a boy. As it turned out, she was sterilized even though she delivered a baby girl.

In many instances LACMC patients were not just subjected to a single incident of coercion but were harassed continually by nurses and doctors. Helena Orozco, a plaintiff in the *Madrigal* trial, had repeatedly declined sterilization throughout her prenatal care at the hospital. She had discussed sterilization with her husband prior to labor, and Mrs. Orozco told the nurses, "We decided not to." However, after numerous solicitations from the doctor and nurses, and while crying from intense pain during labor, Mrs. Orozco signed the consent for sterilization because, in her words, "I just wanted them to leave me alone, sign the papers and get it over with. . . . I was in pain on the table when they were asking me all those questions, and they were poking around my stomach, and pushing with their fingers up there. I just wanted to be left alone. Mrs. Orozco also agreed to the operation because "I thought he [the doctor] meant tying tubes only. Then they could be untied later. . . . If they would have put the word 'sterilization' there, I would not have signed the papers. Because she believed the procedure to be reversible, Mrs. Orozco planned to have her tubes untied in three years and did not find out until a year and a half later that she could never again have children.

Hospital personnel also strategically limited communication between laboring women and their husbands. For example, when a patient adamantly resisted sterilization, the doctor would warn the husband that his wife's health was in danger, hoping that the husband would then pressure his wife to submit to the procedure. Such manipulative gender dynamics were apparent in the case of Dolores Madrigal, who refused sterilization from the outset of her stay at LACMC. After Mrs. Madrigal had refused the recommendations of several nurses that she take care of herself and agree to a tubal ligation, doctors talked with Mr. Madrigal in another room, telling him that his wife would die if she had another child. Ten minutes later, a nurse returned to Mrs. Madrigal and informed her, laughing, that her husband had agreed to the sterilization procedure, and again presented her with a consent form to sign.

Women requiring cesarean section delivery were at greatest risk of coercive sterilization. According to Dr. Benker, once it became clear that a cesarean was going to be necessary, the resident was "extremely aggressive" in pushing for sterilization. Many doctors lied to patients, telling them that state law only allowed three cesarean sections and that sterilization was therefore required after childbirth. Maria Hurtado recalled that her doctor "brought someone from outside and explained to her to ask me why I wanted so many children since the State of California only permitted three Cesareans." While unconscious following the delivery of her child, Mrs. Hurtado was given a tubal ligation without her consent. It was not until requesting birth control during her six-week postpartum visit that she recalled a receptionist at the hospital telling her, "Lady, forever you will not be able to have any more children."

Doctors sometimes told patients that they might even die during future childbirths if they were not sterilized after their cesarean. Upon the cesarean delivery of her third child, Consuelo Hermosillo was advised by her doctor that sterilization would be necessary, because a fourth pregnancy would most likely be life-threatening. While medicated, Ms. Hermosillo signed the consent forms, without full comprehension of their content. Likewise, Estela Benavides feared her doctor's warnings that another child delivered by cesarean could be life-threatening, and she consented to a tubal ligation while hemorrhaging during her labor. She made this hard decision, she stated, out of her commitment to continue to care for her existing children.

"A Clash of Cultures": The Trial of Madrigal V. Quilligan

On June 18, 1975, attorneys for the *Madrigal* plaintiffs filed a class-action civil rights suit in federal district court in Los Angeles, naming USC-Los Angeles County Medical Center, twelve doctors, the State of California, and the U.S. Department of Health, Education, and Welfare as defendants. Three years later, Charles Nabarette and Antonia Hernández began their case in court on May 31, 1978. The lawyers argued that the sterilization of the women without their informed consent constituted a violation of their civil rights and their constitutional right to bear children.

After much dispute, the judge finally decided to allow Dr. Benker to testify. Ms. Hernández began her questioning bluntly: "Did you ever have a conversation with Dr. Quilligan regarding the birth rate of the Mexican and Negro people?" In response, Dr. Benker recounted her memory of her first day of orientation on the obstetrics ward as a medical student in 1970, when she and a group of other medical students met Dr. Quilligan, the head of the ward, in the hallway. Dr. Benker testified that when one of her fellow students commented on the new facilities at the women's building, which were noticeably superior to the hospital's other wings, Dr. Quilligan replied that the department had recently received a federal grant "to show how low we can cut the birth rate of the Negro and Mexican populations in Los Angeles County." When the students appeared surprised by the doctor's remarks, another attending physician referred to the poverty and overpopulation within these populations in an apparent attempt to justify Dr. Quilligan's statement.

While on the witness stand, Dr. Benker recalled several other instances during hospital conferences and meetings when physicians discussed overpopulation and the fertility of Mexican women. In one such incident, Dr. Quilligan claimed that poor minority women in Los Angeles County "were having too many babies," that this was placing a "strain on society," and that it was "socially desirable" that the women be sterilized.

Over continued objections from the defendants' attorney, Dr. Benker began to testify to the many times she witnessed doctors approaching women during labor to request consent to sterilization. Judge Jesse Curtis, responding to Mr. Maskey's objections, halted this line of questioning, claiming, "This case has taken so long already." The judge stated that the doctors were entitled to invoke social motivations for actively encouraging sterilization as long as they had some medical rationale. In one of his many lengthy orations from the bench during Benker's direct examination, Judge Curtis stated: "Suppose he [a doctor] does favor sterilization in every chance he can get. So long as he does not override the will of one of his patients, I do not see that there is anything objectionable. He may believe that in theory one of the big problems is that some families are too big. He is entitled to that belief. He is just not entitled to overpower the will of his patients."

Furthermore, Judge Curtis recognized the cultural and racially based nature of the discussion occurring in the court, but ultimately deemed it inconsequential. In his words,

> There is confusion in this area which arises from a clash of cultures. The plaintiffs are Mexican-Americans who have a culture the based somewhat foreign to ours [*sic*]. They just happened to be Mexican-Americans. There could be other people who, I think in this country, come from other ethnic backgrounds who have more or less the same culture, one which highly values the woman's ability to procreate a family, and particularly the size of the family is a matter of great concern, and also has almost a religious significance. . . .
>
> So, I do not think it is surprising that you might find a doctor who believes that people who are inclined to have big families shouldn't, and particularly for good medical reasons, undertakes to persuade a person not to have a large family. And if that person agrees and is willing to be sterilized, then I cannot see anything wrong with the doctor having suggested it or having convinced the patient, so long as he does not use his powers, his ability, his circumstances to override what would be a reasonable decision on the part of the patient. What I want to know here is: To what extent the doctors had overridden the wishes of the patients, if they had. And if they have in some instances, what is their medical justification for doing it?

The judge quite simply reduced the conflict to one about cultural difference. On the one side we have a culture concerned about overpopulation. On the other is a culture that "highly values a woman's ability to procreate a family." Judge Curtis essentially absolved the doctors of all responsibility for any coercive actions, arguing that it is within their legal limits to attempt to persuade patients to submit to sterilization. With her examination of Dr. Benker so severely curtailed, the plaintiffs' attorney was forced to call an end to Karen Benker's testimony. The defense attorneys, having successfully attacked the relevancy of Benker's testimony during her direct examination, did not cross-examine her.

The article that concludes this chapter is also related to imagery, in this case the way disabled people are portrayed. Segregation and stereotypes have long dominated the lives of disabled persons in this country, though there have been some efforts toward integration, most notably, the Americans with Disabilities Act.[15] How can you, as an individual or member of an organization, take this further and bring the disabled more centrally into civil society, that is, the area of living where government does not ordinarily enter: friendships, colleagueship, casual conversations?

---

[15]See Jonathan Drimmer, "Cripples, Overcomers, and Civil Rights: Tracing the Evolution of Federal Legislation and Social Policy for People with Disabilities," 40 UCLA L. Rev. 1341 (1992–1993).

ASSISTANCE AND TREATMENT
JACQUELINE VAUGHN SWITZER

Well-meaning and often well-educated social workers and reformers attempted to ameliorate the brutality of institutions and the separation mentality by developing tools that would help persons with disabilities live independently. In 1860 Simon Pollack of the Missouri School for the Blind brought a new communications aid to the United States. A system of raised letters and symbols that could be "read" had been developed in France by Louis Braille and later modified by American educators. As often has been the case with the introduction of new technology, however, policymakers argued among themselves over various versions of Braille until 1910, when "American Braille" was adopted as a standard by the American Printing House for the Blind. The language's use remains controversial even today as computerized scanners and portable cassette recorders have reduced the number of persons who actually use Braille to read.

Perhaps the most recognizable aid for disabled persons is the wheelchair. The U.S. Patent Office registered the first design for one in 1869, and a folding model was patented forty years later. Bulky, expensive, and cumbersome, the early models provided some mobility for persons with physical disabilities, but it was not until the 1970s and the advent of wheelchair sports that designs were radically altered. In addition to the lighter weight, racing bike-styled "Quickie," power wheelchairs provided freedom for persons with spinal cord injuries, multiple sclerosis, or other severe disabilities. Unfortunately, while technology moved forward, public policy did not. The availability of such devices remains limited by public funding for health care, insurance carriers attempting to keep the cost of durable medical goods down, and distribution. Moreover, getting a wheelchair is one thing; making a home accessible or finding transportation that can be adapted to accommodate wheelchair users is something else.

Persons who are deaf or hard of hearing have faced a struggle similar to that faced by those who are blind or have limited vision. In the mid-nineteenth century, Bernard Engelsman founded the New York Institution for the Improved Instruction of Deaf Mutes. Using a system he had learned in Vienna, Engelsman began teaching students to read lips and attempt speech. His "oral school" used techniques (oralism) that were the antithesis of the manual or sign language method advocated by Gallaudet and others. Advocates of the two competing approaches battled for scarce resources, and many schools forbade their students from using what had become known as

American Sign Language, or ASL. It took decades for ASL to gain acceptance, and its use remains controversial among some members of the deaf community.

"Treatment" procedures became as controversial as policies to provide assistive devices, especially after media reports flourished that focused on the abuse of persons with disabilities who were being institutionalized. Public attention was captured to some extent in 1946 by the riveting account of life in public mental institutions in Mary Jane Ward's *The Snake Pit*, which was made into a film in 1948, and *Christmas in Purgatory*, a photographic documentation of brutalizing conditions that was published in 1966. By the late 1960s, terms such as "mainstreaming," "normalization," and "residential care" had begun to replace institutionalization in state facilities, which gradually were being shut down.

Debates over treatment continued through the rest of the century, however. Psychotropic medications—known derisively as "chemical strait-jackets"—were developed at the turn of the twentieth century to make people with mental illness more docile and compliant. Yet the use of mind-numbing drugs, along with aversive therapy, remains the treatment of choice in many institutions today. Aversive therapy, for example, often is used to control the actions of people with developmental disabilities, and corporal punishment is common. Disability rights activist Nancy Weiss has documented treatment in U.S. facilities that she equates to that afforded political prisoners.

The contemporary horror of inadequate institutional care is exemplified by what came to be known as "The Willowbrook Wars." The term refers to a series of events that took place at New York's Willowbrook State School, which opened in 1951. Advocates for disabled people provided hundreds of accounts of insufficient medical care, neglect, malnutrition, improper sanitation, forced seclusion, and abuse that resulted from cuts in state funding and poor staffing. An ABC television report in 1972 that showed naked children lying in their own waste and filthy conditions at the facility led to massive protests by parents and eventually a class action lawsuit on behalf of the residents that reduced the size of the facility's population from 5,400 to 250; most of the former patients were placed within community care.

The Willowbrook experience was part of a major change in disability policy—deinstitutionalization—that attempted to bring an end to the warehousing of disabled persons. In 1962 a President's Panel on Mental Retardation commissioned by President John F. Kennedy recommended the development of a wider range of alternatives for people with developmental and psychiatric disabilities. A series of landmark court cases led justices to rule that conditions in institutions were so cruel as to be considered unconstitutional and that people with developmental disabilities had a right to live in the community.

The Stereotypes Continue

Just as the landmark case of *Brown v. Education* in 1954 failed to produce immediate desegregation of the nation's public schools, passage of nondiscriminatory legislation has failed to put an end to the stereotypes that still characterize persons with disabilities. According to several researchers, the problem lies with the media, which have pigeonholed disabled people into common stereotypes. "There is the sad, unlucky disabled person, in need of pity and charity. Or there is the plucky, coura-geous disabled person, celebrated for overcoming a disability and performing seem-ingly superhuman feats, whether holding a job or scaling a mountain. One is the image of Tiny Tim, the other that of the 'super crip.'" In the words of writer Joseph Shapiro, who has covered the disability rights movement in depth, these stereotypes have slowed progress toward full inclusion in American life. "To be seen as patient or in need of charity is to be thought incapable of the same life as others. To be lauded for super-achievement is to suggest that a disabled person can turn our pity into respect only at the point of having accomplished some extraordinary feat."

These images represent a pattern of what researchers Robert Bogdan and Douglas Biklen call "handicapist stereotypes"—seven images use commonly by the media in its depiction of persons with disabilities:

1. *The disabled person as pitiable and pathetic.* This form of continuing negative stereo-typing is found in charity telethons, which perpetuate the image of people with disabilities as objects of pity. Their stories often are told in terms of people who are victims of a tragic fate rather than a social minority.

2. *The disabled person as Supercrip.* These heartwarming stories, says journalism pro-fessor Jack Nelson, depict great courage—or what is often referred to as "disabil-ity chic"—wherein someone likable either succeeds in triumphing or succumbs heroically. The problem, of observer notes, is that a lot of ordinary disabled peo-ple are made feel like failures if they haven't done something extraordinary. Disability advocates are exceptionally harsh and critical of such individuals and their "inspirational" coverage.

3. *The disabled person as sinister, evil, and criminal.* In this stereotype that plays on deeply held fears and prejudices, the disabled villain—especially one with a psy-chiatric illness—is almost always someone who is dangerous, unpredictable, and evil. This perception may lead to unwarranted apprehension and ostracism of people with disabilities, robbing them of their sense of self by regarding them only as exemplars of a stigmatic trait.

4. The disabled person as better off dead. Nelson refers to the "better dead than dis-abled syndrome" as one way in which the media implies that with medical costs soaring and resources limited, a disabled person would seek suicide because life often is unbearable. Society (or the family) is thereby relieved of caring for the disabled individual, who is not whole or useful.

5. *The disabled person as maladjusted—his or her own worst enemy.* "If only disabled per-sons were not so bitter and would accept themselves, they would have better lives" is the translation of this common stereotype. Usually it involves a nondisabled person who helps someone with a disability see the "bright side" of his or her impairment—the mythology that persons with disabilities need guidance because they are unable to make sound judgments.

6. *The disabled person as a burden.* Family responsibility and duty form the core of this stereotype, which is built on the assumption that persons with disabilities need someone else to take care of them. Like the stereotype of disabled persons as better off dead, it engenders the belief that the burden, whether financial or emotional, is so compelling that it ruins families and their lives. In contemporary parlance, it has focused on the hot-button issue of physician-assisted suicide.

7. *The disabled person as unable to live a successful life.* The media has distorted society's views of what it means to be disabled, by limiting the presence of disabled persons in the portrayal of day-to-day life. Although more disabled people are beginning to appear in cameo-like scenes, they are seldom seen in workplace situations or as happy, healthy family members. This legacy of negative images is both damaging and inaccurate.

What is important about these enduring stereotypes, however, is the fact that they have helped frame the policy debate over the civil rights of disabled persons. Richard Scotch notes that the legal precedents for protecting persons with disabilities against discrimination came primarily from the Civil Rights Acts of 1964 and 1968. Both statutes were clear in their goal of protecting individuals facing discrimination because of their race. In the case of disabled persons, however, policy initiatives were made for different reasons: a perceived societal obligation to provide for dependent disabled persons and the assumption that there would be benefits to society from making disabled individuals economically and socially self-sufficient.

Discussion Questions

- What are some of the impacts of structural and institutional discrimination on communities of color? What is their source? How can these impacts be overcome?

- What does it mean for an image to have power? How is this connected to law and policy and attitudes toward the "other"?

- Can media images be dangerous to minority groups? What are some examples?

Chapter 2

MEDIA, CULTURE, AND TECHNOLOGY

If it is true, as the previous chapter argued, that we become, to a certain extent, who we are expected to be, then it is important to consider how these expectations are communicated. While families and friends and community are important in establishing identity, it is the mass media that provide individuals with a window on the wider world. The significance of mass means of communication in individual lives appears to be growing as new technologies are developed and marketed to huge audiences. The web of connections is clearly expanding through social media and wider news nets. This expansion has implications, not just for how we envision our own roles in society, but also for how we see society and its institutions. Students of justice need to be critical and curious about media content and its impact.

The 21st century finds us awash in "media"—a collective term that encompasses every form of mass communication—from books, to television and film, to the Internet. Less than 100 years ago, technology limited the ability of media to transmit information and shape culture. Today, television screens are everywhere. The North American news media broadcast 24 hours a day. Foreign news is readily available via the Internet. A person can ask a news source to send its headlines directly to a cellular phone. If those sources are not enough, blogs—ranging from the serious to the absurd—can either fill in the gaps or become primary sources of information. The ever-expanding range of wireless hotspots ensures that the spaces are shrinking where one is cut off from the enormous flow of information. Constant exposure to the media has an enormous impact on perceptions of justice. Our understanding of social norms, deviant behavior, danger, and just desserts are all heavily influenced by the mass media.

In such an information-saturated environment, it becomes easy to take the media for granted or to tune out its "white noise." The commercial structure of the media seems natural, because that is what we know. We tend to underestimate the role that mass media play in how we "know" the world around us. Meanwhile, new technology has expanded the reach of media in all its forms. In this situation it becomes even more important to understand how media shape culture. such as amplifying what is commercially valuable and ignoring much that cannot easily be marketed for mass consumption. What we know and what we think we know, what we value and what we debate, all are filtered through some sort of media.

Walter Lippmann noted in 1922 that the mass media (primarily print in Lippmann's day) are often "the chief means of contact with the unseen environment."[1] This early insight remains valid today: media transmit and create knowledge by bringing closer what is distant, thereby making the unknown somehow knowable. This ability of media to bring the distant into proximity can have an extraordinarily positive impact on people. News programming, documentaries, entertainment television, films, books, and research reports from all over the world shrink distances and provide us with information that would otherwise be unavailable.

However, the media produces distortions that can have significant consequences. For instance, Victor Kappeler and Gary Potter document how news stories focus on sensational and violent crimes, disproportionately portraying African Americans and Hispanics as criminals.[2] Other important facts about crime—that rates of crime, particularly violent crime, are declining and that most violent crime is perpetrated by someone the victim knows and who is most often of the same race—tend to be ignored.[3] Kappeler and Potter show that the crime-filled United States brought into our living rooms by the nightly news, and the United States people actually live in are really two different places.

Commercialization has made news reporting, in David Altheide's words, "infotainment." The result is a fearful populace looking to authorities for solutions.[4] The authorities reply with a "politics of fear" that capitalizes on concerns that the media and politicians themselves have helped to create.[5] Evidence of this is the fact that penal policies in the United States have grown harsher at the very time that criminal offending became less frequent. Today, the United States has the largest prison population in the world and the highest rate of imprisonment per 100,000 population. These prisoners are disproportionately racial and ethnic minorities. According to the United States

---

[1] Walter Lippmann, *Public Opinion* (New York: Simon and Schuster, 1922), p. 203.

[2] Victor Kappeler and Gary Potter, *The Mythology of Crime and Criminal Justice,* 4th ed. (Long Grove, IL: Waveland Press, Inc., 2005), pp. 20–21.

[3] Ibid., pp. 41–45.

[4] David Altheide, *Creating Fear: News and the Construction of Crisis* (New York: Aldine de Gruyter, 2002).

[5] David Altheide, *Terrorism and the Politics of Fear* (Oxford, U.K.: AltaMira Press, 2006), p. 15.

Department of Justice, 2.3 million people were in federal and state prisons or jails at the end of 2008—with African Americans and Hispanics comprising over 50 percent of all federal and state prison inmates.[6]

Drew Humphries illustrated this phenomenon in her study of the moral panic surrounding "crack mothers" during the late 1980s and early 1990s.[7] Sensationalized accounts of "crack babies" helped spur a series of attempts to prosecute women—mostly African Americans—who had used the drug while pregnant. The campaign was spearheaded by elected county attorneys from white suburban areas where crack cocaine use was not an overwhelming problem. Humphries's work provides a vivid example of how media structures brought the distant "urban problem" of "crack mothers" into proximity for suburban populations and their opinion leaders. Prosecution was made to seem desirable and necessary.

While Lippmann's observations were directed primarily at the news, his insights also apply to entertainment media. Consider, for example, the "*CSI* Effect," a term coined to describe reluctance among juries to convict without the type of air-tight forensic evidence featured on certain police "procedural"-style television shows. For example, a jury may be reluctant to convict in a rape case without some type of DNA evidence conclusively linking the plaintiff to the crime. The *CSI* Effect demonstrates the power of the media to take what is distant and obscure and make it appear to be simple and knowable. People even change their behavior in light of what they think they have learned from television about the proper standard of proof in criminal cases. Jeff Ferrel, Keith Hayward, and Jock Young describe the *CSI* Effect as a "cultural loop."[8] In these loops people begin to use various media representations as the basis to interpret, and act, on real-life situations. In the process, "reality" is subtly altered to match its representation.

The media, Douglas Kellner argues, also "teaches individuals how to fit into the dominant system of norms, values, practices, and institutions and demonstrates punishments for failure to conform."[9] Take for example the science-fiction series *Battlestar Galactica (BSG)*, which follows humanity's near-destruction and quest through space for a new home world. In the midst of spaceship combat, faster-than-light travel, and fighting robots, *BSG* instructs viewers on conventional norms of love, friendship, loyalty, honor, and sacrifice. The series also affirms North American institutional ideals

---

[6]U.S. Department of Justice, Bureau of Justice Statistics, *Prisoners in 2008* (Washington, DC: Office of Justice Programs, 2010), pp. 2, 8.

[7]Drew Humphries, *Crack Mothers: Pregnancy Drugs and the Media* (Columbus, OH: Columbus State University Press, 1999).

[8]Jeff Ferrel, Keith Hayward, and Jock Young, *Cultural Criminology* (London: Sage, 2008), pp. 130–32.

[9]Douglas Kellner, "Toward a Critical Media/Cultural Studies," in *Media/Cultural Studies: Critical Approaches*, edited by Rhonda Hammer and Douglass Kellner (New York: Peter Lang Publishing, 2009), p. 6.

of democratic representation, capitalism, freedom of religion, freedom of speech, and judicial process—all are either unquestioned values in the story, or they triumph in the face of serious challenges. A critic might point out that *BSG* also affirms darker elements of our culture: Militarism, torture, and capital punishment are also legitimated in *BSG*.

In a larger sense, *BSG* is not "just entertainment"; the show has a point of view, one with implications for how people understand concepts like justice and fairness. In other words, this show is ideological because it conveys an understanding about how the world is and how it should function.

Entertainment media do more than simply reaffirm dominant cultural values; they also push forward particular ideologies. For example, in his analysis of reality crime shows, Gray Cavender demonstrates how television shows like *America's Most Wanted (AMW)* and *Unsolved Mysteries (UM)* incorporate a crime-control ideology into their entertainment formats.[10] Cavender argues that these two programs suggest that due-process guarantees interfere with effective police work. They also reinforce the view that crime-control measures need to be harsher, punishments longer, and probation less available. The criminals in the vignettes are typically people on parole or probation who prove not to have been successfully rehabilitated. Another message these programs promote is that law-abiding citizens must be vigilant or criminals will escape unpunished. Both *AMW* and *UM* encourage audiences to call authorities with information about crimes. Thus, underneath the entertainment veneer of *America's Most Wanted* and *Unsolved Mysteries* lies a crime-control ideology that teaches audiences moral lessons that can be easily internalized without really thinking about it.

We also learn moral lessons from the way organizations promote their endeavors via the media. Michael Walker describes how the Arizona Meth Project, an antimethamphetamine drug prevention campaign, deploys images of disease and crime to position drug users as immoral and deserving of punishment. The television spots of the Arizona Meth Project employ "fall from grace" narratives in which innocents who give in to the temptation of drug use—even one time—inevitably become sore-covered deviants who descend from middle-class security into crime, sexual exploitation, homelessness, and insanity.[11] Although the Arizona Meth Project claims it "graphically communicates the risks of Meth use," the campaign also instructs its audience on appropriate, or just, punishments—in this case, framed as rational consequences— for transgressing dominant norms surrounding pleasure-seeking and drug use.[12]

---

[10]Gray Cavender, "In the Shadow of Shadows: Television Reality Crime Programming," in *Entertaining Crime: Television Reality Programs*, edited by Mark Fishman and Gray Cavender (New York: Aldine De Gruyter, 1998), pp. 79–94.

[11]Michael F. Walker, "Dirt, Disease, and Sores; Crazy, Violent Thieves and Whores: The Arizona Meth Project, A Critical Read." Paper delivered at Real and Imagined Bodies, Brown University, Providence, RI. Available from the author.

[12]Arizona Meth Project, "About Us." Retrieved May 15, 2010, from http://www.arizonamethproject .org/About_Us/index.php.

Today, Lippmann's basic idea remains intact, but as media structures and technologies have become more complex and intertwined, the knowledge they produce penetrates more deeply into our social fabric, and the new technologies displace more traditional modes of cultural production. William Leiss, Stephan Kline, and Sut Jhally note, for example, that advertising has eclipsed "church sermons, political oratory, and the words and precepts of family elders" to become the rhetorical force that shapes our worldviews.[13] This argument can be extended more broadly to other forms of mass media. We are in an era when the average American is thought to spend nearly 68 hours per week engaged with some type of media. Thirty of those hours alone are spent watching television.[14] The role of media institutions in the formation and transmission of cultural norms, therefore, should not be underestimated.

The power of the media is the power of persuasion. The structure and functioning of this institution is, obviously, an important element in the study of justice in everyday life. Totalitarian regimes understand and appreciate the power of the mass media, and therefore seek to directly control it at all costs by such means as banning books, controlling television and radio, and limiting Internet access. In the United States, with our constitutional right to free speech and general expectation of freedom from state harassment, it can be easy to miss that vested interests can, and do, dominate media structures, manipulate audiences, and silence alternative or dissenting voices.

Some consider such manipulation essential for a smoothly running society. Edward Bernays, a nephew of Sigmund Freud, believed this to be true. Bernays, who is considered a forefather of the modern public relations industry, began his career by advising corporations such as General Electric, American Tobacco, and United Fruit Company. In 1928, Bernays outlined his thinking on the role of propaganda/public relations in a modern democracy in a book appropriately titled *Propaganda*. The book opens with a dramatic claim bound to stir the interest of politicians: "The conscious and intelligent manipulation of the organized habits of the masses is an important element in a democratic society. Those who manipulate this unseen mechanism of society constitute an invisible government that is the true ruling power of our country."[15] For Bernays, propaganda/public relations practitioners are not only a necessary element in mass democracy—these people are the real governing force in society.

Whether we take Bernays's claim at face value, or approach his boast with skepticism, his assertion raises fundamental questions about the role of the media in a democratic society. We should at least treat Bernays as a warning that something may be amiss, and submit our relationship with our media-dense environment to some fundamental questions about the structure and role of this vast system of cultural meaning. This chapter seeks

---

[13]William Leiss, Stephan Kline, and Sut Jhally, *Social Communication in Advertising* (New York: Routledge, 1997), p. 1.

[14]U.S. Census Bureau. "Media usage and consumer spending: 2000–2010." Retrieved May 15, 2010, from http://www.census.gov/compendia/statab/cats/information_communications/information_sector_services_media_usage.html.

[15]Edward Bernays, *Propaganda* (New York: Ig Publishing, 2005), p. 1

to ask and answer questions concerning the media by proceeding through three sections, the first of which considers overarching theories of media interaction and examines structural issues in the American media system. The section that follows explores the cultural impact of media on American society. The final section offers an overview of the influence of emerging communication technologies on democratic movements.

Media

This section begins with two readings that frame media power in terms of broader issues of justice. James Lull introduces the concept of hegemony to suggest how the media often serve the needs of the most privileged and powerful by legitimating and normalizing their values and interests. This means that many people will defend a view of the world and justice within it that actually works against their own interests. As Herbert Marcuse notes, "a vested interest in the existing system is thus fostered in the instinctual structure of the exploited."[16] The concept of hegemony is useful because it suggests that this indoctrination occurs mostly without our noticing it. Consider, for example, the replacement of the term "estate tax"—with its connotation of wealth—with the more egalitarian term "death tax," which sounds like it hits everyone across the board. In fact, this tax only affects a small number of families with much accumulated wealth, so this name change is inherently misleading. However, the term "death tax" taps into hegemonic norms in the United States of equality and private property. Within this structure, the idea of taxing estates seems both unfair and a violation of the right to property, even to people with minimal assets.

All this is not to say that "The Media" is an all powerful, singular institution that speaks with a unified voice. Dissent occurs within mainstream media structures. Comedy Central's *The Daily Show* often mocks mainstream news as shallow and partisan infotainment that does not serve the needs of a healthy democracy. The show's host, Jon Stewart, even occasionally presents his criticisms in corporate news forums, such as CNN's *Crossfire* and Fox News' *The O'Reilly Factor*. Major motion pictures are also sometimes critical of the status quo. Michael Moore's *Fahrenheit 9/11* questioned the response of the United State to the September 11th attacks at a time when such questions were taboo. Documentaries such as *Food Inc.* and *The Corporation* scrutinize the destructive practices of big business.

Still, it is clear that people with wealth, power, and fame are in the best position to use the media (and other technologies) to their own advantage. Social change is difficult in part because the wealthy and powerful are assumed to be both legitimate and newsworthy, whereas those who challenge the status quo are often seen as deviant and only worthy of coverage when they do something "spectacular or stupid."[17]

---

[16]Herbert Marcuse, *An Essay on Liberation* (Boston, MA: Beacon Press, 1969), p. 16.

[17]Charles J. Stewart, Craig Allen Smith, and Robert E. Denton, *Persuasion and Social Movements* (Long Grove, IL: Waveland Press Inc., 2007), pp. 8–10.

HEGEMONY
JAMES LULL

Hegemony is the power or dominance that one social group holds over others. This can refer to the "asymmetrical interdependence" of political-economic-cultural relations between and among nation-states (Straubhaar, 1991) or differences between and among social classes within a nation. Hegemony is "dominance and subordination in the field of relations structured by power" (Hall, 1985). But hegemony is more than social power itself; it is a method for gaining and maintaining power.

The Italian intellectual Antonio Gramsci—to whom the term hegemony is attributed—broadened materialist Marxist theory into the realm of ideology. According to Gramsci's theory of ideological hegemony, mass media are tools that ruling elites use to "perpetuate their power, wealth, and status [by popularizing] their own philosophy, culture and morality" (Boggs, 1976: 39). The mass media uniquely "introduce elements into individual consciousness that would not otherwise appear there, but will not be rejected by consciousness because they are so commonly shared in the cultural community" (Nordenstreng, 1977: 276). Owners and managers of media industries can produce and reproduce the content, inflections, and tones of ideas favorable to them far more easily than other social groups because they manage key socializing institutions, thereby guaranteeing that their points of view are constantly and attractively cast into the public arena.

Mass-mediated ideologies are corroborated and strengthened by an interlocking system of efficacious information-distributing agencies and taken-for-granted social practices that permeate every aspect of social and cultural reality. Messages supportive of the status quo emanating from schools, businesses, political organizations, trade unions, religious groups, the military, and the mass media all dovetail together ideologically. This inter-articulating, mutually reinforcing process of ideological influence is the essence of hegemony. Society's most entrenched and powerful institutions—which all depend in one way or another on the same sources for economic support—fundamentally agree with each other ideologically.

Hegemony is not a *direct* stimulation of thought or action, but, according to Stuart Hall, is a "framing [of] all competing definitions of reality within [the dominant class's] range, bringing all alternatives within their horizons of thought. [The dominant class] sets the limits—mental and structural—within which subordinate classes 'live' and make sense of their subordination in such a way as to sustain the dominance of those ruling over them" (1977: 333). British social theorist Philip Elliott suggested similarly that the most potent effect of mass media is how they subtly influence their audiences to perceive social roles and routine personal activities. The controlling economic forces in society use the mass media to provide a "rhetoric [through] which these [concepts] are labeled, evaluated, and explained" (1974: 262). Television commercials, for example, encourage audiences to think of themselves as "markets rather than as a public, as consumers rather than citizens" (Gitlin, 1979: 255).

But hegemony does not mature strictly from ideological articulation. Dominant ideological streams must be subsequently reproduced in the activities of our most basic social units—families, workplace networks, and friendship groups in the many sites and undertakings of everyday life. Gramsci's theory of hegemony, therefore, connects ideological representation to culture. Hegemony requires that ideological assertions become self-evident cultural assumptions. Its effectiveness depends on subordinated peoples accepting the dominant ideology as "normal reality or common sense . . . in active forms of experience and consciousness" (Williams, 1976: 145). Because information and entertainment technology is so thoroughly integrated into the everyday realities of modern societies, mass media's social influence is not always recognized, discussed, or criticized, particularly in societies where the overall standard of living is relatively high. Hegemony, therefore, can easily go undetected (Bausinger, 1984).

Hegemony implies a willing agreement by people to be governed by principles, rules, and laws they believe operate in their best interests, even though in actual practice they may not. Social consent can be a more effective means of control than coercion or force. Again, Raymond Williams: "The idea of hegemony, in its wide sense, is . . . especially important in societies [where] electoral politics and public opinion are significant factors, and in which social practice is seen to depend on consent to certain dominant ideas which in fact express the needs of a dominant class" (1976: 145). Thus, in the words of Colombian communication theorist Jesús Martín-Barbero, "one class exercises hegemony to the extent that the dominating class has interests which the subaltern classes recognize as being in some degree their interests too" (1993: 74).

Relationships between and among the major information-diffusing, socializing agencies of a society and the interacting, cumulative, socially accepted ideological orientations they create and sustain is the essence of hegemony. The American television industry, for instance, connects with other large industries, especially advertising companies but also national and multinational corporations that produce, distribute, and market a wide range of commodities. So, for example, commercial TV networks no longer buy original children's television shows. Network executives only want new program ideas associated with successful retail products already marketed to children. By late 1990 more than 20 toy-based TV shows appeared on American commercial TV weekly. Television also has the ability to absorb other major social institutions— organized religion, for instance—and turn them into popular culture. The TV industry also connects with government institutions, including especially the federal agencies that are supposed to regulate telecommunications. The development of American commercial broadcasting is a vivid example of how capitalist economic forces assert their power. Evacuation of the legislatively mandated public service ideal could only have taken place because the Federal Communications Commission stepped aside while commercial interests amassed power and expanded their influence. Symptomatic of the problem is the fact that government regulators typically are recruited from, and return to, the very industries they are supposed to monitor.

Transmedia and transgenre integrations with mutually reinforcing ideological consequences are also commonplace. Popular radio and video songs, for example, can also be commercials. . . . Commercial logos become products themselves and are reproduced on tee-shirts, posters, beach towels, and other informal media. The rhetoric of TV commercials and programs is recycled in the lyrics of rap music and in the routines of stand-up comedians performing live and on television. . . . There are films made for television, magazines published about television, and television news magazines. The most well-known national newspaper in the United States, *USA Today,* is sold nationwide in vending boxes that resemble TV sets. Television commercials appear on Channel One, an educational news channel shown to students in American elementary school classrooms. Logos that advertise only national gasoline, food, and motel chains appear on government highway signs, advising travelers of their availability at upcoming freeway exits. Expensive public relations campaigns of major corporations distribute "informational" supplementary textbooks to elementary and secondary school systems. Major business organizations send digests of their annual reports and other promotional materials to college instructors, hoping this biased information will be incorporated into teaching and research. Similar materials are sent to political and religious leaders so they will pass the information along to their constituencies and congregations.

In the United States, advocacy of alternative political ideologies, parties, and candidates, or suggestions of viable consumer alternatives to the commercial frenzy stimulated and reinforced by advertising and other marketing techniques, are rarely seen on the popular media. Radical ideas typically appear only on underfinanced, noncommercial radio and TV stations and in low-budget print media. These media have tiny public followings compared to commercial television and video outlets, metropolitan daily newspapers, and national magazines. When genuinely divergent views appear on mainstream media, the information is frequently shown in an unfavorable light or is modified and co-opted to surrender to the embrace of mainstream thought. . . . The mass media help create an impression that even society's roughest edges ultimately must conform to the conventional contours of dominant ideologies.

Hegemony as an Incomplete Process

Two of our leading critical theorists, Raymond Williams and Stuart Hall, remind us that hegemony in any political context is indeed fragile. It requires renewal and modification through the assertion and reassertion of power. Hall suggests that "it is crucial to the concept that hegemony is not a 'given' and permanent state of affairs, but it has to be actively won and secured; it can also be lost" (1977: 333). Ideological work is the winning and securing of hegemony over time. . . . . Ideology is composed of "texts that are not closed" according to Hall, who also notes that ideological "counter-tendencies" regularly appear in the seams and cracks of dominant forms (Hall, 1985). Mediated communications ranging from popular television shows to rap and rock music, even graffiti scrawled over surfaces of public spaces, all inscribe messages that challenge central political positions and cultural assumptions.

Audience interpretations and uses of media imagery also eat away at hegemony. Hegemony fails when dominant ideology is weaker than social resistance. Gay subcultures, feminist organizations, environmental groups, radical political parties, music-based formations such as punks, B-boys, Rastafarians, and metal heads all use media and their social networks to endorse counter-hegemonic values and lifestyles. Indeed, we have only just begun to examine the complex relationship between ideological representation and social action.

The second reading in this section, by David Altheide, conceptualizes the mass media as an interactive field with the power to shape our habits of communication and self-perception. Altheide describes a "media logic" composed of particular media technologies, such as television or the Internet, that create symbolic formats, which define communication situations, shape audience expectations, and provide bases for the development of individual identity. Altheide points out that audiences are not simply passive receptors of media messaging; people interact with media.[18] For example, people may select their information sources based on their political views.

Stuart Hall describes media interaction as a process of "encoding" and "decoding." Media producers package, or "encode" messages that audiences "decode." However, like the media itself, audiences are not monolithic, so decoding is not always seamless or perfectly in tune with a producer's intended message.[19] In other words, meaning is created as much by its audience as by its producer—perhaps more so. Nor do audiences simply misinterpret; many times they intentionally transgress against a producer's preferred meaning. For example, in 2006 General Motors sponsored a contest in which people could create an online ad for the Chevy Tahoe SUV. These ads were posted to the General Motors website. In many cases, people used the opportunity to post environmental or antiwar messages critical of SUVs, the companies that produce them, and the people who drive them.[20] In short, while hegemony is a subtle and powerful form of social control, people are not simply "cultural dupes" who always follow the dictates of corporate media. People bring their own understandings of themselves and the world to bear on the media messages they encounter.

[18]David Altheide, "The Mass Media," *in Handbook of Symbolic Interactionism*, edited by Larry T. Reynolds and Nancy J. Herman-Kinney (Walnut Creek, CA: AltaMira Press, 2002), pp. 657–60. Also see The Pew Research Center for The People and The Press, "Pew Research Center Biennial News Consumption Survey, 2004." Retrieved May 10, 2010, from http://people-press.org/reports/pdf/215.pdf.

[19]Stuart Hall, "Encoding and Decoding," *in Culture, Media, Language: Working Papers in Cultural Studies, 1972–1979,* edited by Stuart Hall, Dorothy Hobson, Andrew Lowe, and Paul Willis (New York: Routledge, 1991), pp. 128–38. Also see Kellner (note 9), p. 15.

[20]National Public Radio, "Chevy's Make-Your-Own SUV Ads Go Off Message." Retrieved May 16, 2010, from http://www.npr.org/templates/story/story.php?storyId=5320442.

THE MASS MEDIA
DAVID L. ALTHEIDE

Introduction

Imagine this. A posh English wedding, costing $35,000, was videotaped, but the wedding was reenacted because the mother of the bride was dissatisfied with the footage, "The video was dreadful. . . . There were no shots of the reception, and the video man missed the bride going up the aisle" (*Arizona Republic*, October 19, 1988). This reflects media logic and the growing impact of mass media formats on our everyday lives and social institutions. The mass media are significant for our lives because they are both form and content of cultural categories and experience. As form, the mass media provide the criteria, shape, rhythm, and style of an expanding array of activities, many of which are outside the "communication" process. As content, the new ideas, fashions, vocabularies, and a myriad of types of information (e.g., politics) are acquired through the mass media.

The mass media refer to information technologies that permit "broadcasting" and communication to a large audience. The mass media are critical carriers and definers of popular culture. Traditionally, these media have included print (e.g., books, newspapers, magazines, billboards) and electronic media (e.g., cinema, radio, television), and more recently, various computer communication formats, particularly the Internet. They also include personal communication devices (e.g., audio [CD] players and game players [Gameboys]), as well as pagers and cell phones, especially when the latter are used for "broadcasting" of messages to subscribers of paging and telephone services.

I consider the mass media to be our most important social institution. I regard the "definition of the situation" as the key theoretical construct for the study of social life. Indeed, this is why I study the mass media: They contribute to the definitions of situations in social life. Moreover, I regard social power as the capacity to define a situation for oneself and others. If the mass media contribute to social definitions, then they are also relevant for any attempt to understand "power in society."

There are several points to consider when assessing the process and extent to which popular culture and communication formats contribute to the changing face of identity. First is the massive involvement with media and the gamut of popular culture in the United States and many Western countries. Whether measured in terms of hours viewing television, movie attendance, music and compact disk purchases, popular brands of clothing, or something else, the experience, although far from uniform in our pluralistic society, is enormous. Second, popular culture affords individuals a plethora of styles, personas, and potential role models. Third, popular culture audiences are also participants, albeit in varying degrees. Fourth, the physical and symbolic environment reflects media culture as theme parks, theme cities, shopping malls, and even wars adopt media forms. Fifth, the criteria and frameworks for authenticity, credibility, competence, and acceptability can be widely shared and, indeed, taken for granted as audiences interact in this media context.

Access to Media and Popular Culture

"Normal use" of media is also related to identity and how we are known to others. Three things happen in a media age where identities and products are marketed interchangeably and synergistically. (1) We experience them in the same time, place, and manner. (2) The product and process are reflexive—the product is the identity! Identity appears explicitly and implicitly in numerous advertisements, explicitly and implicitly. (3) Media images "loop" through various media and messages, moving, for example, from initial claim to established fact, to background information to standard. Product labels as key membership categories are a triumph for popular culture and mass mediation. And the freedom to purchase and "become" a member—and participant—reflects the actor's individual freedom and decision making. Social interaction with peers begins to reflect and turn on such familiarity.

The presentation of self has changed drastically. When both actor and audience have at least one foot in popular culture, they hold shared meanings for validating the actor's performance. The mass media promote identity as a resource to satisfy individually oriented needs and interests to "be whoever you want to be." Popular culture's emphasis on entertainment and commodification of the self informs this emphasis. Grossberg, Wartella, and Whitney agree with numerous researchers who have documented the impact of media logic on everyday life: "Ultimately the media's ability to produce people's social identities, in terms of both a sense of unity and difference, may be their most powerful and important effect" (1998: 206).

Media Logic and Social Institutions

Media logic, becomes a way of "seeing" and of interpreting social affairs. This involves an implicit trust that we can communicate the events of our daily lives through the various formats of media. People take for granted that information can be transmitted, ideas presented, moods of joy and sadness expressed, major decisions made, and business conducted through media. But, at the same time, there is a concern that media can and will distort what they present. This fear of media has been defined by some as a conspiracy in which powerful media moguls willfully set out to determine the character of behavior: how people vote, what they buy, what is learned, and what is believed. No doubt there is an intent to shape attitudes and "sell soap," but this is not the most critical factor in understanding the mass media.

I suggest that it is more important theoretically to understand mass communication as an interactive process between media communication as interpreted and acted on by audiences. Technological developments now permit explicit interaction with TV programs, as viewers of videotext can select additional information, as children (and some adults!) participate in TV action games, as "smart sets" enable video participants to draw on rudimentary microprocessors to project images of how one would appear in various clothing styles, and increasingly select programs and media usage to suit their needs (which may also be a commercial enterprise, of course). If current trends continue (e.g., DVD players, CD video recorders that permit "time shifting" with relative ease), TV programming will fundamentally change from a logic of "broadcasting," or offering a few options to a broad socioeconomic audience, to "narrowcasting," or providing essentially personally selected contents and images.

It has long been recognized that TV news was entertainment oriented, but now there are indications that entertainment programs are becoming more like news programs as standard formats mold programming for a culture geared to a media logic that subtly folds TV criteria, discourse, and perspectives into everyday life. One indication was when surveys revealed that a majority of viewers, and especially younger ones, thought that the program *America's Most Wanted* was a news show! From the standpoint of media logic this is hardly surprising since this show, and many like it, incorporate a number of standard TV news formats within its production formula. Another indication is the way in which extended news coverage of events foreshadows future TV movies, and in a sense, becomes a kind of preview or advertisement for "coming attractions."

The Waco debacle that ended in multiple deaths in April 1993 is a good illustration of "news as advertising." Waco, Texas, was the scene of a confrontation between the FBI and a religious leader, David Koresh, and his followers, who would not vacate their compound to answer a range of charges (including child mistreatment and illegal weapons). The fifty-one-day "standoff" ended when a government assault resulted in a horrendous fire that consumed all the inhabitants of the compound. This much-debated action has achieved epic proportions in American popular culture, particularly among "survivor" and "anti-government groups," and was said to be the major motivation for Timothy McVeigh's bombing of the federal building in Oklahoma City a half decade later. What matters for our purposes is that NBC was working on a docudrama of this event before it concluded. As the docudrama formula has been learned and refined from the "production end," the time period between the "real" event and its prime-time airing as a "TV movie" has been reduced to a matter of weeks, and in some cases, days. Commenting on NBC's quick production of a TV movie while the Waco standoff was continuing, ABC senior vice president, Judd Parkin, stated: "Dramatizing such events before they're fully resolved can be irresponsible. In a way, it almost preempts the news" (*Newsweek*, May 24, 1993). As TV networks continue to pursue lucrative ratings, they appear to have stumbled on a surefire way to attract audiences to their TV fare: Simply take news events, which are increasingly being cast in TV formats rich in entertainment value, and then follow up with a made-for-TV movie. After noting that ABC had its own Koresh docudrama in the works, a *Newsweek* reporter discussed what could be termed "advertising news:"

It isn't just their odor of exploitation or their penchant for selling fiction as fact: we've become all too accustomed to that. What's less obvious is the genre's habit, exacerbated by haste, of reducing a complex story to the simplest, most viewer-friendly terms. . . . Still, get ready for a lot more. In high-visibility disasters like Waco, the networks see a way to survival: instantly recognizable "concepts" with a presold market. . . . "We've reached the point," says ABC's Parkin, "where TV movies and news shows are competing for the very same stories." (May 24: 58)

Audience familiarity is nurtured as repeated news coverage of an event provides the familiarity of an event and its connection (often quite distorted) to dominant values and beliefs to "make the report relevant." More than thirty million viewers—one-third of the viewing audience—watched NBC's spectacle about Waco. News as a form of knowledge was transformed through news as entertainment into news as advertising, a preview of coming attractions on television, which in turn adds to the context of experience, understanding, and perspective for future "news events."

As news organizations and the parties they cover share similar views and approaches to what is newsworthy, the line between the journalist and the event has essentially disappeared, producing a "postjournalism" condition:

First, journalistic practices, techniques and approaches are now geared to media formats rather than merely directing their craft at topics; second, the topics, organizations and issues which journalists report about are themselves products of media-journalistic formats and criteria. In a sense, it is as though journalists, and especially TV journalists, are reporting on another entity down the hall from the newsroom. (Altheide and Snow 1991: x)

Public Perception and Social Issues

Mass media materials are organized through an entertainment format that promotes conflict and drama, vicarious and emotional identification, and spontaneity. One example is the increased use of fear. Research on the use and extent of the word *fear* in news reports indicates a sharp increase during the mid-1990s, suggesting the emergence of a discourse of fear. The combination of entertaining news formats with these news sources has forged a fear-generating machine that trades on fostering a common public definition of fear, danger, and dread. Crime and violence has been a staple of entertainment and news programming for decades but has become even more graphic and focused, particularly with numerous "day-time talk shows" and "real TV" programs featuring "real COPS," etc.

Mass media influences on public perceptions can be illustrated with American's views of their own safety. Many Americans perceive themselves to be at great risk and express specific fears about this despite clear evidence showing that Americans today have a comparative advantage in terms of diseases, accidents, nutrition, medical care, and life expectancy. According to numerous public opinion polls, American society is a very fearful society, some believe "the most anxious, frightened society in history." Indeed, 78 percent of Americans think they are subjected to more risk today than their parents were twenty years ago, and a large source of this perception is crime news coverage:

> Why did many Americans suddenly decide last fall, for the first time, to tell national pollsters that crime is "the most important problem facing the country?" Could it have been because last year, for the first time, ABC, CBS and NBC nightly news programs devoted more time to crime than to any other topic? Several media critics think so; as a Los Angeles Times Poll showed early this year, people say their "feelings about crime" are based 65 percent on what they read and see in the media and 21 percent on experience. (*Los Angeles Times*, September 11, 1994: Home Edition, pt., 1)

Although crime and violence are part of the "fear story," there is more to it. For example, the constant coupling of crime and other aspects of urban living with fear has produced a unique perspective about our effective environment. Crime is certainly something to be concerned about, as is any potentially dangerous situation, but the danger per se does not make one fearful, just cautious. Fear is not a thing but a characteristic attributed by someone (e.g., a journalist). Often associated as an attitude pertaining to danger, fear is multifaceted in its actual use in popular culture and especially the news media.

Changing Social Institutions

Media politics has entered the framework of all institutions. This is very apparent in the conduct of police and surveillance activities, and how these are covered and "aided" by news organizations. Serious personal criminal attacks happen rarely, but they are regarded as typical and quite common by American citizens because virtually all mass media reports about crime focus on the most spectacular, dramatic, and violent. Any discussion about crime and justice in the United States today must begin by correcting the audience members' assumptions about crime. With the images of blood, guns, psychopaths, and suffering in front of them and inside their heads, it is quite difficult to offer programmatic criticisms of our current approach to crime and accompanying issues such as prisons, and other modes of dispute resolution, including restitution and negotiation. As long as crime and mayhem are presented in such familiar and "fun" formats, new information will not be forthcoming, but only a recycling of affirmations tied to previous popular culture. And in general, as long as experience is enacted by human beings who participate in mass mediated imagery and orient consumption toward markets and products that look like the status groups, personal identities, and forms of conduct displayed through a host of mass media, media and culture will not only be electronically and technologically joined, they will be meaningfully united as well.

The combination of various media constitutes an interactive communication context. For example, in a study of the "missing children problem," we found that messages about "thousands" if not "millions" of missing children who were abducted, molested and mutilated by strangers were carried on TV news, docudramas, newspapers, billboards, posters, T-shirts, mailings, and milk cartons. Such claims were exaggerated and traded on widespread beliefs about crime and dangerousness. This can also be illustrated with crime news, which seemingly celebrates the inability of the state agencies to protect their citizens. In some cases, this will involve vigilante scenarios by individuals, while in others it will involve vigilante actions by entire audiences. An example is the TV program *America's Most Wanted*, hosted by John Walsh, the man behind much of the "missing children" furor. This show draws some 5,000 calls per week from viewers who report that their neighbors, work associates, and fellow consumers "fit the description" of a "wanted suspect" flashed on TV.

Another example is "gonzo justice," which has emerged as a new cultural form to address the mass mediated public perception of unsuccessful social control. A combination of "public spectacle", moral authority, and news legitimacy, gonzo justice is specifically oriented to mass communication formats and is often celebrated and applauded by mass media writers and commentators. Popular culture provides a way to participate or play with horror, banditry, crime, and justice, as we are presented a range of scenarios and enactments through which we can interactively arrive at meaningful interpretations. The scenario of "out of control" evil calls forth a heroic retort as a kind of narrative response in the mediated drama. Consider a few examples. This first is from Pennsylvania:

> A 311.5 pound man who hasn't made child-support payments for more than a year because he's too overweight to work is under court order to lose 50 pounds or go to jail. . . . "I call it my 'Oprah Winfrey sentence,'" [Judge] Lavelle said . . . . "It's designed to make him lose weight for the benefit of his children, while Oprah (a talk-show host) lost weight for the benefit of her job and future security." (UPI and *Arizona Republic*, June 18, 1989)

This one is from Tennessee:

> A judge ordered Henry Lee McDonald to put a sign in his front-yard for 30 days declaring in 4-inch letters that he "is a thief." U. S. District Court Judge L. Clure Morton instructed McDonald to erect the sign Tuesday as part of his three-year probation for receiving and concealing a stolen car. . . . The sign must be painted black and have 4-inch white capital letters that read: "Henry Lee McDonald bought a stolen car. He is a thief." (UPI and *Tempe Daily News*, January 5, 1984)

Analysis of these materials suggests some identifiable features of gonzo justice that join the news media to legal authority: (1) there must be an act that can be defined and presented as extraordinary, if not excessive and arbitrary; (2) it must be protective or "reclaiming" of a moral (often mythical) dimension; (3) individual initiative (rather than "organizational") is responsible for the reaction; (4) the act is expressive and evocative; (5) the act is intended to be interpreted and presented as an exemplar for others to follow; (6) audience familiarity with other reports about the problem provides a context of experience and meaning; and (7) reports seldom include contrary or challenging statements. In short, what makes gonzo justice peculiar and unique is that we can expect it to be associated with those agencies that are less likely to be seen as affirming and supportive of the cultural myths.

The previous examples suggest that state control work and public order are increasingly occurring through the mass media. Just as judges use gonzo justice to demonstrate (and promote) their moral character and resolve to audiences who know little about their work routines, other bureaucratic workers, like politically ambitious county prosecutors, not only rely on the news media to publicize their "achievements," but actually work with and through the news formats to "do good work."

Conclusion

The mass media and popular culture contribute to the definition of situations and audience expectations and criteria for self–presentations for themselves and others. As audiences spend more time with these formats, the logic of advertising, entertainment, and popular culture becomes taken for granted as a "normal form" of communication.

One way power is manifested is by influencing the definition of a situation. Cultural logics inform this process and are therefore powerful, but we are not controlled by them, and certainly not determined, particularly when one's effective environment contains meanings to challenge the legitimacy, veracity, and relevance of certain procedures. Resistance can follow, but it is likely to be formatted by ecologies of communication. Indeed, the contribution of expanded discourses of control to the narrowing or expansion of resistance modes remains an intriguing area of inquiry.

Although people undoubtedly vary in how they respond to various media content, the most important thing that media do is to set the agenda: "the media may not tell you what to think, but they do tell you what to think about . . . As Lippmann noted long ago, what the media chooses to bring into proximity helps to define the fields of knowledge and debate.

The next reading examines the environment in which media operate and the consequences for citizens. Robert McChesney discusses the impact of corporate ownership on content. McChesney asserts that the profit motive and corporate interests degrade the quality of news and other content, diminishing political participation, even as the amount of available content expands. McChesney refers to this process as the "rich media/poor democracy paradox."

McChesney's insights about corporate power are brought into relief by Gloria Steinem. During her tenure as the editor of *Ms. Magazine*, Steinem experienced the influence and censorship that advertisers exert over content. She describes how corporations can use their economic power to force editors to choose between covering important stories and risking financial ruin. Steinem points out that "even news magazines use "soft" cover stories to sell ads, confuse readers with "advertorials," and occasionally self-censor on subjects known to be a problem with big advertisers." While she notes this practice is media-wide, she contends it is a particularly glaring problem in women's magazines, which become little more than large advertisements. This is an issue of gender equality because dependency on advertising dollars compels women's magazines to avoid controversial, but important, stories on topics such as reproductive rights or the health risks of cosmetics. This denies women information about issues relevant to them. It also reinforces and reproduces traditional gender roles by sticking to safe stories on "appropriate" topics like fashion and romance.

RICH MEDIA, POOR DEMOCRACY: COMMUNICATION POLITICS IN DUBIOUS TIMES
ROBERT WATERMAN MCCHESNEY

Our era rests upon a massive paradox. On the one hand, it is an age of dazzling breakthroughs in communication and information technologies. Communication is so intertwined with the economy and culture that our times have been dubbed the Information Age. Sitting high atop this golden web are a handful of enormous media firms—exceeding by a factor of ten the size of the largest media firms of just fifteen years earlier—that have established global empires and generated massive riches providing news and entertainment to the peoples of the world. This commercial media juggernaut provides a bounty of choices unimaginable a generation or two ago. And it is finding a welcome audience. According to one study, the average American consumed a whopping 11.8 hours of media per day in 1998, up over 13 percent in just three years. As the survey director noted, "The sheer amount of media products and messages consumed by the average American adult is staggering and growing." The rise of the Internet has only accentuated the trend. Although some research suggests that the Internet is replacing some of the time people have spent with other media, other research suggests its more important effect is simply to expand the role of media in people's lives.

On the other hand, our era is increasingly depoliticized; traditional notions of civic and political involvement have shriveled. Elementary understanding of social and political affairs has declined. Turnout for U.S. elections—admittedly not a perfect barometer—has plummeted over the past thirty years. The 2000 presidential election had one of the lowest turnouts of eligible voters in national elections in U.S. history, as just one-half of the eligible voters turned out on election day For poor people—who, as Aristotle noted, are the *raison d'etre* of a democracy, the measure of its strength—electoral democracy has become little more than a charade; exit polls indicate that over one-half of those-who voted in November 2000 came from the wealthiest 20 percent of the population. And, to add insult to injury, the candidate who received the most votes from the poor, Al Gore, actually won the election, but had his victory stolen from him in one of the most brazen examples of corruption in U.S. history. The collapse of the democratic system is palpable, except to those who benefit from the status quo. The cynicism and depoliticization will only continue to increase until the invariable social crisis, that many contend is a long way aways. For the time being, we are living, to employ a phrase coined by Robert-Entman, in a "democracy without citizens."

By conventional reasoning, this is nonsensical. A flowering commercial marketplace of ideas, unencumbered by government censorship or regulation, should generate the most stimulating democratic political culture possible. The response comes that the problem lies elsewhere, that "the people' obviously are not interested in politics or civic issues, because, if they were, it would be in the interests of the wealthy media giants to provide them with such fare. There is an element of truth to that reply, but it is hardly a satisfactory response. Virtually all defenses of the commercial media system justifying the privileges they receive—defenses typically made by the media owners themselves— are based on the notion that media play an important, perhaps a central, role in providing the institutional basis for having an informed and participating citizenry. If this is, indeed, a democracy without citizens, the media system has much to answer for.

I contend that the media have become a significant *antidemocratic* force in the United States. The wealthier and more powerful the corporate media-giants have become, the poorer the prospects for participatory democracy. I am not arguing that *all* media are getting wealthier, of course. Some media firms and sectors are faltering and will falter during this turbulent era. But, on balance, the dominant media firms are larger and more influential than even before, and the media *writ large* are more important in our social life than even before. Nor do I believe the media are the sole or primary cause of the decline of democracy, but that they are a part of the problem and closely linked to many of the other factors. Behind the lustrous glow of new technologies and electronic jargon, the media system has become increasingly concentrated and conglomerated into a relative handful of corporate hands. This concentration accentuates the core tendencies of a profit-driven, advertising-supported media system: hyper-commercialism and denigration of journalism and public service. It is a poison pill for democracy.

This chapter, then, is about the corporate media explosion and the corresponding implosion of public life, the rich media/poor democracy paradox. This paradox has two components. First, it is a political crisis. I mean this in two senses. On the one hand, the nature of our corporate commercial media system has dire implications for our politics and broader culture. On the other hand, the very issue of who controls the media system and for what purposes is not a part of contemporary political debate. Instead, there is the presupposition that a profit-seeking commercial media system is fundamentally sound, and that most problems can be resolved for the most part through less state interference or regulation, which (theoretically) will produce the magic elixir of competition. In view of the extraordinary importance of media and communication in our society, I believe that the subject of how the media are controlled, structured, and subsidized should be at the center of democratic debate. Instead, this subject is nowhere to be found. This is not an accident; it reflects above all the economic, political, and ideological power of the media corporations and their allies. And it has made the prospect of challenging corporate media power, and of democratizing communication, all the more daunting.

The second component of the media/democracy paradox concerns media ideology, in particular the flawed and self-serving manner in which corporate media officers and their supporters use history. The nature of our corporate media system and the lack of democratic debate over the nature of our media system are often defended on the following grounds: communication markets force media firms to "give the people what they want"; commercial media are the innate democratic and "American" system; professionalism in journalism is democratic and protects the public from nefarious influences on the news: new communications technologies are inherently democratic since they undermine the existing commercial media; and, perhaps most important, that the First Amendment to the U.S. Constitution authorizes that corporations and advertisers rule U.S. media without public interference. These are generally presented as truisms, and nearly always history is invoked to provide evidence for each of these claims. In combination these claims have considerable sway in the United States, even among those who are critical of the social order otherwise. It is because of the overall capacity of these myths, which are either lies or half-truths, to strip citizens of their ability to comprehend their own situation and govern their own lives that I characterize these as "dubious" times.

I will address central trends in U.S. media at the dawn of the twenty-first century: the concentration of media industries; the decline of notions of public service in our media culture and a corresponding denigration of journalism; the commercialization of the Internet; and the prospects for renewed politicization in the new century.

Media Concentration

The United States is in the midst of an almost dizzying transformation of its media system, whose main features are concentration and conglomeration. It may seem ironic that these are the dominant structural features when, to the casual observer, the truth can appear quite the opposite. We seem inundated in different media from magazines and radio stations to cable television channels and now, Web sites. But, to no small extent, the astonishing degree of concentrated corporate control over the media is a response to the rapid increase in channels wrought by cable, satellite TV, and digital media. Media firms press to get larger to deal with the uncertainty of the changing terrain wrought by new media technologies. "If you look at the entire chain of entities—studios, networks, stations, cable channels, cable operations, international distribution—you want to be as strong in as many of those as you can," News Corporation president Peter Chernin stated in 1998. "That way, regardless of where the profits move to, you're in a position to gain." Yet, any explanation of media concentration and conglomeration must go beyond media technologies. They also result from changes in laws and regulations that now permit greater concentration in media ownership. But the bottom line, so to speak, is that concentrated media markets tend to be vastly less risky and more profitable for the firms that dominate them.

The U.S. media industries were operated along noncompetitive oligopolistic lines for much of the twentieth century. In the 1940s, for example, broadcasting, film production, motion picture theaters, book publishing, newspaper publishing, magazine publishing, and recorded music were all distinct national oligopolistic markets, each of them dominated by anywhere from a few to a dozen or more firms. In general, these were *different* firms dominating each of these industries, with only a few exceptions. Throughout the twentieth century there were pressing concerns that these concentrated markets would inhibit the flow and range of ideas necessary for a meaningful democracy.

Concentration proceeded in specific media markets throughout the 1990s, with the proportion of the markets controlled by a small number of firms increasing, sometimes marginally and at other times dramatically. The U.S. film production industry has been a tight-knit club effectively controlled by six or seven studios since the 1930s. That remains the case; the six largest U.S. firms accounted for over 90 percent of U.S. theater revenues in 1997. All but sixteen of Hollywood's 148 widely distributed (in six hundred or more theaters) films in 1997 were produced by these six firms, and many of those sixteen were produced by companies that had distribution deals with one of the six majors. The newspaper industry underwent a spectacular consolidation from the 1960s to the 1980s, leaving a half-dozen major chains ruling the roost. The emerging consolidation trend in the newspaper industry is that of "clustering," whereby metropolitan monopoly daily newspapers purchase or otherwise link up with all the smaller dailies in the suburbs and surrounding region.

There were numerous massive media deals, which included Viacom swallowing up CBS to create the third largest media conglomerate in the world; AOL combining with Time Warner in what at the time was largest media deal in history (valued at around $160 billion); and the Tribune Company buying Times Mirror, so that every major newspaper chain is now part of a larger media conglomerate.

It is also clear that many more mergers will take place in the years to come, especially as the few remaining federal restrictions on media ownership are relaxed. It was the FCC's 1999 decision allowing firms to own more than one TV station in a market, for example, that paved the way for the CBS-Viacom deal. When the federal prohibitions are lifted on owning a daily newspaper and a TV station or a cable system and a TV station in the same market look for a wave of colossal deals, as the first-tier media conglomerates grow even fetter.

Denigration of Journalism

Not only is media ownership becoming concentrated into ever fewer extremely large conglomerates, the denigration of journalism continues unabated. By journalism I mean both the product of the commercial news media as well as the journalism of NPR and PBS. After two decades of conservative criticism and corporate inroads, the public system is now fully within the same ideological confines that come naturally to a profit-driven, advertising-supported system. There were several case studies in 1999 and 2000 on the shortcomings of corporate-controlled journalism for a democratic society.

Some of the problems come from the inherent limitations of journalism as conducted by self-interested, profit-motivated companies. Others are due to faults in the professional practice of journalism, faults that date to the beginning of the twentieth century. In particular, the professional reliance upon official sources and the need for a news peg, or event, to justify coverage of a story plays directly into the hands of those who benefit from the status quo. But many problems result from the enhanced corporate pressure to make journalism a source of huge profits; this leads to easy-to-cover trivial stories and an emphasis on the type of news that will have appeal to the upper and upper-middle classes. The combination of all three of these factors leads to the woeful state of U.S. journalism in the twenty-first century.

A long-term problem of local commercial media—notably daily newspapers and television broadcasters—is their consistent reluctance to provide critical investigations of the most important and powerful local commercial interests. Professional standards notwithstanding, there has been a kind of "Eleventh Commandment" in the commercial news media: Thou Shalt Not Cover Big Local Companies and Billionaires Critically. This makes very good economic sense, as the local powers are often major advertisers. It makes sense politically and socially, too, as the media owners and managers run in the same circles as the major shareholders and executives of the local corporate powerhouses. They are not the sort of people or institutions that smart businesses wish to antagonize—and the media are businesses no less than any other profit-maximizing firms. This is truer than ever in an era when investigative journalism of any sort is generally frowned upon as too expensive and bad for profits.

Along these lines, the Boston Herald suspended its consumer affairs columnist. Robin Washington, in the spring of 2000. He had written a series of articles about FleetBoston Financial Corporation, the nation's eighth-largest bank, which not only advertised in the *Herald* but also had outstanding loans to the Herald. The bank contacted the *Herald's* publisher at least twice to complain about the coverage, which emphasized how customers had been getting a higher fee structure since BankBoston and Fleet Financial merged in 1999. The bank did not aim its fire at the accuracy of the findings, only Washington's methods, specifically that he had arranged for a friend to pose as a customer at the bank, Washington's case drew public protest and his suspension was eventually lifted, largely because he was one of only four African-American journalists on an editorial staff of 235.

The lesson to other reporters was one that should have been understood already: the evidentiary and methodological standards for doing critical work on local corporate powerhouses are vastly higher than they are for other institutions. Smart journalists who want successful careers will avoid them, and happy smart journalists will do as others before them; internalize the view that such stories are not really very good journalism anyway.

Another long-term problem of the system is the commercial media's willingness to provide favorable coverage of politicians who provide them with favorable subsidies and regulations. This violates every canon of ethical or professional journalism, too, but its practice is rarely noted. Ben Bagdikian's *The Media Monopoly* used the Freedom of Information Act to uncover how major newspaper chains effectively promised Richard Nixon editorial support in his 1972 reelection campaign if he supported the Newspaper Preservation Act. The deal led to newspaper monopolies in many U.S. cities and made shareholders in newspaper corporations far wealthier than they would have been otherwise. One can only speculate, but perhaps a newspaper industry less involved with the Nixon reelection campaign might have pursued the Watergate story with a modicum of gusto in the five months preceding the 1972 election, possibly sparing the nation a great crisis.

Of course, the tacit quid pro quo of favorable coverage for favorable legislation and regulation rarely draws comment, so it is unusual to find the sort of smoking gun that Bagdikian located. When important legislation affecting media arises on Capitol Hill, for example, the corporations sometimes have the managers of their local stations or the publishers of their local papers call on their representatives in Congress to ask them to support the corporation's position on the bill. No threat or promise about news coverage has to be made; the message is loud and clear.

The corruption of journalistic integrity is always bad, but it becomes obscene under conditions of extreme media concentration, as now exist. This is a primary reason why antitrust needs to be applied to the media industry. In San Francisco a textbook example of the problem arose. Under deposition, it was revealed that a top executive of the Hearst Corporation, owner of the *San Francisco Examiner*, offered favorable editorial coverage to San Francisco mayor Willie Brown—then up for reelection—if Brown would give official blessing to Hearst's purchase of the *San Francisco Chronicle*, the other daily in town. The records show emails and other communications among top Hearst executives approving the offer. Mayor Brown says he made no promises. But in his 1999 re-election campaign against insurgent Tom Ammiano, the *Examiner* portrayed Ammiano harshly, while tending to view Brown with rose-tinted glasses. A Bay Area reporter summed up the situation: "Hearst, like all big media chains these days, sees journalism first and foremost as a business, a way to make money. And when it comes to the bottom line, all ethical rules are off."

Another way to measure the limitations of the contemporary corporate news media is to look at which sorts of stories receive elaborate attention and which receive less coverage or virtually no coverage at all. In the summer of 1999, the deaths of John F. Kennedy Jr., his wife, and her sister were treated by the cable news channels and the media writ large as a story approaching the magnitude of the return of the messiah or the discovery of intelligent life on Mars. Television sets were turned into virtual aquariums for hours as cameras scanned the Atlantic in search of Kennedy's aircraft.

The news was the fates of three private citizens made famous by their lineage, wealth, beauty, and media decision making.

Four months later the news media were presented with another story, the World Trade Organization (WTO) meeting in Seattle. Reporters had long claimed that they could not cover the social and political implications of the global economy because there was no news peg to justify coverage. If they pursued the story it would look as if they were pushing an agenda. Then the WTO meeting and the massive demonstrations that shut it down gave journalists their news peg. But here journalists came into direct conflict with the modern corporate ethos. For one, media corporations are among the largest beneficiaries of the global capitalist economy since they use groups like the WTO and liberalized trade to increase their sales and activities outside the United States. And media's main advertisers tend to be among the largest firms eager to expand their markets across the planet.

Meanwhile, mainstream news and "business news" have effectively morphed in recent decades as the news is increasingly pitched to the richest one-half or one-third of the population. The affairs of Wall Street, the pursuit of profitable investments, and the joys of capitalism are now often taken to be the interests of the general population. The affairs of working-class people have virtually disappeared from the news. Now journalists rely on business or business-oriented think tanks as sources when covering economics stories. These factors place strong pressure on journalists to write favorably about the globalization of capitalism, and to regard the WTO protesters as dubious, if not purely fraudulent.

Compared to reporting on the JFK Jr. plane crash, coverage of the WTO meeting and demonstrations was sparse. There was no week of prime-time special reports on the cable news channels, despite the fact that what was transpiring touched on the most central political and social issues of our age. Indeed, Seattle was not given anywhere near the attention that Elián, Monica, O.J., or JonBenet got. News coverage of the demonstrations tended to emphasize property damage and violence and, even there, it downplayed the activities of the police. There were, to be fair, some outstanding pieces produced by the corporate media, but those were the exceptions to the rule. More of the same took place in April 2000 during the IMF-World Bank meetings and protests in Washington, D.C. The handful of good reports that did appear were lost in the continuous stream of pro-capitalist pieces. The sad truth is that the closer a story gets to corporate power and corporate domination of our society, the less reliable the corporate news media is.

What types of important stories get almost no coverage in the commercial news media? The historical standard is that there is no coverage when the political and economic elites are in agreement. Military spending is a classic example. The United States spends a fortune on the military for no publicly debated or accepted reason. But it serves several important purposes to our economic elite, not the least of which is as a lucrative form of corporate welfare. Since no element of the economic elite is harmed by military spending, and nearly all of them benefit by having an empire to protect profit making worldwide, it rarely gets criticized—unlike federal spending on education or health care or environmental improvements. If a reporter pursued the story of why we are spending some $700 billion on the military and war in 2008, he or she would appear to have an axe to grind and therefore to be unprofessional, since top official sources are not critical of the spending.

In recent years, the increased focus by the commercial news media on the more affluent part of the population has reinforced and extended the class bias in the selection and tenor of material. Stories of great importance to tens of millions of Americans will fall through the cracks because those are not the "right" Americans, according to the standards of the corporate news media. Consider, for example, the widening gulf between the richest and the poorest Americans, throughout the 1980s and 1990s real income declined or was stagnant for the lower 60 percent, while wealth and income for the rich skyrocketed. By 1998, discounting home ownership, the top 10 percent of the population claimed 76 percent of the nation's net worth, and more than half of that is accounted for by the richest 1 percent. The bottom 60 percent has virtually no wealth, aside from some home ownership; by any standard the lowest 60 percent is economically insecure, as it is weighed down by very high levels of personal debt. As Lester Thurow notes, this peacetime rise in class inequality may well be historically unprecedented and is one of the main developments of our age. It has tremendously negative implications for our politics, culture, and social fabric, yet it is barely noted in our journalism except for rare mentions when the occasional economic report points to it. One could say that this can be explained by the lack of a news peg that would justify coverage, but that is hardly tenable when one considers the cacophony of news media reports on any economic boom or blip. In the crescendo of news media praise for the genius of contemporary capitalism, it is almost unthinkable to criticize the economy as deeply flawed. To do so would seemingly reveal one as a candidate for an honorary position in the Flat-Earth Society. The *Washington Post* has gone so far as to describe ours as a nearly "perfect economy." And it does, indeed, appear more and more perfect the higher one goes up the socioeconomic ladder, which points to the exact vantage point of the corporate news media.

The Internet

Moving on from journalism, the most striking media and communication development since January 1999 has been the rapid commercialization and expansion of the Internet. It is ironic that the media giants use the rise of the Internet and the prospect of new competition to justify their mega-mergers because, if anything, the Internet is spurring more concentration in media ownership, as well as other corporate sectors. The Internet will not launch a wave of commercially viable challengers to the existing media giants. Merely being able to launch a Web site is not sufficient to contend with the enormous market advantages of the media giants as they colonize the Internet. Recent evidence has borne that out in spades. Indeed, when AOL announced its deal with Time Warner, that pretty much hammered the nail in the coffin that the Internet would launch a new wave of media competition and drive the traditional media giants into extinction. For what AOL paid for Time Warner, it could have duplicated Time Warner's physical assets many times over. But what it needed was Time Warner's semi-monopolistic market position, which is nearly priceless.

As all communication switches to digital format, what seems most likely is that the corporate media giants will increasingly merge and partner with the few remaining corporate computer and telecommunication giants. We will have a global communication oligopoly of ten to twelve unbelievably huge firms, rather than a media oligopoly of six to eight believably huge ones.

But the bankruptcy of communication policymaking is most apparent where it is the most important: with the rise of the Internet and digital communication systems. The shadowy history of how the Internet went from being a public-sector creation to being the province of Wall Street needs to be written, but this much is known: both political parties are thoroughly in the pay of the firms and sectors that benefited by the expansion of the commercialized Internet. The explicit policy of both parties was to fan the flames of this expansion as much as possible, all with the aim of making the Internet ubiquitous as quickly as possible. If the corporations have their way, soon it will be virtually impossible even to raise the issue of how the Internet should develop because its course will have been set in stone, or at least in code, and will be protected by powerful lobbies. Even more important, there will no longer be any option about whether one wishes to participate in the "e-society." It will be all but mandatory, if one is to participate in U.S. life. All along the way we will be told of the great advantages we will enjoy by being online most of the time, of the unimaginable power and control over our lives it will give us. The commercialized Internet will soon appear as natural to us as our system of roads.

The analogy to automobiles is intentional, as the Internet in many ways is coming to play the same role in the twenty-first-century economy and social structure that cars have over the past seventy-five years or so. When automobiles were introduced—and especially after their prices came down—they provided revolutionary mobility for people. Who could not want to have a car? Soon networks of roads were built with public funds and the suburban sprawl that has engulfed so much of our countryside began in earnest. It became impossible to survive in the United States, except in a handful of locations, without having an automobile. Not one car per family either, but one per adult. Cars became as American as apple pie. And then, slowly, by the final third of the twentieth century it became clear that the toll automobiles were taking on human life was enormous. Air pollution, atomized suburban living conditions, the decline of the cities, traffic congestion, and a myriad of other social problems related to the automobile began to draw attention. Yet the problems were difficult to address because the automobile had become such an ingrained part of the society. One could speculate that, had the American people democratically considered all the pros and cons of the automobile back before, say, the 1940s, they might have opted to emphasize mass transit and downplay the usage of cars. But that was a debate that powerful interests made certain we never had.

Could the same be true of the Internet? Is the "Damn the Torpedoes" Internet policy a bit like driving at night on a strange mountain road at a hundred miles an hour with the headlights off? Might there be a dark side to the commercial cyberworld? Already there are concerns about Internet privacy, concerns that the ability to expand commerce necessarily also means the ability of corporations and governments to keep much closer tabs, on individuals. Some foresee a panoptic society where traditional notions of personal privacy will be virtually eliminated. There are concerns as well that the new digital system will make it possible for poor people to be entirely written out of the world experienced by the middle and upper classes, making political democracy that much more fragile. Similarly, scholarly research is beginning to show that those who spend the most time online risk becoming more antisocial and increasingly unhappy. In short, there are serious questions that have been pushed aside in the mad dash to commercialize the Internet. They will only get taken up, I suspect, years from now when they will be written as laments.

As with the automobile, the primary justification for this Internet commercialism is economic. As the automobile provided the basis for the expansion of twentieth-century industrial capitalism, so, we are told, the Internet and digital technology will provide the basis for economic growth in twenty-first-century capitalism. This is not debated so much as it is reiterated. Some of the claims about the Internet and the economy are clearly false, such as the popular cry that the Internet would smash up traditional giant corporations and create an economy dominated by small, hungry, lean and mean Internet-based entrepreneurial firms operating in competitive markets. A more important claim is that the Internet will provide the basis for sustained investment and economic growth that will raise living standards and the quality of life for generations, much as the automobile did. It is probably too early to pass judgment on that issue, but one 2000 study finds little evidence that the Internet will stimulate massive investment and economic growth.

Even if one accepts that the Internet is to some extent the foundation of our current and future economic success, the important social questions remain: Who in the economy truly benefits? How much do the benefits spread to the bulk of the population—and at what social cost? So far the benefits are passing to a relatively small sector of the population, and there is little reason at present to anticipate the type of job creation associated with the auto industry with all of its related industries like oil, steel, rubber, glass, and construction. Only in a political and media culture where the affairs of Wall Street investors are presumed to be the same as the interests of the average person can these issues be ignored.

Prospects for Media Reform

Across the United States there is growing interest in media reform, ranging from local media literacy campaigns in schools to campaigns for revamping public television and radio at the national level. The objective, in the end, is to reduce the power of Wall Street and Madison Avenue and increase the power of everyone else. Antitrust is crucial, but it is not sufficient. Even more competitive media markets would leave too much power in the hands of owners and advertisers; that is why we need a viable, heterogenous nonprofit and noncommercial sector. Media reform activity continues to grow. This issue is not just the province of the political Left. Indeed, political conservatives like Phyllis Schlafly have worked with progressive media reform groups like Ralph Nader's Commercial Alert to challenge advertising and commercialism in public schools, an issue closely related to media reform. A May 1999 national survey sponsored by the Project on Media Ownership concluded that a majority of Americans from all backgrounds supported the sort of structural media reform that is off-limits to debate in mainstream political circles. (No wonder the media giants do not want this to become a public issue!)

I would go so far as to say that media reform is not an issue that is best cast along left-right lines. It is better thought of as elementary to democracy. To the extent people not on the left support rudimentary democracy, they can and should support media reform as providing the basic groundwork for a democratic political culture.

Prospects for Political Renewal

There have been indications that we are entering an era of renewed politicization. On college campuses, for example, the 1999–2000 year saw an explosion of student organizing against sweatshops on some two hundred campuses. What has been striking to me is the growth in interest in anti-capitalist political organizing at a rate unprecedented for a quarter of a century. Also apparent, and so very refreshing, is that political organizing, though very serious, is also fun for the first time for students in a very long time. "With a joie de vivre that the American economic left has probably lacked since before WWL," an observer wrote, "college students are increasingly engaged in well-organized, thoughtful and morally outraged resistance to corporate power." This new political culture provides a marked contrast to the wet blanket of the phony corporate world pitched at the "youth market," with commercially sponsored "alternative" music events and contrived MTV hipness, all aimed at turning young people upside down and shaking the money out of their pockets. An alternative political culture is emerging along with a movement, much in evidence at the astonishing demonstrations in Seattle for the WTO meeting in late 1999 and in Washington, D.C., for the IMF-World Bank meetings in April 2000. A big part of this movement is the importance of alternative media, and the explicit critique of the limitations of corporate media. The new movement "appears to have legs," one business writer informed his readers. "The world's financial and corporate elites would do well to listen up."

Nor are campuses the only site of activism. Movements against the death penalty and against police brutality are growing across the nation, especially in communities of color. The labor movement is in the midst of a renaissance of sorts, as more union shops get organized, especially among low-paid minority and women workers. Environmental activism, too, is going on all around the nation. The most exciting moments are when these various concerns—about class exploitation, about the environment, about racism—converge and draw people together. Such is the case with the anti-sweatshop movement, the environmental justice movement, the anti-WTO/IMF-World Bank movement, and the movements to organize low-wage workers. If a new and powerful Left is going to emerge in the United States, this is where the embryo will be found.

Almost all of this is taking place beneath the radar of the corporate news media, with their reliance on official sources and their close ties to those at the top of the social pecking order. Indeed, it is the lack of attention to these issues in the media, or the distorted nature of the coverage when there is attention, that underlines the importance of media activism to the new generation of activists. Similarly, the national electoral system is largely immune to these developments; awash in massive campaign contributions from billionaires and multimillionaires, the Democrats and Republicans spend a fortune on manipulative and insulting advertisements aimed at the dwindling numbers that take them seriously. The corporate media rake in this money for TV ads, highlight only the activities of politicians who support their agenda, and then pretend that this charade has something to do with democracy.

It is with this new progressive movement that the fate of media reform resides. Media reform cannot win without widespread support and such support needs to be organized as part of a broad anti-corporate, pro-democracy movement. If progressive forces can just get media reform on the agenda, merely make it part of legitimate debate, they will find that it has considerable support from outside the ranks of the Left. (It may even encourage people to take a closer and more sympathetic look at the Left.) This has been the pattern abroad: where Left parties have gotten media issues into debate, the mainstream parties could no longer blindly serve the corporate media-masters. And this point is well understood by the media giants, which do everything within their considerable power to see that there is not even the beginnings of public discussion of media policy.

We are in precarious times. The corporate media system is consolidating into the hands of fewer and fewer enormous firms at a rapid rate, providing a hypercommercialized fare suited to wealthy shareholders and advertisers, not citizens. At the same time, there is a budding movement for media reform which is part and parcel of a broader anti-corporate movement At present the smart money says that the big guys will win and the wise move is to accept the inevitable and abandon any hope of social change. But the same smart money once said that communism was going to last forever unless overthrown from without, and that South African apartheid could never be removed peacefully so it was best to work with the status quo white regime. Smart money is often more interested in protecting money than in being smart. Nobody can predict the future, especially in turbulent times like these. All we can do is attempt to understand how the world works so we can try to protect and expand those values we deem important. And if enough people come together to protect and expand democratic values—as it is in their interest to do—anything can happen.

Concluding this section, John Stauber and Sheldon Rampton describe how public-relations professionals are quite deliberate in their efforts to manipulate the habits of the masses, that is, to "manufacture consent." They show that "news" is often little more than well-disguised propaganda that serves vested interests while limiting the ability of citizens to stay accurately informed of issues that have serious consequences on their lives. The effort extends from global warming to the effects of junk food (and, we can safely assume, everything in between).

ALL THE NEWS THAT'S FIT TO PRINT

JOHN STAUBER SHELDON RAMPTON

It's to the point where Brit Hume, the ABC correspondent at the White House, plays tennis with George Bush. Tom Friedman of the New York Times is very close to Jim Baker. You find these relationships are so close that reporters don't challenge the subjects of their stories, they just tell you what the government is saying. In other words, they have become stenographers for power and not journalists.

—JEFF COHEN
Executive Director,
Fairness & Accuracy In Reporting (FAIR)

If popular culture is any guide at all to the imagination of the American people, there is something sacred about the news. Journalists, along with private detectives and police, seem to occupy a special place as the ministers of truth and wisdom in our society. The archetypal image for all three professions is the "little guy" with the common touch—picture Columbo, Lou Grant or Phil Marlowe— dressed in cheap clothes, cynical, smoking a cigar, fond of a drink at the local tavern, working odd hours, bothering people, persistent, smart beneath that rumpled exterior, piecing together clues, finding contradictions, relentless and inquisitive, refusing to let go of an investigation until the truth is exposed and the villains receive their just punishment. This image of the journalistic profession has been the backdrop for a number of popular plays, novels, films and television shows, including "Citizen Kane," "His Girl Friday," "Meet John Doe," "The Front Page," "The Paper" and "Murphy Brown." Of course mild-mannered reporter Clark Kent is the alter-ego of Superman, the ultimate comic-book hero, who spends much of his time rescuing fellow reporters Lois Lane and Jimmy Olsen when their journalistic curiosity gets them into trouble. Hollywood turned to real life in "All the President's Men," in which Robert Redford and Dustin Hoffman portray *Washington Post* reporters Bob Woodward and Carl Bernstein in their investigation of President Nixon's role in the Watergate scandal. The final scene of the movie visually dramatizes the power of the press when the camera zooms in on a clattering newsroom teletype as it prints out a sequence of bulletins from the Watergate affair, culminating in the terse headline: "NIXON RESIGNS."

From "All the News That's Fit to Print," from *Toxic Sludge is Good for You: Lies, Damn Lies, and the Public Relations Industry* by John Stauber. Courtesy of the Center for Media and Democracy, http://www.prwatch.org, http://www.sourcewatch.org, and http://www.banksterusa.org

But schoolbooks often fail to mention that Woodward and Bernstein were virtually alone in their dogged pursuit of the Watergate scandal, which occurred in the midst of a presidential election yet had absolutely no impact on the election outcome. According to Project Censored, a phone call from the Nixon White House was all it took to persuade CBS chair William Paley to scale back Walter Cronkite's attempt to do an extraordinary two-part series about Watergate on the *CBS Evening News* before the election. Nixon was re-elected by an overwhelming margin, and wasn't forced to resign until two years after the burglary. Even then, the real "heroes" include a still-unknown whistleblower dubbed "Deep Throat" and Nixon's own arrogance in leaving behind expletive-loaded tape recordings of his self-incriminating involvement in a cover-up. Even Woodward and Bernstein were never able to explain important aspects about the scandal, such as White House motivations behind the Watergate break-in, or Deep Throat's reasons for coming forward.

Hard Pressed

The romantic mythology surrounding the journalistic profession attracts many more would-be reporters than there are jobs available. In reality, as most working reporters readily admit, the profession is a far cry from its image. Reporters are notoriously underpaid and overworked. While researching this book, we encountered one reporter with a small-town daily paper who was earning an annual income of $13,000 in 1994 while working 60-hour weeks—less than he could have earned flipping hamburgers. Sitting below a poster of Rush Limbaugh which the newspaper management had mounted on the wall of his break room, the reporter described how the paper had ordered him and his fellow reporters to falsify time cards so it would appear they were only working 40 hours per week—thus enabling management to violate minimum-wage laws. We contacted a state labor official who assured us that if the reporter kept good records, he could document the fraud and force the paper to pay him for his uncompensated labor. The reporter, however, was afraid that he would be fired if he filed a complaint, and we were left wondering: Is someone who collaborates this easily with covering up his own exploitation even *capable* of investigating and exposing the larger wrongs in his community?

In a democracy, a free and independent press is counted upon to provide the information and opinions that fuel public debate, expose corruption, illuminate major social issues, and enable an informed citizenry to make participatory decisions. Today's reality, however, is ever more distant from this lofty ideal. Journalism is in fact in demise, and its collapse is opening ever more opportunities for PR practitioners to increase their influence in the news room.

Today the number of PR flacks in the United States outnumbers working journalists, and the gap is widening. A working reporter is deluged daily with dozens if not hundreds of phone calls, letters, faxes and now e-mailed press releases. Pam Berns, the publisher of *Chicago Life* magazine, estimates that her office receives at least 100 PR contacts each and every day. "It's annoying and overwhelming," says Berns.

Is It Real Or Is It Memorex?

The use of radio and video news releases is a little-known practice which took hold during the 1980s, when PR firms discovered that they could film, edit and produce their own news segments—even entire programs—and that broadcasters would play the segments as "news," often with no editing. When Gray & Company began producing a radio program for its clients called "Washington Spotlight," the Mutual Radio Network came to Gray and *asked* to carry it. "PR firms would not send out packaged radio and television stories if no one was using them," notes author Susan Trento. "Not only technology, but economics made things easier for PR firms in the 1980s"

Video news releases, known as VNRs, typically come packaged with two versions of the story the PR firm is trying to promote. The first version is fully edited, with voiceovers already included or with a script indicating where the station's local news anchor should read his or her lines. The second version is known as "B-roll," and consists of the raw footage that was used to produce the fully-edited version. The receiving station can edit the B-roll footage itself, or combine it with other footage received from other sources. "There are two economics at work here on the television side," explains a Gray & Company executive. "The big stations don't want prepackaged, pretaped. They have the money, the budget, and the manpower to put their own together. But the smaller stations across the country lap up stuff like this."

MediaLink, a PR firm that distributed about half of the 4,000 VNRs made available to newscasters in 1991, conducted a survey of 92 newsrooms and found that all 92 used VNRs supplied free by PR firms and subtly slanted to sell a clients' products and ideas while appearing to be "real" TV news. On June 13, 1991, for example, the *CBS Evening News* ran a segment on the hazards of automatic safety belts. According to David Lieberman, author of a 1992 article titled "Fake News," the safety belt tape "was part of a 'video news release' created by . . . . a lobby group largely supported by lawyers."

"VNRs are as much a public relations fixture as the print news release," stated George Glazer, a senior vice-president of Hill & Knowlton. "In fact, many public relations firms are well into the second generation of VNR technology. We use satellite transmissions from our own facilities almost on a daily basis, and wait eagerly for fiber optics systems to allow us to dial into nationwide networks. . . . With few exceptions, broadcasters as a group have refused to participate in any kinds of standards establishment for VNRs, in part because they rarely will admit to using them on the air. . . . There are truly hundreds of examples of self-denial on the part of broadcasters when it comes to admitting that VNRs are used." Following a beverage-tampering scare on the West Coast, for example, a VNR was mailed out to all three TV stations in the first city to report the problem. All three stations used the VNR in at least one newscast the following day, along with five other stations in the region. When asked later, however, all three stations denied that they had broadcast the material.

In 1985; Trento reports, Gray & Company distributed a VNR featuring a canned interview with one of its clients, the ruthless King Hassan II of Morocco. The segment's airing on CNN provoked a scandal with reporters claiming they had been tricked into airing paid propaganda. An executive at Gray & Company scoffed at the media's hypocrisy: "I used to read in *Broadcasting* the cache of letters from news directors after the story broke about electronic news releases saying, 'How despicable. Never in a thousand years!' And they were people I had talked to who had called me back so that they had the right coordinates on the satellite so that they could take the feed. They knew exactly who we were. They called us all the time. They asked us for stuff. They told us they couldn't get it. They forgot to turn their downlink on, and could we send them a hard copy FedEx overnight because they'd use it tomorrow night."

"I was personally aggrieved at all this sort of self-righteousness of the media when that story broke," said another Gray & Company executive. "They are free to use it. Not use it. Use it for B-roll. Write their own scripts. Most of them take it straight off the air and broadcast it. Rip and read. Rip and read."

Watching the Detectives

In theory, journalism is a "watchdog" profession, which serves the public by finding and reporting on abuses of power. In practice, reporters live under closer scrutiny than the people they are supposed to be monitoring.

Former *Wall Street Journal* reporter Dean Rotbart has carved a niche for himself within the PR industry by compiling dossiers on his former colleagues so that his corporate clients know how to manipulate individual members of the media. Rotbart's firm—called TJFR Products and Services—publishes this information in high-priced newsletters and delivers customized workshops and reports.

Rotbart told a 1993 meeting of the Public Relations Society of America that his workshops and newsletters help PR professionals know "what a journalist is thinking. . . . One of the services we provide is taking biographies of reporters from all over the country—something like 6,000 bios—in our computer system, and if at any point you get a call from a journalist and don't know who it is, call up and we will fax you that bio within an hour."

These bios are a regular feature in a new Rotbart publication, the *TJFR Environmental News Reporter*. Promotional literature boasts that this $395-a-year PR resource is "tailored to serve the needs of communications professionals who deal with environmental issues. . . . Let us be your eyes and ears when the environmental media convene. . . . Gather vital information on key journalists . . . Who's the boss? . . . How do you break the ice? . . . Not only will you find news on journalists, we'll tell you what they want from you and what strategies you can employ with them to generate more positive stories and better manage potentially negative situations."

The premier issue of Rotbart's newsletter includes a long piece on CNN's Environment Unit, with biographies of all its top staff. It explains, for example, that Peter Dykstra worked for Greenpeace for 11 years and attended Boston University's College of Communications. The issue also contains an interview with Emilia Askari of the *Detroit Free Press*. The accompanying bio explains that Askari is president of the Society of Environmental Journalists and "enjoys all kinds of outdoor activities and tutors illiterate adults with Literacy Volunteers of America." In addition to this information, the story tells PR managers whom to contact if they want to complain about something that Askari writes: "Chain of command: Reports to Bob Campbell, assistant city editor."

Some PR firms specialize in tracking specific issues and compiling reports on the journalists writing stories. Rowan & Blewitt, a Washington, DC, PR firm, conducted in depth analyses for the dairy industry, analyzing media coverage of the rBGH issue to "help answer these questions: Has the coverage been sensationalistic. . . Has the coverage favored the anti-[rBGH] views?. . .How does the coverage of [rBGH] compare with the volume of coverage on Alar? Air emissions? . . . Alaskan oil spills?" Detailed charts and graphs examined virtually every story on rBGH over an extended period of time. Another media monitoring firm, CARMA International, also worked on the rBGH account and ranked individual reporters based on whether their stories were "favorable" or "unfavorable" to rBGH.

PR firms also hire real journalists to participate in training sessions so flacks can hone their skills in handling media situations. In *Sierra Magazine*, reporter Dashka Slater describes her experience working for Robert J. Meyers and Associates, a Houston-based consulting firm that hired her and two other journalists to help ARCO Petroleum practice its PR plan for handling the news media following environmental disasters. In a staged run-through of an oil spill, Slater and the other reporters were assigned to play the part of the "predatory press." Professional actors were brought in to play the part of environmentalists. ARCO employees and government officials played themselves. "The drills give company flacks the opportunity to practice varnishing the truth just in case the mop-up doesn't go as planned," wrote Slater. "Mostly the company and government spokespeople did what they had learned to do in numerous media-training workshops: convey as little information as possible in as many words as possible." In the past 6 years Meyers and Associates have conducted more than 400 such training drills.

Experts Agree

The advertising industry learned years ago that one of the best ways to influence an audience is to put its message in the mouth of a publicly-trusted expert such as a scientist, doctor or university professor. A whole genre of TV commercials has evolved featuring actors dressed in white laboratory coats who announce that "research proves" their brand is the best product on the market. The PR industry has also mastered the art of using "third party" experts, a ruse which almost never fails to hoodwink supposedly cynical reporters.

Via the internet, for example, public relations representatives "assist" the news media through an on-line service called Profnet, based at the State University of New York in Stony Brook. Journalists in search of information are invited to simply e-mail their request to Profnet, which distributes it to over 800 PR representatives of research institutions in 16 countries. The flacks then find professors or researchers to answer the questions. Needless to say, this "free" information helps shape the spin of the story in a direction the PR representative is trying to promote.

Corporations also fund "nonprofit research institutes" which provide "third party experts" to advocate on their behalf. The American Council on Science and Health (ACSH), for example, is a commonly-used industry front group that produces PR ammunition for the food processing and chemical industries. Headed by Elizabeth Whelan, ACSH routinely represents itself as an "independent," "objective" science institute. This claim was dissected by Howard Kurtz of the *Washington Post* in the March 1990 *Columbia Journalism Review*, which studied the special interests that fund ACSH. Kurtz reported that Whelan praises the nutritional virtues of fast food and receives money from Burger King. She downplays the link between a high fat diet and heart disease, while receiving funding from Oscar Mayer, Frito Lay and Land O'Lakes. She defends saccharin and receives money from Coca-Cola, Pepsi, NutraSweet and the National Soft Drink Association. Whelan attacks a Nebraska businessman's crusade against fatty tropical oils—the unhealthy oils in movie popcorn—while she is in the pay of palm oil special interests. "There has never been a case of ill health linked to the regulated, approved use of pesticides in this country," she claims, while taking money from a host of pesticide makers. And Whelan speaks harshly of mainstream environmentalists, such as the Natural Resources Defense Council. Speaking to the Bangor *Daily News*, Whelan described the NRDC as an "ideologically fueled project" whose "target is the free-enterprise, corporate America system. I think they hate the word 'profit' and they'll do anything that will involve corporate confrontation."

Whelan defends her "scientific" views by saying that her findings have undergone "peer review" by experts among the scientists affiliated with her group. But Michael Jacobson of the Center for Science in the Public Interest dismisses the bona fides of such "peer review" scientists: "They don't exactly publish in leading scientific journals. They publish pamphlets that are reviewed by their professional cronies of the regulated industries. It's science that's forced through a sieve of conservative philosophy."

Journalists rarely check the background of sources, so Whelan and the American Council on Science and Health are often quoted in the news as "scientific experts." For example, in a show hosted by Walter Cronkite titled "Big Fears, Little Risks," Cronkite introduced Whelan as one of "a growing number of scientists who fear that overstating the risk of environmental chemicals is actually threatening the health of Americans." In *Fortune* magazine, Whelan appeared as the source in a story by Ann Reilly Dowd which stated, "A big part of the problem is that America's environmental policy making has increasingly been driven more by media hype and partisan politics than by sensible science. . . . Despite the waves of panic that roll over America each year, some 500 scientists surveyed by the American Council on Science and Health have concluded that the threat to life from environmental hazards is negligible." Neither Cronkite nor Dowd explained that the ACSH is an industry front group.

Revolving Doors

Media critics note that the media habitually fails to report on itself; it also fails to report on the PR industry. To do so would reveal the extent of its dependency on PR for access, sources, quotes, stories and ideas. According to authors Jeff and Marie Blyskal, "the press has grown frighteningly dependent on public relations people. Outsiders—the reading and viewing public—would have a hard time discovering this on their own because the dependence on PR is part of behind-the-scenes press functioning. . . Meanwhile, like an alcoholic who can't believe he has a drinking problem, members of the press are too close to their own addiction to PR to realize there is anything wrong. In fact, the press which has a seemingly inborn cynical, arrogant, down-the-nose view of public relations, seems sadly self-deceptive about the true press/PR relationship."

Canned news and industry-supplied "experts" are effective because they appeal to budget-conscious news organizations. When a TV news show airs a video news release, the PR firm that produced the segment pays for all the costs of scripting, filming and editing. Likewise, PR-supplied experts enable reporters to produce authentic-sounding stories with a minimum of time and effort. The public rarely notices the self-serving bias that creeps into the news along with these subtle subsidies.

Sometimes the financial pressures that influence the news are more direct. In Canada, PR giant Burson-Marsteller's work for the British Columbia timber industry became the subject of investigation by Ben Parfitt, forestry reporter for the daily *Vancouver Sun*. In 1991, however, Burson-Marsteller picked up the *Sun* as a client, and editorial policy shifted. Before Burson-Marsteller went to work for the *Sun*, the paper employed five full-time reporters to cover forestry, fisheries, native affairs, energy and mines, and environment. Today only the environment position remains, and the reporter on that beat has been instructed to cover environmental issues in Greater Vancouver and the lower mainland, an area which is conveniently distant from the Clayoquot Sound, where Burson-Marsteller is helping fell one of the last large areas of intact coastal temperate rainforest in the world.

Corporate advertisers have enormous power to influence news coverage, despite editors' statements to the contrary. Large corporations pump $100 billion per year in advertising dollars into the coffers of the US media alone. Ben Bagdikian points out that "selecting news in order to make advertising more effective is becoming so common that it has achieved the status of scientific precision and publishing wisdom." PR executive Robert Dilenschneider admits that "the notion, that business and editorial decisions in the press and media are totally separate is largely a myth."

Mergers, buyouts and new electronic technologies are all hastening the crumbling of walls that supposedly separate news reporting, advertising, and PR. Two of the biggest global PR firms, Burson-Marsteller and Hill & Knowlton, are owned by two of the biggest advertising conglomerates, respectively Young & Rubicam and the WPP Group. These two PR/advertising giants purchase billions of dollars of media print space, TV and radio time. Their clients include Philip Morris, McDonald's, Ford Motor Company, Johnson & Johnson, AT&T, Pepsi, Coca-Cola, NutraSweet, Revlon, Reebok, and hundreds of other major advertisers.

Discussion Questions

- Consider the power of hegemony. How does it limit our ability to address and fix structural problems, such as poverty, that stubbornly persist in North American society?

- Altheide asserts that media provides a basis for people to construct their identities. Does this support hegemony? How or how not?

- What role might McChesney say the corporate media plays in maintaining hegemony?

- How can average citizens resist hidden propaganda/public relations messaging in the news media?

- How is censorship in the United States different or not different from the stereo-type of censorship in repressive regimes? What are the implications of these differences?

Culture

How do the media affect a societies' core cultural beliefs? Culture is inherently social, that is, created through human interaction, but it is not easy to define.[21] For our purposes, culture can perhaps best be described as a set of widely shared beliefs about social situations, institutions, values, and norms. The fact that these beliefs are held in some sense collectively should not be read to mean that everyone thinks they are just. As Ferrel, Hayward, and Young remind us, culture "operates less as an entity or environment than as an uncertain dynamic by which groups large and small construct, question, and contest the collective experience of everyday life."[22]

Consider resistance to the type of stereotyping described in Chapter 2 of this volume. The slogan "Black is Beautiful" arose in the 1960s when activists challenged the inferior and unattractive identity that whites had constructed for them. Second-wave feminists have challenged cultural norms that restrict women's roles in society, and disability-rights activists are undertaking a similar campaign. Culture, in short, is "contested" space.

Also, beliefs, once firmly held by millions of people, do sometimes change with time; they are not grounded in some essential nature of a phenomenon. Consider changing attitudes toward the rights of homosexuals to marry, the role of women in the military, and men who choose the role of stay-at-home parent. Thus culture can also be described as "unstable."

Where does justice enter this discussion? Can the media play a positive role in redefining cultural understandings? The obstacles are formidable. Noam Chomsky provides a brief history of propaganda in America and discusses how it can weaken the ability of citizens to engage in decision making and alter both the form and meaning of "democracy."

In the next reading, Pepi Leistyna is pessimistic, suggesting how entertainment television shapes perceptions of social class in America across lines of race and gender. He notes the focus on (upper) middle-class norms and the failure to deal with the realities of working-class life. Working-class people are often portrayed as lazy buffoons who have found their natural place in the class hierarchy. Sometimes the story line varies to include "escape" fantasies where those from the working-class move up through hard work and individual initiative. In the process, these shows affirm hegemonic ideals of social mobility, meritocracy, and a colorblind society.

---

[21]"Culture," in *Cultural Theory: The Key Concepts*, edited by Andrew Edgar and Peter Sedgwick (New York: Routledge, 2002), p. 102.

[22]Ferrel, Hayward, and Young, *Cultural Criminology*, p. 7.

Social Class and Entertainment Television: What's So Real and New about Reality TV?

Pepi Leistyna

Corporate bodies take the fact that culture shapes our sense of political agency very seriously and mediates the relations between everyday struggles and structures of power. In fact, in this age of postmodern technologies that can saturate society with media messages, elite private interests have worked diligently to monopolize the means of production and distribution of information and ideas so as to be able to more effectively circulate, legitimate, and reproduce a vision of the world that suits their needs. One of the pedagogical forces that needs to be watched more closely is entertainment television.

Television in the United States is largely controlled by five massive transnational corporations: Time Warner (which among its many assets, owns and operates CNN, Turner Classic Movies, HBO, Court TV, TNT, TBS, and the Cartoon Network); Disney (owns ABC, ESPN, the Disney Channel, The History Channel, A&E, Biography, Military History, Lifetime, E, The Style Network, and Soapnet); News Corporation (owns Fox, National Geographic Channel, Direct TV, FX, and STAR); General Electric (owns NBC, Telemundo, Bravo, MSNBC, CNBC, Sci Fi, Paxon, the USA Network, and Sundance—which is a joint venture with CBS); and Viacom (owns CBS, MTV, Showtime, Comedy Central, BET, TV Land, VH1, CMT, Nick at Nite, Spike TV, and Nickelodeon). It's important to look critically at the stories these corporate-managed media channels script and ask: whose interests are served by such representations, and what alternative visions of the world are available to the public?

When it comes to labor in the United States, network television has a long history of constructing tales about the lives of working people that reinforce classist, racist, and sexist stereotypes that serve to justify the inequities inherent in capitalism's class structure.

What's Been the Norm?

The working class has always found its image on entertainment television. In the early years of broadcasting, working-class and immigrant families appeared regularly on shows like *I Remember Mama* (1949–1957), *The Goldbergs* (1949–1955), and *Life with Luigi* (1952–1953), which featured Norwegian, Jewish, and Italian families.

As TV evolved as a commercially sponsored medium, advertisers took the reins in steering the creation and production of programs, including script writing and hiring

From "Social Class and Entertainment Television" by Pepi Leistyna, from *Media/Cultural Studies: Critical Approaches*, edited by Rhonda Hammer and Douglas Kellner, pp. 339–348, 353–354. Peter Lang, 2009.

of talent. Advertisers worked diligently to redefine the meaning of the American Dream from the search for a better life, to the pursuit of a consumer lifestyle. Working together, producers and advertisers understood that associating products with middle- and upper-class lifestyles would increase both ratings and sales. They effectively perpetuated the myth that buying products would bring about class mobility. Unlike on radio, where many of the earlier shows got their start, on television you can really see what the assimilation process is supposed to look like, according to the advertising-driven media. It's the acquisition of consumer goods, becoming less ethnic, and looking more like middle-class American families with aspirations. The stark contrast between the gritty image of working-class life, and the shiny sanitized world of consumer advertising, proved to be irreconcilable. As television became more consolidated in the late 50's and the early 60's, working-class and immigrant families would gradually disappear. On the contrary, programs that could provide a pristine setting for product placement and articulate the needs of a healthy, successful middle-class family living the American dream would take center stage—shows such as: *I Married Joan* (1952–1955), *The Adventures of Ozzy and Harriet* (1952–1966), *Make Room for Daddy* (1953–1965), *Father Knows Best* (1954–1960), *Leave it to Beaver* (1957–1963), *Dennis the Menace* (1959–1963), and *The Dick Van Dyke Show* (1961–1969).

In the 1950s as the white working class was disappearing into the classless middle, African Americans and other racially subordinated groups continued to endure the horrors of white supremacy, coupled with the exploitative logic of capital. Disregarding these harsh realities, TV's fantasy land only allowed people of color to be visible as happy servants or entertainers on programs like *Beulah* (1950–1953) and *The Nat "King" Cole Show* (1956–1957).

In order to gain broader access to television, blacks and other marginalized groups would have to learn to play by TV's rules—namely to have faith in the American Dream. While this logic has served television's commercial imperatives, it has also reduced struggles for economic justice and social equality to a simple matter of inclusion.

In the post-civil rights era, the arrival of African Americans onto primetime television with shows like *Sanford and Son* (1972–1977), *Fat Albert and the Cosby Kids* (1972–1980), *Good Times* (1974–1979), *Grady* (1975–1976), *What's Happening* (1976–1979), and *That's My Momma* (1974–1975), suggests that there is no need for the redistribution of wealth and power because on TV, there is plenty of room for everyone. As Marlon Riggs (1991) notes in his documentary film *Color Adjustment*, in large part these sitcoms cast ghetto life in a happy light where opportunity was simply a question of initiative. He also reveals how *Good Times* showed real potential to take on some of the harsh realities of class exploitation and racism—potential that was quickly extinguished because of the transparent political content of some of the earlier episodes. And of course, in the spirit of the American Dream and meritocracy, by the last episode—as with so many of these programs, the family escapes the ghetto and moves into the middle class.

The other storyline running through black sitcoms during this period dealt with this idea of "moving on up," but these shows didn't address economic hardship at all. The best known example is *The Jeffersons* (1975–1985) with the self-made man, George Jefferson. George's hard work and entrepreneurial spirit ensure the success of his dry cleaning business and consequently allows his family to "move on up" to the East Side. As Robin Kelly argues:

> He proves that black people are successful, so therefore the Civil Rights Movement is over. He proves that there is no need for affirmative action because he is a self-made man. He proves that there is no need for welfare because these people can make it on their own. (interview in Class *Dismissed*, 2005)

The Cosby Show (1984–1992) was also controversial in this respect. While the sitcom provided an important non-stereotypical image of a black family that countered the overwhelmingly pejorative representations that preceded it, the show nonetheless disregarded the harsh realities faced by poor and working-class people of color, and it made it look like the middle class is open to anyone. It's important to note that, while still very popular, the show went off the air the year of the Los Angeles uprisings.

This same ideology of openness and arrival is embedded in more recent shows that feature African Americans such as *Martin* (1992–1997), *The Hughleys* (1998–2002), *The Bernie Mac Show* (2001–present), *My Wife and Kids* (2001–2005), *All of Us* (2003–present), and *That's So Raven* (2003–present). While these shows depict the everyday lives of people, they are scripted outside of the reality that 30.4% of black workers and 39.8% of Latino/a workers earn low wages. The median income of racially subordinated families is $25,700, as compared with white families—$45,200. The unemployment rate for African Americans and Latino/as over the years has remained more than double that of whites. While about 10% of white children live in poverty in the United States, over 30% of African American and Latino/a kids experience economic hardship. Representations that capture these realities are at best few and far between.

There have been some black working-class characters on situation comedies; for example, the *Fresh Prince of Bel Air* (1990–1996). This character played by actor Will Smith is having some trouble in the ghetto, so he's shipped off to live with his rich relatives in Bel Air—leaving his single mom behind in the hood. In this post-Cosby world, there is no need for government programs to provide much-needed social services and economic support because there are wealthy black families that can rescue troubled youth and offer them all of the necessities for social advancement.

With the exception of a few prominent roles (featuring middle- and upper-middle-class characters) on shows like *ER* (1994–present), *Law & Order: Special Victims Unit* (1999–present), and *Crey's Anatomy* (2005–present), Asian Americans are still largely excluded from prime time, or relegated to bit parts. And while the growing importance of the Latino/a demographic has resulted in a small increase in representations [e.g., *The Brothers Garcia* (2000–2004), *Resurrection Blvd.* (2000–2002), and *American Family* (2002–2004)], most Latinos are still confined to cable and Spanish-language networks, and are overwhelmingly middle class. The only show to feature a working-class Latino character since *Chico and the Man* (1974–1978) is *The George Lopez Show* (2002–present). But unlike the characters of the ghetto sitcom era who are trying to move out of the working class, George Lopez has already left it behind and moved up to the comfortable familiarity of the middle-class family sitcom.

The George Lopez Show is a perfect example of how the American dream is supposed to work. A former assembly line worker, George is promoted to manager of the factory. Suddenly he has no problems. He lives in a beautiful space. His family has no problems other than what typical American middle-class families supposedly go through. And the only thing that marks him as working class is his mom and his buddies back at the factory that refer to him as "Mr. Clipboard." It's pretty comical that the producers chose to use *Low Rider* as the theme song for the show. While this is a song about urban Latino/a culture, there's a total disconnect between the song and who this middle-class character is—there's nothing *Low Rider* about George Lopez. In fact, if anything, the show eclipses the reality that the overwhelming majority of Latino/as in the United States suffer the abuses of immigration discrimination, labor exploitation, unemployment, and racism.

Women with Class

While they have never been excluded like other underrepresented groups, television largely ignores the economic realities faced by so many women in this country. Across the board, women earn less than men regardless of education, and they often work a double shift as part of the paid labor force, and as unpaid caretakers of the home and family. On average, women make 77 cents to a man's dollar. Median income for men in the United States is $40,800; for women, it is $31,200. The leading occupations for women are all lower-middle and working-class jobs. In addition, the majority of jobs at the bottom of the economic scale are held by women, especially women of color. In 2003, "33.9% of Black women and 45.8% of Latinas earned low wages." Not only does television disregard these realities, it rarely even depicts work as an economic necessity. This is evident in older shows that feature female characters such as *Bewitched* (1964–1972) and *The Brady Bunch* (1969–1974) (where even Alice, the family maid, is happy and carefree), and in more recent programs like *Friends* (1994–2004) and *Sex & the City* (1998–2004).

In the last three decades, the number of households headed by single moms has remained fairly constant, at around 80%. With an average income of only $24,000, single moms experience poverty at a rate that is substantially higher (28%) than the national average (13%). Single moms, in shows like *Julia* (1968–1971), *The Partridge Family* (1970–1974), *One Day at a Time* (1975–1984), *Murphy Brown* (1983–1998), *Ally McBeal* (1997–2002), *Judging Amy* (1999–2005), *The Parkers* (1999–2004), *The Gilmore Girls* (2000–present), and *Reba* (2001–present) don't reflect the reality of single mothers' lives.

Class Bozos

In order to reinforce its middle-class ideology, television must account for the members of the working class who haven't made it. TV has reproduced the deeply ingrained belief that worker's inadequacies are to blame for their lack of advancement. In reality, most Americans do not change their class position, and the boundaries of social class are now more restrictive than ever. Television representations either perpetuate the idea that the cream always rises to the top, or they reinforce stereotypes about workers' failure to succeed due to their inferior qualities such as bad taste, lack of intelligence, reactionary politics, poor work ethic, and dysfunctional family values.

One of the flaws that is supposedly characteristic of the working class that is widely circulated in popular culture, and in which TV plays an important role in that circulation, pertains to taste, lifestyle, and leisure. A stereotypical image that we get is a bunch of slobs sitting around on some cheesy couch drinking beer, preferably brown bottle or can beer, and starring endlessly at the tube. Given their love of junk culture, we don't get the sense that they are deserving of the finer things in life—they wouldn't appreciate them anyway. On entertainment television, we don't get the idea that working-class characters are economically deprived; rather, their low tolerance and limited access to the 'virtues of high culture' are attributed to personal taste and choice. When working-class characters do try to move out of this space and hob-knob with the middle and upper classes, it's made really laughable because they're so awkward in this new environment—they don't have the cultural capital to navigate it.

Another debilitating characteristic of this group of people, according to the stereotype, is that working-class men lack intelligence. It's obvious they weren't good students. They often fumble the language and a lot of basic stuff just goes right over their heads. The classic character of the lovable but laughable buffoon that is still very much with us today was played by Jackie Gleason in *The Honeymooners* (1955–1956), in the character of Ralph Cramden.

The *Honeymooners* is also an important prototype for a particular gender dynamic. Because these guys are so lacking in common sense, and the wives are obviously smarter, it's the women who end up ruling the roost. What we end up with is a reversal of traditional gender roles where these guys are essentially incapable of taking their place at the head of the household.

It's not just the wives. In a typical working-class household, even the kids are smarter than the dad. This is really evident in shows like *The Simpsons* (1989–present), in the father son relationship in *Married with Children* (1987–1997), and in *Still Standing* (2002–present).

The working class is being blamed for not being educated enough to compete in a global economy, and yet we have one of the most educated workforces in the world, regardless of the fact that our public education system is highly class based. It's also ironic that given this claim of lack of education, corporations are moving to 'third world' countries where there is enormous illiteracy in order to find "cheap" labor.

On corporate-run TV, there is a recurring representation that the working class has no interest in education as they wallow in anti-intellectualism. They have no interest in reading, unless it's the sports page, the comics, or a tabloid of some sort. The history of the working class fighting for public education is nowhere to be found. There's a reason for these stereotypes: they distract us from the structural realities, especially the unequal distribution of resources in public education that inhibit people's lives. But what's worse is they disregard the fact that the overwhelming majority of working-class parents really do care about their kids' education.

The working class is also represented as being disinterested in politics, which is ridiculous if you think about working-class history, and the struggle for basic rights and a living wage. When we do get characters that are interested in politics, they're almost always staunch conservatives, bigots, and closed-minded. The archetypal figure here is Archie Bunker from *All in the Family* (1971–1979), a character that for a long time was a stand-in for working-class guys.

Perhaps the most blatant representational crime against the working class by this corporate media is this image of this lazy, incompetent worker, who's complacent and not interested in improving his or her lot in life. These characters have no leadership skills and they are in constant need of supervision. In this era of globalization with enormous job loss, outsourcing and off-shoring, corporations need a scapegoat for their avarice activity, and the scapegoat is the working class who is not working hard enough and yet, since 1975, productivity is way up (163%); who's asking for too much money, and yet wages are stagnant (115%) and profits are through the roof (758%).

When it comes to family values, in the late 1980s and early 1990s there's a dramatic shift away from the omnipresent image of the happy, homogenous, nuclear family. This era that is often referred to as "Loser TV," gave birth to shows like *Married with Children, The Simpsons, Jerry Springer* (1991–present), and *Beavis and Butthead* (1993–1997). These shows appear at the tail end of eight years of Ronald Reagan, when the country was going through some serious economic turmoil. But instead of looking at downsizing, layoffs, unemployment, and corporate greed, these working-class couples are seen as the poster child of bad parenting, and hence the source of all society's ills. They certainly don't have the wisdom, discipline, and morality of the middle-class parents of other shows.

These families give rise to a couple different kinds of children, either they are smart and talented, which reinforces the myth of meritocracy—these kids are going to make it out regardless of the circumstances, or they are deviant in a number of ways—the Bart Simpson type.

The two biggest troublemakers are definitely Beavis and Butthead. These guys celebrate stupidity, and they live for sex and violence. The show plays on a generation of youth raised on a media-saturated society of junk culture, commodity, and alienation where the parents are driven out of the home and into the labor force, and where the TV becomes the babysitter and the role model. As Doug Kellner notes, there surely is an element of working-class revenge for these two guys who come from broken homes in a disintegrating community, where school and work in the fast-food industry are meaningless, and where they are downwardly mobile with a bleak future, if any. Shows like *The Simpsons* and *Beavis and Butthead* do offer a critique of our corporate-driven society. These guys know that something is wrong. But the problem is that their actions are just individualized acts of rebellion—their response is to trash stuff. As a consequence, such behavior ends up being self-destructive, rather than transformative.

Race, Deviance, and Class

Outside of the comic frame, there is a different and more threatening image of the working class on crime shows. Because this genre does not use class as a lens to view criminal behavior, deviance is most often framed in racial or cultural terms. The 70s and 80s are filled with cop shows that criminalize the black culture. The more recent incarnation of such shows [e.g., *Cops* (1989–present), *Homicide: Life on the Street* (1993–1999), *NYPD Blue* (1993–2005), *Oz* (1997–2003), *The Shield* (2002–present), and *Dog the Bounty Hunter* (2004–present)] continue to do important ideological work. They justify the growing prison system that now has a record 2.1 million people behind bars—over 70% of whom are non-white. African American males make up the largest number of those entering prisons each year in the United States. Racially subordinated women are also being incarcerated in epidemic proportions. As Loic Wacquant (2002) states, "The astounding upsurge in Black incarceration in the past three decades results from the obsolescence of the ghetto as a device for caste control and the correlative need for a substitute apparatus for keeping (unskilled) African Americans in a subordinate and confined position—physically, socially, and symbolically" (p. 23). And of course, these images are scripted outside of any analysis of racism and the poverty caused by capitalism. 37 million people in this country live in poverty, a number that is up 1.1 million from 2003. According to the U.S. Department of Agriculture, there are 25.5 million people who rely on food stamps to avoid hunger—a number that is up 2 million from 2004. 6.8 million families live in poverty. 17% of the nation's children, or about 12 million kids, are compelled to endure inhumane economic conditions. An Urban Institute study recently revealed that about 3.5 million people are homeless in the U.S. (a number projected to increase 5% each year), and 1.3 million (or 39%) of them are children.

The largest group of poor people in the United States is white. Yet we have a very limited understanding of who they are, because their images historically have been so few and far between. And because whiteness is associated with a dominant culture, poor and working-class whites are usually portrayed as cultural outcasts or a subculture. And while TV mocks their condition, it gladly uses their image to entertain us.

The rural working class is nearly invisible in mainstream culture. What we find on television are these twisted comedic images, which, like the ghetto sitcoms, really pastoralize poverty. The earlier images were of hillbilly characters popularized on shows like *Ma & Pa Kettle* (1954) and *The Real McCoys* (1951–1963). And these are followed by the 'idiot sitcom era,' with country bumpkin shows like *The Beverly Hillbillies* (1962–1971), *Andy Griffith* (1961–1968), *Gomer Pyle* (1964–1970), *Green Acres* (1965–1971), and *Petticoat Junction* (1963–1970), which featured characters who were simple-minded, non-threatening, and really easy to laugh at. These shows would be followed by *Hee-Haw* (1969–1993), *The Dukes of Hazard* (1979–1985), *Newhart* (1982–1990), *Enos* (1980–1981), and *The Dukes* (1983–1984).

The guy who resurrected the hillbilly and has given it new life as "redneck pride," is Jeff Foxworthy. From comedy tours to films to a cable show, *Blue Collar* TV (2004–present), being a redneck seems like a lifestyle which includes NASCAR and country music. What Foxworthy has done, is to take what in reality is an economic position and make it look like a lifestyle choice.

As the effects of the economic downturn become more visible, so is this more threatening image of the white poor who're being popularized as white trash. All these types, the hillbilly, the redneck, and white trash are racially coded terms to describe a genetic subset of white people—lowlifes. So Jerry Springer, who introduces his show with a television in the trashcan, is where all the qualities associated with white trash are on display: a lack of desire to work, sexual perversion, incest, and so on. In a similar spirit, *Geraldo* (1987–1998—hosted by Geraldo Rivera), created a perverse spectacle that was described by *Newsweek* as "trash TV." It's interesting because this is a multiracial world—it's a sort of equal opportunity spectacle. The common link that brings them all together is social class.

While presented with a touch of seriousness and professionalism, there is a similar entertainment strategy used on talk shows such as *Sally Jesse Raphael* (1985–2002), *Montel Williams* (1991–present), *Jenny Jones* (1991–2003), *Riki Lake* (1993–2004), and *The Maury Povich Show* (1998–present). They often have programs about working-class children who are out of control. A popular response is to send these deviant youth to military boot camp or prison and televise the spectacle.

Courtroom series also play a role in reproducing the image of working-class cheats and buffoons [e.g., *Judge Judy* (1996–present) and *Judge Joe Brown* (1998–present)].

Class Action

While television has long, used the image of the working class to entertain us, current labor conditions are no laughing matter. Today's workers face a declining standard of living and the loss of job security. They also risk falling victim to corporate greed and malfeasance such as the recent atrocities of Enron, Tyco, Walmart, Worldcom, or any of the other over 20,000 acts of corporate lawbreaking that are documented annually.

Regardless of the neoliberal promise of prosperity for all, it's more than obvious that the structural dimensions of social class within this economic logic remain profoundly in place. In fact, economic conditions for millions of people in the United States, and for billions of people worldwide, are worsening as a direct result of privatization, deregulation, and restructuring as well as by the ways in which elite private powers have been successful in using the State to protect corporate interests and dismantle many of the rights and protections achieved locally and internationally by grassroots activists, organized labor, and social democracies.

Corporate media's narrow, unrealistic images conceal the extent of this assault on America's workforce, so we can no longer afford to ignore TV's framing of the working class or see it as just entertainment.

The media reform movement has already begun to educate the general population about the political economy of the mass media—that is, ownership and regulation of this industry—and challenge the FCC and Congress to democratize the airwaves and new technologies, and to diversify representations that reflect both the new realities of work and the changing face of the working class in the United States.

A key component of any activist effort should be to encourage the wide-spread development of critical media literacy, that is, the ability to read the values and beliefs embedded in the knowledge that is circulated throughout society, so as to be able to defend ourselves from propaganda and participate in its eradication. A critical model of media literacy is primarily concerned with the kinds of theories and practices that encourage people to develop an understanding of the interconnecting relationships among ideology, power, meaning, and identity that constitute *culture*. Literacy of this sort entails understanding culture as a pedagogical force in which the multiplicity of aural and visual signifying systems that people are inundated with every day, through language, TV, advertising, radio, print journalism, music, film, and so on, are ideological and formative rather than merely vehicles for expression or reflections of reality. They are the conduits through which values and beliefs that work to shape how people see, interpret, and act as socialized and political beings are promoted.

Critical media literacy encourages us to not only think about culture politically, but also to think about politics culturally, and is thus rooted in a democratic project that emphasizes new theories and languages of critique, resistance, and possibility capable of engaging the oppressive social practices that maintain the de facto social code in the United States. These new theories and languages provide the necessary analytic stepping stones for realizing a truly democratic process through which we can better identify the sociopolitical realities that shape our lives, and where necessary, transform our practices. In any battle for economic justice and racial and social equality, TV in the hands of the public can play a pivotal role.

Discussion Questions

- What are the dangers of a "spectator democracy"? What characteristics of a spectator democracy do you see at work in the United States? ?

- How do familiar media portrayals of oppressed and marginalized groups support and recreate structures of domination?

- Use Altheide's descriptions of media and identity formation to explain how advertisers have been able to equate the American Dream with a consumer lifestyle.

- What is "counter-hegemonic" about rap, hippies, and other forms of nonstandard living? Is "living green" counter-hegemonic?

- Is it even possible for resistant cultural forms, such as rap, to avoid being commercialized and drained of political meaning?

Technology

Advances in technology over the last 25 years have had a significant impact on the lives of many. iPods and MP3 players can hold thousands of songs, video games have the quality of film, and people can download movies onto their laptops. Today, most technologies are more powerful, smaller, cheaper, and more versatile than at any time previously.

These advances are not merely limited to "fun." Beyond the static images of the X-ray, medical researchers can use technologies such as magnetic resonance imaging (MRI) and positron emission tomography (PET) to "look" inside the brain and "see" real-time reactions to stimuli such as drugs or stress. Warfare has also entered a technological age, one that arguably blurs the lines between combat and video games. From the trench warfare of World War I, the United States has "evolved" into an era of sanitized, robotic warfare where missile-carrying, remote-controlled "drones" carry out attacks. The United States Army has even developed a video game, *America's Army*, as a recruiting tool targeted at a generation of young people reared on Xbox® and PlayStation®.

With these advances, increased surveillance and decreased privacy have both become issues. In 2005, researchers from the American Civil Liberties Union walked through lower Manhattan and mapped the locations of over 4000 surveillance cameras. The social networking site Facebook created controversy as it sought to increase the amount of users' personal information that the company shared with advertisers. Beyond these high-profile concerns, it is worth considering the information trail a person leaves simply by entering a grocery store and paying with a debit card while using a "preferred customer" ID. Technology can and does enrich people lives, but at the same time, technology carries with it the potential for a panoptic society, where we are all watched all the time, echoing George Orwell's 1984.

The last section of this chapter focuses on the potential that emerging media technologies hold for activism and democratic involvement. Technology and media are inseparable—the media is composed of technologies that shape the forms of its messages. When we think about media and technology, there may be a tendency to think of the exciting advances of the last century, such as the radio, television, and the Internet. However, we should also think about those technologies that today seem mundane and boring, such as the printing press, paper, and even the alphabet. Each of these technologies created a revolution in communication, increasing its range, scope, and rapidity. Each had the potential to create a critical mass of educated and informed citizens and to expand democratic involvement. At the same time, as noted earlier, each of these technologies was open to manipulation by those concerned with maintaining the status quo and/or expanding their own power.

Today, with the exponential expansion of new communication technologies such as the Internet, text-messaging, and social networking sites, we are arguably in the middle of another media/communication revolution. Some, like Robert McChesney, would argue that the Internet has already been colonized by corporate forces and risks becoming little more than an interactive version of other corporate media. Yet there are interesting cases of media resistance to state power. The Internet giant Google shut down its China website over censorship issues. The company also launched a tool that allows users to see government requests for information from around the world, helping citizens to monitor their governments.

Technology can also help a social movement take shape. In their analysis of the Internet as a participatory political space, Merlyna Lim and Mark Kann conclude, "The more promising forms of online politics are not bound within a framework of conventional politics. Activities that don't fit into the traditional political framework, such as political blogging and political remix, thrive on the Internet."

Lim and Kann argue that the Internet represents the possibility of greater direct political involvement by people who may not otherwise have a political voice. Blogging and political remix (i.e., using multiple media to create politically oriented videos posted on sites like YouTube or personal blogs) represent expanded access to the mediated public sphere. Previous technologies, such as newspapers, radio, and television restricted this access to professionals and political insiders. Moreover, the Internet allows for people to connect across vast distances to form political movements. In short, "the Internet may become a more powerful gateway for people formerly on the sidelines to become local, even global activists."

Elsewhere, Lim has described how Internet cafes in Indonesia circumvented state-controlled information and facilitated the development of a "resistance identity" among young people against the Suharto regime. Another example of technology in the service of social reform occurred after the 2009 presidential election in Iran. Protestors used new social media, principally Facebook and Twitter, to organize resistance to the regime and to circumvent the state-controlled media. They were able to broadcast information about their struggle to the world.

The final selection in this chapter offers a critical perspective on new technologies. The story Holman tells here emerges from a single web site. This reading, interesting and important in its own right, also implicitly suggests that students undertake their own critical reading of the web pages they browse. Critical reading is particularly important when the product involves the potential for exploitation of vulnerable people.

SURFING FOR A SHAMAN: ANALYZING AN AYAHUASCA WEBSITE

CHRISTINE HOLMAN
ARIZONA STATE UNIVERSITY, UNITED STATES

Introduction

Ayahuasca seems to appeal to people unconcerned with traditional modals of life, people searching for the extraordinary, the remarkable and unusual facets of life. That there even exists a tourist industry to serve this population strikes me as amazing. That this industry is heavily advertised and available to anyone with financial means to undertake a trip, that it is not a hush-hush experience available only to a select few in the psychedelic drug underground, is perhaps even more astonishing (Grunwell, 1998, p. 62).

As Grunwell suggests, indigenous and mestizo communities in the Amazon Basin have been experiencing a unique type of tourism recently: ayahuasca tourism. Sometimes referred to as drug tourism or spiritual tourism, this new form typically involves non-indigenous, Western tourists who purchase all-inclusive trips to the Peruvian jungles to participate in shaman-led ceremonies that include the drinking of the hallucinogenic tea ayahuasca. Considered to be the most widely consumed hallucinogen in Amazonia, ayhuasaca produces intensely vivid, colorful and sometimes frightening hallucinations or visions. Ingested by indigenous peoples for centuries, ayahuasca has been used by shamans in providing healing services to their local communities. While several studies have examined ayahuasca tourism and argue that it is increasing in popularity, few have investigated this trend and its implications for local culture/peoples in depth and no studies have examined the Internet's role in the evolution of this industry.

Though some may describe spiritual tourists as those who take a "modern secular pilgrimage," ayahuasca tourists differ from such "pilgrims" insofar as their primary motivation is for an individualistic, spiritual and/or transformational experience, one that is neither connected to a specific religion nor directed toward a particular site or space. It is this motivational, individual, experiential aspect, combined with a self-described lack of affiliation with any organized religion, which differentiates the spiritual tourist from either the religious tourist or the modern pilgrim.

This study is designed to advance a deeper understanding of the phenomenon of spiritual tourism by interrogating the structures of knowledge and power, and image and representation utilizing a post-colonial framework. It seeks to broaden our understanding of ayahuasca tourism by examining the primary medium through which it is marketed and sold, the Internet website. Specifically, it analyzes the commodification of the ayahuasca ceremony and investigates whether or not the means by which this tourism is advertised reflects the exoticization of the local communities from whom the ceremony originates.

Drawing from Said's (1993) definition of imperialism, cultural imperialism can be described as a practice, a theory and and/or an attitude of domination or superiority of the West over other, typically non-Western cultures. One way to understand spiritual tourism is to analyze the ways in which it serves as a vehicle for Western tourists to appropriate indigenous culture via the tourists' participation in the ayahuasca ceremony. This appropriation occurs in the context of what Mary Louise Pratt (1992) calls the "contact zone." Pratt describes the contact zone as "social spaces where disparate cultures meet, clash, and grapple with each other, often in highly asymmetrical relations of domination and subordination—like colonialism, slavery, or their aftermaths as they are lived out across the globe today" (p. 4). Pratt's work informs this study by providing a conceptual framework from which to analyze the discourse on the ayahuasca websites. In addition to situating spiritual tourism as occurring in a "contact zone," the language on the websites is examined to understand to what extent it reflects what Pratt calls moments of "anti-conquest". Pratt defines anti-conquest as "strategies of representation whereby European bourgeois subjects seek to secure their innocence in the same moment as they assert their European hegemony" (p. 7).

The "Blue Morpho Tours" (www.bluemorpho.com) website was chosen as the site for this in-depth analysis due to its appearance on Dogpile.com as the most frequently visited website from the search term "ayahuasca tour." According to Fairclough (2003), the website can be considered a promotional genre, a characterization of the new Capitalism, wherein there has been a proliferation of genres which have the implicit or explicit purpose of selling commodities, brands or individuals (p. 35). Here, a single site analysis seeks to obtain a rich, comprehensive understanding of a particular phenomenon. While it is clear that the website functions to provide communication, findings from this detailed analysis suggest that its purpose is much more strategic: to attract potential tourists who are willing to pay $1940.00 to participate in an "all-inclusive" nine-day "workshop/retreat" (includes five ayahuasca sessions). Thus, Internet analysis has emerged as a critical medium in understanding social processes and serves as an appropriate method herein.

Three primary themes or discourses emerged from this analysis. These included the "Corporate Discourse," the "New Age" and the "Exotic Discourse." Additional findings included the near exclusion of indigenous or mestizo actors on the sites (with the exception of the shamans), and the presentation of the broker as "host," subsequently moving from the role of middleman to that of primary host, thus maintaining the host/guest dichotomy discussed previously, while at the same time effectively removing the local host.

The very first line of the Blue Morpho site asserts that Blue Morpho "specializes" in "all inclusive Shamanic Workshops . . ." Phrases such as "specialize," "all inclusive," "workshops," and "excellent service" are utilized multiple times throughout the site and can each be attributed to a broader corporate, capitalistic discourse—a far cry from the spiritual, shamanic and transformative descriptors used on other pages of the site. Moving from the first line to the last line of the paragraph of the Home Page, one finds this discourse reflected most succinctly and prominently, as it is the final piece of text which the tourist sees, before, presumably, moving on to the next page (Shamanic Workshops): "Blue Morpho is dedicated to our clients' enjoyment of the experience. Our goal is for our guests to return to Iquitos beaming from their adventure into the jungle and impressed by our professionalism and commitment to service." In the "About Blue Morpho" section, one is informed that the company has "already lead over 800 satisfied tourists to the camp," thus providing a strong "track record" of "satisfied tourists," language more appropriate to business brochure providing a service than a tour group providing a spiritual experience.

In the text, the tourist is referred to by various names. Ranked in order of those terms used most often, the tourist was referred to as: "guest(s)," "tourist," "traveler," "client," "participant," and "person(s)." Notably, the word "guest" was used five times more often than the next term, "tourist," suggesting that the relationship between the purchaser of the tour and the provider of the tour is one of "host" and "guest." While this finding may seem to contrast with a Corporate Discourse, it is actually similar to popular corporate language. For example, if one takes into account the linguistic turns in other customer-service oriented businesses, one will notice that even such retailers as McDonald's and Disneyland refer to their customers as "guests." Fairclough (2003) refers to this process as recontextualization, whereby the elements of one social practice (e.g., business transactions) are appropriated by and/or inserted to another (e.g., spiritual retreats), thus transforming the shamanic experience in a particular, corporate-oriented manner (pp. 22–23).

Another example of such genre mixing can be found on the "About Blue Morpho" section whereby the "traveler" is offered the "opportunity to experience the realities of the mystical world surrounded by untamed wilderness in a safe and well-organized workshop."

Discussing both the "mystical world" and a "well-organized workshop" in the same sentence reflects the appropriation of the spiritual nature of the ceremonies offered. This recontextualization of the Corporate Discourse within the New Age or Spiritual Discourse is one way in which the ayahuasca ceremony, in particular, and indigenous spirituality more broadly have become appropriated and commodified.

Similar to the Corporate Discourse, but perhaps less surprising, is the inclusion of several elements of the website text that cluster together to form the New Age Discourse. While the term "New Age" is both amorphous and contentious in the religious and sociological literatures, it is used here to draw out its main features as noted by Wood (2007), a "discursive emphasis upon the self and that self authority is paramount" (p. 27); that New Agers are concerned with "spirituality" instead of religion, that they are individual "seekers" of spirituality; and that the individuals most likely to participate in the New Age experiences tend to be "white, educated [and] middle class."

Multiple nouns, verbs and descriptors were dedicated to the shamanic and spiritual dimensions of the tour. Additionally, 42 photos on the site illustrate the shamans, the ayahuasca, and/or the Ceremonial House. Of the textual elements, "spiritual" or "Spirit" was employed the most often throughout the site. Other frequently employed terms included "sacred," "visionary," "transformational," and "personal growth"; the phrase "sacred, visionary plant" (ayahusaca) was employed six times. The tourist is invited to come to the "center for shamanism . . . deep in the Peruvian Amazon rain forest where traditional shamanic methods and study could be offered in the environment where these techniques developed."

There is a conspicuous exclusion of local people as evidenced through both the verbal and visual elements on the site. Social actors were tracked to note the inclusion/exclusion of particular groups or individuals. "Locals," be they indigenous or mestizo inhabitants of that area of the Peruvian Amazon, were mostly suppressed, with the exception of the shamans (as noted earlier) and the people who work as the "camp staff." Neither the locals nor the "local community" were identified in any way (e.g., no information was provided on the group's race, ethnicity, or region of residence).

Aside from the minimal information regarding the camp staff, there are only three other places where any type of local community is mentioned, albeit briefly. The first reference is on the Home Page, "Ceremonies with traditional shamans *(curanderos)* who currently practice native shamanism in local communities!" Interestingly, this is the only place in the entire text where an exclamation point is used, leading one to perhaps assume that this is a deliberate move to authenticate the shamans who work at the camp thereby affirming their legitimacy. The second reference to the "locals" occurs on the "Shamanic Workshops" pages within the "Shamanism Workshop Activity and Ceremony List." The locals are mentioned only in the following sentence, "The Amazon is home to thousands of medicinal plants used by the locals to cure many illnesses ranging from headaches to cancer." Again, there is no mention of who these locals are or how they cure these many illnesses, thus pushing the locals to the periphery.

The third reference to the "locals" is on "Lodge & Meals" page, within the paragraph on "Location":

> The Blue Morpho Shamanic Center and Jungle lodge sits on privately owned 180 acres of Primary Forest 53 Km from Iquitos off the Iquitos Nauta road. We employ locals in all levels of employment, aiding their struggling economy. We contribute to town projects, and donate clothing and household items to the families.

The individual presentation of each team member, highlighted by both a quality photograph and a detailed biography serves as a sharp contrast to the single paragraph in this section, describing the entire "Blue Morpho Staff:"

> The Blue Morpho Staff: The Blue Morpho staff is in charge of the kitchen and food, cleaning, laundry, grounds maintenance, and assistance during cer-

emonies. They work hard during trips to provide excellent service, tasty food and a clean environment. They are also of great assistance during ceremonies by giving support and helping people to the bathroom in times of need.

Finally, the staff are the only employees described as helping people "to the bathroom" in times of need. This bathroom assistance is likely shorthand for helping people to wash and/or change themselves during or after a ceremony, as ayahuasca is a purgative, causing most people to vomit or experience diarrhea after drinking it. No other team members are listed as providing this type of care-taking to the tourist, thus reinforcing the binary between those who are skilled (who lead the tourist) and those who are unskilled (who clean the tourist), limiting the role and potential of the ethnic other.

From a post-colonial perspective, this paper examines how the Internet may inadvertently function as a tool of imperialism instead of as an instrument of equality and social change.

Key findings of this comprehensive study of the Blue Morpho website suggest that business and spiritual discourses were combined to most strategically advertise the ayahuasca tour and, in turn, local actors were largely removed from the site, rendering them extinct in this process of appropriation. Through the use of Corporate Discourse, the privileging of place over people and the paternalistic references to the "locals" whom the tour broker employs, it appears that the discourse on this ayahuasca tour website reflects the broader tendencies of neocolonialism and cultural commodification within the spiritual tourism industry. The near absence of any reference to the historical, social or traditional context of the ayahuasca plant and ceremony serves to commodify the experience of ayahuasca by severing it from its indigenous roots, making it seem a historical and more easily appropriated as a product for purchase in an all-inclusive retreat package, available to anyone with enough time and money to take the tour.

In sum, this study suggests that contemporary spiritual tourism, in contrast to its predecessors religious and pilgrimage tourism, can be theorized best as a form of postmodern tourism (Munt, 1994), wherein the discourses of consumerism and individualism are coupled with a quest for the authentic, ethnic other, situated in the current stage of economic and cultural globalization. Through an examination of the power of online representation, this study questions the democratic potential of the Internet and suggests that instead of improving the lives of the marginalized, it may instead be replicating the imperialistic processes of appropriation and commodification.

Discussion Questions

- What could be some limitations of blogging and remix that Lim and Kann allude to? Why are these important to consider in a discussion of Internet activism?

- What challenges do new media technologies present to current hegemonic structures?

- What challenges do current hegemonic structures present to new media technologies?

Chapter 3

LAW, POLICY, AND SOCIAL CHANGE

The impact of the mass media on what people think and do, the previous chapter suggests, can be quite subtle and hard to trace. Law and policy seem much more tangible, at least at first glance. But, as anyone who has ever violated a posted speed limit knows from personal experience, law on the books and law in action can be quite different things. Laws do not necessarily lose their power because some people violate them without detection. The relationship between obedience to law, respect for law, and a deeper sense of law's legitimacy is complex and will be explored in this chapter, always with an eye to the issue of justice and social change.

What is the relationship between the law, policy, social change, and justice? Let's start with law. We are all aware of unjust laws, particularly those of past eras. For some well-known examples, consider the network of laws that defined and perpetuated slavery and Jim Crow segregation, the state and federal laws that prohibited women from voting or serving on juries or teaching while pregnant, the federal government's exclusion of Japanese Americans from their homes during World War II, or the laws that criminalized the dissemination of birth-control information. We have had laws that disqualified children with disabilities from attending public schools and requirements that all children pray in school. Many of these laws had been reviewed by courts and upheld before they were finally changed. History teaches us that not everything that is legal is also just.

The law seems to be an instrument of prevailing values, and yet it is also something more than that in many people's minds. Justice is the standard by which we evaluate law. Even if justice does not prevail at first, we tend to expect that it can prevail in the end.

119

Americans have a tradition of using the courts in the struggle to make law and policy more just, encouraged by a venerable Constitution that speaks to basic values and a tendency to see issues in legal terms. Our legal traditions make the Constitution our "higher" law against which ordinary laws can be measured. This is not to say that every wrong can be righted by making (and succeeding with) a constitutional claim, but that the legal system of the United States encourages the idea of social change through litigation. Many other countries have adopted this strategy of allowing constitutional litigation, though not always by ordinary citizens. But even where litigation is a well-travelled path to seeking justice, it is not the only path. People clash over the justice of laws and policies every day in legislative chambers, in organizations, within families, and among friends and strangers.

Some philosophers argue that an unjust law is no law at all. Many American Indian nations would go further, challenging the legitimacy of Western-imposed legal structures.[1] Others disagree, contending that law is no more than the will of the sovereign, and in a democratic country, that's us. Still, most of us expect more of law than simple order and obedience. People fight hard to achieve more just laws and policies in order to, it is hoped, change the world for the better. These sites of struggle include the criminal-justice system, with its familiar themes of deterrence, retribution, and due process. Justice issues in law and policy range much further, however. The struggle for justice includes issues of social welfare and equality of opportunity on the job, in schooling, and in training. Also at risk are basic freedoms to speak, assemble, and to be free of undue governmental surveillance.

The fight for justice goes on because these are battles worth fighting. Law, which sets forth general standards, and policy, which details how implementation will occur, are unavoidable parts of daily life. They are the social-ordering devices that make various layers of government work, but they also help to create order in the private sector. Law and policy, in short, are deeply implicated in our economic, political, and social worlds. It is not surprising then that the effort to create social change often focuses first on law and policy, rather than on changing public attitudes. And besides, bringing a lawsuit or petitioning to have a policy changed is much easier than attempting to change public attitudes. The goal is not always to create justice in law; sometimes it is enough simply to avoid injustice, which can be done with a lawsuit designed to block implementation of a law.

The power of law to do injustice, even as it claims to do justice, is well-known to anyone familiar with failures of the criminal law. Consider, for example, the case of Johnnie Earl Lindsey. In September 2008, Johnnie Earl Lindsey was released from prison. He had spent nearly 26 years incarcerated for a rape that he did not commit. He became a suspect when the victim was shown a photo lineup nearly one year after the assault. Mr. Lindsey's supervisor testified at the trial that he was at work during the time of the rape and therefore could not have been the rapist, but a jury nevertheless found him guilty, based largely on the testimony of the victim. Eyewitness testimony is notoriously unreliable, but jurors often believe otherwise.

---

[1] Barbara Gray (Kanatiiosh) and Pat Lauderdale, "The Web of Justice: Restorative Justice Has Presented Only Part of the Story." *Wicazo Sa Review*, vol. 21 (1): 29–41 (Spring 2006).

Fortunately for Mr. Lindsey, his case was reviewed by the Innocence Project of Texas. The Innocence Project reexamines closed cases using sophisticated methods of analysis, like DNA testing, that were generally not employed or not available at the time of the original conviction. Nearly half of the Texas cases reviewed by this group have been reversed based on DNA evidence. Thanks in part to this group of change agents, the state of Texas leads the nation in the number of wrongful convictions overturned by DNA evidence. Of course, this statistic also raises questions about the fairness of criminal trials in that state. This case serves as a reminder of the fragility and capacity for error in institutions charged with doing justice.

This chapter examines the dynamic relationship between legal and social change. Law sometimes precipitates social change, but also often follows social changes that were underway at the time a law was enacted. The sequence of events can be even more confusing when courts are involved in the law making. An interesting example is legalized racial segregation. "Separate But Equal" was constitutional before the Supreme Court decided *Brown V. Board of Education,* but it was under attack in many places, including in the Court's own decisions, which had begun to look critically at whether educational opportunities for Black Americans really were equal. How did these social concerns with segregation develop? It appears that World War II played a role. Black soldiers complained bitterly about racial segregation in the service of their nation. After the war, our Cold War foes liked to point out the American hypocrisy of venerating equality while continuing to subordinate citizens by race. Ending "Separate But Equal" became a way to strengthen the nation's position on the world stage, as well as an honorable cause in its own right.

The first section of this chapter discusses problems raised by law and policy, principally in the area of race. The section that follows describes some of the ways that social movements, organizations, and individuals have used law to initiate social change. This suggests another important aspect of law: its capacity to shape popular conceptions of what matters about individuals. Sexual orientation is considered a significant aspect of social identity, in part because the law has quite a bit to say about sexual relations. Citizenship status is important, not because it has any significance in nature, but because law and policies make it important. Law and policy, in short, shape—and are shaped by—prevailing beliefs about the social order.

Law and Policy

Laws are a system of rules. Some rules prohibit or mandate certain behavior (e.g., you must pay your taxes, you must not run red lights when driving). Other kinds of laws are about laws—they specify how laws should work (e.g., requiring that only legislatures can make rules about taxes, but allowing the Internal Revenue Service to fill in certain details).[2]

---

[2]See H. L. A. Hart, *The Concept of Law* (New York: Oxford University Press, 1997, first published in 1961). Hart contended that law should be seen as a system of primary and secondary rules, in which the primary rules set forth basic duties of individuals, while the secondary rules establish how those primary rules will be enacted and implemented. He intended his two-level conceptualization to challenge the earlier, simpler view of John Austin that law is simply what the ruler says it is, the so-called "command" theory of law.

This layering of rules and rules about rules creates a complex, functioning legal system. The layering becomes more complex when various levels of government are factored in, each with its proper scope of jurisdiction and all within an overall hierarchy of importance. These are examples of rules about rules generally found in constitutional documents.

Policies add another layer of complexity. Within government, policies are a final layer of legal ordering. They must be within the scope of an agency's authority and follow other legal strictures (e.g., nondiscrimination, Sunshine laws) to be valid. The policies that a government agency develops do not require legislative action in order to take effect. But the legislature that created the agency may decide that the agency is moving in the wrong direction and intervene to reshape the law and thus reshape policy. Social movements advocate for some policies and against others, taking their arguments to the agencies themselves, to legislatures, and to the courts.

Outside of government, companies and organizations also develop policies. The standards to which they must adhere are frequently lower than for agency policies. Whether an organization like the Jaycees or a country club that opens its doors for some public functions can restrict membership or participation by sex or religion, for example, has been a matter of hot dispute.

Consider just a few areas in which law and policy operate: There are laws telling administrative officials what they can and cannot do, and volumes of administratively created policies setting forth standards for businesses and regulated entities, like airports. Contract law looks in a different direction. It allows all of us to be law-givers in limited ways (e.g., when we rent an apartment and sign a lease), and it helps businesses conduct affairs. Tort law specifies the standards for compensation after an injury, determining, for example, what constitutes negligence, and what will be classified as simply an unavoidable (and noncompensable) misfortune. Some laws outline how we can properly give things to other people, such as those that set forth the requirements for making a valid will or gift. And we are all familiar with the criminal law that sets standards for social behavior and the laws and policies that set forth rules for how criminal investigations and proceedings will be conducted in order to ensure fairness. Constitutional law is a kind of umbrella sitting above all these types of law, setting forth the powers of government and the limits on what officials can legitimately do.

The complexity of law creates a need for legal assistance. The United States, Deborah Rhode argues, has plenty of lawyers, but a dearth of legal assistance. How can a nation be the richest in the world in terms of the lawyers per capita, but still starved for basic legal assistance, not just for the poor, but for the majority of the population? The answer lies in the organization of law.

ACCESS TO JUSTICE
DEBORAH L. RHODE

"Equal justice under law" is one of America's most proudly proclaimed and widely violated legal principles. It embellishes courthouse entrances, ceremonial occasions, and constitutional decisions. But it comes nowhere close to describing the legal system in practice. Millions of Americans lack any access to justice, let alone equal access. According to most estimates, about four-fifths of the civil legal needs of the poor, and two- to three-fifths of the needs of middle-income individuals, remain unmet. Government legal aid and criminal defense budgets are capped at ludicrous levels, which make effective assistance of counsel a statistical impossibility for most low-income litigants. We tolerate a system in which money often matters more than merit, and equal protection principles are routinely subverted in practice.

This is not, of course, the only legal context in which rhetoric outruns reality. But it is one of the most disturbing, given the fundamental rights at issue. A commitment to equal justice is central to the legitimacy of democratic processes. And many nations come far closer than our own to realizing this ideal in practice. It is a shameful irony that the country with the world's most lawyers has one of the least adequate systems for legal assistance. It is more shameful still that the inequities attract so little concern. Over the last two decades, national spending on legal aid has been cut by a third, and increasing restrictions have been placed on the clients and causes that government-funded programs can represent. Groups that are the most politically vulnerable are now the most legally vulnerable as well. Federally funded programs may not take cases involving the "unworthy" poor, defined expansively to include prisoners, undocumented aliens, women seeking abortions, and school desegregation plaintiffs.

Although indigent criminal defendants are theoretically entitled to effective assistance of counsel, few actually receive it. Over 90 percent of cases are resolved by guilty pleas, generally without any factual investigation. Court-appointed lawyers' preparation is often minimal, sometimes taking less time than the average American spends showering before work. In the small minority of cases that go to trial, convictions have been upheld where defense counsel were asleep, on drugs, suffering from mental illness, or parking their cars during key parts of the prosecution's case.

What perpetuates the problem is the lack of public recognition that there is a serious problem. Although most Americans agree that the wealthy have advantages in the justice system, about four-fifths believe that it is still the "best in the world." About the

---

From *Access to Justice* by Deborah L. Rhode, pp. 3–17. Oxford University Press, 2004.

same number also believe, incorrectly, that the poor are entitled to counsel in civil cases. Only a third of Americans think that low-income individuals would have difficulty finding legal assistance, a perception wildly out of touch with reality. Fewer than 1 percent of lawyers are in legal aid practice, which works out to about one lawyer for every 1,400 poor or near-poor persons in the United States.

The criminal justice system reflects an even wider gap between public perceptions and daily realities. Americans generally believe that the process coddles criminals, whose lawyers routinely get them off on technicalities. Such assumptions come largely from movies, television, and the highly publicized trials in which zealous advocacy is the norm. Counsel for O. J. Simpson and the Oklahoma bombers left no stones unturned. But they were charging by the stone. Most defense counsel cannot, and no media glare is available to encourage adequate preparation. Few Americans have any clear appreciation of what passes for justice among the have-nots. And those who do are not necessarily motivated to respond. The groups most in need of legal assistance have the least access to political leverage that could secure it. A common attitude, expressed with uncommon candor by one chair of a state legislative budget committee, is that he did not really "care whether indigents [were] represented or not."

This reading is about why all of us *should* care about access to justice. It is not only the poor who are priced out of the current system. Millions of Americans, including those of moderate income, suffer untold misery because legal protections that are available in principle are inaccessible in practice. Domestic violence victims cannot obtain protective orders, elderly medical patients cannot collect health benefits, disabled children are denied educational services, defrauded consumers lack affordable remedies. . . . The list is long and the costs incalculable. Moreover, those who attempt to navigate the system unassisted confront unnecessary obstacles at every turn. In most family, housing, bankruptcy, and small claims courts, the majority of litigants lack legal representation. Yet the system has been designed by and for lawyers, and too little effort has been made to ensure that it is fair or even comprehensible to the average claimant.

This reading briefly discusses the shameful gap between our rhetorical commitments and daily practices concerning access to justice and gives an overview of our current pathologies and essential prescriptions. Discussion then turns to a different diagnosis of the problem: the widespread view that America has too much law and lawyering, rather than too little. Yet while some of the public's concerns about frivolous litigation and excessive expense have ample basis, most of the prevailing wisdom about litigiousness rests on flawed premises and points to misconceived solutions. What should be of greatest concern are not excessive lawsuits but inaccessible rights and remedies. The basic conclusion is straightforward. Given the increasing centrality of law in American life, we can no longer afford a system that most citizens cannot themselves afford.

Defining the Goal: Access for Whom? For What? How Much? And Who Should Decide?
In theory, "equal justice under law" is difficult to oppose. In practice, however, it begins to unravel at key points, beginning with what we mean by "justice." In most

discussions, "equal justice" implies equal access to the justice system. The underlying assumption is that social justice is available through procedural justice. But that, of course, is a dubious proposition. Those who receive their "day in court" do not always feel that "justice has been done," and with reason. The role that money plays in legal, legislative, and judicial selection processes often skews the law in predictable directions. Even those who win in court can lose in life. Formal rights can be prohibitively expensive to enforce, successful plaintiffs can be informally blacklisted, and legislatures may overturn legal rulings that lack political support.

These difficulties are seldom acknowledged in discussions of access to justice, which assume that more is better, and that the trick is how to achieve it. But even from a purely procedural standpoint, that assumption leaves a host of conceptual complexities unaddressed. What constitutes a "legal need"? A vast array of conflicts and concerns could give rise to legal action. How much claiming and blaming is our society prepared to subsidize? Does access to law also require access to legal assistance, and if so, how much is enough? For what, for whom, from whom? Should government support go to only the officially poor or to all those who cannot realistically afford lawyers? Under what circumstances do individuals need full-blown representation by attorneys, as opposed to other less expensive forms of assistance? How do legal needs compare with other claims on our collective resources? And, most important, who should decide?

The complexities are compounded if we also think seriously about what would make justice truly "equal." Equal to what? Although there is broad agreement that the quality of justice should not depend on the ability to pay, there is little corresponding consensus on an alternative. How do we deal with disparities in incentives, resources, and legal ability? True equality in legal assistance would presumably require not only massive public expenditures but also the restriction of private expenditures. And, as R. H. Tawney once noted about equal opportunity generally, it is not clear what would alarm proponents most, "the denial of the principle or the attempt to apply it." If cost were no constraint, what would prevent excessive resort to expensive procedural processes? Our ideal world is surely not one in which all disputes are fully adjudicated, but can we develop more equitable limiting principles than ability to pay?

These questions cannot be resolved in the abstract, however, a few general observations can help put such concerns into broader context. By virtually any measure, our nation falls well short of providing even minimal, let alone equal, access to justice for Americans of limited means. Unlike most other industrialized nations, the United States recognizes no right to legal assistance for civil matters and courts have exercised their discretion to appoint counsel in only a narrow category of cases. Legislative budgets have been equally restrictive. The federal government, which provides about two-thirds of the funding for civil legal aid, now spends only about $8 per year for those living in poverty. Less than 1 percent of the nation's total expenditures on lawyers goes to help the seventh of the population that is poor enough to qualify for legal assistance. The inadequacies in criminal defense for indigents are of similar magnitude. On average, court-appointed lawyers receive only about an eighth of the resources available to prosecutors. Moreover, millions of Americans who are above poverty thresholds are also priced out of the legal process for the vast majority of their legal concerns.

These inequities are particularly appalling for a nation that considers itself a global leader in human rights. Equal justice may be an implausible aspiration, but more accessible legal institutions are within our reach. Many nations with comparable justice systems and far fewer lawyers than the United States do much better at making basic rights available. These countries typically provide more sources of low-cost legal assistance, and more substantial government subsidies for low-income residents. For example, according to the most recent comparative research available, the United States allocates only about a sixteenth per capita of what Great Britain budgets for civil legal assistance, a sixth of what New Zealand provides, and a third of what some Canadian provinces guarantee. The following chapters leave no doubt that realistic reforms in our nation's delivery of legal services could go a long way to insuring that more Americans can assert their most fundamental rights. To make that possible the public needs a clearer sense of its own stake in the reform agenda.

The Increasing Role of Law and the Rationale for Legal Assistance

As commentators since Alexis de Tocqueville have noted, law and lawyers occupy a distinctively central role in American society. The importance that we attach to legal institutions has deep ideological and structural roots. It is not surprising that a nation founded by individuals escaping from governmental persecution should be wary of state power and protective of individual rights. Cross-national studies find that Americans are less willing than citizens of other nations to trust a centralized government to address social problems and to meet social welfare needs. This distrust is reflected and reinforced by political institutions that give courts a crucial role in constraining state power, safeguarding individual rights, and shaping public policy. The United States relies on legal institutions to protect fundamental values such as freedom of speech, due process, and equal opportunity that are central to our cultural heritage and constitutional traditions. This nation also finds privately financed lawsuits to be a fiscally attractive way of enforcing statutory requirements without spending taxpayer dollars on legal costs. Much of this country's environmental, health, safety, consumer, and antidiscrimination regulation occurs through litigation.

Moreover, despite policymakers' frequent laments about legalization, the role and reach of law is increasing, a trend that reflects broader global forces. As patterns of life become more complex and interdependent, the need for legal regulation becomes correspondingly greater. In Western industrialized countries, improvements in the standard of living have also led to increased expectations about the functions of law in maintaining that standard. Throughout the last half century, many societies have come to expect what legal historian Lawrence Friedman labels "total justice." Unsafe conditions, abusive marriages, discriminatory conduct, and inadequacies in social services that were once accepted as a matter of course now prompt demands for legal remedies and for assistance in obtaining them. More and more of our everyday life is hedged about by law. Family, work, and commercial relationships are subject to a growing array of legal obligations and protections. As law becomes increasingly crucial and complex, access to legal services also becomes increasingly critical.

The Right to Legal Assistance

That need for legal assistance has not been entirely lost on judicial and legislative decision makers, but neither have they taken the steps necessary to insure it. In 1932 the U.S. Supreme Court offered the common sense observation that an individual's "right to be heard [in legal proceedings] would be, in many cases, of little avail if it did not comprehend the right to be heard by counsel." In the years that followed, judges gradually built on that recognition to find a constitutional right to lawyers for indigent criminal defendants. However, courts have largely failed to extend guarantees of legal assistance to civil contexts, even where crucial interests are at issue. In the leading decision on point, *Lassiter v. Department of Social Services*, the Supreme Court interpreted the due process clause to require appointment of counsel in civil cases only if the proceeding would otherwise prove fundamentally unfair. In making that determination, courts must consider three basic factors: "the private interests at stake, the government's interest, and the risk that [lack of counsel] will lead to an erroneous decision."

Although that standard is not unreasonable on its face, courts have applied it in such restrictive fashion that counsel is almost never required in civil cases. The *Lassiter* decision itself is a representative example. There, an incarcerated woman lost parental rights after a hearing at which she had no attorney. In the majority's view, such legal assistance would not have made a "determinative difference," given the state's strong factual case and the absence of "troublesome points of law." Lower courts have proven similarly reluctant to guarantee lawyers or to ensure their compensation, even in contexts where their aid would clearly be critical.

This reluctance is problematic on several grounds. Some civil proceedings implicate interests as significant as those involved in many minor criminal proceedings where counsel is required. It is, for example, a cruel irony that in cases involving protective orders for victims of domestic violence, defendants who face little risk of significant sanctions are entitled to lawyers, while victims whose lives are in jeopardy are not. The rationale for subsidized representation seems particularly strong in cases like *Lassiter*, where fundamental interests are at issue, legal standards are imprecise and subjective, proceedings are formal and adversarial, and resources between the parties are grossly imbalanced. Under such circumstances, opportunities for legal assistance are crucial to the legitimacy of the justice system. As the Supreme Court has recognized in other contexts, the "right to sue and defend" is a right "conservative of all other rights, and lies at the foundation of an orderly government." Providing representation necessary to make those rights meaningful fosters values central to the rule of law and social justice. For many individuals, legal aid is equally critical in legislative and administrative contexts. Such assistance is the only way that millions of Americans can participate in these governance processes. Not only does access to legal services help prevent erroneous decisions, it also affirms a respect for human dignity and procedural fairness that are core democratic ideals.

Courts' reluctance to extend the right to legal assistance has more to do with pragmatic than principled considerations. As law professor Geoffrey Hazard has noted, no "politically sober judge, however anguished by injustice unfolding before her eyes," could welcome the battles involved in trying to establish some broadly enforceable right to counsel. Given legislatures' repeated refusal to fund legal assistance at anything close to realistic levels, courts are understandably wary about stepping into the breach.

Political Opposition to Legal Services

Political opposition to guaranteed legal services builds on several longstanding concerns; the first is that much of the assistance that poverty lawyers provide may in fact worsen the plight of the poor. One commonly cited example involves representation of "deadbeat" tenants or consumers. Landlords and merchants forced to litigate such matters allegedly pass on their costs in increased rents or prices to other, equally impoverished but more deserving individuals who manage to honor their financial obligations. A further objection is that even if some legal services do help the poor, it is inefficient to provide those services in kind rather than through cash transfers. Any broad-based entitlement to legal aid assertedly would encourage over-investments in law, as opposed to other purchases that the poor might value more, such as food, medicine, education, or housing. Critics note that poor people with unmet legal needs rarely spend their discretionary income on lawyers. And it is by no means clear that clients, if given the choice, would invest in the kinds of impact litigation that legal services attorneys often prefer.

These claims raise several difficulties that do not emerge clearly in public debate. To begin with, the value of legal assistance cannot be gauged only by what the poor are willing and able to pay. Those who cannot meet their most basic subsistence needs also cannot make many purchases that would prove cost-effective in the longer term. That is part of what traps them in poverty. Yet even for those individuals, legal services may be a highly efficient use of resources. A few hours of legal work can result in benefits far exceeding their costs. Reviews of legal services programs reveal countless examples, such as brain-damaged children and elderly citizens on fixed incomes who receive essential medical treatment, or impoverished nursing mothers who gain protection from dangerous pesticides. For many forms of legal assistance, it would be difficult, if not impossible, to attach a precise dollar value, but the benefits may be enormous and enduring. Government-subsidized assistance makes it possible for millions of poor people to leave violent marriages.

Moreover, law is a public good. Protecting legal rights often has value beyond what those rights are worth to any single client. Holding employers of farm workers accountable for unsafe field conditions, making landlords liable for violations of housing codes, or imposing penalties for consumer fraud can provide an essential deterrent against future abuse. Contrary to critics' claims, it is by no means clear that the costs of defending such lawsuits will all be passed on to other poor people, or that those costs are excessive in light of the deterrent value that they serve. Understaffed legal services offices have little reason to spend scarce resources litigating meritless cases that critics endlessly invoke. This is not to suggest that society in general or the poor in particular would benefit if every potential claim were fully litigated. But neither is ability to pay an effective way of screening out frivolous cases. America's gross inequalities in access to justice are an embarrassment to a nation that considers its legal system a model for the civilized world.

Criminal Defense

In criminal cases, over three-quarters of defendants facing felony charges are poor enough to qualify for court-appointed counsel. Legal assistance for these defendants takes three main forms: competitive contracts, individual case assignments, and public defender programs. As with Tolstoy's unhappy families, each of these systems breeds unhappiness in its own way.

Under competitive bidding systems, lawyers offer to provide representation for all, or a specified percentage of a jurisdiction's criminal cases, in exchange for a fixed price, irrespective of the number or complexity of matters involved. Such systems discourage effective assistance by selecting attorneys who are willing to accept a high volume of defendants at low cost. Annual caseloads can climb as high as 900 felony matters or several thousand misdemeanors. Rarely can these lawyers afford to do adequate investigation, file necessary motions, or take a matter to trial. "Meet 'em, greet 'em and plead 'em" is standard practice among contract attorneys. In one all too typical example, a lawyer who agreed to handle a county's entire criminal caseload for $25,000 filed only three motions in five years.

Similar disincentives for effective representation occur under other systems. Some assign private practitioners on a case-by-case basis. These lawyers receive minimal flat fees or hourly rates, coupled with a ceiling on total compensation. Limits of $1,000 are common for felony cases, and some states allow less than half that amount. Teenagers selling sodas on the beach make higher rates than these attorneys. Low ceilings apply even for defendants facing the death penalty, and attorneys subject to such compensation caps have ended up with hourly rates below $4. For most court-appointed lawyers, thorough preparation is a quick route to financial ruin. Analogous problems often arise in the remaining jurisdictions, which rely on public defender offices. Although the quality of representation in some of these offices is quite high, others operate with crushing caseloads.

Under all of these systems, the vast majority of court-appointed counsel lack sufficient resources to hire the experts and investigators who are often essential to an effective defense. The same is true for defendants who retain their own counsel. Most of these individuals are just over the line of indigence and cannot afford substantial legal expenses. Their lawyers typically charge a flat fee, payable in advance, which creates obvious disincentives to prepare thoroughly or proceed to trial.

Many defense counsel also face nonfinancial pressures to curtail their representation. A quick plea spares lawyers the strain and potential humiliation of an unsuccessful trial. Such bargains also preserve good working relationships with judges and prosecutors, who confront their own, often overwhelming caseload demands. Indeed, a reputation for thorough representation on behalf of the accused is unlikely to work to counsel's advantage among the judiciary who control appointments. Judges coping with already unmanageable caseloads have been reluctant to appoint "obstructionist" lawyers who routinely raise technical defenses or demand lengthy trials. Taken together, these financial and non-financial pressures help explain why over 90 percent of defendants plead guilty, generally before their counsel does any factual investigation.

The problem is compounded by the lack of accountability for inadequate performance. Neither market forces nor judicial and bar oversight structures provide a significant check on shoddy representation. Defendants typically lack sufficient information to second guess lawyers' plea recommendations and trial strategies. Even if clients doubt the adequacy of their counsel, they can seldom do much about it. Indigent defendants have no right to select their attorneys, and court-appointed lawyers do not depend for their livelihood on the satisfaction of clients.

Nor is "mere negligence" enough to trigger bar disciplinary action, establish malpractice liability, or overturn convictions based on ineffective assistance of counsel. Convicted criminals are generally unsympathetic litigants. To establish their lawyer's civil liability, they must also establish their own innocence. To obtain a reversal of a conviction, they must show specific errors falling below "prevailing professional norms" and a "reasonable probability" that "but for counsel's unprofessional errors, the results would have been different." That burden is almost impossible to meet. In one representative survey, over 99 percent of ineffective assistance claims were unsuccessful. Tolerance for ineptitude and inexperience runs even to capital cases. Defendants have been executed despite their lawyers' lack of any prior trial experience, ignorance of all relevant death penalty precedents, or failure to present any mitigating evidence. As one expert puts it, too many capital cases end up in the hands of lawyers who have "never tried a case before and never should again."

Civil Contexts

Many low-income civil litigants fare no better. As noted earlier, legal services offices can handle less than a fifth of the needs of eligible clients and often are able to offer only brief advice, not the full range of assistance that is necessary. In some jurisdictions, poor people must wait over two years before seeing a lawyer for matters like divorce that are not considered emergencies, and other offices exclude such cases entirely. Legal aid programs that accept federal funds may not accept entire categories of clients who have nowhere else to go, such as prisoners or undocumented immigrants. Unrealistic income eligibility ceilings also exclude many individuals just over the poverty line who also cannot afford counsel. The result is that millions of Americans are locked out of law entirely. Millions more attempt to represent themselves in a system stacked against them.

Self-Representation and Nonlawyer Assistance

The last quarter century has witnessed a rapid growth in self-representation and in related materials and businesses. Kits, manuals, interactive computer programs, on-line information, form processing services, and courthouse facilitators have emerged to assist those priced out of the market for lawyers. But especially for the individuals who need help most, those of limited income and education, such forms of assistance fall far short. Much of the difficulty lies with judicial and bar leaders who have resisted access to law without lawyers. On issues like procedural simplification and lay services, the legal profession has often contributed more to the problem than the solution.

Procedural Hurdles

In courts that handle housing, bankruptcy, small claims, and family matters, parties without lawyers are less the exception than the rule. Cases in which at least one side is unrepresented are far more common than those in which both sides have counsel. In some jurisdictions, over four-fifths of these matters involve self-represented "pro se" litigants. Yet a majority of surveyed courts have no formal pro se assistance services, such as facilitators who can advise parties, or interactive computer kiosks that can help them complete legal forms. Many of the services that are available are unusable by those who need help most: low-income litigants with limited computer competence and English language skills.

All too often, parties without lawyers confront procedures of excessive and bewildering complexity, and forms with archaic jargon left over from medieval England. Court clerks and mediators are instructed not to give legal "advice," since that would constitute "unauthorized practice of law." Even courts that have pro se facilitators caution them against answering any "should" questions, such as "which form should I file?" The result is that many parties with valid claims are unable to advance them. Pro se litigants in family and housing courts achieve less favorable results than litigants with lawyers who raise similar issues.

Some courts are openly hostile to unrepresented parties, whom they view as tying up the system or attempting to gain tactical advantages. Even the most sympathetic judges often have been unwilling to push for reforms that will antagonize lawyers whose economic interests are threatened by pro se assistance. Particularly for elected judges, support from the organized bar is critical to their reputation, election campaigns, and advancement. And encouraging parties to dispense with lawyers wins few friends in the circles that matter most.

The Lawyer's Monopoly

Similar considerations have worked against other efforts to broaden access to non-lawyer providers of legal services. Almost all of the scholarly experts and commissions that have studied the issue have recommended increased opportunities for such lay assistance. Almost all of the major decisions by judges and bar associations have ignored those recommendations. Nonlawyers who engage in law-related activities are subject to criminal prohibitions that are inconsistently interpreted, unevenly enforced, and inappropriately applied. The dominant approach is to prohibit individuals who are not members of the state bar from providing personalized legal advice. For example, independent paralegals generally may type documents but may not answer even simple legal questions or correct obvious errors. The American Bar Association has recently taken actions to strengthen enforcement of these prohibitions, and many state and local bars have launched similar efforts. Yet research concerning nonlawyer specialists in other countries and in American administrative tribunals suggests that these individuals are generally at least as qualified as lawyers to provide assistance on routine matters where legal needs are greatest. Concerns about unqualified or unethical lay assistance could be addressed through more narrowly drawn prohibitions and licensing structures for nonlawyer providers.

Unrepresented Parties

A profession truly committed to access to justice would not only support such reforms, it would also rethink the rules governing lawyers' dealings with unrepresented parties. In response to massive opposition from attorneys, the ABA rejected a proposed ethical standard that would have prevented lawyers from "unfairly exploiting" pro se litigants' ignorance of the law and from "procur[ing] an unconscionable result." According to opponents, "parties `too cheap to hire a lawyer' should not be `coddled' by special treatment." Under the rule ultimately approved, lawyers' sole responsibilities are to avoid implying that they are disinterested, to refrain from giving advice that is not disinterested, and to make "reasonable efforts" to correct misunderstandings concerning their role. Such minimal obligations have proven totally inadequate to curb overreaching behavior. Counsel for more powerful litigants in landlord-tenant, consumer, and family law disputes have often misled weaker unrepresented parties into waiving important rights and accepting inadequate settlements. Since these individuals typically do not know, cannot prove, or cannot afford lawsuits to prove that they were misinformed by opposing counsel, such conduct has rarely resulted in any disciplinary sanctions or legal remedies.

Inadequate Resources

Further problems arise in the small number of civil cases where courts or legislatures have mandated appointment of counsel for indigent litigants. As in criminal matters, ludicrously inadequate compensation discourages effective representation. Even where legal assistance is adequate, court time is not. Overcrowded caseloads lead to rubber stamp review in matters that most affect ordinary Americans. Judges who spend weeks presiding over minor commercial disputes may have less than five minutes available to decide the future of an abused or neglected child. Equal justice is what we put on courthouse doors, not what happens inside them.

The Limitations of Lawyers' Pro Bono Service

A final context in which rhetoric outruns reality involves lawyers' charitable "pro bono publico" service. Bar ethical codes and judicial decisions have long maintained that lawyers have a responsibility to assist those who cannot afford counsel. Leaders of the profession have endlessly applauded the "quiet heroism" of their colleagues in discharging that responsibility. A constant refrain in bar publications is that "no other profession . . . is as charitable with its time and money."

Such claims suggest more about the profession's capacity for self-delusion than self-sacrifice. Pro bono assistance has never addressed more than a tiny fraction of the public's needs for assistance, and neither courts nor bar associations have been willing to require significant public service contributions. The scope of judicial power to compel lawyers to provide unpaid legal assistance remains unsettled, largely because the power has so rarely been exercised. The Supreme Court has never definitively resolved the issue, although some of its language and summary rulings imply that the judiciary has inherent authority to require such assistance at least in criminal cases. Lower court decisions are mixed, but most have upheld mandatory court appointments as long as the required amount of service is not "unreasonable." Yet in the face of strong resistance and inadequate performance by many lawyers, courts have been reluctant to exercise their appointment power. They have been even less willing to adopt ethical rules requiring a minimum amount of pro bono service. State codes of conduct include only aspirational standards, which typically call for twenty to fifty hours a year of unpaid assistance (or the financial equivalent) primarily to persons of limited means or other charitable causes.

How many lawyers meet these aspirational standards and how much service they actually provide to the poor is impossible to determine with any precision. Information is spotty because only three states mandate reporting of contribution levels, and because many lawyers take liberties with the definition of "pro bono" and include any uncompensated or undercompensated work. However, the best available research suggests that the American legal profession averages less than half an hour a week and under half a dollar a day in pro bono contributions, little of which goes to the poor. Most goes to assist family, friends, and charitable causes that largely benefit middle and upper income groups. Fewer than 10 percent of lawyers accept referrals from legal aid or bar-sponsored poverty-related programs. Pro bono participation by the profession's most affluent members reflects a particularly dispiriting distance between the bar's idealized image and actual practices. Only a third of the nation's large law firms have committed themselves to meet the ABA's Pro Bono Challenge, which requires contributions equivalent to 3 to 5 percent of gross revenues, and fewer still meet that goal. Lawyers at the nation's one hundred most financially successful firms have typically averaged eight minutes per day on pro bono service.

Defining the Challenge

It is a national disgrace that civil legal aid programs now reflect less than 1 percent of the nation's legal expenditures and that a majority of Americans have a justice system that they cannot afford to use. It is a professional disgrace that pro bono service occupies less than 1 percent of lawyers' working hours and that the organized bar has so often put its own economic interests ahead of the public's. We can and must do better.

To be sure, this country has come a considerable distance since 1919, when Reginald Heber Smith published his landmark account of *Justice and the Poor*. At that time, most indigent criminal defendants had no right to counsel and the entire nation had only about sixty full-time legal aid attorneys with a combined budget of less than $200,000. Yet despite our substantial progress, we are nowhere close to the goal that Smith envisioned, which is also engraved on the entrance of the U.S. Supreme Court: "Equal Justice under Law." That should remain our aspiration. And it should not just decorate our courthouse doors; it should guide what happens inside them.

The need for legal assistance is perhaps greatest when one's liberty is at stake. A person accused of a serious crime needs to know what rights he or she has in confronting the power of the state and what the likely consequences of conviction are. The system for providing representation to people who cannot afford it is not well-funded, which creates a bias against the poor in the criminal-justice process. Race also matters from the earliest stages of the criminal process. Blacks come into contact with the police much more often than whites, and prosecutors and juries have been shown to treat Black and white defendants differently.

The election of the first African-American president has not changed this system, which in the modern era has more to do with differing levels of economic resources, different levels of social capital, and persistent forms of institutionalized racism. The law no longer explicitly disadvantages people of color who are accused of crimes. But racialized attributions continue, and social isolation by race tends to perpetuate this problem. Should law intervene at this more basic level, for example, to prevent schools from sponsoring racially separate high school proms, which is the practice in some areas?

Scholars who study this issue suggest that racism has morphed into a different, still potent, form. Tim Wise has labeled this new form "Racism 2.0." Other race scholars, such as Patricia J. Williams and Eduardo Bonilla-Silva, describe the phenomenon of *color-blind racism*, a term introduced earlier in this volume. In "Racism Without Racists," Bonilla-Silva describes a shift from overt racism to covert racism. While the prevailing norm rejects racist slurs and name-calling, other kinds of racial talk are considered acceptable. He describes four varieties of contemporary racism, some of which may surprise you:

- *Abstract liberalism* uses ideas associated with political and economic liberalism (e.g., social policy failure, choice, and individualism) in abstract manners to explain racial matters.

- *Naturalization* is a frame in which whites can explain away racial phenomena (e.g., segregation in schools and housing, high instances of people of color in prisons) by suggesting that they are natural occurrences.

- *Cultural racism* is a frame that relies on cultural stereotypes such as "Mexicans do not put much emphasis on education" or "Blacks are lazy and commit more crimes."

- *Minimization of racism* suggests that discrimination is no longer the central factor affecting people of color.

This typology of racisms can readily be translated into arguments that explain away vast racial differences in incarceration rates and in rates of the imposition of the death penalty.[3]

> Approximately thirty-five percent of all persons executed in the United States since 1976 have been Black, even though Blacks constitute only twelve percent of the United States population. The odds of receiving a death sentence are nearly four times higher if the defendant is black than if he or she is white.[4]

Black defendants have an even higher chance of receiving the death penalty if their victim is white.[5]

> Changes in sentencing law and policy, not increases in crime rates, explain most of the six-fold increase in the national prison population. These changes have significantly impacted racial disparities in sentencing, as well as increased the use of "one size fits all" mandatory minimum sentences that allow little consideration for individual characteristics.[6]

Black defendants who have used these and other statistics to show racial bias in the criminal-justice system have been firmly rebuffed by the highest tribunal in the United States. The U.S. Supreme Court has so far been unwilling to recognize racial discrimination as a constitutional violation on the basis of statistics showing significant racial disproportion in sentencing. Instead, the 14th Amendment's guarantee of equal protection of the laws without regard to race (or certain other individual characteristics) has been interpreted to forbid only *intentional* racial discrimination, as Doris Marie Provine explains in the following brief excerpt.

THE SUPREME COURT'S ROADBLOCK TO CONSTITUTIONAL RELIEF
DORIS MARIE PROVINE

"No State shall . . . deny to any person within its jurisdiction the equal protection of the laws." This brief phrase, somewhat obscure in its precise meaning, concludes the first section of the Fourteenth Amendment, which lays out several other important rights of citizenship. Congress adopted the

---

[3]Rudolph J. Gerber and John M. Johnson, *The Top Ten Death Penalty Myths: The Politics of Crime Control* (Westport, CT: Praeger Publishers, 2007), p. 44.

[4]Capital Punishment Project, *Race and the Death Penalty* (Washington, DC: American Civil Liberties Union, 2004).

[5]Gerber and Johnson. *The Top Ten Death Penalty Myths*, p. 45.

[6]The Sentencing Project, *Sentencing Policy* (Washington, DC: Author, 2010).

Fourteenth Amendment in 1868 to guarantee the civil rights of the nation's newly freed slaves. The necessity for a federal guarantee was obvious. The southern states had subordinated the former slaves economically, socially, and politically through the notorious Black Codes. President Andrew Johnson had vetoed the first congressional effort to turn back this tide of incapacitating state law, the 1866 Civil Rights Act. The Fourteenth Amendment provided the necessary legal foundation for the reconstruction effort that was then taking shape, but its major significance came much later, after a long period of Jim Crow legislation segregated facilities of all sorts in the South—from water fountains to cemeteries and orphanages.

The Supreme Court arrived late to the problem of racial disadvantage, and its engagement since that time has been fitful. Not until 1938 did the Court acknowledge that it has special responsibilities toward "discrete and insular minorities" like African Americans. It failed to fully embrace this standard, however, until the 1960s, bypassing an obvious opportunity in its 1954 school desegregation decision, *Brown v. Board of Education*. The Court finally became actively engaged with equal protection doctrine at about the same time that Congress was developing the 1964 Civil Rights Act. As the justices began to demand a higher standard for government action, they also expanded the coverage of the guarantee to other disadvantaged groups, including white women.

The early emphasis on alleviating oppression of powerless groups, Evan Gerstmann and others have argued, was turned on its head in the 1980s, as the Supreme Court developed a generalized suspicion of classifications based on group membership. The concern, in other words, shifted from protecting powerless minorities by requiring a high level of scrutiny of any rule that affected them, to a presumption against *any* racial classification, including those designed to benefit long-oppressed minorities. The Constitution's equal protection guarantee, in effect, has become a broad mandate for government not to arbitrarily single out any individual or group.

How can courts determine whether government is acting against a minority out of spite or without any legitimate purpose? Legislatures never announce invidious intentions. Courts must draw their own conclusions on the basis of the legislature's handiwork. In the early civil rights era, this task was made easier by the presumption that white southerners would always attempt to preserve their race privileges. Officials might deny discriminating, but the evidence of racial exclusion spoke louder than their words. The absence of Black voters in a district, for example, undermined the credibility of local officials who claimed that their rules were neutral.

The problem of intent arises not just in Fourteenth Amendment equal protection claims, but also in the enforcement of the 1964 Civil Rights Act's equality guarantee. The Supreme Court came closest to letting evidence of impact alone justify intervention in a 1971 race discrimination case arising under the Civil Rights Act. In *Griggs v. Duke Power Company*, the Court declared that the company's newly imposed test requirement violated the Civil Rights Act because it excluded almost all local Blacks in the area from decent jobs. There was no dissent from this result or reasoning.

By 1976, however, the Supreme Court had retreated. In *Washington v. Davis,* it reversed a court of appeals decision that had relied on *Griggs* in finding disparate racial impact sufficient to establish a constitutional violation. The issue was whether a verbal aptitude test that the District of Columbia was using in hiring police officers violated the Constitution's equal protection guarantee. The test disproportionately excluded African American applicants from consideration, but the Court decided that racial disproportion alone was not enough to violate the Constitution's equal protection clause: "A law, neutral on its face and serving ends otherwise within the power of government to pursue, is [not] invalid under the Equal Protection Clause simply because it may affect a greater proportion of one race than another." While litigants might still use impact-based arguments to show violations of statutory guarantees, these arguments would not be sufficient to invalidate rules or procedures on constitutional grounds.

The Supreme Court has been reasonably consistent since *Washington v. Davis* in ruling that there must be evidence of intent to discriminate before the government's action will be deemed to violate the equal protection clause. The Court's 1987 decision in *McCleskey v. Kemp* reaffirmed this line of cases and has become the major point of reference in subsequent cases. One study found that in the decade following *McCleskey,* not a single claimant had prevailed in a claim alleging racial discrimination by government—*McCleskey* is usually cited in denying relief.

Cognitive Psychology on Racism in Law

How does the reasoning in *McCleskey* stand up to what is currently known about the psychology of racial discrimination? Should discrimination be conceptualized as typically intentional, as *McCleskey* and its companion cases presume? Law is biased toward willed behavior because it is less morally problematic to assume that what we do is under our conscious control. But as a theory of discrimination, does this approach leave out most of what it should contain? If the life of the law has been experience, as Justice Oliver Wendell Holmes famously proclaimed, shouldn't the experience of life inform the law?

The past thirty years of social psychological research, Linda Krieger and Susan Fiske (2006) assert, offers several major insights relevant to antidiscrimination law. One of them is that unconscious expectations, including stereotypes, influence perception. Perception, this research suggests, is not passive. It is highly selective in making sense of reality, relying on cues that derive from preexisting frameworks, or schemas. The irony is that we are completely unaware of all this. "We experience the world," Susan Fiske and Shelley Taylor assert, "as if our schemas have added nothing to it" (1991, 99).

Controlled experiments suggest that people use visually prominent physical features, such as race, gender, age, and apparent occupation or region of origin, to cue schemas, which in turn evoke certain expectations that had measurable effects on thinking. Schemas associated with race, age, and religion are, in effect, stereotypes. They may be simple or complex, for example "white southern Baptist" might function as a schema for some people. One indication that schemas are operating is that people are dramatically slowed down in their mental processing if there is a mismatch between their stereo-typical expectations and the reality they encounter in a test. Words alone (for example, *female* or *old*) influence reaction times in directions suggestive of stereotypes and prejudice.

This research proceeds from the starting point that modern racism less hostile than its antecedents, but probably no less widespread. Some researchers propose the term *aversive racism* to describe attitudes commonly held by white Americans who are genuinely committed to tolerance and who, at the same time, hold negative stereotypes about African Americans and other racial and ethnic groups: "These factors converge to produce attitudinal ambivalence, uncertainty and fear in interracial encounters, and racist behavior that is manifested in indirect and subtle ways" (Eagly and Chaiken 1998, 285). The invocation of racial and other stereotypes affects thinking in at least four ways, according to Eliot Smith's review of mental representation and memory in the *Harvard book of Social Psychology*:

- Ambiguous behaviors may be interpreted as confirming the stereotype.

- Stereotype-consistent behavior will tend to reconfirm the stereotype while inconsistent behavior will be thought exceptional or attributable to chance.

- The stereotype, rather than the individual's behavior, may be used for the basis of judgment.

- Recall will be affected, and stereotype-inconsistent characteristics will tend to be forgotten. (1998, 405)

Racial stereotypes tend to persist not just because of selective information processing, but also because of the way people differentiate themselves from others, what cognitive psychologists call the outgroup homogeneity effect. Individuals tend to accentuate differences from groups they perceive as different from themselves, at the same time minimizing differences among individuals in the out group. The effect is robust, occuring across various kinds of ingroup/outgroup combinations, including students in neighboring colleges, members of related professions, and racial groups.

Another processing error relevant to racism is "the fundamental attribution error," a tendency to attribute another person's behavior to character, rather than situation. We make this error in judging others, but tend to forgive our own lapses: "Instead of realizing that there are situational forces, such as social norms or roles, that produce particular behavior, people generally see another's behavior as freely chosen and as representing that other person's stable qualities."

All of these processing errors are made worse by a human tendency to assume that everyone else sees things as we do, what cognitive psychologists call the false consensus effect: "People not only overestimate how typical their own behavior is, they also overestimate the typicality of their feelings, beliefs, and opinions. The false consensus effect may be a chief vehicle by which people maintain that their own beliefs or opinions are right" (Fiske and Taylor 1991, 78–79). It also helps people justify imposing their own beliefs on others.

These findings suggest the difficulty of eliminating prejudice, rooted as it is in basic modes of thought. The question of how to uproot it has engaged researchers for at least two decades. A basic finding is that negative stereotypes must be actively resisted to be avoided. Patricia Devine likens the process to breaking a bad habit: "The individual must (a) initially decide to stop the old behavior, (b) remember the resolution, and (c) try repeatedly and decide repeatedly to eliminate the habit" (1989, 15). The old stereotype remains, but it is no longer used. Resisting old stereotypes requires effort and is not always successful: "The non-prejudiced responses take time, attention, and effort. To the extent that any (or all) of these are limited, the outcome is likely to be stereotype-congruent or prejudice-like responses" (1989, 16; and see Devine et al. 2002).

This brief survey suggests a fundamental conflict with the legal approach to discrimination. The racism that law treats as exceptional, psychology considers mundane. Law looks for motives to discriminate, while psychology postulates that the architecture of our thinking predisposes us to racism and other forms of stereotyping by group. Were judges to acknowledge in their decisions what psychologists have established in their experiments, what would discrimination law look like?

Reconceptualizing Racism and Disparate Impact in Law

If the U.S. Supreme Court were to accept the idea that racial stereotypes and prejudice are endemic in society, courts would look differently at disparate-impact claims. Judges would be more ready to attribute racial disadvantage to individual "wiring" problems and to institutionalized practices built on stereotypical thinking, rather than intentional prejudice. They would not accept assertions of nonprejudice at face value, even from Congress. They would be interested in helping to ferret out discrimination.

Were the judicial branch to accept the reality of unconscious racism, the whole tenor of public debate about racial discrimination would change. Policymakers would have to be concerned about disparate racial impact and embedded racism. They would need to monitor their own decisions to avoid racial stereotyping. There would be a premium on designing institutions that operate stereotype-free. If decision makers took these responsibilities seriously, public debate about race would be more engaged with policy description than name calling, and government would be pressing institutions to measure the impact of their procedures to avoid institutionalizing disadvantage.

In its early years under the Johnson administration, the Equal Economic Opportunity Commission took this approach, pressuring companies to address patterns of exclusion, rather than focusing on specific acts of discrimination. This policy was carried forward under President Nixon. Although impact is still relevant in the government's enforcement actions, courts have become less willing to press for change in the past two decades. Linda Krieger, a law professor and employment rights litigator, writes of the difficulty of winning Title VII employment discrimination cases with only disparate impact data. Courts, she has found, are looking for evidence of prejudice because they assume that discrimination is intentional. She noted the difficulty of making this kind of showing in a case she litigated: "To be blunt, to establish that my client had been wronged, I would have to prove that the plant manager was a racist and a liar" (1995, 1163).

Conclusion

A comforting myth about the American system of government is that, over time, judicial decisions help us move progressively closer to our nation's foundational values. The way the Supreme Court has handled the problem of racial discrimination, however, belies that myth. Instead of broadening and deepening American understanding of discrimination in line with our core commitment to racial equality, the Court has narrowed and rigidified its approach in the past two decades. Current constitutional doctrine makes only the most blatant type of discriminatory treatment actionable, which means that the judiciary has little to contribute to the resolution of contemporary racial inequities.

The conflict between law and justice is certainly felt within the lower reaches of the judicial branch, among the judges and magistrates who see drug defendants face to face as they impose punishment. "Justice," as one acute observer noted, "is personal. It always begins and ends with specific, concrete persons" (J. Johnson 1995, 201).

Racial profiling, one law-enforcement practice that has received critical attention from government and the media, is only the tip of a constitutional iceberg. The whole architecture of the anti-drug effort is vulnerable to criticism for racial bias. If courts and policymakers were to go in this direction, they would also be obliged to consider the long tradition of particularly harsh punishment for other crimes committed by Black citizens. Taking impact seriously would also extend courts into forms of discrimination outside the criminal justice system. Racial impact is a source of useful information wherever there is evidence of disadvantage—for example public education, land use, and employment. The absence of courts from the struggle for racial justice allows many old wounds to fester.

The Court's refusal to consider the psychological underpinning of modern racism has left virtually undisturbed a criminal-justice system that disproportionately targets Black Americans.[7] The Court's logic seems to suggest that no degree of racial difference, no matter how extreme, would in itself be evidence of racism.

The next reading features testimony by Kemba Smith, who details her personal story of being incarcerated on drug charges. Smith also discusses the war on drugs and ways in which drug laws and prison terms can be targeted toward minorities and the poor. Her reflections may make you think about the possibility of struggles for legal and social change coming from within prisons. Prison activism is an often unheralded aspect of the American experience. Alan Eladio Gomez discusses how Chicanos and Puerto Rican independence advocates began to work together in Leavenworth Federal Penitentiary from 1969 to 1972, and the effects that these experiences had

---

[7]Jennifer L. Eberhardt, Paul G. Davies, Valerie J. Purdie-Vaughns, and Sheri Lynn Johnson, "Looking Deathworthy: Perceived Stereotypicality of Black Defendants Predicts Capital-Sentencing Outcomes," *Psychological Science*, vol. 17 (5): 383–86.

on the Chicano Movement and beyond. The prisoners created a newspaper and a political organization that helped to mobilize lawsuits, strikes, and solidarity outside the prison. As Gomez observes, "These political and educational projects challenged the logic of a prison regime based on racial divisions, while simultaneously establishing political links that would continue to resonate throughout the 1970s and into the present."[8]

Testimony of Kemba Smith
Kemba Smith

Members of the Commission, my name is Kemba Smith, and only a little over five years ago, I was identified by an inmate number, and today I am speaking on behalf of those currently incarcerated, those who are in district court today, and for those in the future who are being sentenced under federal mandatory minimum drug sentences.

Three days before Christmas 2000, President Bill Clinton commuted my sentence of 24.5 years for a drug conspiracy charge. If he had not done so, this morning, instead of talking to you, I would still be in Federal prison until the year 2016. If my parents had not waged a campaign in the news media, in the churches, and among the criminal justice reform community, I would not have been freed from prison to raise my 11-year old son.

I grew up as the only child of professional parents in a Richmond, Virginia suburb, leading an advantaged and sheltered childhood. After graduating from high school in 1989, I left the security of my family to continue my education at Hampton University in Hampton, Virginia. I was not a drug trafficker. I was a college student and at the age of 19, away from the protective watch of my mother and father and in an attempt to "fit in", I met a man while a sophomore in college who I became romantically involved with and unbeknownst to me at the time, according to the government, he was head of a violent 4 million dollar crack cocaine ring. He eventually became verbally and physically abusive, for which I had to seek medical attention. I continued to be in a relationship with him for over 3.5 years in which during this time he increasingly drew me into his drug activities. The prosecutor stated during

---

[8]Alan Eladio Gomez, " 'Nuestras Vidas Corren Casi Paralelas': Chicanos, Independentistas, and the Prison Rebellions in Leavenworth, 1969–1972," in *Behind Bars: Latino/as and Prison in the United States,* edited by Suzanne Oboler (New York: Palgrave Macmillan, 2009), pp. 67–96.

---

my court hearings that I never handled, used or sold any of the drugs involved in the conspiracy. Yet, I was sentenced as a first-time nonviolent drug offender to 24.5 years, one for every year of my life. I remained in prison from the moment I turned myself in September 1994, 7 months pregnant with my first child, until December 22, 2000. My boyfriend at the time, did not do any time, he was killed.

After my boyfriend was murdered, the U.S. government came after me and held me accountable for the total amount of drugs within the conspiracy, which was 255 kilograms of crack cocaine, even though according to the government's investigation, the drug dealing started two years before I even met him. I did not traffic in drugs, but I knew my boyfriend did. I knew while living with him that he did not have a job and we were living off of the proceeds of his drug crimes. I never claimed total innocence and this is the reason why I pled guilty. The prosecutor added extra incentive in negotiating the guilty plea stating that he would allow me a bond so that I could go home until sentencing to give birth to my son and that I would only receive a two-year sentence. Unfortunately, due to his unethical conduct, after pleading guilty I remained in jail.

Minutes after giving birth in a hospital, guarded by two prison officials, the U.S. Marshall Service walked into my room and ordered that I be shackled to the bed, and two days later my son was taken away. I was sent back to a cold jail cell with my breast gorging and in extreme pain. If my parents had not been able to take and raise my son, my parental rights would have been terminated.

Since being released from prison in 2000, I graduated from Virginia Union University with a bachelor's degree in Social Work, worked at a law firm for over 4 years, bought a home and I am currently a first year law student at Howard University. I have spoken across the country to youth audiences, inspiring them to become educated about injustices in the U.S. criminal justice system, and hoping that they will recognize that there are consequences to their life choices. But most importantly, I am raising my only child who is now eleven years old. Unfortunately, my burden is that I represent the thousands of others still currently incarcerated, some my friends, who I left behind that deserve an opportunity to raise their children, as well.

Mandatory minimum sentences are sentences, usually of imprisonment, created by legislative bodies that must be imposed by a court upon a finding of guilt based upon either that fact or some other fact, not withstanding any other factors that are traditionally relevant to a just sentence, including the degree of culpability and the accused's role in the offense.

U.S. law provides that any person who is an accessory to a crime or who aids or abets the commission of a crime is a principal and is treated and punished exactly like the principal perpetrator of an offense. In the Anti-Drug Abuse Act of 1988. Congress applied the mandatory minimum sentences it enacted in 1986 to the crimes of attempt and conspiracy in the Controlled Substances Act.

The consequence is that the most minor participants in the activities of a drug trafficker are charged with all of the crimes of the drug trafficker. This means they are facing the equivalent punishment. The threat of imprisonment for 20 or 30 years or more leads many to plead guilty and seek a departure below the mandatory minimum sentence.

In 1986, the U.S. Department of Justice insisted on a provision to the mandatory minimums to permit the government to move the court to sentence below the statutory mandatory minimum if the government found that the defendant had provided "substantial assistance in the investigation or prosecution of another person who has committed an offense."

Many women are unwilling to provide this "substantial assistance" in order to be loyal to the man they love, even if they are not married. This results in what has been called "the girlfriend problem." The drug trafficker pleads guilty, cooperates in the prosecution of his colleagues, and is sentenced below the mandatory minimum. His girlfriend, having no information about the criminal organization other than the acts of her boyfriend, feels morally and emotionally compelled not to testify against him. Therefore she is unable to qualify for the "substantial assistance" departure and receives the full mandatory minimum sentence even though, in fact, her culpability is substantially less than that of the principal offender.

Aside from mandatory minimum sentencing, various features of drug enforcement in the United States have a racially disparate impact.

The United States Housing Act of 1937 was amended by section 5101 of the Anti-Drug Abuse Act of 1988 to permit the termination of a lease in a public housing facility "if any member of the tenant's household, or a guest or other person under the tenant's control . . . engage[s] in criminal activity, including drug-related criminal activity, on or near public housing premises, while the tenant is a tenant in public housing." This has been implemented as the "one strike and you're out" public housing provision that has resulted in the eviction of public housing tenants. This policy was recently unanimously upheld by the United States Supreme Court in *Department of Housing and Urban Development v. Rucker*, 535 U.S. 125 (2002). Mrs. Rucker's daughter was found with cocaine and a crack pipe three blocks away from her apartment, and Mrs. Rucker was evicted.

A person with a drug conviction has a lifetime ban from food assistance and temporary assistance to needy families.

Any student convicted of any drug offense (even a summary citation for simple possession) shall be denied Federal higher education financial aid (P.L. 105-244, sec. 483(f); 20 U.S.C. §1091 (r). Such sanctions are not applied to convicted murderers, rapists or child molesters.

A non-U.S. citizen convicted of a drug offense or regulation (other than one involving less than 30 grams of marijuana) must be barred from entry into the United States, or deported from the United States, no matter when the offense took place.

It is evident that the people who are disproportionately impacted by these federal drug sentencing laws are people of color and I am not ashamed to say again that I represent those who are currently incarcerated, people just like me who are capable of being productive taxpaying citizens.

When the U.S. Congress created the mandatory minimum sentences and collateral consequences for drug offenses, they may not have been acting with the intent to inflict special punishment upon people of color, but that has unquestionably been the effect.

Turning now more specifically to policies that guide the implementation of law, an interesting question arises when policies are not compatible with the law. This is not necessarily a bad thing. Many states long ago passed statutes criminalizing adultery and fornication (sexual relations outside of matrimony), but police departments and prosecutors often adopt policies of not enforcing such laws. Would it be better if every law were enforced? That way the legislature would have an incentive to keep laws up-to-date with public sentiments. Of course, that would put a tremendous drain on policing and other administrative resources because legislatures routinely pass more laws than government can actually enforce. Sometimes laws are adopted, not to be enforced, but to signal political commitments.

The disjuncture between law "on the books" and the way relevant agencies actually implement law raises many questions, not just about legislative intent in framing the law, but also about agency discretion in implementing it. One bundle of issues concerns discretion far down the implementation line, at the level of the individual "street-level bureaucrat." A neighborhood police officer (a.k.a., street-level bureaucrat) who lets certain kinds of law-breaking pass without intervention is exercising discretion informally given by her police department, or even higher authorities. Probably everyone can think of examples of nonenforcement of traffic or criminal laws, perhaps even an incident involving oneself.

The issue of discretion is complex. On the positive side, discretion helpfully allows an official to weigh competing circumstances and move accordingly. On the negative side, discretion makes it harder to detect corruption, inefficiency, and discrimination. Not surprisingly, social-change advocates and legislatures often call for reduction or elimination of discretion at the agency or street level. One does not hear as often the argument that some laws or policies are simply unenforceable in light of the problem of discretionary enforcement. The much-discussed "don't ask, don't tell" policy that the American armed services adopted regarding military service by homosexuals, however, is one example.

This issue of whether justice sometimes demands nonenforcement of law has arisen in Arizona recently. In this case, some police chiefs are making the case that local police should not routinely attempt to enforce federal immigration law, while others strongly disagree with that position. For some local residents, the issue echoes concerns raised after a 1997 "round-up" that resulted in the deportation of 432 people from Chandler, Arizona, a fast-growing city within the metro Phoenix area. Local police and border patrol agents coordinated efforts for the five-day operation, making stops without probable cause and committing other violations. The operation resulted in a federal civil-rights lawsuit that concluded with a settlement on behalf of victims, including a promise by the City of Chandler to not engage in similar mass enforcement-actions in the future.[9]

The issue took on new urgency in April 2010 when Arizona adopted a law mandating that local police actively seek to ascertain legal status under certain circumstances.[10] Before this law was adopted, police departments around the state (and nation) had varied in interpreting their responsibility to assist the federal government in detecting unauthorized immigrants.[11] Some Arizona departments had limited their inquiries about legal status to situations involving serious crime. The policy was usually not clearly spelled out in writing, but it was understood within departments and by the city governments that employ them that police have many priorities, not all of which are compatible with inquiring about immigration status.

A major concern for police chiefs and city governments was that people without proper documentation, or who had family members in that situation, would be afraid to contact the police if they were victimized by crime or observed suspicious activity. The idea was that if some members of the community feel constrained by fear of deportation of themselves or loved ones, the whole community is rendered less secure. Many individual police officers agreed with this reasoning, but some did not, so there was considerable variation in how these policies of nuanced enforcement were being carried out.

To better ensure that police departments and individual officers would follow the state's new mandate, the legislature gave citizens the right to sue a police department for not complying with the new law. The new law permits any Arizona citizen, to sue an Arizona police department for a policy not compatible with the state's mandate. This citizen-suit provision is clearly designed to limit the discretion of local police departments and local governments (cities and counties) to fashion their own policies in this complex area. It remains unclear how individual police officers will respond in actual stops, a layer of discretionary decision making that the state law does not address directly.

One of the concerns that some observers have with laws like Arizona's is that police officers will engage in racial profiling, focusing on one racial or ethnic group for questions about legal status, when, in reality, anyone of any racial or ethnic group can be an undocumented immigrant. A white person could get a pass, either because an officer's suspicions would not be aroused or because an officer might have been racially selective about whom to stop in the first place. Racial profiling and pretextual stops are

---

[9]For a description of the injustices perpetuated in this raid, see Mary Romero and Marwah Serag, "Violation of Latino Civil Rights Resulting from INS and Local Police's Use of Race, Culture and Class Profiling: The Case of the Chandler Roundup in Arizona," *Cleveland State Law Review*, vol. 52 (1&2): 75–96 (2005).

[10]Support Our Law Enforcement and Safe Neighborhoods Act. S.B. 1070 (Arizona State Senate, April 23, 2010).

[11]See Scott H. Decker, Paul G. Lewis, Doris Marie Provine and Monica W. Varsanyi, "On the Frontier of Local Law Enforcement: Local Police and Federal Immigration Law," in *Immigration, Crime, and Justice* (vol. 13 in series *Sociology of Crime, Law, and Deviance*), edited by William F. McDonald (Bingley, UK: Emerald/JAI Press, 2009), pp. 261–77.

familiar justice issues, not just in the context of immigrants who may lack documentation, but in cases involving African American citizens suspected of selling or buying illegal drugs or other crimes. While the studies vary in how much racial profiling is occurring in highway and other stops, it does seem clear that Americans tend to associate negative traits with darker skinned people.

This lesson about difference is learned early. A recent study found that children associated positive traits (i.e., being smart, nice, good, good-looking) with lighter skin tones. The children associated negative traits (i.e., dumb, mean, bad, ugly) with darker skin tones.[12] This study was patterned after a famous one conducted by Kenneth and Mamie Clark (and cited favorably in *Brown v. Board of Education*). The Clarks asked 53 Black children to pick from four dolls—two with white skin and two with brown skin. The children were asked which dolls they would like to play with and which dolls were nice. Ninety-four percent of the children chose the white doll.[13]

The impact of stereotypical thinking ranges widely, raising troubling questions about how to deal with it in social policy. Consider, for example, the issue of hiring. It is difficult for government to attempt to second-guess hiring decisions with policies designed to end racial discrimination. Yet at the same time, it is unjust that some members of society are without a well-functioning legal remedy. How can hiring, which generally leaves much discretion in the hands of employers, be regulated to eliminate the influence of negative racial stereotypes? The reading below by Bertrand and Mullainathan suggests that this will not be easy.

ARE EMILY AND GREG MORE EMPLOYABLE THAN LAKISHA AND JAMAL? A FIELD EXPERIMENT ON LABOR MARKET DISCRIMINATION
MARIANNE BERTRAND AND SENDHIL MULLAINATHAN

Every measure of economic success reveals significant racial inequality in the U.S. labor market. Compared to Whites, African-Americans are twice as likely to be unemployed and earn nearly 25 percent less when they are employed. This inequality has sparked a debate as to whether employers treat members of different races differently. When faced with observably similar African-American and White applicants, do they favor the White one? Some argue yes, citing either employer prejudice or employer perception that race signals lower productivity. Others argue that differential treatment by race is a relic of the past, eliminated by

[12]Anderson Cooper, CNN Pilot *Demonstration*, April 28, 2010.
[13]Kenneth B. Clark and Mamie P. Clark, *Racial Identification and Preference in Negro Children* (Racial Identification and Preference, 1947).

"Are Emily and Greg More Employable than LaKisha and Jamal?" by Marianne Bertrand and Sendhil Mullainathan, *American Economic Review*, American Economic Association, vol. 94(4), September 2004, pp. 991–1009. Reprinted by permission of *American Economic Review* and the authors.

some combination of employer enlightenment, affirmative action programs and the profit-maximization motive. In fact, many in this latter camp even feel that stringent enforcement of affirmative action programs has produced an environment of reverse discrimination. They would argue that faced with identical candidates, employers might favor the African-American one. Data limitations make it difficult to empirically test these views. Since researchers possess far less data than employers do, White and African-American workers that appear similar to researchers may look very different to employers. So any racial difference in labor market outcomes could just as easily be attributed to differences that are observable to employers but unobservable to researchers.

To circumvent this difficulty, we conduct a field experiment that builds on the correspondence testing methodology that has been primarily used in the past to study minority outcomes in the United Kingdom. We send resumes in response to help-wanted ads in Chicago and Boston newspapers and measure callback for interview for each sent resume. We experimentally manipulate perception of race via the name of the fictitious job applicant. We randomly assign very White-sounding names (such as Emily Walsh or Greg Baker) to half the resumes and very African-American-sounding names (such as Lakisha Washington or Jamal Jones) to the other half. Because we are also interested in how credentials affect the racial gap in callback, we experimentally vary the quality of the resumes used in response to a given ad. Higher-quality applicants have on average a little more labor market experience and fewer holes in their employment history; they are also more likely to have an e-mail address, have completed some certification degree, possess foreign language skills, or have been awarded some honors. In practice, we typically send four resumes in response to each ad: two higher-quality and two lower-quality ones. We randomly assign to one of the higher- and one of the lower-quality resumes an African-American-sounding name. In total, we respond to over 1,300 employment ads in the sales, administrative support, clerical, and customer-services job categories and send nearly 5,000 resumes. The ads we respond to cover a large spectrum of job quality, from cashier work at retail establishments and clerical work in a mail room, to office and sales management positions.

We find large racial differences in callback rates. Applicants with White names need to send about 10 resumes to get one callback whereas applicants with African-American names need to send about 15 resumes. This 50-percent gap in callback is statistically significant. A White name yields as many more callbacks as an additional eight years of experience on a resume. Since applicants' names are randomly assigned, this gap can only be attributed to the name manipulation.

Race also affects the reward to having a better resume. Whites with higher-quality resumes receive nearly 30-percent more callbacks than Whites with lower-quality resumes. On the other hand, having a higher-quality resume has a smaller effect for African-Americans. In other words, the gap between Whites and African-Americans widens with resume quality. While one may have expected improved credentials to alleviate employers' fear that African-American applicants are deficient in some unobservable skills, this is not the case in our data.

The experiment also reveals several other aspects of the differential treatment by race. First, since we randomly assign applicants' postal addresses to the resumes, we can study the effect of neighborhood of residence on the likelihood of callback. We find that living in a wealthier (or more educated or Whiter) neighborhood increases callback rates. But, interestingly, African-Americans are not helped more than Whites by living in a "better" neighborhood. Second, the racial gap we measure in different industries does not appear correlated to Census-based measures of the racial gap in wages. The same is true for the racial gap we measure in different occupations. In fact, we find that the racial gaps in callback are statistically indistinguishable across all the occupation and industry categories covered in the experiment. Federal contractors, who are thought to be more severely constrained by affirmative action laws, do not treat the African-American resumes more preferentially; neither do larger employers or employers who explicitly state that they are "Equal Opportunity Employers." In Chicago, we find a slightly smaller racial gap when employers are located in more African-American neighborhoods.

Previous Research

With conventional labor force and household surveys, it is difficult to study whether differential treatment occurs in the labor market. Armed only with survey data, researchers usually measure differential treatment by comparing the labor market performance of Whites and African-Americans (or men and women) for which they observe similar sets of skills. But such comparisons can be quite misleading. Standard labor force surveys do not contain all the characteristics that employers observe when hiring, promoting, or setting wages. So one can never be sure that the minority and nonminority workers being compared are truly similar from the employers' perspective. As a consequence, any measured differences in outcomes could be attributed to these unobserved (to the researcher) factors.

This difficulty with conventional data has led some authors to instead rely on pseudo-experiments. Claudia Goldin and Cecilia Rouse (2000), for example, examine the effect of blind auditioning on the hiring process of orchestras. By observing the treatment of female candidates before and after the introduction of blind auditions, they try to measure the amount of sex discrimination. When such pseudo-experiments can be found, the resulting study can be very informative; but finding such experiments has proven to be extremely challenging.

A different set of studies, known as audit studies, attempts to place comparable minority and White actors into actual social and economic settings and measure how each group fares in these settings. Labor market audit studies send comparable minority (African-American or Hispanic) and White auditors in for interviews and measure whether one is more likely to get the job than the other. While the results vary somewhat across studies, minority auditors tend to perform worse on average: they are less likely to get called back for a second interview and, conditional on getting called back, less likely to get hired.

These audit studies provide some of the cleanest nonlaboratory evidence of differential treatment by race. But they also have weaknesses, most of which have been highlighted in Heckman and Siegelman (1992) and Heckman (1998). First, these studies require that both members of the auditor pair are identical in all dimensions that might affect productivity in employers' eyes, except for race. To accomplish this, researchers typically match auditors on several characteristics (height, weight, age, dialect, dressing style, hairdo) and train them for several days to coordinate interviewing styles. Yet, critics note that this is unlikely to erase the numerous differences that exist between the auditors in a pair.

Another weakness of the audit studies is that they are not double-blind. Auditors know the purpose of the study. As Turner et al. (1991) note: "The first day of training also included an introduction to employment discrimination, equal employment opportunity, and a review of project design and methodology." This may generate conscious or subconscious motives among auditors to generate data consistent or inconsistent with their beliefs about race issues in America. As psychologists know very well, these demand effects can be quite strong. It is very difficult to insure that auditors will not want to do "a good job." Since they know the goal of the experiment, they can alter their behavior in front of employers to express (indirectly) their own views. Even a small belief by auditors that employers treat minorities differently can result in measured differences in treatment. This effect is further magnified by the fact that auditors are not in fact seeking jobs and are therefore more free to let their beliefs affect the interview process.

Finally, audit studies are extremely expensive, making it difficult to generate large enough samples to understand nuances and possible mitigating factors. Also, these budgetary constraints worsen the problem of mismatched auditor pairs. Cost considerations force the use of a limited number of pairs of auditors, meaning that any one mismatched pair can easily drive the results. In fact, these studies generally tend to find significant differences in outcomes across pairs.

Our study circumvents these problems. First, because we only rely on resumes and not people, we can be sure to generate comparability across race. In fact, since race is randomly assigned to each resume, the same resume will sometimes be associated with an African-American name and sometimes with a White name. This guarantees that any differences we find are caused solely by the race manipulation. Second, the use of paper resumes insulates us from demand effects. While the research assistants know the purpose of the study, our protocol allows little room for conscious or subconscious deviations from the set procedures. Moreover, we can objectively measure whether the randomization occurred as expected. This kind of objective measurement is impossible in the case of the previous audit studies. Finally, because of relatively low marginal cost, we can send out a large number of resumes. Besides giving us more precise estimates, this larger sample size also allows us to examine the nature of the differential treatment from many more angles.

Three main sets of questions arise when interpreting the results above. First, does a higher callback rate for White applicants imply that employers are discriminating against African-Americans? Second, does our design only isolate the effect of race or is the name manipulation conveying some other factors than race? Third, how do our results relate to different models of racial discrimination?

Callback Rates

Our results indicate that for two identical individuals engaging in an identical job search, the one with an African-American name would receive fewer interviews. Does differential treatment within our experiment imply that employers are discriminating against African-Americans (whether it is rational, prejudice-based, or other form of discrimination)? In other words, could the lower callback rate we record for African-American resumes *within our experiment* be consistent with a racially neutral review of the *entire pool* of resumes the surveyed employers receive?

In a racially neutral review process, employers would rank order resumes based on their quality and call back all applicants that are above a certain threshold. Because names are randomized, the White and African-American resumes we send should rank similarly on average. So, irrespective of the skill and racial composition of the applicant pool, a race-blind selection rule would generate equal treatment of Whites and African-Americans. So our results must imply that employers use race as a factor when reviewing resumes, which matches the legal definition of discrimination.

Potential Confounds

While the names we have used in this experiment strongly signal racial origin, they may also signal some other personal trait. More specifically, one might be concerned that employers are inferring social background from the personal name. When employers read a name like "Tyrone" or "Latoya," they may assume that the person comes from a disadvantaged background. In the extreme form of this social background interpretation, employers do not care at all about race but are discriminating only against the social background conveyed by the names we have chosen.

While plausible, we feel that some of our earlier results are hard to reconcile with this interpretation. For example, we found that while employers value "better" addresses, African-Americans are not helped more than Whites by living in Whiter or more educated neighborhoods. If the African-American names we have chosen mainly signal negative social background, one might have expected the estimated name gap to be lower for better addresses. Also, if the names mainly signal social background, one might have expected the name gap to be higher for jobs that rely more on soft skills or require more interpersonal interactions.

We, however, directly address this alternative interpretation by examining the average social background of babies born with the names used in the experiment. We were able to obtain birth certificate data on mother's education (less than high school, high school or more) for babies born in Massachusetts between 1970 and 1986. For each first name in our experiment, we compute the fraction of babies with that name and, in that gender-race cell, whose mothers have at least completed a high school degree.

In Table 8, we display the average callback rate for each first name along with this proxy for social background. Within each race-gender group, the names are ranked by increasing callback rate. Interestingly, there is significant variation in callback rates by name. Of course, chance alone could produce such variation because of the

Table 8—Callback Rate and Mother's Education by First Name

White female			African-American female		
Name	Percent callback	Mother education	Name	Percent callback	Mother education
Emily	7.9	96.6	Aisha	2.2	77.2
Anne	8.3	93.1	Keisha	3.8	68.8
Jill	8.4	92.3	Tamika	5.5	61.5
Allison	9.5	95.7	Lakisha	5.5	55.6
Laurie	9.7	93.4	Tanisha	5.8	64.0
Sarah	9.8	97.9	Latoya	8.4	55.5
Meredith	10.2	81.8	Kenya	8.7	70.2
Carrie	13.1	80.7	Latonya	9.1	31.3
Kristen	13.1	93.4	Ebony	9.6	65.6
Average		91.7	Average		61.0
Overall		83.9	Overall		70.2
Correlation	−0.318	($p = 0.404$)	Correlation	−0.383	($p = 0.309$)

White male			African-American male		
Name	Percent callback	Mother education	Name	Percent callback	Mother education
Todd	5.9	87.7	Rasheed	3.0	77.3
Neil	6.6	85.7	Tremayne	4.3	—
Geoffrey	6.8	96.0	Kareem	4.7	67.4
Brett	6.8	93.9	Darnell	4.8	66.1
Brendan	7.7	96.7	Tyrone	5.3	64.0
Greg	7.8	88.3	Hakim	5.5	73.7
Matthew	9.0	93.1	Jamal	6.6	73.9
Jay	13.4	85.4	Leroy	9.4	53.3
Brad	15.9	90.5	Jermaine	9.6	57.5
Average		91.7	Average		66.7
Overall		83.5	Overall		68.9
Correlation	−0.0251	($p = 0.949$)	Correlation	−0.595	($p = 0.120$)

Notes: This table reports, for each first name used in the experiment, callback rate and average mother education. Mother education for a given first name is defined as the percent of babies born with that name in Massachusetts between 1970 and 1986 whose mother had at least completed a high school degree (see text for details). Within each sex/race group, first names are ranked by increasing callback rate. "Average" reports, within each race-gender group, the average mother education for all the babies born with one of the names used in the experiment. "Overall" reports, within each race-gender group, average mother education for all babies born in Massachusetts between 1970 and 1986 in that race-gender group. "Correlation" reports the Spearman rank order correlation between callback rate and mother education *within* each race-gender group as well as the *p*-value for the test of independence.

rather small number of observations in each cell (about 200 for the female names and 70 for the male names).

The row labeled "Average" reports the average fraction of mothers that have at least completed high school for the set of names listed in that gender-race group. The row labeled "Overall" reports the average fraction of mothers that have at least completed high school for the full sample of births in that gender-race group. For example, 83.9 percent of White female babies born between 1970 and 1986 have mothers with at least a high school degree; 91.7 percent of the White female babies with one of the names used in the experiment have mothers with at least a high school degree.

Consistent with a social background interpretation, the African-American names we have chosen fall below the African-American average. For African-American male names, however, the gap between the experimental names and the population average is negligible. For White names, both the male and female names are above the population average.

But, more interestingly to us, there is substantial between-name heterogeneity in social background. African-American babies named Kenya or Jamal are affiliated with much higher mothers' education than African-American babies named Latonya or Leroy. Conversely, White babies named Carrie or Neil have lower social background than those named Emily or Geoffrey. This allows for a direct test of the social background hypothesis within our sample: are names associated with a worse social background discriminated against more? In the last row in each gender-race group, we report the rank-order correlation between callback rates and mother's education. The social background hypothesis predicts a positive correlation. Yet, for all four categories, we find the exact opposite. The p-values indicate that we cannot reject independence at standard significance levels except in the case of African-American males where we can almost reject it at the 10-percent level ($p = 0.120$). In summary, this test suggests little evidence that social background drives the measured race gap.

Names might also influence our results through familiarity. One could argue that the African-American names used in the experiment simply appear odd to human resource managers and that any odd name is discriminated against. But as noted earlier, the names we have selected are not particularly uncommon among African-Americans. We have also performed a similar exercise to that of Table 8 and measured the rank-order correlation between name-specific callback rates and name frequency within each gender-race group. We found no systematic positive correlation.

Conclusion

This Study suggests that African-Americans face differential treatment when searching for jobs and this may still be a factor in why they do poorly in the labor market. Job applicants with African-American names get far fewer callbacks for each resume they send out. Equally importantly, applicants with African-American names find it hard to overcome this hurdle in callbacks by improving their observable skills or credentials.

Taken at face value, our results on differential returns to skill have possibly important policy implications. They suggest that training programs alone may not be enough to alleviate the racial gap in labor market outcomes. For training to work, some general-equilibrium force outside the context of our experiment would have to be at play. In fact, if African-Americans recognize how employers reward their skills, they may rationally be less willing than Whites to even participate in these programs.

Affirmative-action programs are one solution to the problem of racial discrimination in hiring (and in admission to institutions of higher learning). These are governmental (and sometimes private-company) policies that explicitly or implicitly take race into account in an effort to level the playing field. How to do this fairly has proven a nettlesome issue in our purportedly "post-racial" society. The issue is clouded by lack of knowledge about how extensively law and policy have favored whites in the past. Most New Deal policies, and arguably, even the GI Bill of Rights adopted after World War II, were designed to preserve white supremacy by denying benefits to Blacks who would have otherwise been qualified for them. The federal government subsidized housing, for example, in areas with racially restrictive covenants that excluded Blacks and other non-white races. Ira Katznelson describes this as a form of affirmative action for whites.[14] The justice of current affirmative-action efforts should be viewed with enough historical perspective to take account of the advantages the American system has created for whites.

WHITE IDENTITY AND AFFIRMATIVE ACTION
BEVERLY DANIEL TATUM, PH.D.

What Is Affirmative Action?

There has been much public debate about affirmative action since its inception, with little attempt to clarify concepts. Politicians' interchangeable use of the terms *affirmative action* and *quotas* have contributed to the confusion, perhaps intentionally. The term *quota* has a repugnant history of discrimination and exclusion. For example, earlier in the twentieth century, quotas were used to limit how many Jews would be admitted to prestigious institutions of higher learning.

But despite common public perceptions, most affirmative action programs do not involve quotas, though they may involve goals. The difference between a goal and a

[14]Ira Katznelson. *When Affirmative Action Was White: An Untold History of Racial Inequality in Twentieth-Century America* (New York: W.W. Norton and Company, 2005).

quota is an important one. Quotas, defined here as fixed numerical allocations, are illegal, unless court-ordered as a temporary remedy for a well-documented, proven pattern of racially-motivated discrimination. Unlike a quota, goals are voluntary, legal, and may even be exceeded. Goals are not a ceiling meant to limit (as quotas did in the past). Instead, goals provide a necessary target toward which to aim. As any long-range planner knows, goals are necessary in order to chart one's course of action, and to evaluate one's progress. Goals are an essential component of effective affirmative action programs.

The term *affirmative action* was introduced into our language and legal system by Executive Order 11246, signed by President Lyndon Johnson in 1965. This order obligated federal contractors to "take affirmative action to ensure that applicants are employed, and that employees are treated during employment without regard to their race, color, religion, sex, or national origin." As set forth by this order, contractors were to commit themselves to "apply every good faith effort" to use procedures that would result in equal employment opportunity for historically disadvantaged groups. The groups targeted for this "affirmative action" were White women, and men and women of color (specifically defined by the federal government as American Indian/Alaska Natives, Asian or Pacific Islanders, Blacks, and Hispanics). In the 1970s, legislation broadened the protected groups to include persons with disabilities and Vietnam veterans. Though Executive Order 11246 required affirmative action, it did not specify exactly what affirmative action programs should look like.

Given this lack of specificity, it is not surprising that there is great variety in the way affirmative action programs have been developed and implemented around the country. The executive order had as its goal equal employment opportunity. But in practice, because of continuing patterns of discrimination, that goal cannot be reached without positive steps—affirmative actions—to create that equality of opportunity. Consequently, affirmative action can be defined as attempts to make progress toward actual, rather than hypothetical, equality of opportunity for those groups which are currently under-represented in significant positions in society by explicitly taking into account the defining characteristics—sex or race, for example—that have been the basis for discrimination. These attempts can be categorized as either *process-oriented* or *goal-oriented*.

Process-oriented programs focus on creating a fair application process, assuming that a fair process will result in a fair outcome. If a job opening has been advertised widely, and anyone who is interested has a chance to apply, and all applicants receive similar treatment (i.e., standard interview questions, same evaluation criteria and procedures), the process is presumed to be fair. The search committee can freely choose the "best" candidate knowing that no discrimination has taken place. Under such circumstances, the "best" candidate will sometimes be a person of color, "too good to ignore." In theory, such would seem to be the case, and because process-oriented programs seem consistent with the American ideal of the meritocracy, most people support this kind of affirmative action. At the very least, it is an improvement over the "old boy network" that filled positions before outsiders even had a chance to apply.

Goal-oriented affirmative action also provides an open process. However, when the qualified pool of applicants has been identified, those among the pool who move the organization closer to its diversity hiring goals are favored. If the finalist hired was qualified but not the "best" choice in the eyes of those who don't share the goal, the decision is often criticized as "reverse discrimination."

Though the process-oriented emphasis is more palatable to some than the goal-oriented emphasis, in practice the process-oriented approach is often quite ineffective. Despite the attempts to insure a fair process, search committee after search committee finds the "best" person is yet another member of the dominant group. What goes wrong? Some answers may be found in the research of social psychologist John Dovidio and his colleagues.

Aversive Racism and Affirmative Action

In "Resistance to Affirmative Action: The Implications of Aversive Racism," John Dovidio, Jeffrey Mann, and Samuel Gaertner argue that White opposition to affirmative action programs is largely rooted in a subtle but pervasive form of racism they call "aversive racism." Aversive racism is defined as "an attitudinal adaptation resulting from an assimilation of an egalitarian value system with prejudice and with racist beliefs." In other words, most Americans have internalized the espoused cultural values of fairness and justice for all at the same time that they have been breathing the "smog" of racial biases and stereotypes pervading the popular culture. "The existence, both of almost unavoidable racial biases and of the desire to be egalitarian and racially tolerant, forms the basis of the ambivalence that aversive racists experience."

Pointing to the findings of several impressive research studies, these social psychologists argue that because aversive racists see themselves as nonprejudiced and racially tolerant, they generally do not behave in overtly racist ways. When the norms for appropriate, non-discriminatory behavior are clear and unambiguous, they "do the right thing," because to behave otherwise would threaten the non-prejudiced self-image they hold. However, Dovidio and his colleagues assert that in situations when it is not clear what the "right thing" is, or if an action can be justified on the basis of some factor other than race, negative feelings toward Blacks will surface. In these ambiguous situations, an aversive racist can discriminate against Blacks without threatening his racially tolerant self-image.

For example, in a study in which White college students were asked to evaluate Black and White people on a simple "good-bad" basis, where choosing *bad* rather than *good* to describe Blacks might clearly indicate bias, the students consistently rated both Blacks and Whites positively. However, when the task was changed slightly to rating Blacks and Whites on a more subtle continuum of goodness, Whites were consistently rated better than Blacks. For instance, when the rating choice was "ambitious-not lazy," Blacks, were not rated as more lazy than Whites, but Whites were evaluated as more ambitious than Blacks. Repeated findings of this nature led these researchers to conclude that a subtle but important bias was operating. In the eyes of the aversive racists, Blacks are not worse, but Whites are better.

How might such a bias affect hiring decisions? Would this kind of bias affect how the competence of Black and White candidates might be evaluated? To explore this question, a study was conducted in which White college students were asked to rate college applicants who on the basis of transcript information were strongly qualified, moderately qualified, or weakly qualified. In some cases the applicant was identified as Black, in other cases as White. When the applicant was weakly qualified, there was no discrimination between Black and White applicants. Both were rejected. When the applicant had moderate qualifications, Whites were evaluated slightly better than Blacks, but not significantly so. However, when the applicant had strong qualifications, there was a significant difference between how strong White candidates and strong Black candidates were rated. Though the information that had been provided about the candidates was identical, the Black applicants were evaluated significantly less positively than the White applicants. The subtle bias that Dovidio and his colleagues have identified does not occur at all levels, but it occurs when you might least expect it, when the Black candidate is highly qualified. In this and other similar studies, Blacks could be seen as good; but Whites with the same credentials were consistently rated as better.

The bias was even more apparent when the Black person being rated was in a position superior to the White evaluator. While high-ability White supervisors were accepted by subordinate White raters as being somewhat more intelligent than themselves, White evaluators consistently described high-ability Black supervisors as significantly less intelligent than themselves. So even when the Black supervisor is more competent than the White subordinate, the White again sees the situation as though a Black person less qualified than themselves is being given preferential treatment. The researchers speculate that the bias is accentuated in this scenario because the possibility of being subordinated to a Black person threatens deeply held (though perhaps unconscious) notions of White superiority.

Social psychologists Susan Clayton and Sandra Tangri also discuss the illusory nature of "objective" evaluation, and offer another reason that the pattern of underestimating the abilities of competent Black candidates is so widespread. They suggest that when an evaluator expects a weak performance and sees a strong one, the strong performance is attributed to unstable causes such as luck or effort. Unlike "innate" ability, luck or effort can change and are therefore unreliable. However, strong performances based on ability will probably be repeated. Strong performances attributed to ability (the explanation likely used for White male candidates) are viewed more positively and more often rewarded than performances assumed to be based on luck or an unusual effort.

Dovidio and colleagues conclude:

> The aversive racism framework has important and direct implication for the implementation of affirmative action–type policies. Affirmative action has often been interpreted as, "when all things are equal, take the minority person." Our research suggests that even when things are equal, they may not be perceived as equal—particularly when the minority person is well-qualified and

the situation has personal relevance to the non-minority person. Because Whites tend to misperceive the competence of Blacks relative to themselves, resistance to affirmative action may appear quite legitimate to the protesters. Insufficient competence, not race, becomes the rationale justifying resistance.

The particular irony is that the more competent the Black person is, the more likely this bias is to occur.

The research that has been discussed here has been framed in terms of Black-White relationships. Of course, affirmative action programs may also involve other people of color as well as White women. Yet the Black-White emphasis in the aversive racism framework seems well placed when we consider that researchers have found that negative attitudes toward affirmative action are expressed most strongly when Blacks are identified as the target beneficiaries. As Audrey Murrell and her colleagues point out, "whereas giving preference based on nonmerit factors is perceived as unfair, giving such preference to Blacks is perceived as more unfair."

Now we can see why affirmative action efforts focusing on the process rather than the outcome are likely to be ineffective. There are too many opportunities for evaluator bias to manifest itself—in the initial recruitment and screening of applicants, in the interview process, and ultimately in the final selection. Competent candidates of color are likely to be weeded out all along the way. Those that make it to the final selection process may in fact be "too good to ignore," but as the research suggests and as I have seen in some of my own search committee experiences, for Black candidates "too good to ignore" can mean too good to hire.

"Not a Prejudiced Bone in Their Bodies": A Case Example

During the first nine years of my teaching career, I taught on two different campuses. In each case, I was the only Black female faculty member throughout my tenure. Though both institutions identified themselves as "equal employment opportunity/affirmative action employers," my experience on search committees in those settings taught me a lot about why there weren't more Black women or many Black men on campus. Black applicants "too good to be ignored" regularly were ignored, sometimes because they were too good. "Can't hire him, he's too good, he won't stay." "She's good, but not exactly what we had in mind." "He gave a brilliant talk, but there's just something about him, I can't quite put my finger on it."

In at least one instance, I thought I could put my finger on it, and did. When I raised questions about racial bias, I was told by the chair of the search committee, "I've known all of these [White] people for years. There's not a prejudiced bone in their bodies." I replied, "You know, I don't think anyone on the committee would intentionally discriminate, but I know that people feel most comfortable with people like themselves, with the kind of people they've grown up around, that they play golf with. When interacting with someone who doesn't fit that description, there may be a kind of uneasiness that is hard to articulate. So when I sit in a committee meeting, and White people all agree that a Black candidate is well qualified for the position, better than the competing White candidates in fact, but then they say things like, `I'm not sure if he's the right person for the job,' `I'm not sure what kind of colleague he'd be, I just didn't feel comfortable with him,' I think we have a problem."

We did have a problem. In this case, rather than offer the Black candidate the position, it was declared a failed search and the position was advertised again the following year. I was not asked to serve on the next search committee, and perhaps not surprisingly, there were no Black candidates in the pool of finalists the second time around. Did the Black candidate recognize the discrimination that I believe occurred, or was it seen as just another rejected application? I don't know. But this case highlighted for me one of the reasons that affirmative action is still needed. As social psychologist Faye Crosby writes,

> Affirmative action is needed to lessen bias in the paid labor force because affirmative action is the only legal remedy in the United States for discrimination that does not require the victims (or someone with a stake in their welfare) to notice their condition and come forward with a grievance on their own behalf. . . . In affirmative action, designated individuals monitor the operations of institutions and so can notice (and correct) injustices in the absence of any complaint. This monitoring role is crucial because an accumulation of studies' have shown that it is very difficult to detect discrimination on a case-by-case basis, even when the case involves the self.

When we examine the aggregate data, case after case, hiring decision after hiring decision, the idiosyncrasies of particular cases recede and the discriminatory pattern can emerge. Then we can make a change.

Discussion Questions

- Why do you believe the United States has the highest incarceration rate in the world?

- What is meant by the prison-industrial complex? Is this notion real?

- Did Kemba Smith's testimony alter your view of drug dealers? If so, how?

- Why do you think the Supreme Court is unwilling to consider racially dispro-portionate results as an indication that the constitutional mandate of equality has been violated?

- Why are affirmative action policies viewed as fundamentally unfair by many people, while disability policies are usually viewed more positively?

- What are some other ways, besides those described above, in which law and policy build in advantages for one racial or ethnic group over another?

- How would you describe the relationship between justice and law?

Social Change

Social change is a complex process because it involves both institutional readjustments and changes in prevailing thinking about social issues. Consider, for example, the issue of domestic violence. Feminists helped policy makers reconceptualize domestic violence. What had been considered a matter internal to families became a crime deserving of a meaningful response from police, prosecutors, and courts. This significant achievement has not been problem free, however, as a solution to safety for women and vulnerable family members. Social inequality and social identity affect women's willingness to report domestic violence. Immigration status and national origin, for example, have a discernable impact on how women understand domestic violence and what they feel empowered to do about it.[15]

Social change efforts often involve public protest. How such events are conducted, what media coverage they receive, and how decision makers react all help determine how effective protest will be as a tool for social change in any particular case. After the passage of Arizona's new immigration law, for example, there were rallies and vigils from groups opposing the legislation. Lawsuits were filed and boycotts were instituted. Meanwhile, law enforcement began to consider how it would enforce the new law, and educational efforts were instituted. The response has had an organized character, at least on the surface.

Other causes have provoked what appear to be more spontaneous forms of protest. Consider, for example, the 1995 Million Man March on Washington[16] or the famous August 28, 1963, protest demanding federal civil rights legislation. On that day, more than 250,000 people of all races marched on Washington, DC, to lobby for equality, freedom, and jobs, culminating more than a decade of protest and resistance to segregation and racial subordination.[17] Before that giant audience, Dr. Martin Luther King Jr. delivered his famous, "I Have a Dream[18]" speech. The passion of the people that marched on Washington and their many supporters was in large part responsible for the passage of the Civil Rights Act of 1964.[19] Protest works, at least sometimes.

The issue is how to mobilize individuals and groups with shared concerns. The process of mobilization is itself an educational experience for those who participate, and protesters hope, for those who witness the effort. Education can also be a mobilizing experience. Consider this description of prisoners who drew upon what they were learning to create changes in their circumstances and in themselves. Alan Gomez,

[15]Edna Erez, Madelaine Adelman, and Carol Gregory, "Intersections of Immigration and Domestic Violence," *Feminist Criminology*, vol. 4 (1): 32–56 (2009).

[16]Under the leadership of the Nation of Islam leader Louis Farrakhan, African American men from around the country gathered on the National Mall to show America a positive picture of black men.

[17]Patrik Henry Bass, *Like a Mighty Stream: The March on Washington, August 28, 1963.* (Philadelphia: Running Press, 2002).

[18]Dr. Martin Luther King Jr., "I Have a Dream," in *A Call To Conscience: The Landmark Speeches of Dr. Martin Luther King, Jr.*, edited by Clayborne Carson, Kris Shepard, and Andrew Young (New York: Warner Books, 2001), pp. 75–88.

[19]Civil Rights Act of 1964, H.R. 7152 (Congress of the United States of America, January 7, 1964).

whose work was cited earlier in this chapter, observed how education affected the lives of the prisoners he studied:

> Inmates organized GED and cultural history courses, created social and cultural groups, published journals and newspapers, acted as prison lawyers or writ writers to defend themselves in a court of law. All of these efforts not only led to changes in prison policies and constitutional law, but perhaps most importantly transformed the lives of these inmates in a positive manner.[20]

In the next reading, David Meyer considers the relationship between social movements, mobilization, and policy change. He details the influence that participatory democracy has over social policy reform, using examples of the Bonus Marchers and opposition to the Vietnam War. Think about what general lessons you can draw from his historical examples.

THE POLICY CONNECTION: HOW MOVEMENTS MATTER
DAVID S. MEYER

At the height of the Great Depression, in the spring of 1932, unemployed veterans of the First World War (then called the "Great War"), desperate for work, called for the federal government to pay them their service bonus, amounting to no more than $1,000 — and often much less—immediately rather than waiting until 1945, when the bonus was originally scheduled to be paid. Across the country, groups of veterans started separate marches to Washington, D.C., where the federal government might consider such a demand, conducting parades along the way. As reports of the marches spread, new marches started, and other veterans (sometimes surreptitiously) rode freight trains, organized car caravans, or hitchhiked. Ultimately more than twenty thousand veterans would converge on the Capitol.

In February of 1932, a Democratic congressman from Texas had introduced a bill calling for the accelerated payment of the bonus, but the bill faced opposition from both the right (too expensive!) and the left (why not money for all people in need, rather than just veterans?). The Bonus Marchers hoped that their presence would force Congress to vote on the bill and that then they would be able to defeat its opponents at the polls in November. At once, the idea behind the Bonus March was

---

[20]Gomez, *Behind Bars*, pp. 67–96.

From *The Politics of Protest*: Social Movement in America by David S. Meyer, pp. 162–180. Oxford University Press 2007.

both radical (government spending provoked by direct action) and profoundly conservative (money directed to veterans who had proved their patriotism, delivered through the most conventional political means). The eventual outcomes of this bold idea illustrate much about protest politics in America and draw our attention directly to the relationships among protest, institutional politics, and public policy.

By the end of May 1932, the first three hundred marchers from Oregon had reached the outskirts of Washington, with thousands more following on their heels. President Herbert Hoover and District of Columbia Police Superintendent Pelham Glassford welcomed the veterans, guardedly, warning them about associating with Socialists and Communists. Glassford, himself a veteran of the war, met frequently with the "Bonus Expeditionary Forces," numbering more than five thousand by early June, and arranged for a safe campground in Anacostia, across the Potomac River from the District of Columbia. He also helped the marchers set up their camps and makeshift kitchens and raised money from local merchants to find food for the marchers. The Bonus Marchers asked him to serve as their "secretary-treasurer," and he agreed, even while still preparing to protect the Capitol from the veterans, including securing tear gas for the district's police force. At the same time, the newly appointed chief of staff of the U.S. Army, Douglas MacArthur, much less sympathetic than Glassford, developed his own militarized plans to control the marchers and the streets of Washington.

On June 7, the Bonus Army conducted its first large parade, displaying in an orderly fashion decorated war heroes, disabled veterans, and veterans (including African Americans from diverse backgrounds and regions of the country. They emphasized their service, their patriotism, and their discipline, winning some support from Congress and the press in the process. Implicitly, they also emphasized their desperation, because men with jobs could not spend months traveling to the Capitol and camp out on lawns to support a demand for a relatively small cash payment. Their parades were complemented by organized visits to the offices of members of Congress, a kind of grassroots lobbying. Although some members of Congress expressed sympathy for the marchers, others proclaimed that they would never vote for such a payment when under the implicit pressure of men encamped at the national capital.

On June 17, the Bonus Army gathered outside the Capitol while the Senate considered the Bonus Bill inside. When the Bonus Bill was soundly defeated (62–18), the veterans were forced to reconsider their strategy. Although they marched in an orderly fashion back to the camp across the river, they refused to leave the city; indeed, more Bonus Marchers continued to arrive, with close to twenty thousand veterans encamped throughout Washington most in Camp Anacostia. In response to legislative defeat, the veterans refocused on extending their message to reach a new audience, the broader public, rather than just Congress, and expanded their demands to include relief for all needy people. They also welcomed some families into their camps, stressing the presence of women and children within their ranks Some of their leaders traveled to other cities on the East Coast to raise money to feed the marchers.

The tensions of the long encampment affected everyone as the marchers grew frustrated and the police impatient. A faction of Communist veterans tried to press others to escalate their rhetoric and to include the White House in their targets for protest, and District of Columbia police conducted preemptive arrests on those near the White House. The end of July, as Congress prepared to adjourn its legislative session, authorities grew more determined to clear the veterans out of the city. Local and national officials issued eviction orders to the encamped veterans, and General MacArthur and the army began enforcing those orders on July 28, overrunning the camps, using tear gas, and burning the shacks the protesters were living in. Most of the veterans fled the encampments in the face of the army's superior force, but some men fought back by throwing rocks, effectively encouraging MacArthur's strategy of relatively aggressive force. Seeking to justify the use bayonets and tear gas, MacArthur, publicly supported by President Hoover (who kept his own misgivings private), suggested that a strong Communist presence had hijacked Bonus March effort and that many of the men present weren't even veterans. Both charges proved false, but the veterans were routed from the Capitol, and pictures and movies of the burning shacks filled newsreels across the country.

In November 1932, Franklin Delano Roosevelt defeated Hoover's bid for reelection by a landslide. When Bonus Marchers reappeared in early 1933, President Roosevelt arranged for lodging, food, and bathrooms at an army post in Virginia and provided ready transport for veterans who wished to demonstrate in the capital. Roosevelt received a delegation.

Bonus veterans at the White House, and his wife, Eleanor, followed by newsreel cameras, visited their encampment. Although Roosevelt initially opposed paying the bonus, he offered the veterans priority for employment in the newly established Civilian Conservation Corps; by 1936, in the context of a rapidly expanding set of relief programs and the beginnings of a social safety net, he agreed to pay the bonus as well (Amenta 1998).

The story of the Bonus March cuts through many of the issues involving protest movements and American politics and focuses our attention particularly on the interaction of movements with the larger policy process.

To begin, the Bonus Marchers continued what had already become a well-established tradition of personally carrying their claims to Washington. It began, according to Lucy Barber (2002), in 1894 with Coxey's Army, an offshoot of Populist dissatisfaction with American politics that marched to call for public spending to create jobs, employing what activists called a "petition with boots." The tactic and the space were emulated in 1913 by the suffragettes, who paraded throughout the city and called for the extension of the franchise. The Mall has become a common place for people with grievances. In our time, we see the same space used, and then imitated, by all sorts of contemporary movements, ranging from the Million Man March, which called for African American men to gain control of their communities, to the Million Mom March, which called for governments at all levels to work for handgun control.

Groups go to Washington for a number of reasons, not the least of these being that it is where government works, where decisions are made, policies made, and money allocated. Demonstrating near the buildings that house American government, activists send a direct message to legislators, to the Supreme Court, and to the president. More than that, by demonstrating in Washington, they try to use the nation's press to speak to their allies across the country and to inspire other sorts of action, including the most routine conventional politics as laid out in the Constitution. The demonstration is an expression of a cause, an expression of a constituency, and an analysis about what is to be done.

Tracing Social Movement Influence

The Bonus Marchers got exactly what they initially demanded within four years of the protest, as Franklin Roosevelt initiated a massive transformation of federal government official welfare policies (Amenta 1998). Indeed, full payment of the bonus was a very large piece of that transformation. The legacies of most movement effects, however, play out over a longer period of time and are more difficult to trace. Take, for example, the movement against American involvement in the Vietnam War.

There were already all kinds of good reasons to oppose U.S. participation in the Vietnam War in 1965, when Lyndon Johnson announced that he would increase the American military presence in Vietnam by nearly fifty thousand troops. Providing these men meant expanding the military draft, and the expanded draft turned a distant issue, them in faraway Vietnam, into a proximate one and stoked the fledgling antiwar movement draft provided both a focus for the antiwar movement and a sense of urgency on college campuses to do something to stop the war.

The salience of the draft invigorated what had formerly been small pacifist and peace organizations mobilizing and coordinating the initial opposition to the war, flooding local chapters and national events with larger numbers of new activists than any of the organizations was prepared to handle. The expanded draft created much greater potential audiences for the committed peace lobby. It helped groups such as Students for a Democratic Society (SDS), which expressed a broad commitment to comprehensive democratic change in the United States, to spread quickly across American college campuses

The rapid growth of the antiwar movement also created difficulties for those who would organize it. New recruits to organizations working against the war didn't necessarily share commitments to pacifism or "participatory democracy." The newly swollen armed organizations also provided a larger venue, as well as the prospects of higher payoff for everyone involved in the movement, encouraging internecine fights about ideology and tactics. Many organizations didn't survive.

More significant for this chapter, the larger, more volatile, more public, and more diverse antiwar movement made life even more difficult for government seeking, minimally, domestic peace. In his memoirs, Richard Nixon (1978: 396–404) claims that the antiwar protesters constrained his options in Vietnam, preempting his using nuclear weapons in Vietnam—or even his making a credible threat to use nuclear weapons. Of course, at the time President Nixon repeatedly proclaimed that the antiwar movement would not affect his policies. Politicians are understandably reluctant to admit that social movements affected their conduct. Such an admission could only undermine the politicians' credibility.

Still, politicians respond to movements, even if they don't acknowledge doing so. Richard Nixon certainly did. One obvious response to the antiwar movement was extending the franchise to eighteen-year-olds, who were already eligible for the draft. Another response was instituting a draft lottery before ultimately ending the draft. Of course, it wasn't only the political problems at home that encouraged the end of the draft. Conscripts created discipline problems in the field and were more likely to attack their own officers with guns and grenades than were volunteers.

The end of the draft in 1972, following ratification of the twenty-sixth Amendment the previous year, altered the political terrain dramatically for the antiwar movement. As electoral possibilities for organizing opened, organizers simultaneously lost some portion of the zealous new converts, terrified for their own lives even as they opposed the war. James Fallows (1981: 136) observes, "the history of Vietnam demonstrated the difference between abstract and self-interested actions. Resistance to the war went up in proportion as the effects of the war (primarily, the draft) touched the children of influential families." Although the antiwar movement may well have won, as U.S. involvement in Vietnam ultimately ended, the pacifists lost their connections with movement politics, and broader claims about invigorated and genuine democracy, as expressed by SDS, mostly disappeared from American political life or were reformulated in much more moderate terms as procedural reforms.

Social Movements and Policy Change

In the 1960s, at the height of a range of social movements, scholars sought to determine whether protest, as an addition to more routine politics, helps activists get what they want. The initial answers, focusing on movements on behalf of the poor were positive. For people poorly positioned in the political system, protest and disruption proved to be a way to get their concerns taken to a broader audience and, sometimes, to have them addressed. Frances Fox Piven and Richard Cloward looked particularly at social welfare spending, finding that government often increased spending on social welfare in response to political unrest; essentially, spending was a way to buy quiet during difficult political times. Absent political turmoil, however, that spending could be withdrawn.

Sociologist William Gamson, writing at about the same time, looked at a broader range of social movements. He randomly selected fifty-three groups that had challenged government to act on a broad variety of issues between 1800 and 1945, then followed the historical record forward fifteen years from the height of a challenge. If some of what a group had wanted became policy (new advantages) or if it won formal recognition as a legitimate political player (acceptance), Gamson coded it as a winner, then set out to discover the characteristics of groups that won or lost. This pioneering analysis, however, raised more questions than it answered. For example, how can you tell which group affected policy change when more than one group was involved and they were all doing different things? How did groups translate their efforts into policy change? Why did policy responses seem to come in flurries and at defined times, rather than gradually in direct responses to movements?

In fact, the policy process is long and complicated, with many steps between an idea for reform and the adoption and implementation of a new policy. This is particularly true in the United States where Madison and the founders designed a system that they intended to slow the process of political change. Even in the simplest model of policy reform, recounted in grade school as "how a bill becomes a law," introduction of a policy proposal in one House in Congress is followed by committee hearings, revisions, consideration in the other House of Congress, followed by more revisions, negotiations between leaders of both Houses of Congress, and then presidential approval. It's not surprising that social movement activism can weigh in more heavily in the earlier stages in the policy process, when much of the activity takes place in public and many officials have the opportunity to act, than in later stages of the process when rules are more rigid, the number of significant factors smaller, and much of the action takes place behind closed doors. In order to understand the relationship between social movements and public policy, we need to recognize a longer and more complicated policy process, and to realize that even when social movements affect change, they rarely get all they want.

How Movements Matter

By recognizing the add-on role that movements play in the normal policy process, we can see how social movements sometimes matter, identifying the means through which successful movement activists exercise influence.

An active social movement alters the calculations that those inside mainstream politics—and in office—make about their actions. When a mobilized effort demonstrates strength and commitment, it can make the current policy course untenable or make long-simmering ideas appear suddenly viable. At the same time, mainstream political figures suddenly have to address the same broader audience engaged by the movement, and they must explain and justify their policies more frequently and in more detail. As we saw with the Bonus March, President Hoover had to explain why, in a time of widespread unemployment, he didn't favor helping veterans with a relatively small cash payment. Similarly, during the period of antiapartheid protests in Washington, D.C., President Reagan was forced to explain his policies toward South Africa far more frequently than were any of his predecessor all of whom had managed essentially the same policy. Richard Nixon, facing the antiwar movement, had to explain again and again just what his plan for peace was, and each subsequent version was a little different. More outside attention to the content of policy and policymaking process can make more substantial reforms possible.

The institutionalization of movement concerns can mean changes in policies, if not in what activists ask for; it also makes it harder for activists to mobilize active support in the same way. Generally, organizers see their most visible policy demand, be it banning DDT, passing a voting rights act or an equal rights amendment, or freezing the nuclear arms race, as the leading edge in a broad movement to remake the world. Institutionalization of concerns means, to varying degrees, settling for something less than that. Thus, appointees to the Arms Control and Disarmament Agency learn to speak of only the first objective in the agency's name, and opponents of pollution learn to negotiate acceptable levels of contaminants. And feminists learn to rely on legislators who make it easier to convict and punish rapists, even if ignoring larger oppressions in society.

For elected officials, understanding this reality means the constant search for balancing points on policy to stabilize their political environment: giving enough to quell disturbances, but not so much as to generate disruption from the other side. For activists, understanding this reality means making hard calculations about the costs, as well as the benefits, of concessions on matters of policy and political inclusion. It also means there is always work to be done.

How Stories Matter

Organizers can use stories of movements of the past to spur or support new efforts. Narratives of past influence can maintain the enthusiasm of the faithful, mobilize new activists by providing a plan for contemporary actions, and make sense of current political challenges. That the civil rights movement is broadly accepted as a cause of significant improvements in the lives of millions has been a source of inspiration for other social movements—on the right as well as the left—providing a sense that movement efforts in the service of a moral cause against great odds are worthwhile. In contrast, when movement efforts are viewed by those who initiated them as costly and ultimately futile, recruiting activists in the future may be difficult.

In looking at the stories of influence told by social movement activists and their competitors, we can identify the implicit negotiations in constructing accepted narratives of influence. Perhaps the most successful case, that of the civil rights movement for African Americans, demonstrates both the extent and limits of success claimed. Although the movement is widely given credit for winning basic civil rights, its popular image emphasizes charismatic leadership, rather than political organizing, most notably in the eventual inclusion of Martin Luther King Jr. in the pantheon of national heroes. The frequently told story of Rosa Parks's civil disobedience on a bus in Montgomery in December 1955 is taken out of the organizational and political context of the day. Parks is remembered as a tired old lady, with rarely a mention of her connections to long-standing organizations such as the NAACP and the Highlander Folk School's leadership programs.

In short, although the movement's influence is acknowledged, the movement itself is often portrayed as something inevitable or mystical, almost apart from politics, and not something that people today could organize. Even in a story of influence, the neglect of context and organization in favor of spontaneity or magic, what

Taylor (1989) terms a myth of "immaculate conception," undermines the prospects of subsequent mobilization, giving little clear direction to today's organizers.

American Politics: You Can't Ever Get All You Want

Most activists are always going to be able to find disappointments in the outcomes of their efforts. First, because movements are comprised of coalitions, in which people and groups unify around common demands, many activists are going to see their most cherished goals left out of the movement campaign, much less any ultimate policy reform. Second, the nature of the American political system prizes compromise, even as politicians and organizers are rewarded for using polemics outside of *government*. Whereas mobilization is generally based on promising more than you can deliver, legislation is based on making sure you deliver whatever you carl. Third, because the ultimate translation of protest into policy is undertaken by mainstream political figures, including elected officials and bureaucrats, social movement activists will always have to compete with more established figures to get their story out. And those established figures will have an incentive to oversell the programs they enact.

In American politics, polemical rhetoric dominates. Politicians talk about "saving Social Security", fighting a "war" against drugs after losing another one against poverty, or adopting "zero tolerance" for crime or environmental pollution. *There is a mismatch between political rhetoric that emphasizes absolutes and a political process that prizes compromise and incrementalism.* Thus, the dynamics of contemporary American politics virtually mandate that *most people are going to be disappointed most of the time.*

Paradoxically, disappointment is most likely for the movements that achieve the most. Effecting social and political change is a result of the process of institutionalization, that is, getting people into positions of power and, even more importantly, getting your ideas into mainstream culture and politics. Social movements carry new ideas to a broader audience, and when they succeed in getting their ideas into the mainstream, they lose control of how those ideas are presented. American social movements are poorly positioned to reject institutional figures who claim to speak for them. An opponent of government regulation of pollution can claim to be an environmentalist, and the more successful a movement has been, the more attractive its labels are—and the easier they are to poach. People with no previous connection to a movement such as the women's movement, for example, can claim to be feminists—or environmentalists or animal rights supporters or peace activists. In doing so, they make explicit claims not only about their own identity, but also about the politics and identity of the larger movements.

In the article that concludes this chapter, Willie V. Bryan, describes the fight to amend the Civil Rights Act of 1964 to prohibit discrimination in employment based on physical and mental disability. He shows how persons with disabilities fought to gain minority status and thereby gain the protection afforded other minority groups.

STRUGGLE FOR FREEDOM:
DISABILITY RIGHTS MOVEMENTS
WILLIE V. BRYAN

Lack of Concern

Since World War II, there has been an increasing emphasis on human and civil rights in the United States. Minorities and women have spoken out on their own behalf attempting to gain the privileges, freedoms, and rights guaranteed for all Americans by the Constitution. While legal and social ground has been won and lost throughout the years, many minorities and women now enjoy a somewhat more equal existence in the United States than some fifty years ago. Still, the battle for equality is far from victorious. While other groups continue their struggle, individuals with disabilities have joined forces to end discrimination in their lives and claim a life of equality in the United States.

The Civil Rights movement of the sixties resulted in legislation designed to bar discrimination based on sex, race, and national origin; however, prohibition of discrimination based on physical and/or mental disabilities was not included. As Thomas D. Schneid reminds us, a bill introduced in Congress in 1971 to amend Title VI of the Civil Rights Act of 1964 to prohibit discrimination based on physical or mental disability died in committee. Similarly, in 1972, another bill introduced in Congress, this time to amend Title VII of the Civil Rights Act to bar discrimination in employment based upon physical or mental disabilities, also died in committee. This may be seen as somewhat of a barometer of the level of concern lawmakers and many other nondisabled Americans had with regard to the civil rights of persons with disabilities.

Perhaps the lack of concern demonstrated by these actions of Congress is more of a reflection of ignorance of the needs and capabilities of persons with disabilities rather than a blatant desire to deny the civil rights of a group of people. At the time, the thought was that employers should not be forced to hire persons who could not adequately perform the required tasks. Persons with disabilities and their friends certainly were not advocating employment of nonqualified persons; they were simply asking that employers be required to look beyond a person's limitation to see abilities and attempt to match them with the required job. Employers also had a number of misconceptions with regard to employing persons with disabilities, such as they would not be able to secure insurance for the person and the company's insurance premiums would increase. Another major misconception was the belief that persons with disabilities were unsafe employees. This erroneous belief was held despite safety records indicating that persons with disabilities had fewer accidents than nondisabled employees. Many employers were aware that by making modifications to the work site and/or its environment, a significant number of jobs could be made accessible to persons with disabilities; however, these same employers harbored the belief that making these accommodations would be too expensive. Again, this belief was held even though the DuPont Company had demonstrated that many changes to a work site could be done inexpensively.

These and other misconceptions were firmly held by employers because persons with disabilities and their advocates did not vigorously dispute them. The lack of opposition to discrimination against persons with disabilities with respect to employment allowed longheld stereotypes and prejudices to continue unchallenged. Activism would be necessary to dramatize the extent of the lack of concern for the rights of persons with disabilities and cause action to be taken to correct the neglect that had become an accepted method of treatment of persons with disabilities.

Minority Status

Until recently, persons with disabilities were not widely considered a minority group. In fact, it was not until the Rehabilitation Act of 1973 that they were considered a "class" of people. Persons with disabilities are members of other groups of people, they are male or female, and they have an ethnic identity; their rights and privileges are associated with whatever cultural and/or gender group they belong. It is ironic that with regard to human rights their disabilities were secondary to their cultural and/or gender identity, but with regard to their rights as citizens, their disabilities were primary, overshadowing gender and/or cultural identity. Since disability groups were not considered a culture at the time, the person with a disability was viewed as a "disabled member of another class."

Another reason for the lack of class status is that there are large numbers of disabilities and each one is considered a separate condition within its own group identity. For example, there are persons who have disabilities resulting from polio, arthritis, visual impairments, hearing impairments, lupus, mental illness, mental retardation, amputations, and paralysis, to mention only a few. In most cases, there was and continues to be associations or foundations which are considered the official representative for all who have a particular condition. This has the effect of segregating disabilities into distinct disease groups, thus causing each disabling condition to stand alone and not be part of a larger whole. This internal segregation combined with society's segregation of persons with disabilities has been devastating to efforts of persons with disabilities to unite and demand their constitutional rights.

Although it would not be until the passage of the Rehabilitation Act of 1973 that persons with disabilities would obtain the classification of minority status and be officially viewed as a class of people, several years before the passage of the act they began to think of themselves as a minority. And more importantly, they began to view their life conditions as having been deprived of their basic human rights similar to other minority groups. They also began to think of themselves as being oppressed and disenfranchised. With this realization, they began to unite and to speak openly about the manner in which they were being excluded from full participation in society's activities. Thinking of themselves as oppressed minorities, they also thought of the manner in which other minority groups had placed their agenda before the American people; thus a "grassroots disability rights movement" began which has resulted in the passage of the ADA in 1990.

Grassroots Movement

Despite the concern exhibited by charitable organizations and Congress, the one aspect often missing was the involvement of persons with disabilities. For example, much of the legislation prior to the Rehabilitation Act of 1973 had been developed with little, if any, input from persons with disabilities. Charitable organizations established telethons to raise funds for research and/or provide services without giving much thought to the negative images being projected. This was "business as usual" or stated another way, it was the continuation of the paternalistic attitude that has existed in America for many decades. Perhaps without meaning harm to persons with disabilities, nondisabled persons have treated them as though they are incapable of determining and expressing how they would like to live their lives. Regardless of how well-intended the motivation of a non-oppressed person there are some things he/she will either overlook or not understand with regard to the effects of being oppressed. Therefore it is imperative that those affected must be involved in determining the best methods for eliminating the problems created by oppression.

Independent Living Movement

The quest for independence by most Americans does not occur by accident, but is a quality that is taught and reinforced to every American youth, both by formal teaching and by example. American history is replete with both fictional and factual persons accomplishing or attempting to accomplish extraordinary deeds to establish or maintain their independence.

Independence is therefore highly valued in American society; it is considered an essential building block in constructing and maintaining a democracy. Freedom, to an extent, is reliant upon its citizens having the independence to build better lives for themselves and in the process of accomplishing their dreams, they lift freedom and democracy to new levels. Conversely, being dependent is devalued in American society and those that are considered so are often assigned lower positions on the social totem pole. To many, the word "dependent" denotes lack of initiative, laziness, and a burden upon society. Although public and private social welfare agencies and organizations including hospitals, clinics, and rehabilitation centers, to mention a few, have been developed to assist persons who by virtue of illness, accident, or birth defects must rely upon assistive services, the recipients are often viewed in a negative light and at best given sympathy instead of empathy and understanding.

Given the value placed on independence by American society, no one should be amazed that persons with disabilities began to recognize and resent the limited role society drafted for them. They correctly perceived that society equated disability with dependency. They also recognized that this perception created a very low ceiling and an almost insurmountable wall around their abilities to function and achieve.

In the early seventies, persons with disabilities began to realize that to be truly free they must take and maintain control of their lives. This train of thought resulted in the development of Independent Living Centers (ILCs). Dejong provides a brief history of the genesis of Independent Living Centers as he reveals that a small group of persons with disabilities at the University of Illinois and at the University of California at Berkeley moved out of their residential hospital setting into the community and organized their own system for delivery of survival services. The centers established by these students became the blueprint by which future centers would be established. As might be expected, since the inception of these centers, the scope of services has expanded. Even so, the idea of persons with disabilities taking greater control of their lives remains the same. Perhaps Dejong best summarizes the independent living philosophy when he said the dignity of risk is what the independent movement is all about. Without the possibility of failure, a person with a disability is said to lack true independence and the mark of one's humanity: the right to choose for good or evil.

When one considers that the independent living movement was initiated by persons with disabilities, many of whom were persons with severe disabilities such as spinal cord injuries, it became quite apparent that these individuals exhibited courage of the highest magnitude. Although prior to the movement they lived in conditions that made them almost totally dependent upon others, it was a safe environment; therefore, moving from this safe environment to face the many uncertainties created by a society with many barriers and obstacles certainly qualifies the founding members as pioneers.

More Than Work

Work is so much a central part of most Americans' lives that it, in part, defines who we are. It is common for Americans to describe someone by identifying their occupation. For example, we may identify someone as Mary Smith the attorney, or John Smith the teacher. Work has been the defining feature in American lives for many years. The Puritan work ethic is a standard by which Americans often judge each other. While we no longer subscribe to the theory of hard work for all, we most certainly subscribe to the idea of work for all. Work provides us with economic power to purchase goods and services which in part by virtue of the amount and types of goods we accumulate determines our social standing in America. Social condemnation is the reward for those that are able to work but do not. Work not only is a means by which we develop, maintain or improve our societal standing in American society, it also is patriotic. In a capitalist society, it is through the production of products that our nation develops its standing in the world as compared to other nations.

Obviously, work has many important meanings to Americans and American society. Considering the position work holds in American life, it is easy to understand why virtually all rehabilitation legislation prior to the 1972 Rehabilitation Act emphasized "vocational rehabilitation." In fact, when we speak of rehabilitating a person with a disability we think the ultimate goal of the rehabilitation process is to make the person ready for a job. There is one thing wrong with this approach: what about the person who is unable to work because of the severity or perhaps type of disability? Unless they and/or their families have sufficient financial resources, they have to rely upon sympathy and charity of others as well as some social welfare assistance from the federal government. Because of the social stigma of not working and receiving charity, these persons' independence, self-dignity, and ability to participate as full American citizens are in jeopardy.

Perhaps these reasons, as well as others, caused the disability rights movement leaders to lobby Congress to deemphasize "vocational" in the Rehabilitation Act of 1972. It is unfortunate that the Nixon Administration did not comprehend what persons with disabilities were saying as they lobbied for removal of "vocational" from the rehabilitation act. In part, what they were saying, and perhaps today we are just beginning to hear, is that a person's worth, self-respect, and dignity should not be measured by employment and moreover measured by whether employed in a job, especially if that person is unable to work. The leaders were wise to note that no person with a disability would be totally free until all persons with disabilities had opportunities to more fully participate in American life. Again it was this type of thinking that led them to push for independent living centers, and the abolishment of the segregation of persons with disabilities so they could not only become more involved in American society, but also make decisions that would effect the quality of their lives. In short, they recognized that to be free, life for a person with a disability meant more than being able to work.

Discussion Questions

- Is there a tipping point that causes people to react and begin to protest, or are the moments when protest occurs more a function of charismatic leadership that precipitates social change?

- What roles do negative changes in law and policy have in influencing social protests?

- In what ways might protests against long-standing laws be different in character than those brought about by a notable change in law, for example, the Arizona statute mandating local police involvement in the enforcement of federal immigration law?

- Persons with disabilities have fought to be treated equally; is it possible that the Americans with Disabilities Act actually forces employers to treat persons with disabilities differently from others?

Chapter 4

HUMAN RIGHTS, MIGRATION, AND CITIZENSHIP

The topics we have introduced up until this point have focused mainly on the United States and its culture, economy, and politics. This chapter and the one that follows take us to a broader, global level, where the issues of justice and how to reach it are more complex than ever. One way to approach these issues is to begin with the powerful concept that all humans have a basic set of rights that should be honored. Why? Because we are all human beings—nothing more is required. This perspective raises critical questions about the role of nation states in matters of justice. A key question in this chapter is whether human rights can be achieved in a world broken into so many separate pieces. Does citizenship, which confers rights to people as citizens, conflict with human rights, which confers rights to people as people?

You are probably well aware of many of the rights citizens enjoy—the right to vote, for example, and for United States citizens, many other rights associated with freedom of speech and criminal proceedings, as well as the right to certain government benefits and consular assistance when an American citizen goes abroad. There are also advantages on the job market. Of course, there are also obligations too, including, for men, the possibility of mandatory military service. Do citizens in a democracy also have a duty to be well informed, even critically minded, toward their government? "Eternal vigilance," Thomas Jefferson argued, is "the price of democracy." What about differences in the ability to make one's voice heard—can anything be done about that? How serious a problem is discrimination?

The well-worn term "second-class citizenship" suggests that all citizens do not enjoy the same rights and privileges, despite "equality under law." Law often reinforces inequality—slavery is a notorious example. It is helpful also to consider the case of white women, whose citizenship was never an issue, but who were for over a century oppressed by laws that restricted their right to hold or accumulate property, gave them little recourse against abuse or abandonment by their husbands, and, until they won a hard-fought battle for the franchise, prevented them from voting in elections. The battle for formal equality has finally been won, but laws continue to create disadvantages for some citizens. This raises the question of citizen apathy. Why are voters so willing to let oppressive laws stand and to ignore other serious problems by not voting or not taking the time to be well-informed? This is a question that this chapter examines.

The benefits of citizenship are perhaps most evident to people who do not have it. Stateless persons are in a terrible predicament, enjoying no rights that they can count on because governments remain the source of enforceable rights. When the Nazi regime declared Jews noncitizens of the Reich, for example, they became stateless persons, losing the right to have rights.[1] Do citizens have a moral duty to assist such people? To treat them fairly? And what about the related problem of people working and residing without citizenship in the nation where they live? Sometimes people come with legal authorization to remain, and sometimes they come without it. Governments are attempting to crack down on residents without authorization, but at the same time nations are competing for certain kinds of workers and are opening their doors wider to trade and foreign investment. There are benefits to open economies and free flow of labor because capitalism is more and more a globally organized phenomenon. But this flow creates problems, both for labor and for governments. Global capitalism challenges the power of individual nations to determine their own destinies. Massive human migration is another challenge for governments, which still operate on the basis that they have national sovereignty, that is, power to do what they consider best for their own citizens, even at the expense of noncitizens.

The shrinking globe raises new questions about our duties toward one another, not so much as citizens of any particular nation or workers engaged in common tasks, but as beings connected by our shared humanity. The idea that there are some interests so basic that they belong to all humans simply because they are human can be traced at least to the Enlightenment period of the 18th century. Not until after World War II, however, did governments begin to negotiate specific human rights that they would pledge to promote. World War II was a wake-up call to leaders around the world of the need to specify what is, and is not, acceptable in any nation's laws. One important result was the United Nations Declaration of Human Rights, adopted by the United Nations General Assembly in 1948. Many of the provisions bear a striking resemblance

---

[1]Hannah Arendt made this observation on p. 395 of *The Origins of Totalitarianism*, New York: Harcourt Brace Jovanovich, 1979, originally published in 1951. More recently Giorgio Agamben revisited this problem, suggesting that humans without the protection of a government are *homo sacer*, in a condition where all they have is their biological existence, or "bare life" (*Homo Sacer: Sovereign Power and Bare Life*, Stanford, CA: Stanford University Press, 1998).

to individual rights long guaranteed by democratic nations, though some go beyond what most of these governments promise to provide their citizens.

This chapter considers the relationship between individuals and government. What does justice demand in this area? Advocates of natural law believe that individuals have inherent rights that governments must respect. Some of these ideas have been incorporated into contemporary regimes of human rights and civil rights. Citizenship undoubtedly helps ensure that government will respect basic rights, but what of noncitizens? Do they have rights? What rights? And why does this matter? These are questions we reach in this chapter.

Human Rights

The idea that people have god-given or natural rights that government cannot legitimately infringe upon is very old and continues to play an important role in ideas about the proper role of government. This idea that there are inherent limits of government's legitimate power is particularly compelling. It underlies many political struggles, both violent and nonviolent. One well-known example is the Magna Carta, which English nobles drafted in 1215 to challenge the divine right of kings to govern as they saw fit. In the 18th century, the concept of natural rights became the basis for successful popular revolutions. The French "Rights of Man" and the American Declaration of Independence each drew on the idea that individual rights were a fundamental aspect of humanity, and thus must be respected by government.

This idea continues to have a strong, and arguably growing, following. Martin Luther King framed his advocacy for full civil rights for African Americans in terms of a higher law. He claimed a moral duty to resist injustice, including segregation and other forms of discrimination. Recall that racial segregation was widespread at the time and had only recently been declared unconstitutional in the context of public schooling (Brown v. Board of Education (347 U.S.483 (1954)).

King delivered his famous "Letter from Birmingham Jail" on April 16, 1963. He had been arrested a few days earlier for violating Alabama's law against mass demonstrations. There was no mass demonstration, however. King and Ralph Abernathy had marched from the 6th Avenue Baptist Church into a waiting police wagon, suggesting a highly symbolic protest. That same day, eight white Birmingham clergy wrote to criticize their strategy, calling it "unwise and untimely," and urging restraint. King's moving letter links the passion of the civil-rights struggle to the key idea that animates the human rights movement; that is, that all humans are equal in deserving respect and equal consideration before the law.

But how does this process of realization for the need for rights occur when government opposes any change in the status quo? One way of drawing attention to the issue is through civil disobedience, a type of political action that attempts to persuade people that they need changes, using moral example and suffering to make the point. Violence directed toward authorities, advocates of this approach believe, would not have the same political effect. The idea that civil disobedience can achieve social justice has a long pedigree. Sophocles produced the still-famous play *Antigone* in 442 B.C. The young Antigone rejects King Creon's order not to bury her warrior brother, arguing that the higher law compels a proper burial. Her defiance of the king results in her death. Her act, however, helps to undermine King Creon's credibility as a leader and brings misfortune to his realm.

The power of nonviolent resistance to authority is also evident in the successful struggles of American and British suffragettes to win the right to vote, and in the life of Mahatma Gandhi, who effectively used civil disobedience to draw attention to the injustice of continued British colonial rule in India in the early 1900s. Like the suffragettes, Gandhi's strategy was organized, mass nonviolent disobedience to laws that he and his supporters considered unjust and discriminatory. Arrest and even violence is to be expected and prepared for; the essential thing is not to strike back (see "Passive Resistance," *Swaraj: The Indian Home Rule* [Chapter 17], Ahmedabad, Gujarat [India]: Navjivan Press [1938]).

Martin Luther King was aware of the Universal Declaration of Human Rights when he wrote his letter in the Birmingham jail, but he chose not to make it the basis of his justification for his actions, perhaps because he knew that the immediate struggle was to gain basic civil rights, such as freedom from discrimination and race-based oppression for African Americans, and because he knew that the language of civil rights was more familiar and congenial to Americans. Yet from a human-rights perspective, King's famous letter could be considered a first step in a larger struggle for equal opportunity. He emphasized human dignity and decent treatment, which are key concepts in human-rights advocacy. These resoundingly secular goals have a practical quality—if you want peace and justice for yourself and others, you must honor human rights.

The concept of human rights first took on clear-cut dimensions in the drafting of the Universal Declaration of Human Rights, which almost all nations in the world have endorsed. Eleanor Roosevelt, widow of President Franklin Delano Roosevelt, was appointed by President Truman to take a leadership role in drafting a human-rights statement, and she did so with gusto. (For a fascinating, almost blow-by-blow account of the struggle to produce this document, see Mary Ann Glendon, *A World Made New: Eleanor Roosevelt and the Universal Declaration of Human Rights*, New York: Random House, 2001.)

Human rights claims legitimacy on the basis of the human condition, which is vulnerability, and the universal human desire to have a dignified life. The rights that flow from this base are broad. The Declaration of Human Rights sets forth rights to housing and employment and to found a family, along with more traditional civil rights and liberties. The idea that governments owe such duties to their citizens, however, is hotly contested, particularly in the United States. Americans tend to see rights in terms of an individual's right to self-expression, opportunity, and fair play—those rights guaranteed by the U.S. Constitution. This tendency to emphasize negative rights to be free of government interference, rather than positive rights to the enjoyment of basic support, tends to dampen American interest in human rights, at least on the home front. The United States has refused to ratify most human-rights conventions and exempted itself from some of those it has signed. The United States has not, for example, ratified the UN Convention on the Rights of the Child, which sets forth civil, political, economic, social, and cultural rights of children. Nor, almost alone among nations, has it ratified the Convention on the Elimination of All Forms of Discrimination against Women. It has, however, signed the Convention against Torture and Other Cruel, Inhuman or Degrading Treatment, which requires proactive measures to prevent acts of torture and prohibits torture under all circumstances and use of evidence obtained through torture.

Take a careful look at the rights set forth in the Universal Declaration of Human Rights, which appears below. Each of these rights is designed to promote and protect human dignity, but to people familiar with the civil rights and liberties guaranteed by the American Constitution, some of the items will seem very specific and perhaps unattainable. It would be helpful to compare and contrast the relatively young Declaration of Human Rights with the 200-year-old guarantees found in the amendments to the U.S. Constitution. Think about the differences you find.

UNIVERSAL DECLARATION OF HUMAN RIGHTS
UNITED NATIONS

Preamble

Whereas recognition of the inherent dignity and of the equal and inalienable rights of all members of the human family is the foundation of freedom, justice and peace in the world,

Whereas disregard and contempt for human rights have resulted in barbarous acts which have outraged the conscience of mankind, and the advent of a world in which human beings shall enjoy freedom of speech and belief and freedom from fear and want has been proclaimed as the highest aspiration of the common people,

Whereas it is essential, if man is not to be compelled to have recourse, as a last resort, to rebellion against tyranny and oppression, that human rights should be protected by the rule of law,

Whereas it is essential to promote the development of friendly relations between nations,

---

Universal Declaration of Human Rights. Adopted and proclaimed by General Assembly Resolution 217 A (III) of 10 December 1948. Reprinted by permission of the United Nations.

Whereas the peoples of the United Nations have in the Charter reaffirmed their faith in fundamental human rights, in the dignity and worth of the human person and in the equal rights of men and women and have determined to promote social progress and better standards of life in larger freedom,

Whereas Member States have pledged themselves to achieve, in co-operation with the United Nations, the promotion of universal respect for and observance of human rights and fundamental freedoms,

Whereas a common understanding of these rights and freedoms is of the greatest importance for the full realization of this pledge,

Now, therefore,

The General Assembly

Proclaims this Universal Declaration of Human Rights as a common standard of achievement for all peoples and all nations, to the end that every individual and every organ of society, keeping this Declaration constantly in mind, shall strive by teaching and education to promote respect for these rights and freedoms and by progressive measures, national and international, to secure their universal and effective recognition and observance, both among the peoples of Member States themselves and among the peoples of territories under their jurisdiction.

Article 1

All human beings are born free and equal in dignity and rights. They are endowed with reason and conscience and should act towards one another in a spirit of brotherhood.

Article 2

Everyone is entitled to all the rights and freedoms set forth in this Declaration, without distinction of any kind, such as race, colour, sex, language, religion, political or other opinion, national or social origin, property, birth or other status.

Furthermore, no distinction shall be made on the basis of the political, jurisdictional or international status of the country or territory to which a person belongs, whether it be independent, trust, non-self-governing or under any other limitation of sovereignty.

Article 3

Everyone has the right to life, liberty and the security of person.

Article 4

No one shall be held in slavery or servitude; slavery and the slave trade shall be prohibited in all their forms.

Article 5

No one shall be subjected to torture or to cruel, inhuman or degrading treatment or punishment.

Article 6

Everyone has the right to recognition everywhere as a person before the law.

Article 7

All are equal before the law and are entitled without any discrimination to equal protection against any discrimination in violation of this Declaration and against any incitement to such discrimination.

Article 8

Everyone has the right to an effective remedy by the competent national tribunals for acts violating the fundamental rights granted him by the constitution or by law.

Article 9

No one shall be subjected to arbitrary arrest, detention or exile.

Article 10

Everyone is entitled in full equality to a fair, and public hearing by an independent and impartial tribunal, in the determination of his rights and obligations and of any criminal charge against him.

Article 11

Everyone charged with a penal offence has the right to be presumed innocent until proven guilty according to law in a public trial at which he has had all the guarantees necessary for his defence. No one shall be held guilty of any penal offence on account of any act or omission which did not constitute a penal offence, under national or international law, at the time when it was committed. Nor shall a heavier penalty be imposed than the one that was applicable at the time the penal offence was committed.

Article 12

No one shall be subjected to arbitrary interference with his privacy, family, home or correspondence, nor to attacks upon his honour and reputation. Everyone has the right to the protection of the law against such interference or attacks.

Article 13

1. Everyone has the right to freedom of movement and residence within the borders of each State.

2. Everyone has the right to leave any country, including his own, and to return to his country.

Article 14

1. Everyone has the right to seek and to enjoy in other countries asylum from persecution.

2. This right may not be invoked in the case of prosecutions genuinely arising from non-political crimes or from acts contrary to the purposes and principles of the United Nations.

Article 15

1. Everyone has the right to a nationality.

2. No one shall be arbitrarily deprived of his nationality nor denied the right to change his nationality.

Article 16

1. Men and women of full age, without any limitation due to race, nationality or religion, have the right to marry and to found a family. They are entitled to equal rights as to marriage, during marriage and at its dissolution.

2. Marriage shall be entered into only with the free and full consent of the intending spouses.

3. The family is the natural and fundamental group unit of society and is entitled to protection by society and the State.

Article 17

1. Everyone has the right to own property alone as well as in association with others.

2. No one shall be arbitrarily deprived of his property.

Article 18

Everyone has the right to freedom of thought, conscience and religion; this right includes freedom to change his religion or belief, and freedom, either alone or in community with others and in public or private, to manifest his religion or belief in teaching, practice, worship and observance.

Article 19

Everyone has the right to freedom of opinion and expression; this right includes freedom to hold opinions without interference and to seek, receive and impart information and ideas through any media and regardless of frontiers.

Article 20

1. Everyone has the right to freedom of peaceful assembly and association.

2. No one may be compelled to belong to an association.

Article 21

1. Everyone has the right to take part in the government of his country, directly or through freely chosen representatives.

2. Everyone has the right of equal access to public service in his country.

3. The will of the people shall be the basis of the authority of government; this will shall be expressed in periodic and genuine elections which shall be by universal and equal suffrage and shall be held by secret vote or by equivalent free voting procedures.

Article 22

Everyone, as a member of society, has the right to social security and is entitled to realization, through national effort and international co-operation and in accordance with the organization and resources of each State, of the economic, social and cultural rights indispensable for his dignity and the free development of his personality.

Article 23

1. Everyone has the right to work, to free choice of employment, to just and favourable conditions of work and to protection against unemployment.

2. Everyone, without any discrimination, has the right to equal pay for equal work.

3. Everyone who works has the right to just and favourable remuneration ensuring for himself and his family an existence worthy of human dignity, and supplemented, if necessary, by other means of social protection.

4. Everyone has the right to form and to join trade unions for the protection of his interests.

Article 24

Everyone has the right to rest and leisure, including reasonable limitation of working hours and periodic holidays with pay.

Article 25

1. Everyone has the right to a standard of living adequate for the health and well-being of himself and of his family, including food, clothing, housing and medical care and necessary social services, and the right to security in the event of unemployment, sickness, disability, widowhood, old age or other lack of livelihood in circumstances beyond his control.

2. Motherhood and childhood are entitled to special care and assistance. All children, whether born in or out of wedlock, shall enjoy the same social protection.

Article 26

1. Everyone has the right to education. Education shall be free, at least in the elementary and fundamental stages. Elementary education shall be compulsory. Technical and professional education shall be made generally available and higher education shall be equally accessible to all on the basis of merit.

2. Education shall be directed to the full development of the human personality and to the strengthening of respect for human rights and fundamental freedoms. It shall promote understanding, tolerance and friendship among all nations, racial or religious groups, and shall further the activities of the United Nations for the maintenance of peace.

3. Parents have a prior right to choose the kind of education that shall be given to their children.

Article 27

1. Everyone has the right freely to participate in the cultural life of the community, to enjoy the arts and to share in scientific advancement and its benefits.

2. Everyone has the right to the protection of the moral and material interests resulting from any scientific, literary or artistic production of which he is the author.

Article 28

Everyone is entitled to a social and international order in which the rights and freedoms set forth in this Declaration can be fully realized.

Article 29

1. Everyone has duties to the community in which alone the free and full development of his personality is possible.

2. In the exercise of his rights and freedoms, everyone shall be subject only to such limitations as are determined by law solely for the purpose of securing due recognition and respect for the rights and freedoms of others and of meeting the just requirements of morality, public order and the general welfare in a democratic society.

3. These rights and freedoms may in no case be exercised contrary to the purposes and principles of the United Nations.

Article 30

Nothing in this Declaration may be interpreted as implying for any State, group or person any right to engage in any activity or to perform any act aimed at the destruction of any of the rights and freedoms set forth herein.

Jack Donnelly provides a helpful guide to the theory behind the Declaration in the selection that follows, beginning with a discussion of what it means to have a right to something. This discussion lays the groundwork for specifying what human rights are in legal and political discourse. Donnelly then takes on the difficult question of whether humans have an inherent "nature" or whether we are essentially blank slates upon which our society writes a script. And what about the Declaration itself? Can it claim timelessness and universality when it was composed in a particular place, by a particular group of people bound by their own cultural and other limitations? Is this important?

THE CONCEPT OF HUMAN RIGHTS
JACK DONNELLY

Human rights—droits de *l'homme*, *derechos humanos*, *Menschenrechte*, "the rights of man"—are, literally, the rights that one has because one is human. What does it mean to have a right? How are being human and having rights related?

1. How Rights "Work"

To have a right to *x* is to be *entitled* to *x*. It is owed to you, belongs to you in particular. And if *x* is threatened or denied, right-holders are authorized to make special claims that ordinarily "trump" utility, social policy, and other moral or political grounds for action.

Rights are not reducible to the correlative duties of those against whom they are held. If Anne has a right to *x* with respect to Bob, it is more than simply desirable, good, or even right that Anne enjoy *x*. She is entitled to it. Should Bob fail to discharge his obligations, besides acting improperly (i.e., violating standards of rectitude) and harming Anne, he violates her rights, making him subject to special remedial claims and sanctions.

Neither is having a right reducible to enjoying a benefit. Rather than a passive beneficiary of Bob's obligation, Anne is actively in charge of the relationship, as suggested by the language of "exercising" rights. She may assert her right to *x*. If he fails to discharge his obligation, she may press further claims against Bob, choose not to pursue the matter, or even excuse him, largely at her own discretion. Rights empower, not just benefit, those who hold them.

2. Special Features of Human Rights

Human rights are, literally, the rights that one has simply because one is a human being.

Human rights are *equal* rights: one either is or is not a human being, and therefore has the same human rights as everyone else (or none at all). They are also *inalienable* rights: one cannot stop being human, no matter how badly one behaves nor how barbarously one is treated. And they are *universal* rights, in the sense that today we consider all members of the species *Homo sapiens* "human beings," and thus holders of human rights.

A. Human Rights as Rights

We do not have human rights to all things that are good, or even all *important* good things. For example, we are not entitled—do not have (human) rights—to love, charity, or compassion. Parents who abuse the trust of children wreak havoc with millions of lives every day. We do not, however, have a human right to loving, supportive parents. In fact, to recognize such a right would transform family relations in ways that many people would find unappealing or even destructive.

Most good things are not the objects of human rights. The emphasis on human rights in contemporary international society thus implies selecting certain values for special emphasis. But it also involves selecting a particular mechanism—rights—to advance those values.

B. Human Rights, Legal Change, and Political Legitimacy

Human rights traditionally have been thought of as moral rights of the highest order. They have also become, as we will see in more detail later, international (and in some cases national and regional) legal rights. Many states and local jurisdictions have human rights statutes. And the object of many human rights can be claimed as "ordinary" legal rights in most national legal systems.

Armed with multiple claims, right-holders typically use the "lowest" right available. For example, in the United States, as in most countries, protection against racial discrimination on the job is available on several grounds. Depending on one's employment agreement, a grievance may be all that is required, or a legal action based on the contract. If that fails (or is unavailable), one may be able to bring suit under a local ordinance or a state nondiscrimination statute. Federal statutes and the Constitution may offer remedies at still higher levels. In unusual cases, one may (be forced to) resort to international human rights claims. In addition, a victim of discrimination may appeal to considerations of justice or righteousness and claim moral (rather than legal) rights.

One can—and usually does—go very far before human rights arguments become necessary. An appeal to human rights usually testifies to the absence of enforceable positive (legal) rights and suggests that everything else has been tried and failed, leaving one with nothing else (except perhaps violence). For example, homosexuals in the United States often claim their human right against discrimination because U.S. courts have held that constitutional prohibitions of discrimination do not apply to sexual preference.

Rights are a sort of "last resort"; they usually are claimed only when things are not going well. Claims of human rights are the final resort in the realm of rights; no higher rights appeal is available.

A set of human rights can be seen as a standard of political legitimacy. The Universal Declaration of Human Rights, for example, presents itself as a "standard of achievement for all peoples and all nations." To the extent that governments protect human rights, they are legitimate.

No less important, though, human rights authorize and empower citizens to act to vindicate their rights; to insist that these standards be realized; to struggle to create a world in which they enjoy (the objects of) their rights. Human rights claims express not merely aspirations, suggestions, requests, or laudable ideas, but rights-based demands for change.

We must therefore not fall into the trap of speaking of human rights simply as demands for rights, what Joel Feinberg calls rights in a "manifesto sense" (1980: 153). Human rights do imply a manifesto for political change. That does not, however, make them any less truly rights. Claiming a human right, in addition to suggesting that one ought to have or enjoy a parallel legal right, involves exercising a (human) right that one already has. And in contrast to other grounds on which legal rights might be demanded—for example, justice, utility, self-interest, or beneficence—human rights claims rest on a prior moral (and international legal) entitlement.

Legal rights ground legal claims to protect already established legal entitlements. Human rights ground moral claims to strengthen or add to existing legal entitlements. That does not make human rights stronger or weaker, just different. They are human (rather than legal) rights. If they did not function differently, there would be no need for them.

3. Human Rights and Human Nature

We can now turn from the "rights" to the "human" side of "human rights." This involves charting the complex relationship between human rights and "human nature."

A. The Source of Human Rights

From where do we get human rights? Legal rights have the law as their source. Contracts create contractual rights. Human rights would appear to have humanity or human nature as their source. With legal rights, however, we can point to statute or custom as the mechanism by which the right is created. With contractual rights we have the act of contracting. How does "being human" give one rights?

The source of human rights is man's moral nature, which is only loosely linked to the "human nature" defined by scientifically ascertainable needs. The "human nature" that grounds human rights is a *prescriptive* moral account of human possibility. The scientist's human nature says that beyond this we cannot go. The moral nature that grounds human rights says that beneath this we must not permit ourselves to fall.

Human rights are "needed" not for life but for a life of dignity. "There is a human right to x" implies that people who enjoy a right to x will live richer and more fully human lives. Conversely, those unable to enjoy (the objects of) their human rights will to that extent be estranged from their moral nature.

B. Human Rights and The Social Construction of Human Nature

Human rights theories and documents point beyond actual conditions of existence—beyond the "real" in the sense of what has already been realized—to the possible, which is viewed as a deeper human moral reality. Human rights are less about the way people "are" than about what they might become. They are about moral rather than natural or juridical persons.

The Universal Declaration of Human Rights, for example, tells us little about life in many countries. And where it does, that is in large measure because those rights have shaped society in their image. Where theory and practice converge, it is largely because the posited rights have shaped society, and human beings, in their image. And where they diverge, claims of human rights point to the need to bring (legal and political) practice into line with (moral) theory.

The Universal Declaration, like any list of human rights, specifies minimum conditions for a dignified life, a life worthy of a human being. Even wealthy and powerful countries regularly fall far short of these requirements. As we have seen, however, this is precisely when, and perhaps even why, having human rights is so important: they demand, as rights, the social changes required to realize the underlying moral vision of human nature.

Human rights are at once a utopian ideal and a realistic practice for implementing that ideal. They say, in effect, "Treat a person like a human being and you'll get a human being." But they also say "Here's how you treat someone as a human being," and proceed to enumerate a list of human rights.

Human rights seek to fuse moral vision and political practice. The relationship between human nature, human rights, and political society is "dialectical." Human rights shape political society, so as to shape human beings, so as to realize the possibilities of human nature, which provided the basis for these rights in the first place.

Human rights thus are constitutive, no less than regulative, rules. We are most immediately familiar with their regulative aspects: "No one shall be subjected to torture or to cruel, inhuman or degrading treatment or punishment"; "Everyone has the right to work, to free choice of employment, to just and favorable conditions of work and to protection against unemployment." No less important, however, human rights *constitute* individuals as a particular kind of political subject: free and equal rights-bearing citizens. And by establishing the requirements and limits of legitimate government, human rights seek to constitute states of a particular kind.

C. Analytic and Substantive Theories

If we were faced with an array of competing and contradictory lists of human rights clamoring for either philosophical or political attention, this inability to defend a particular theory of human nature might be a serious shortcoming. Fortunately, there is a remarkable international normative consensus on the list of rights contained in the Universal Declaration and the International Human Rights Covenants.

4. The State and International Human Rights

If human rights are held universally—that is, equally and by all—one might imagine that they hold (universally) against all other individuals and groups. Such a conception is inherently plausible and in many ways morally attractive. It is not, however, the dominant contemporary international understanding.

A. National Implementation of International Human Rights

Internationally recognized human rights impose obligations on and are exercised against sovereign territorial states. "Everyone has a right to *x*" in contemporary international practice means "Each state has the authority and responsibility to implement and protect the right to *x* within its territory." The Universal Declaration presents itself as "a common standard of achievement for all peoples and nations"—and the states that represent them. The Covenants create obligations only for states, and states have international human rights obligations only to *their own* nationals (and foreign nationals in their territory or otherwise subject to their jurisdiction or control).

Human rights norms have been largely internationalized. Their implementation, however, remains almost exclusively national. Contemporary international (and regional) human rights regimes are supervisory mechanisms that monitor relations between states and citizens. They are not alternatives to a fundamentally statist conception of human rights. Even in the strong European regional human rights regime, the supervisory organs of the European Court of Human Rights regulate relations between states and their nationals or residents.

The centrality of states in the contemporary construction of international human rights is also clear in the substance of recognized rights. Some, most notably rights of political participation, are typically (although not universally) restricted to citizens. Many obligations—for example, to provide education and social insurance—apply only to residents. Virtually all apply to foreign nationals only while they are subject to the jurisdiction of that state.

Foreign states have no internationally recognized human rights obligation to protect foreign nationals abroad from, for example, torture. They are not even at liberty to use more than persuasive means on behalf of, for example, foreign victims of torture. Current norms of state sovereignty still prohibit states from acting coercively abroad against torture and virtually all other violations of human rights.

This focus on state-citizen relations is also embedded in our ordinary language. The human rights of a person who is beaten by the police have been violated, but it is an ordinary crime, not a human rights violation, to receive an otherwise identical beating at the hands of a thief or an irascible neighbor. Internationally, we distinguish human rights violations from war crimes. Even when comparable suffering is inflicted on innocent civilians, we draw a sharp categorical distinction based on whether the perpetrator is (an agent of) one's own government or a foreign state.

Although neither necessary nor inevitable, this state-centric conception of human rights has deep historical roots. The idea of human rights received its first mature expression in, and remains deeply enmeshed with, liberal social contract theory, the only major tradition of political theory that assumes that individuals are endowed with equal and inalienable rights. And the contractarian notion of the state as an instrument for the protection, implementation, and effective realization of natural rights is strikingly similar to the conception of the state in international human rights instruments. Both measure the legitimacy of the state largely by its performance in implementing human rights.

The restriction of international human rights obligations to nationals, residents, and visitors also reflects the central role of the sovereign state in modern politics. Since at least the sixteenth century, states have struggled, with considerable success, to consolidate their internal authority over competing local powers. Simultaneously, early modern states struggled, with even greater success, to free themselves from imperial and papal authority. Their late modern successors have jealously, zealously, and (for all the talk of globalization) largely successfully fought attempts to reinstitute supranational authority.

With power and authority thus doubly concentrated, the modern state has emerged as both the principal threat to the enjoyment of human rights and the essential institution for their effective implementation and enforcement. Although human rights advocates have generally had an adversarial relationship with states, both sides of this relationship between the state and human rights require emphasis.

B. Principal Violator and Essential Protector

Early advocates of natural (human) rights emphasized keeping the state out of the private lives and property of its citizens. In later eras, working men, racial and religious minorities, women, and the colonized, among other dispossessed groups, asserted their human rights against states that appeared to them principally as instruments of repression and domination. In recent decades, most human rights advocates, as symbolized by the work of groups such as Amnesty International, have focused on preventing state abuses of individual rights. Given the immense power and reach of the modern state, this emphasis on controlling state power has been, and remains, both prudent and productive.

The human rights strategy of control over the state has had two principal dimensions. Negatively, it prohibits a wide range of state interferences in the personal, social, and political lives of citizens, acting both individually and collectively. But beyond carving out zones of state exclusion, human rights place the people above and in positive control of their government. Political authority is vested in a free citizenry endowed with extensive rights of political participation (rights to vote, freedom of association, free speech, etc.).

Precisely because of its political dominance in the contemporary world, however, the state is the central institution available for effectively implementing internationally recognized human rights. "Failed states" such as Somalia suggest that one of the few things as frightening in the contemporary world as an efficiently repressive state is no state at all. Therefore, beyond preventing state-based wrongs, human rights require the state to provide certain (civil, political, economic, social, and cultural) goods, services, and opportunities.

This more positive human rights vision of the state also goes back to seventeenth and eighteenth century social contract theories. Contractarians such as Locke, Kant, and Paine emphasized that the rights one possesses naturally, simply as a human being, could not be enjoyed in a state of nature. Society and government are essential to the enjoyment of natural or human rights. In fact, within the contractarian tradition the legitimacy of a state can largely be measured by the extent to which it implements and protects natural rights.

The essential role of the state in securing the enjoyment of human rights is, if anything, even clearer when we turn from theory to practice. The struggle of dispossessed groups has typically been a struggle for full legal and political recognition by the state, and thus inclusion among those whose rights are protected by the state. Opponents of racial, religious, ethnic, and gender discrimination, political persecution, torture, disappearances, and massacre typically have sought not simply to end abuses but to transform the state from a predator into a protector of rights.

The need for an active state has always been especially clear for economic and social human rights. Even early bourgeois arguments emphasizing the natural right to property stressed the importance of active state protection. In fact, the "classic" liberalism of the eighteenth and nineteenth centuries saw the state as, in large measure, a mechanism to give legal form and protection to private property rights. Since the late nineteenth century, as our conceptions of the proper range of economic and social rights have expanded, the politics of economic and social rights has emphasized state provision where market and family mechanisms fail to ensure enjoyment of these rights.

A positive role for the state, however, is no less central to civil and political rights. The effective implementation of the right to nondiscrimination, for example, often requires extensive positive actions to realize the underlying value of equality. Even procedural rights such as due process entail substantial positive endeavors with respect to police, courts, and administrative procedures. And free, fair, and open elections do not happen through state restraint and inaction. The state must not merely refrain from certain harmful actions but create a political environment that fosters the development of active, engaged, autonomous citizens.

Because human rights first emerged in an era of personal, and thus often arbitrary, rule, an initial emphasis on individual liberty and state restraint was understandable. As the intrusive and coercive powers of the state have grown—steadily, and to now frightening dimensions—an emphasis on controlling the state continues to make immense political sense. The language of human rights abuses and violations continues, quite properly, to focus our attention on combating active state threats to human rights.

Nonetheless, a state that does no active harm itself is not enough. The state must also include protecting individuals against abuses by other individuals and private groups. The "classic" right to personal security, for example, is about safety against physical assaults by private actors, not just attacks by agents of the state. The state, although needing to be tamed, is in the contemporary world the principal institution we rely on to tame social forces no less dangerous to the rights, interests, and dignity of individuals, families, and communities.

Other strategies have been tried or proposed to control the destructive capacities of the state and harness its capabilities to realize important human goods and values. The virtue or wisdom of leaders, party members, or clerics, the expertise of technocrats, and the special skills and social position of the military have seemed to many to be attractive alternatives to human rights as bases of political order and legitimacy. But the human rights approach of individual rights and popular empowerment has proved far more effective than any alternative yet tried—or at least that is how I read the remarkably consistent collapse of dictatorships of the left and right alike over the past two decades in Latin America, Central and Eastern Europe, Africa, and Asia (although not [yet?] in most of the Middle East).

The final reading in this section illustrates human-rights theory in action. The principal author of this document is Liu Xiaobo, a Chinese professor and prominent dissident who has long protested the lack of basic freedoms in contemporary China. He argues that his country has paid too much attention to economic development and not enough to the basic rights and needs of its people. In light of the 100th anniversary of the Chinese constitution, which occurred in 2008, Liu and his colleagues drew up a proposed charter of rights, which they named Charter 08. A diverse group of intellectuals, retired Communist Party officials, workers, peasants, and business persons—303 people in all—then signed on to the document and publicized it. Within the next year, 10,000 people added their names to Charter 08, despite a news blackout and internet censorship. As a result of his activities, Liu was convicted of subversion and sentenced to 11 years of imprisonment on Christmas Day, 2009. No one else has been convicted, although the censorship continues. The United States and the European Union have urged China to free Liu, and hundreds of international writers have also called for his release. China has labeled these actions "a gross interference" in its internal affairs. Liu Xiaobo was awarded the Nobel Peace Prize for 2010 for what the Nobel committee described as "his long and non-violent struggle for fundamental human rights in China." The Chinese government reacted to this news with anger and threats of reprisals against the nations that attended the ceremony.

It should be clear by now that the realm of human rights is largely about aspirations for justice. Yet the concept of rights implies that there should be mechanisms for their guarantee, including courts to adjudicate competing rights claims. The question then is how do people become persuaded that an aspirational right can become a concrete legal reality? Perhaps, it is the experience of what we perceive to be wrongs against them that motivates us to advocate for change in our everyday laws and sometimes, our fundamental constitutional documents.

CHARTER 08

LIU XIAOBO

December 09, 2008

A group of 303 Chinese writers, intellectuals, lawyers, journalists, retired Party officials, workers, peasants, and businessmen have issued an open letter—the "Charter 08"—calling for legal reforms, democracy and protection of human rights in China. An English translation of the Charter by Human Rights in China is below.

Preamble

This year is the 100th year of China's Constitution, the 60th anniversary of the *Universal Declaration of Human Rights,* the 30th anniversary of the birth of the Democracy Wall, and the 10th year since China signed the *International Covenant of Civil and Political Rights.* After experiencing a prolonged period of human rights disasters and a tortuous struggle and resistance, the awakening Chinese citizens are increasingly and more clearly recognizing that freedom, equality, and human rights are universal common values shared by all humankind, and that democracy, a republic, and constitutionalism constitute the basic structural framework of modern governance. A "modernization" bereft of these universal values and this basic political framework is a disastrous process that deprives humans of their rights, corrodes human nature, and destroys human dignity. Where will China head in the 21st century? Continue a "modernization" under this kind of authoritarian rule? Or recognize universal values, assimilate into the mainstream civilization, and build a democratic political system? This is a major decision that cannot be avoided.

The "New China" established in 1949 is a "people's republic" in name only. In fact, it is under the "Party's dominion." The ruling power monopolizes all the political, economic and social resources. It created a string of human rights catastrophes such as the Anti-Rightist Campaign, the Great Leap Forward, the Cultural Revolution, June 4, and attacks on non-governmental religious activities and on the rights defense movement, causing tens of millions of deaths, and exacted a disastrous price on the people and the country.

The "reform and opening up" of the late 20th century extricated China from the pervasive poverty and absolute power in the Mao Zedong era, and substantially increased private wealth and the standard of living of the masses. Individual economic freedom

English translation by Human Rights in China, excerpted here courtesy of Human Rights in China. The full text of Charter 08 in English translation is available in Human Rights in China, "Freedom of Expression on Trial in China," *China Rights Forum,* 2010, no. 1, http://www.hrichina.org/public/contents/173687

and social privileges were partially restored, a civil society began to grow, and the calls for human rights and political freedom among the people increased by the day. Those in power, as they were implementing economic reforms aimed at marketization and privatization, also began to move from a position of rejecting human rights to one of gradually recognizing them. In 1997 and 1998, the Chinese government signed two important international human rights treaties. In 2004, the National People's Congress amended the Constitution to include language to "respect and safeguard human rights." And this year, [the government] has promised to formulate and implement a "National Human Rights Action Plan." However, this political progress stops at the paper stage. There are laws but there is no rule of law. There is a constitution but no constitutional governance. And there is still the political reality that is obvious for all to see. The power bloc continues to insist on maintaining the authoritarian regime, rejecting political reform. This has caused corruption in officialdom, difficulty in establishing rule of law, and no protection of human rights, the loss of ethics, the polarization of society, warped economic development, damages in the natural and human environments, no systematic protection of the rights to property and the pursuit of happiness, the accumulation of countless social conflicts, and the continuous rise of resentment. In particular, the intensification of hostility between government officials and the ordinary people, and the dramatic rise of mass incidents, illustrate a catastrophic loss of control in the making, and the anachronism of the current system has reached a point where change must occur.

Our Fundamental Concepts

At this historical juncture of the future destiny of China, it is necessary to rethink the last 100 years of modernization and reaffirm the following concepts:

Freedom: Freedom is at the core of universal values. The rights of speech, publication, belief, assembly, association, movement, and to demonstrate are all the concrete realizations of freedom. If freedom is not flourishing, then there is no modern civilization of which to speak.

Human Rights: Human rights are not bestowed by the state, but are rights that each person is born with and enjoys. To ensure human rights must be the foundation of the first objective of government and lawful public authority, and is also the inherent demand of "putting people first." The past political calamities of China are all closely related to the disregard of human rights by the ruling authorities.

Equality: Each individual, regardless of social status, occupation, gender, economic situation, ethnic group, skin color, religion, or political belief, is equal in human dignity and freedom. The principle of equality before the law and a citizen's society must be implemented; the principle of equality of economic, cultural, and political rights must be implemented.

Republicanism: Republicanism is "governing together; living peacefully together," that is, the decentralization of power and balancing of interests, that is comprised of diverse interests, different social groups, pluralistic culture and groups seeking religious belief, on the foundation of equal participation, peaceful competition, public discussion, and peaceful handling of public affairs.

Democracy: The most basic meaning is that sovereignty resides in the people and the people elect government. Democracy has the following basic characteristics: (1) the legitimacy of government comes from the people, the source of government power is the people; (2) government must be chosen by the people; (3) citizens enjoy the right to vote, important civil servants and officials of all levels should be produced through elections at fixed times; (4) the decisions of the majority must be respected while protecting the basic rights of the minority. In a word, democracy will become the modern tool for making government one "from the people, by the people, and for the people."

Constitutionalism: Constitutionalism is the principle of protecting basic constitutionally-guaranteed freedoms and rights of citizens through law and a rule of law, delimiting the boundaries of government power and actions, and providing corresponding systemic capacity.

In China, the era of imperial power has long passed and will not return; in the world, authoritarian systems are approaching the dusk of their endings. The only fundamental way out for China: citizens should become the true masters of the nation, throw off the consciousness of reliance on a wise ruler or honest and upright official, make widely public civic consciousness of the centrality of rights and the responsibility of participation, and practice freedom, democracy, and respect for law.

Conclusion

China, as a great nation of the world, one of the five permanent members of the United Nations Security Council, and a member of the Human Rights Council, should contribute to peace for humankind and progress in human rights. But to people's regret, among the great nations of the world, China, alone, still clings to an authoritarian political way of life. As a result, it has caused an unbroken chain of human rights disasters and social crises, held back the development of the Chinese people, and hindered the progress of human civilization. This situation must change! The reform of political democratization can no longer be delayed.

Because of this, we, with a civic spirit that dares to act, publish the "Charter 08." We hope that all Chinese citizens who share this sense of crisis, responsibility and mission, without distinction between the government or the public, regardless of status, will hold back our differences to seek common ground, actively participate in this citizens' movement, and jointly promote the great transformation of the Chinese society, so that we can establish a free, democratic and constitutional nation in the near future and fulfill the dreams that our people have pursued tirelessly for more than a hundred years.

Discussion Questions

- Gandhi claims that passive resistance to law works better than violence. Do you agree?

- King calls his antagonists "brothers" and claims to act out of love. How can he lead a struggle against those he professes to love?

- When is civil disobedience just? Is negotiation an essential first step in the process?

- Is it a fair criticism to complain that the Declaration of Human Rights is culture-bound and limited by the time in which it was written? Is this a significant objection?

- The Declaration of Human Rights does not have the force of law. It sets out goals, not rules, that must be followed. The U.S. Declaration of Independence is similar. It is a beacon designed to inspire, not an enforceable document. What kind of actions do you think the drafters of the Declaration of Human Rights envisioned from its adoption?

- Was Liu Xiaobo's action in creating and publicizing this document an example of civil disobedience? If so, is his suffering the consequences (11 years of imprisonment) part of what may make his stance effective?

- Did world leaders advance the cause of human rights when they complained publicly about China's actions toward Liu Xiaobo? Could such complaints make things worse for Liu Xiaobo?

- Should the idea of American citizenship include more than a guarantee against government infringement of basic rights? Should the victims of Hurricane Katrina in New Orleans have had an enforceable right to the government's help, for example?

Migration

Humans are on the move as never before, thanks to improvements in international transit and communication networks. This trend toward greater human mobility raises many important questions about the relationship between residents of a nation and governments. Migrants, we can assume, are entitled to human rights, but guaranteeing these rights can be difficult. Nations are becoming a mixture of peoples that includes recent migrants as well as people who have strong roots, both in their adopted and in their original communities. This trend is impressively large. The International Organization for Migration estimated in December 2009 that there were 214 million immigrants in the world. At about the same time a Gallup poll estimated that nearly 16 percent of the world's adults (about 700 million people) would relocate if they could. How should migrants be incorporated into the national political community and its social life? This is a contentious political issue because demographic shifts tend to provoke cultural and economic changes that can easily be perceived as threatening. There is also worry that government is not listening, or rather that it is listening only to conglomerates that are looking for cheap labor and investment opportunities. As Brysk and Shafir assert, "Globalization creates a citizenship gap" in which global markets take on new importance. National governments are less important players than in the past, rendering individual citizens less able to influence government and less likely to be protected by it (2004: 6).[2]

For citizens, this may mean that migration seems "out of control," with people rushing to fill jobs that are not supposed to be available to them, crossing national boundaries that are supposed to be secure. Market forces seem to overwhelm government's efforts to control the flow of people. But it should be remembered that national governments are not simply victims of market forces. They are also players in the effort to grow their economies with foreign workers, partly to keep pace with what other governments are doing in the race to maintain their standing and wealth. The well-educated immigrant with valuable skills who can increase a nation's productivity is much in demand.

People with less education and more common skills are also in demand when jobs are plentiful, but for these workers, governments tend to prefer more temporary arrangements with limited benefits because economies fluctuate in their need for labor. The inflexibility of governments in responding to the need for labor creates incentives for businesses to hire people who immigrate without legal authorization. These people are, historian Mae Ngai suggests, "impossible subjects" supported by policies that accept their presence for some purposes, for example, working and buying goods and services, but deny them legal status.[3] Racism and xenophobia amplify fears of citizens about these new residents and about migration in general. The result of these converging forces, some suggest, is a moral

---

[2]Allison Brysk and Gershon Shafir, "Citizenship and Human Rights in an Era of Globalization," from the Introduction to *People Out of Place: Globalization, Human Rights, and the Citizenship Gap* (New York: Routledge/Taylor and Francis, 2004).

[3]Mae Ngae, *Impossible Subjects: Illegal Aliens and the Making of Modern America* (Princeton, NJ: Princeton University Press, 2005).

panic in which emotion overtakes reason, and migrants become the butt of deeper anxieties concerning the pace of change and the ability of the nation to absorb new people and cultural change without losing its way.[4] Some observers see a kind of inside-out process, where white fears are redirected to justify racialized violence against nonwhites:

> Anti-immigration discourse inverts violence, projecting it onto racialized bodies to create the condition of possibility for state sanctioned white-on-color violence, which, in turn, may legitimately terrorize entire populations. This dynamic creates such a climate of uncertainty among immigrants and their allies that it undermines their capacity to organize, thereby (re)producing a docile, readily exploitable labor force. It produces a spatial arrangement within the United States in which whites benefit from this violence: they may move freely, buy cheaply, and retain social control, all the while believing it is they who are under siege.[5]

For some immigrants, the potential for violence and oppression by majority populations is not only an issue in the receiving state. People flee wars and violence to save their lives and those of their loved ones, often on foot under dire circumstances. They are refugees seeking shelter in neighboring nations, hoping for an end to the violence in their own country, or seeking relocation to a safer place. Over a million people streamed into refugee camps in Kosovo after racialized massacres of Muslim residents by the Bosnian Serbs in Srebrenica and elsewhere.[6] International relief organizations support refugee camps in many nations near violent areas. Kenya, for example, hosts refugees from Somalia, which is in the grip of a long civil war. Sometimes people take a different route to escape danger, travelling directly to nations perceived to be safe, where they seek asylum.

There is a strong world-wide consensus about the need to assist people fleeing violence and persecution in their home countries. World War II and the German persecution of the Jews, gypsies, homosexuals, and political dissidents brought home the need for action. A United Nations convention setting forth a definition of refugees and rights of people granted asylum was approved in 1951 and took effect in 1954. Nearly 150 nations have signed on, promising, at a minimum, not to force anyone back into harm's way, and at a maximum, to open their doors wide to refugees and those who can prove that they are legitimate candidates for asylum. The United States, for example, gives refugees the same basic rights as U.S. citizens and the right to seek naturalization after five years. Refugees and asylees make up about 13 percent of those offered

---

[4]See Catherine Dauvergne, *Making People Illegal: What Globalization Means for Migration* (Cambridge: Cambridge University Press, 2008), especially p. 2. For a general discussion of moral panics, see Gilbert Herdt (ed.), *Moral Panics, Sex Panics* (New York: NYU Press, 2009), pp. 7–9.

[5]Aimee Marie Carrillo Rowe, "Whose 'America'? The Politics of Rhetoric and Space in the Formation of U.S. Nationalism," *Radical History Review*, vol. 89 (spring): pp. 115–34 (2004).

[6]John Hagan describes the violence of the Bosnian conflict in graphic terms, such as the ethnic cleansing in Prijedor, in which whole families were first forced into detention camps and then killed, raped, or sexually enslaved. The subsequent prosecution of Slobodan Milosevic and others for war crimes was an attempt to bring some closure to these terrible events. See *Justice in the Balkans: Prosecuting War Crimes in the Hague Tribunal*, Chicago: University of Chicago Press, 2003.

permanent residence; most of the rest are migrants seeking reunification with family members already here or people coming for employment purposes.

Rights on paper may, however, be different from rights in fact. The reading below suggests, in dramatic terms, the need to think carefully about how government treats migrants. The setting is the period shortly after the terrorist attack on the World Trade Center and the Pentagon on September 11, 2001. Professor Sheikh describes what political theorist Giorgio Agamben would call a "state of exception," when government selectively, for some segment of the population, suspends the rule of law, including individual rights. Agamben argues that states of exception are becoming more frequent, not just in the United States, but around the world, as governments declare states of emergency that demand increased governmental powers over individuals.[7]

RACIALIZING, CRIMINALIZING, AND SILENCING 9/11 DEPORTEES
IRUM SHEIKH

SINCE SEPTEMBER 11, 2001, the U.S. government has continued to arrest and deport immigrants predominantly from Muslim countries on the suspicion of terrorism. The stories all follow a familiar pattern: the arrest of a Muslim or Muslim-looking individual, sizzling news stories about the individual's connection to al-Qaeda, and, months later, deportation on minor charges unrelated to terrorism. Deportation occurs quietly, in vivid contrast to the arrest. But even when the media does follow through on the stories, the deportees are described as lawbreakers, illegals, and suspected terrorists—not distinguishing among these terms. Weeks or months later, more headlines appear about the arrest of yet another alleged terrorist. These sensational arrests keep the general public preoccupied with the fear of new attacks by Muslim terrorists who are intent on killing Americans.

Over the last five years, I have interviewed more than forty individuals and researched fifty other cases connected with terrorism. In reviewing these, I found a pattern very similar to what I have just described.

Racializing Muslims and Muslim-Looking Individuals
Michael Omi and Howard Winant argue that racial categories are socially constructed and are constantly being contested and transformed. Racialization can be defined

---

[7]Giorgio Agamben, *State of Exception*, translated by Kevin Attell (Chicago: University of Chicago Press, 2005).

---

as a political process through which frameworks for defining racial difference are manipulated by institutional actors and used to subjugate specific groups. This usually results in the creation of a field of discourse that imputes negative stereotypes to racialized minorities. Latinos, African Americans, Native Americans, and Asian Americans are the primary groups that Omi and Winant refer to in their discussion of racialization in the United States.

In the case of Arab Americans and Muslim noncitizens, the racialization process draws on interpretations which associate phenotype with religion, resulting in profiles that are based on what a Muslim "looks like." In addition, the post-9/11 racialization process equates Islam with terrorism. Within this framework, it is relatively uncontroversial for an enforcement officer to frame a Muslim-looking individual as a terrorist and later deport him on minor immigration and/or criminal charges. In the vast majority of cases, Muslims and Muslim-looking individuals who are detained on and deported under immigration charges have no connection to terrorism.

This process of framing immigration detainees as terrorists was not limited to the actions of lower-level enforcement officers. Top administration officials, including President George W. Bush and Attorney General John Ashcroft, were very keen to inform the public about the success of the government's intelligence operation. For example, speaking in October 2001, the attorney general stated:

> Our anti-terrorism offensive has arrested or detained nearly 1,000 individuals as part of the September 11 terrorism investigation. Those who violated the law remain in custody. Taking suspected terrorists in violation of the law off the streets and keeping them locked up is our clear strategy to prevent terrorism within our own borders.

In June 2002, when most of the detainees had been deported or released, President Bush praised the Department of Homeland Security by declaring that the homeland defense coalition, "has hauled in about 2,400 of these terrorists, these killers—there's still a lot of them out there."

In public, government officials boasted about the success of the intelligence operation. Behind closed doors, however, some were skeptical about these arrests. Colleen Rowley, an FBI whistleblower and *Time* magazine's Person of the Year for 2002, characterized these arrests as a public relations strategy. In her letter dated March 6, 2003, addressed to the FBI director, Rowley pointed out:

> After 9-11, Headquarters encouraged more and more detentions for what seem to be essentially PR purposes. Field offices were required to report daily the number of detentions in order to supply grist for statements on our progress in fighting terrorism. . . . Particular vigilance may be required to head off undue pressure (including subtle encouragement) to detain or "round up" suspects—particularly those of Arabic origin.

This PR strategy becomes more apparent when we look at the patterns of arrests and the way they were carried out after September 11, 2001. For example, on September 13, 2001, dozens of FBI agents raided the one-bedroom apartment of a naturalized Pakistani citizen who worked as a pilot for United Airlines. All of the streets adjoining the apartment were sealed off with yellow "Do not enter" tape. Floodlights lit up the night, creating a circuslike atmosphere, inviting curiosity and an audience. Local television and newspaper reports sensationalized the investigation. As a consequence, this retired U.S. Air Force major was recast as a "mysterious . . . pilot" over night. According to a news article, FBI agents found "terrorist paraphernalia" in the pilot's house; in fact, they had found spy novels written in Urdu. Neighbors and other residents living in the area watched the FBI investigation and became concerned.

Ahmed Khalifa, an Egyptian, was a medical student with a valid tourist visa who was kept in a high-security jail in New York for months. He was brought to jail in a motorcade of police cars with blaring sirens. He felt that through the spectacle of the motorcade, FBI agents wanted to show the public that they were doing their job. In my interview with him, he explained that everyone on the street was staring at the motorcade with frightened expressions.

On November 28, 2001, two police officers paraded a Pakistani American businessman in handcuffs through downtown Manhattan from the East side police precinct to the West side precinct. Apparently, the fingerprinting machine at the former was too busy, and the officers decided to walk instead of driving the five or six blocks. Syed Ali has described his walk in handcuffs through downtown Manhattan as a setup that was designed to show off the success of federal agents in capturing another supposed "terrorist suspect."

Through these theatrics, federal agents effectively framed Muslims as terrorists in the national imagination. These actions were also used to appease the fears and concerns of the general public, and to attract the attention of the media and politicians. In many ways, these dramatizations resembled the staged FBI raids of Japanese American communities during World War II. And just as members of the media were present for many of the government raids on Japanese American communities, so were they for the FBI's post-9/11 raids on Muslims. Hungry for quick answers and eager to satisfy the curiosity of the general public, the media ran stories of these investigations, and arrests without confirming or checking sources. The mainstream media televised and published images of Muslim-looking men in chains, implying their connection to terrorism on the basis of little more than their religion, ethnicity, and racial appearance.

As the government paraded shackled, Muslim-looking bodies, it also reinforced popular stereotypes about Muslim males. Immediately after the attacks of September 11, 2001, the state launched the Terrorism Information and Prevention System (also known as Operation TIPS). Through Operation TIPS, the state encouraged the public to call FBI hotlines with leads on suspicious persons. By September 18, one week after the attacks, "the FBI had received more than 96,000 tips or potential leads from the public, including more than 54,000 through an internet site." Most of the callers attributed suspicious activities to "Arab men." In one of her speeches, Colleen Rowley describes the kinds of tips that were often received through the FBI hotlines right after September 11:

> The most common "citizen tip" we receive is something to the effect of, "I don't want you to think I'm prejudiced because I'm not, but I just have to

report this because one never knows and I'm worried and I thought the FBI should check it out." This precedes a piece of general information about an "Arab" or "Middle-Eastern" man who the tipster lives by or works with that contains little or nothing specific to potential terrorism activities.

This was not simply a matter of thousands of U.S. citizens "turning racist" over night. These attitudes developed in response to a climate of fear that had been created by the state and reinforced through repeated references to the "arrest of 1,000 terrorists" and slogans like "United We Stand." President Bush defined *patriotism* with binary statements, like "Either you are with us, or you are with the terrorists." Even when it became clear that Operation TIPS was not providing any substantial information about terrorists, the state continued to encourage the public to report "suspicious people."

Displays of American flags on houses, cars, and office buildings were a common spectacle after September 11, 2001. Within this context it became very easy for state officials and right-wing groups to label people as unpatriotic if they questioned brutal interrogations, detentions, and deportations. This climate led many people to see the racial profiling of Muslim-looking individuals as a civic duty. It also emboldened some U.S. citizens to engage in hate crimes and racially motivated killings. On September 15, 2001, Balbir Singh Sodhi, a Sikh immigrant from India, was shot to death in Mesa, Arizona, while he was planting flowers outside his Chevron station. After killing him, Frank Roque drove to an Afghani family's house and opened fire but missed the people inside. Later, he shot at a man of Lebanese heritage at a nearby convenience store, but missed him also. Mesa police arrested him a few hours later as he yelled that he was a patriot and an American.

On November 26, 2001, two Somali men praying in a parking lot in Texas City, Texas, were reported as taking part in "suspicious activity." Arrested on minor technical violations, they were released after a day. Ahmad Abdou El-Khier, an Egyptian, was picked up after a hotel clerk in Maryland told police that he appeared suspicious. He was initially charged with trespassing at the hotel where he was staying. He was deported on November 30, 2001, on a separate immigration violation. Ali Yaghi, a Palestinian with a Jordanian passport, was deported after five months of solitary confinement. He was arrested in October 2001 in Albany, New York, because a neighbor called to say that he was expressing anti-American sentiment and dancing in the streets. He, too, was deported on an immigration violation. Ali Raza, a Pakistani American, was picked up from his home in New York City in October 2001 after the police received a tip from a concerned neighbor who insisted that "people make bombs there." He spent about six months in jail for an immigration violation.

These attitudes toward Muslims and Muslim-looking individuals have not subsided. As recently as December 2006, talk radio host Jerry Klein suggested that all Muslims in the United States should be identified with a crescent-shaped tattoo or a distinctive armband. One of the callers responded, "Not only do you tattoo them in the middle of their forehead but you ship them out of this country. . . . They are here to kill us." Another called and suggested that tattoos and other identifying markers don't go far enough, "What good is identifying them?. . . You have to set up encampments like during World War Two with the Japanese and Germans."

Unfortunately, these opinions are shared by a cross section of the American public. A Gallup Poll in the summer of 2006 showed that 39 percent were in favor of requiring Muslims in the United States, including American citizens, to carry special identification. A third of those polled thought that Muslims in the United States sympathized with al-Qaeda.

The discourse on national security has been a truly hegemonic force negating the human rights and civil liberties of Arabs and Muslims and, specifically, young males. Through the eyes of the state, these infringements on the rights of Muslims and their families were small sacrifices when compared against the greater goal of national security. Even when the details of many of these cases were brought to light, the circumstances of the post-9/11 climate were still seen to justify the interrogations, detentions, and deportations.

Even though civil and human rights groups questioned the governments's discriminatory practices, the discourse of illegality and criminal aliens prevailed. Most newspapers and television stations uncritically accepted the government's rationale, and in situations when the media publicized these arrests, the undocumented or criminal status of the detainee was highlighted without any additional context.

These immigration violators included people with expired visas, people without employment authorization (who had only been granted a visiting visa), people with incomplete paperwork, and others who failed to inform the immigration office of a change in address. The heavy concentration of undocumented immigrants in high-security jails also suggests that the government targeted vulnerable individuals. Because many of them were new to the country, undocumented Muslims were unfamiliar with the U.S. immigration and legal system and lacked resources and connections to the right people. Sandra Nicholas, an attorney who worked with several of these detainees, describes a typical immigration courtroom in the days after September 11, 2001, as follows:

> I was going in for their first hearings. And it was a mob scene when I got there. There were forty or fifty prisoners shackled to each other, packed into courtrooms. Relatives, lawyers, court personnel, guards, were all just wandering around the halls and trying to get things organized. . . . It was so chaotic. I said, oh, my God what a mess. . . . It was like a zoo, a three-ring circus. I have never seen such chaos in the immigration court. Everybody was still very anxious and nervous because of 9/11. The judges did not want to erroneously free someone who might be a terrorist. . . . All of [the detainees] were in on [immigration charges]—anyone who would interview them . . . anybody in their right mind talking to these guys would know in a minute that they were not terrorists. . . . They would not know how to light the match . . . how to get the fuse into the bomb. . . . They were the guys who overstayed the visas. . . . They just wanted to send money back home.

Nonetheless, the attorney general was pleased to claim that "our antiterrorism offensive has arrested or detained nearly 1,000 individuals as part of the September 11 terrorism investigation,"

This concentration on undocumented immigrants was deliberate and systematic. Individuals who had legal status were generally let go. For example, in October 2001 enforcement officials entered the Brooklyn apartment of five Arab men. One out of the five had a green card and thus was not arrested. The remaining four were classified as "high interest" cases, which translated into having a strong connection with terrorism. These four spent months in a high-security jail in New York. Months later, they were deported for expired visas and working on a visiting visa.

The Office of the Inspector General's (OIG) 2003 report criticized the Department of Justice for violating the legal, human, and civil rights of individuals arrested during their post-9/11 investigations. The report noted that men without any connection to terrorism were placed in solitary confinement and held under restrictive conditions for weeks and even months. Held incommunicado, these pretrial detainees "were locked down 23 hours a day, were placed in four-man holds during movement, had restricted phone call and visitation privileges, and had less ability to obtain and communicate with legal counsel [than ordinary prisoners]."

The sense of shame and guilt that Japanese Americans felt in the aftermath of the internment was, arguably, even more intense for post-9/11 detainees. They were much more alienated from each other than the Japanese American internees and were returned to home communities that did not necessarily understand or sympathize with their situation. As explained earlier, the U.S. government capitalized on the notion that all post-9/11 detainees were guilty of immigration or criminal violations. To further complicate matters, no meaningful assistance from human rights or legal organizations materialized after they arrived in their homelands. In addition, deportees were often reluctant to take legal action because they are afraid of the retaliation that could follow if they talked about their experience. One of the deportees expressed these fears in my interview with him:

> When I came back, I was thinking that I should publish the entire story in detail, in twenty to thirty episodes, in a local newspaper. . . . But later, I thought that this writing could harm me. I met a person. His son was detained in the U.S. . . . I told him that I want to write about this incident in detail in the newspapers. He said, "You should try to forget all the things that happened to you. If you write something against the FBI, it could be constructed against you. It could create some problems for you in the future." I became quiet and decided not to write. Otherwise, I had a lot of things to write about."

Rising rates of immigration challenge governments, not only to avoid panicky reactions to events, but also to govern justly in ordinary times. But what is justice in a setting that involves people of varying legal status? Some governments decide that the best course is to draw a bright line between citizens and noncitizens, providing citizens, but no one else, with the right to political expression and voice in government. The United States Constitution suggests a different course. It consistently speaks in terms of the rights of persons, not the rights of citizens. Local police departments often take a similar view, believing that good policing requires treating all residents equally and encouraging trust from all members of the community. Making a community secure, they argue, involves everyone's participation, regardless of legal status. Police officers must somehow balance the pressure to assist in the enforcement of federal immigration laws with their own sense of fairness and community trust. A national survey of chiefs of police suggests that officers in their day-to-day work do attempt such a balance.

Chiefs reported that their officers draw distinctions between violent crimes and those like shoplifting and traffic infractions that are perceived to be less serious when they encounter someone who may lack legal status.[8]

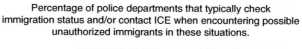

Percentage of police departments that typically check immigration status and/or contact ICE when encountering possible unauthorized immigrants in these situations.

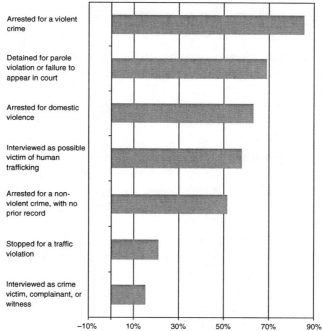

[8]This finding is based on a national survey of police executives conducted in 2007–2008. Results can be found in Scott H. Decker, Paul G. Lewis, Doris Marie Provine, and Monica W. Varsanyi, "On the Frontier of Local Law Enforcement: Local Police and Federal Immigration Law," in *Immigration, Crime, and Justice*, edited by William F. McDonald, vol. 13 in *Sociology of Crime, Law, and Deviance* (Bingley, UK: Emerald/JAI Press, 2009), pp. 261–77. See a summary of this research at http://ccj.asu.edu/research/immigration-research-section/current-project/immigration-and-local-policing-results-from-a-national-survey-of-law-enforcement-executives-a-paper-presented-for-the-police-foundation/view.

In an increasingly mobile world, where people often have strong ties to more than one nation, it may be a mistake to draw sharp lines according to the legal status of residents. In the excerpt below, Seyla Benhabib suggests a more flexible approach that allows a degree of political voice to every resident and that encourages movement toward full citizenship; she calls this approach "cosmopolitan federalism." This would mean a commitment to the political and social incorporation of immigrants, including those without legal authorization. Residents without citizenship would not have the same voice as citizens, but they would have some voice, and they would eventually qualify for citizenship. She argues not for open borders, but for porous borders that recognize the existence of noncitizens and their need to participate in self-governance.

COSMOPOLITAN FEDERALISM
SEYLA BENHABIB

On April 4, 2003, US newspapers reported the case of Lance Corporal Jose Gutierrez, aged twenty-seven, who died in a tank battle outside Umm Qasr in Iraq on March 21, 2003 (Weiner 2003). Corporal Gutierrez was an undocumented immigrant from Guatemala, an orphan who had reached the United States through clandestine means and who joined the Marines in California. His case is by no means unusual: over a dozen legal and undocumented immigrants—mainly from Mexico and Central America—who were members of the US armed forces stationed in Iraq have lost their lives since March 2003. It is estimated that about 37,000 immigrants serve in the US armed forces, making up about 3 percent of the population on active duty (Swarns 2003). Their sad stories led both conservative and liberal lawmakers to propose hastily passed bills to grant these slain soldiers, and in some cases their spouses and children, posthumous citizenship. Some suggested that immigrants who join the armed forces be granted citizenship immediately, while still others advocated the reduction of the current waiting period for the granting of citizenship to those in the military from three to two years.

This is by no means the first time that immigrants have served in the US army. With the abolition of universal conscription, however, joining the army has become a venue of upward mobility for large numbers of low-income legal and undocumented migrants. We thus have the disturbing case of individuals dying for a country that denies them voting rights, that is, if they are legal permanent residents waiting to become "naturalized"; and if they are undocumented migrants, as was the case with Corporal Gutierrez, they do not even have the right to obtain a driving license or to open a bank account.

From *The Rights of Others* by Seyla Benhabib. Reprinted with the permission of Cambridge University Press.

The hasty efforts of American lawmakers to respond to these anomalous and intuitively unfair situations are indicative of the more general scrambling of the lines between territoriality, sovereignty, and citizenship. Those who carry out the ultimate sacrifice for the democratic people by giving their lives for it are not always its members in good standing. Furthermore, some are asked to die for a country that denies them the right to vote on those very laws which order them to take up arms against another people. Despite being the largest immigrant nation in the world, the American conception of citizenship has remained remarkably unitary at the level of granting political rights, by making "naturalization" a precondition for political voice. This practice is usually defended with the argument that since the granting of citizenship to legal migrants is fairly open, transparent, and speedy in the United States, it is not unfair to make the acquisition of citizenship a precondition for political voice.

This defense, however, does not attend to the facts on the ground: there are at the present an estimated 7 million undocumented immigrants in the United States, many of whom are active and contributing members of the labor force, in farms, hospitals, hotels, and sanitation facilities, others of whom send their children to school, who are active in the community and on school boards. The status of being an undocumented immigrant does not mean having no voice at all. However, these individuals, who may service hospitals, whether as nurses or as orderlies, are themselves scared to become sick and dependent on hospital facilities. Not having one's papers in order in our societies is a form of civil death.

The causes of their "illegality" can vary from illogical bureaucratic mishaps and mistakes to their desperate attempts to escape their home countries via smugglers known as "coyotes." The status of illegality does not stamp the other as an alien. Clearly, a democratic adjustment of the practices of legal incorporation is needed so as to normalize undocumented immigrants.

While undocumented-migrant status means civil death and political silencing, the lack of political voice for legal permanent residents means their effective disenfranchisement. An increasing number of individuals wish to retain dual citizenship or to live in one country on a long-term basis while not abdicating their original nationality. Making the exercise of democratic voice dependent upon one's nationality status alone, as the United States laws do, flies in the face of the complex interdependence of the lives of peoples across borders and territories. While the United States has remained impervious to many calls to facilitate dual citizenship, countries such as Mexico and the Dominican Republic permit their large diasporic populations to retain certain citizenship rights at home, including voting in local and national elections and, in the case of the Dominican Republic and Colombia, even running for and holding office. Throughout Southeast Asia, India, and Latin America; "flexible citizenship" (Ong 1999) is emerging as the norm.

These empirical developments are not only indicators of trends toward the disaggregation of citizenship; whether recognized as such by democratic lawmakers or not, they also herald transformations of *democratic sovereignty*. Democratic sovereignty is based on three regulative ideals: that the people are the author as well as the subject of the laws; the ideal of a unified *demos;* and the idea of a self-enclosed and autochthonous territory over which the *demos* governs. The latter two ideals are indefensible both on normative and on empirical grounds. The unity of the *demos* ought to be understood not as if it were a harmonious given, but rather as a process of self-constitution, through more or less conscious struggles of inclusion and exclusion.

Furthermore, the ideal of territorial self-sufficiency flies in the face of the tremendous interdependence of the peoples of the world—a process which has been speeded up by the phenomenon of globalization. The emergence of international law and the spread of international human rights norms are developments which parallel the spread of globalization. As economic, military, and communicational interdependence increase, as tourism and crossborder mobility are intensified, a body of norms and regulations emerges to govern the activity of international civil society. The traditional view, which traces the legitimacy of international law to treaties among sovereign states alone, is no longer adequate to understand the legal complexities of a global civil society. Along with the obsolescence of this model, the ideal of territorial autochthony [that is, roughly, legitimacy arising out of native traditions] must be discarded as well.

The core of democratic self-governance is the ideal of public autonomy, namely, the principle that those who are subject to the law should also be its authors. How can democratic voice and public autonomy be reconfigured if we dispense with the faulty ideals of a people's homogeneity and territorial autochthony? Can democratic representation be organized so as to transcend the nation-state configuration? The new reconfiguration of democratic voice gives rise to subnational as well as transnational modes of citizenship. Within the European Union in particular, there is a return to citizenship in the city and in the transnational institutions of the EU. "Flexible citizenship," particularly in the case of Central American countries, is another such attempt to multiply voice and the sites for the exercise of democratic citizenship.

Non-territorially based models of representation are certainly possible: one can be represented by some individual or a body of individuals by virtue of one's linguistic identity, ethnic heritage (as was proposed by Otto Bauer for the nationalities of middle and central Europe after World War I); religious affiliation, professional activities, and affected interests. Representation can run along many lines besides territorial residency. The discourse principle of legitimacy, which enjoins that all those who are affected by the consequences of the adoption of a norm have a say in its articulation certainly leads to the multiplication of sites of representation and discursive involvement. For example, the community of those affected by the fall of acid rain cuts across the Canadian/USA border and unites these individuals around shared interests, concerns, and activities. Globalization, insofar as it increases both the intensity and the interconnectedness of human actions around the world, results in the creation of new sites and new logics of representation.

Yet there is a crucial link between democratic self-governance and territorial representation. Precisely because democracies enact laws that are supposed to bind those who legitimately authorize them, the scope of democratic legitimacy cannot extend beyond the *demos* which has circumscribed itself as a people upon a given territory. Democratic laws require closure precisely because democratic representation, must be accountable to a specific people. I see no way to cut this Gordian knot linking territoriality, representation, and democratic voice. Certainly, representative institutions based on other principles will exist and they ought to proliferate.

The intuition that there may be a crucial link between territorial size and form of government is old in the history of western political thought, and it is one that I accept. Unlike communitarians and liberal nationalists, however, who view this link primarily as being based upon a cultural bond of identity, I am concerned with the logic of democratic representation, which requires closure for the sake of maintaining democratic legitimacy. Certainly, identification and solidarity are not unimportant, but they need to be leavened through democratic attachments and constitutional norms. In the spirit of Kant, therefore, I have pleaded for moral universalism and cosmopolitan federalism. I have not advocated *open* but rather *porous* borders; I have pleaded for first-admittance rights for refugees and asylum seekers but have accepted the right of democracies to regulate the transition from first admission to full membership; I have also argued for subjecting laws governing naturalization to human rights norms and rejected the claim of a sovereign people not to permit naturalization and to bar the eventual citizenship of aliens in its midst. For some, these proposals will go too far in the direction of rootless cosmopolitanism; for others, they will not go far enough. I believe that the best way to approach political membership at the dawn of a new century is by accepting the challenge of conflicting moral visions and political commitments suggested by one of the slogans of the Immigrant Workers' Freedom Ride: "No human is illegal."

Benhabib clearly believes that it is time to end the traditional idea that citizenship is a singular status, linking an individual to the nation state in which he or she is born. She argues that there is too much human movement and interaction for this idea to survive without producing a lot of injustice. One solution might be to abolish citizenship altogether or to create a singular global citizenship that would promote an international civil society. Human rights could be the currency of this global realm, obviating the need for state-based bills of rights. In a global community, as Charles Lee points out: "Everyone is a legitimate and official citizen of the worldwide community [and] there will be no such thing as illegal aliens or excluded foreigners. Moreover, global citizens and officials will have to somehow account for the material disparity between regions as a pressing 'domestic' issue rather than disregarding it as a matter of another state's internal mismanagement."[9] Another, perhaps more

---

[9]Charles T. Lee, "Undocumented Workers' Subversive Citizenship Acts," *Peace Review: A Journal of Social Justice,* vol. 20: 330–38 (2008).

practical, solution to the citizenship/migration/globalization problem might be multiple affiliations that would legitimate political participation where one worked and resided and would link transnational locales, much as Benhabib envisions in the selection you read. Lee adds an intriguing thought, suggesting that unauthorized migrants are already pointing the way to such new citizenship rules and arrangements.

Note that Benhabib favorably mentions Immanuel Kant in this excerpt. Here is the original document to which she refers. Impressively, this document was written in 1795 and has remained influential since then. Kant's position on immigrants and visitors is part of a larger set of principles for perpetual peace in the world, which he regarded as theoretically achievable and possibly politically feasible too, if only politicians would take on this goal.

THIRD DEFINITIVE ARTICLE FOR A PERPETUAL PEACE
IMMANUEL KANT

"The Law of World Citizenship Shall Be Limited to Conditions of Universal Hospitality"

Here, as in the preceding articles, it is not a question of philanthropy but of right. Hospitality means the right of a stranger not to be treated as an enemy when he arrives in the land of another. One may refuse to receive him when this can be done without causing his destruction; but, so long as he peacefully occupies his place, one may not treat him with hostility. It is not the right to be a permanent visitor that one may demand. A special beneficent agreement would be needed in order to give an outsider a right to become a fellow inhabitant for a certain length of time. It is only a right of temporary sojourn, a right to associate, which all men have. They have it by virtue of their common possession of the surface of the earth, where, as a globe, they cannot infinitely disperse and hence must finally tolerate the presence of each other. Originally, no one had more right than another to a particular part of the earth.

Uninhabitable parts of the earth—the sea and the deserts—divide this community of all men, but the ship and the camel (the desert ship) enable them to approach each other across these unruled regions and to establish communication by using the common right to the face of the earth, which belongs to human beings generally. The inhospitality of the inhabitants of coasts (for instance, of the Barbary Coast) in robbing ships in neighboring seas or enslaving stranded travelers, or the inhospitality of the inhabitants of the deserts (for instance, the Bedouin Arabs) who view contact with nomadic tribes as conferring the right to plunder them, is thus opposed to natural law, even though it extends the right of hospitality, i.e., the privilege of foreign arrivals, no further than to conditions of the possibility of seeking to communicate with the prior inhabitants. In this way distant parts of the world can come into peaceable relations with each other, and these are finally publicly established by law. Thus the human race can gradually be brought closer and closer to a constitution establishing world citizenship.

But to this perfection compare the inhospitable actions of the civilized and especially of the commercial states of our part of the world. The injustice which they show to lands and peoples they visit (which is equivalent to conquering them) is carried by them to terrifying lengths. America, the lands inhabited by the Negro, the Spice Islands, the Cape, etc., were at the time of their discovery considered by these civilized intruders as lands without owners, for they counted the inhabitants as nothing. In East India (Hindustan), under the pretense of establishing economic undertakings, they brought in foreign soldiers and used them to oppress the natives, excited widespread wars among the various states, spread famine, rebellion, perfidy, and the whole litany of evils which afflict mankind.

Since the narrower or wider community of the peoples of the earth has developed so far that a violation of rights in one place is felt throughout the world, the idea of a law of world citizenship is no high-flown or exaggerated notion. It is a supplement to the unwritten code of the civil and international law, indispensable for the maintenance of the public human rights and hence also of perpetual peace. One cannot flatter oneself into believing one can approach this peace except under the condition outlined here.

Discussion Questions

- Would it be fair to say that law enforcement suffered a moral panic in the wake of the 9/11 attack? What, if anything, can be done to prevent such occurrences?

- Should immigrants from countries that have in the past produced terrorists be treated differently than other immigrants? What does your answer imply for the United States? Consider, for example, the Oklahoma City bombing of the federal office building for which Timothy James McVeigh, a U.S. citizen and Army veteran, was convicted. Or the suicide attack by the American software engineer who, out of anger with the IRS, flew his plane into the agency's building in Austin, Texas, in February 2010.

- What do you make of Agamben's claim that states of exception are becoming more frequent?

- Kant wrote this document during the height of European expansion over the entire globe. The goal was new markets for goods and resources for European manufacturers and consumers. Kant wanted to bring more justice to the process of globalization that was occurring then. Does his advice seem desirable and/or feasible for the contemporary period?

- Does Benhabib provide a sufficiently detailed roadmap as to what "cosmopolitan federalism" might involve? How might this goal realistically be achieved? Is it fair to native-born and naturalized citizens?

Citizenship

Citizenship is a status conferred by governments, sometimes based on one's origin of birth, sometimes on a series of steps one must take (naturalized citizens), and sometimes conferred by law or treaty, as happened in the 1867 Treaty of Purchase that transferred Alaska from Russia to the United States. In that case some local residents received citizenship, but others (the so-called "uncivilized tribes") did not, a distinction that courts attempted to apply based on earlier Russian interactions with the residents.[10] However acquired, citizenship confers important benefits to those who hold this status.

Citizens of democratic nations like to think that their voices matter. Indeed, the idea that the citizens control their government, with their views represented in the process of law-making, is a keystone of democratic theory. But if citizens want to be governed responsibly and effectively, they must pay attention to what is going on politically. This means not just being well-informed about issues, but also being well-informed about cultural and social differences in human populations. Political philosopher Martha Nussbaum suggests that education in cultural diversity is an essential ingredient for effective governance in the contemporary world because the decisions we make now affect groups differently and because one nation's decisions often involve people from other societies with different value systems:

> All modern democracies are inescapably plural. As citizens within each nation we are frequently called upon to make decisions that require some understanding of racial and ethnic and religious groups in that nation, and of the situation of its women and its sexual minorities. As citizens we are also increasingly called upon to understand how issues such as agriculture, human rights, ecology, even business and industry, are generating discussions that bring people together from many different nations. This must happen more and more, if effective solutions to pressing human problems are to be found (2002: 291).[11]

The implications for education in Nussbaum's remarks are clear—no nation is an island, and no nation is homogeneous. Education must recognize and take account of these differences within and among nations. Taking this problem of education one step further, how can we be sure that our governing process fully represents our own national diversity? If government is to represent *all* the people, we must find ways to avoid steam-rolling minorities, who, by definition, cannot outvote the majority. This is a matter of justice, but also effective governance. In life, as in government, the best decisions occur when all perspectives are considered.

---

[10]Arthur Mason traces this history in "Of Enlightenment and Alaska Early Moderns," *Identities: Global Studies in Power and Culture,*" vol. 7 (4): 411–429 (2010). He applies a framework developed by Pierre Bourdieu to examine the social history of the Alaska Native Alutiiq. The elites in this native population were able to maintain a position under Russian domination that later allowed them to acquire American citizenship, further amplifying social-class differences in this population.

[11]Martha Nussbaum, "Education for Citizenship in an Era of Global Connection," *Studies in Philosophy and Education,* vol. 21 (4–5): 289–303 (2002).

The first reading in this section addresses the problem of representation for all groups within a society and offers a solution. The author is another political philosopher of great repute, Iris Marion Young. Her argument may seem complex, but it is really quite straightforward. She argues for mechanisms that protect oppressed minorities and that give them opportunities to promote their interests and views. She contrasts her position with those who believe that equality requires the same treatment for all. Where there is pre-existing inequality and injustice, she suggests, the same-treatment approach actually perpetuates inequality. The same-treatment approach, by ignoring differences in access and voice, fosters what Stephen Castles[12] calls "differentiated" citizenship," in which everyone has the same formal citizenship rights, but in which ethnic minorities and indigenous peoples, among others, are excluded from real political and social rights (2005: 689).

Professor Young's argument for taking active steps to level the playing field in governance may sound familiar: Does it remind you of the debate over affirmative action in higher education and employment? Both are concerned with taking account of existing differences to achieve more just results in areas of importance for the whole society. But they differ in their focus of concern. The emphasis in the reading below is on achieving voice for all in the democratic process.

POLITY AND GROUP DIFFERENCE: A CRITIQUE OF THE IDEAL OF UNIVERSAL CITIZENSHIP
IRIS MARION YOUNG

An ideal of universal citizenship has driven the emancipatory momentum of modern political life. During this angry, sometimes bloody, political struggle in the nineteenth and twentieth centuries, many among the excluded and disadvantaged thought that winning full citizenship status, that is, equal political and civil rights, would lead to their freedom and equality. Now, however, when citizenship rights have been formally extended to all groups in liberal capitalist societies, some groups still find themselves treated as second-class citizens. Social movements of oppressed and excluded groups have recently asked why extension of equal citizenship rights has not led to social justice and equality. Part of the answer is straightforwardly Marxist: those social activities that most determine the status of individuals and groups are anarchic and oligarchic; economic life is not sufficiently under the control of citizens to affect the unequal status and treatment of groups. I think this is an important and correct diagnosis of why equal citizenship has not

---

[12]Stephen Castles, "Hierarchical Citizenship in a World of Unequal Nation-States," *PSOnline*, http://www.apasanet.org (October 2005): 689–92.

From "Polity and Group Difference: A Critique of the Ideal of Universal Citizenship" by Iris Marion Young, from *Ethics*, Vol. 99, No. 2, (Jan. 1989).

eliminated oppression, but in this article I reflect on another reason more intrinsic to the meaning of politics and citizenship as expressed in much modern thought.

I argue that the inclusion and participation of everyone in public discussion and decision making requires mechanisms for group representation. Where differences in capacities, culture, values, and behavioral styles exist among groups, but some of these groups are privileged, strict adherence to a principle of equal treatment tends to perpetuate oppression or disadvantage. The inclusion and participation of everyone in social and political institutions therefore sometimes requires the articulation of special rights that attend to group differences in order to undermine oppression and disadvantage.

I. Citizenship as Generality

In a society where some groups are privileged while others are oppressed, insisting that as citizens persons should leave behind their particular affiliations and experiences to adopt a general point of view serves only to reinforce that privilege; for the perspectives and interests of the privileged will tend to dominate this unified public, marginalizing or silencing those of other groups.

Instead of a universal citizenship in the sense of this generality, we need a group differentiated citizenship and a heterogeneous public. In a heterogeneous public, differences are publicly recognized and acknowledged as irreducible, by which I mean that persons from one perspective or history can never completely understand and adopt the point of view of those with other group-based perspectives and histories. Yet commitment to the need and desire to decide together the society's policies fosters communication across those differences.

II. Differentiated Citizenship as Group Representation

In her study of the functioning of a New England Town Meeting government, Jane Mansbridge discusses how women, blacks, working-class people, and poor people tend to participate less and have their interests represented less than whites, middle-class professionals, and men. Even though all citizens have the right to participate in the decision-making process, the experience and perspectives of some groups tend to be silenced for many reasons. White middle-class men assume authority more than others and they are more practiced at speaking persuasively; mothers and old people often find it more difficult than others to get to meetings. Amy Gutmann also discusses how participatory democratic structures tend to silence disadvantaged groups. She offers the example of community control of schools, where increased democracy led to increased segregation in many cities because the more privileged and articulate whites were able to promote their perceived interests against blacks' just demand for equal treatment in an integrated system. Such cases indicate that when participatory democratic structures define citizenship in universalistic and unified terms, they tend to reproduce existing group oppression.

If we are not to be forced to trace a utopian circle, we need to solve now the "paradox of democracy" by which social power makes some citizens more equal than others, and equality of citizenship makes some people more powerful citizens. That solution lies at least in part in providing institutionalized means for the explicit recognition and representation of oppressed groups. Before discussing principles and practices involved in such a solution, however, it is necessary to say something about what a group is and when a group is oppressed.

The concept of a social group has become politically important because recent emancipatory and leftist social movements have mobilized around group identity rather than exclusively class or economic interests. In many cases such mobilization has consisted in embracing and positively defining a despised or devalued ethnic or racial identity. In the women's movement, gay rights movement, or elders' movements, differential social status based on age, sexuality, physical capacity, or the division of labor has been taken up as a positive group identity for political mobilization.

I shall not attempt to define a social group here, but I shall point to several marks which distinguish a social group from other collectivities of people. A social group involves first of all an affinity with other persons by which they identify with one another, and by which other people identify them. A person's particular sense of history, understanding of social relations and personal possibilities, her or his mode of reasoning, values, and expressive styles are constituted at least partly by her or his group identity. Many group definitions come from the outside, from other groups that label and stereotype certain people. In such circumstances the despised group members often find their affinity in their oppression.

As products of social relations, groups are fluid; they come into being and may fade away. Homosexual practices have existed in many societies and historical periods, for example, but gay male group identification exists only in the West in the twentieth century. Group identity may become salient only under specific circumstances, when in interaction with other groups. Most people in modern societies have multiple group identifications, moreover, and therefore groups themselves are not discrete unities. Every group has group differences cutting across it.

I think that group differentiation is an inevitable and desirable process in modern societies. We need not settle that question, however. I merely assume that ours is now a group differentiated society, and that it will continue to be so for some time to come. Our political problem is that some of our groups are privileged and others are oppressed.

But what is oppression? Briefly, a group is oppressed when one or more of the following conditions occurs to all or a large portion of its members: (1) the benefits of their work or energy go to others without those others reciprocally benefiting them (exploitation); (2) they are excluded from participation in major social activities, which in our society means primarily a workplace (marginalization); (3) they live and work under the authority of others, and have little work autonomy and authority over others themselves (powerlessness); (4) as a group they are stereotyped at the same time that their experience and situation is invisible in the society in general, and they have little opportunity and little audience for the expression of their experience and perspective on social events (cultural imperialism); (5) group members suffer random violence and harassment motivated by group hatred or fear. In the United States today at least the following groups are oppressed in one or more of these ways: women, blacks, Native Americans, Chicanos, Puerto Ricans and other Spanish-speaking Americans, Asian Americans, gay men, lesbians, working-class people, poor people, old people, and mentally and physically disabled people.

Perhaps in some utopian future there will be a society without group oppression and disadvantage. We cannot develop political principles by starting with the assumption of a completely just society, however, but must begin from within the general historical and social conditions in which we exist. This means that we must develop participatory democratic theory, not on the assumption of an undifferentiated humanity, but rather on the assumption that there are group differences and that some groups are actually or potentially oppressed or disadvantaged.

I assert, then, the following principle: a democratic public, however that is constituted, should provide mechanisms for the effective representation and recognition of the distinct voices and perspectives of those of its constituent groups that are oppressed or disadvantaged within it. Such group representation implies institutional mechanisms and public resources supporting three activities: (1) self-organization of group members so that they gain a sense of collective empowerment and a reflective understanding of their collective experience and interests in the context of the society; (2) voicing a group's analysis of how social policy proposals affect them, and generating policy proposals themselves, in institutionalized contexts where decision makers are obliged to show that they have taken these perspectives into consideration; (3) having veto power regarding specific policies that affect a group directly, for example, reproductive rights for women, or use of reservation lands for Native Americans.

The principles call for specific representation only for oppressed or disadvantaged groups, because privileged groups already are represented.

Social and economic privilege means, among other things, that the groups which have it behave as though they have a right to speak and be heard, that others treat them as though they have that right, and that they have the material, personal, and organizational resources that enable them to speak and be heard in public. The privileged are usually not inclined to protect and further the interests of the oppressed partly because their social position prevents them from understanding those interests, and partly because to some degree their privilege depends on the continued oppression of others. So a major reason for explicit representation of oppressed groups in discussion and decision making is to undermine oppression. Such group representation also exposes in public the specificity of the assumptions and experience of the privileged. For unless confronted with different perspectives on social relations and events, different values and language, most people tend to assert their own perspective as universal.

Group representation is the best means to promote just outcomes to democratic decision-making processes. The argument for this claim relies on Habermas's conception of communicative ethics. In the absence of a Philosopher King who reads transcendent normative verities, the only ground for a claim that a policy or decision is just is that it has been arrived at by a public which has truly promoted free expression of all needs and points of view.

The introduction of such differentiation and particularity into democratic procedures does not encourage the expression of narrow self-interest; indeed, group representation is the best antidote to self-deceiving self-interest masked as an impartial or general interest. In a democratically structured public where social inequality is mitigated through group representation, individuals or groups cannot simply assert that they want something; they must say that justice requires or allows that they have it. Group representation provides the opportunity for some to express their needs or interests who would not likely be heard without that representation.

Group representation best institutionalizes fairness under circumstances of social oppression and domination. But group representation also maximizes knowledge expressed in discussion, and thus promotes practical wisdom. Group differences not only involve different needs, interests, and goals, but probably more important, different social locations and experiences from which social facts and policies are understood.

Emancipatory social movements in recent years have developed some political practices committed to the idea of a heterogeneous public, and they have at least partly or temporarily instituted such publics. Some political organizations, unions, and feminist groups have formal caucuses for groups (such as blacks, Latinos, women, gay men and lesbians, and disabled or old people) whose perspectives might be silenced without them. Frequently these organizations have procedures for caucus voice in organization discussion and caucus representation in decision making, and some organizations also require representation of members of specific groups in leadership bodies. Under the influence of these social movements asserting group difference, during some years even the Democratic party, at both national and state levels, has instituted delegate rules that include provisions for group representation.

Though its realization is far from assured, the ideal of a "rainbow coalition" expresses such a heterogeneous public with forms of group representation. Ideally, a rainbow coalition affirms the presence and supports the claims of each of the oppressed groups or political movements constituting it, and it arrives at a political program not by voicing some "principles of unity" that hide differences but rather by allowing each constituency to analyze economic and social issues from the perspective of its experience. This implies that each group maintains autonomy in relating to its constituency, and that decision-making bodies and procedures provide for group representation.

What groups deserve representation? Clear candidates for group representation in policy making in the United States are women, blacks, Native Americans, old people, poor people, disabled people, gay men and lesbians, Spanish-speaking Americans, young people, and nonprofessional workers. But it may not be necessary to ensure specific representation of all these groups in all public contexts and in all policy discussions. Representation should be designated whenever the group's history and social situation provide a particular perspective on the issues, when the interests of its members are specifically affected, and when its perceptions and interests are not likely to receive expression without that representation.

What should be the mechanisms of group representation? Earlier I stated that the self-organization of the group is one of the aspects of a principle of group representation. Members of the group must meet together in democratic forums to discuss issues and formulate group positions and proposals. This principle of group representation should be understood as part of a larger program for democratized decision-making processes. Public life and decision-making processes should be transformed so that all citizens have significantly greater opportunities for participation in discussion and decision making. All citizens should have access to neighborhood or district assemblies where they participate in discussion and decision making. In such a more participatory democratic scheme, members of oppressed groups would also have group assemblies, which would delegate group representatives.

III. Universal Righs and Special Rights

Contemporary social movements seeking full inclusion and participation of oppressed and disadvantaged groups now find themselves faced with a dilemma of difference. On the one hand, they must continue to deny that there are any essential differences between men and women, whites and blacks, able-bodied and disabled people, which justify denying women, blacks, or disabled people the opportunity to do anything that others are free to do or to be included in any institution or position. On the other hand, they have found it necessary to affirm that there are often group-based differences between men and women, whites and blacks, able-bodied and disabled people that make application of a strict principle of equal treatment, especially in competition for positions, unfair because these differences put those groups at a disadvantage. For example, white middle-class men as a group are socialized into the behavioral styles of a particular kind of articulateness, coolness, and competent authoritativeness that are most rewarded in professional and managerial life. To the degree that there are group differences that disadvantage, fairness seems to call for acknowledging rather than being blind to them.

Though in many respects the law is now blind to group differences, the society is not, and some groups continue to be marked as deviant and as the other. In everyday interactions, images, and decision making, assumptions continue to be made about women, blacks, Latinos, gay men, lesbians, old people, and other marked groups, which continue to justify exclusions, avoidances, paternalism, and authoritarian treatment. Continued racist, sexist, homophobic, ageist, and ableist behaviors and institutions create particular circumstances for these groups, usually disadvantaging them in their opportunity to develop their capacities and giving them particular experiences and knowledge. Finally, in part because they have been segregated and excluded from one another, and in part because they have particular histories and traditions, there are cultural differences among social groups—differences in language, style of living, body comportment and gesture, values, and perspectives on society.

Where group differences in capacities, values, and behavioral or cognitive styles exist, equal treatment in the allocation of reward according to rules of merit composition will reinforce and perpetuate disadvantage. Equal treatment requires everyone to be measured according to the same norms, but in fact there are no "neutral" norms of behavior and performance. Where some groups are privileged and others oppressed, the formulation of law, policy, and the rules of private institutions tend to be biased in favor of the privileged groups, because their particular experience implicitly sets the norm. Thus where there are group differences in capacities, socialization, values, and cognitive and cultural styles, only attending to such differences can enable the inclusion and participation of all groups in political and economic institutions. This implies that instead of always formulating rights and rules in universal terms that are blind to difference, some groups sometimes deserve special rights.

Whether they involve quotas or not, affirmative action programs violate a principle of equal treatment because they are race or gender conscious in setting criteria for school admissions, jobs, or promotions. These policies are usually defended in one of two ways. Giving preference to race or gender is understood either as just compensation for groups that have suffered discrimination in the past, or as compensation for the present disadvantage these groups suffer because of that history of discrimination and exclusion. I do not wish to quarrel with either of these justifications for the differential treatment based on race or gender implied by affirmative action policies. I want to suggest that in addition we can understand affirmative action policies as compensating for the cultural biases of standards and evaluators used by the schools or employers. These standards and evaluators reflect at least to some degree the specific life and cultural experience of dominant groups—whites, Anglos, or men. In a group-differentiated society, moreover, the development of truly neutral standards and evaluations is difficult or impossible, because female, black, or Latino cultural experience and the dominant cultures are in many respects not reducible to a common measure. Thus affirmative action policies compensate for the dominance of one set of cultural attributes. Such an interpretation of affirmative action locates the "problem" that affirmative action solves partly in the understandable biases of evaluators and their standards, rather than only in specific differences of the disadvantaged group.

Although they are not a matter of different treatment as such, comparable worth policies similarly claim to challenge cultural biases in traditional evaluation in the worth of female-dominated occupations, and in doing so require attending to differences. Schemes of equal pay for work of comparable worth require that predominantly male and predominantly female jobs have similar wage structures if they involve similar degrees of skill, difficulty, stress, and so on. The problem in implementing these policies, of course, lies in designing methods of comparing the jobs, which often are very different. Most schemes of comparison choose to minimize sex differences by using supposedly gender-neutral criteria, such as educational attainment, speed of work, whether it involves manipulation of symbols, decision making, and so on. Some writers have suggested, however, that standard classifications of job traits may be systematically biased to keep specific kinds of tasks involved in many female-dominated occupations hidden. Many female-dominated occupations involve gender-specific kinds of labor—such as nurturing, smoothing over social relations, or the exhibition of sexuality—which most task observation ignores. A fair assessment of the skills and complexity of many female-dominated jobs may therefore involve paying explicit attention to gender differences in kinds of jobs rather than applying gender-blind categories of comparison.

Finally, linguistic and cultural minorities ought to have the right to maintain their language and culture and at the same time be entitled to all the benefits of citizenship, as well as valuable education and career opportunities. This right implies a positive obligation on the part of governments and other public bodies to print documents and to provide services in the native language of recognized linguistic minorities, and to provide bilingual instruction in schools. Cultural assimilation should not be a condition of full social participation, because it requires a person to transform his or her sense of identity, and when it is realized on a group level it means altering or annihilating the group's identity. This principle does not apply to any persons who do not identify with majority language or culture within a society, but only to sizeable linguistic or cultural minorities living in distinct though not necessarily segregated communities. In the United States, then, special rights for cultural minorities applies at least to Spanish-speaking Americans and Native Americans.

The universalist finds a contradiction in asserting both that formerly segregated groups have a right to inclusion and that these groups have a right to different treatment. There is no contradiction here, however, if attending to difference is necessary in order to make participation and inclusion possible. Groups with different circumstances or forms of life should be able to participate together in public institutions without shedding their distinct identities or suffering disadvantage because of them. The goal is not to give special compensation to the deviant until they achieve normality, but rather to denormalize the way institutions formulate their rules by revealing the plural circumstances and needs that exist, or ought to exist, within them.

To achieve justice, democracies need not only a way of hearing the voices of all citizens, but also good counsel from those citizens. In short, citizens must be reasonably knowledgeable about social problems and policy proposals to exercise their rights effectively and wisely. This requirement suggests a dilemma. Citizens depend on government for much of their information, but government officials will often find it more convenient to provide misinformation than correct information, or to obscure awkward facts. And citizens are not necessarily motivated to dig for the truth. The problem goes deeper. Citizens may not even be motivated to overcome their own preexisting prejudices to accept correct information when it is offered to them.

The authors of our next reading argue that misinformation is at least as serious a problem as lack of information in democratic governance. This article explores the problem of preconceived ideas and shows how preconceptions get in the way of absorbing information that contradicts those preconceptions. It is as if people are wired to be certain in their views, even when those views are incorrect. The authors mean *us*: Do you plead guilty to sticking to what you think you know and resisting contradictory new information, even when it might be more accurate? The brief excerpt below is from a much longer article that provides empirical evidence of resistance to correct information about the costs of government programs.

MISINFORMATION AND THE CURRENCY OF DEMOCRATIC CITIZENSHIP

JAMES H. KUKLINSKI, PAUL J. QUIRK, JENNIFER JERIT,
DAVID SCHWIEDER, AND ROBERT F. RICH

Citizens must have ready access to factual information that facilitates the evaluation of public policy. This information should be specific to the policy deliberations taking place among political leaders, for domain-specific facts best enable people to connect to policy debates. Citizens must then use these facts to inform their preferences. They must absorb and apply the facts to overcome areas of ignorance or to correct mistaken conceptions. The more facts they bring to bear, the better, and some facts are always better than no facts. What is crucial is that preferences stem from facts, objective data about the world. If both conditions are met, the thinking goes, then representative democracy is on solid footing.

Fulfilling the first condition is a prerequisite to meeting the second; citizens can use facts only if the political system disseminates them. Generally speaking, the American political system fares poorly on this count. Those best positioned to provide relevant facts, elected officials and members of the media, lack the incentive to do so. Politicians want their preferred policies to prevail, and so they employ manipulative rhetoric and create themes and images that will sway the electorate in the desired direction. When elected officials do cite facts, it is to dramatize their own cause, not to educate and elucidate. In the same vein, television news, the dominant source of information in American society, seeks to gain and maintain its viewers' interest. Rather than present general facts and place them in context, it reports specific events and personal situations, and the more vivid, the better. If facts are the currency of citizenship, then the American polity is in a chronically impecunious state.

The empirical investigations reported below represent our initial effort to find out. They show that, in general, citizens tend to resist facts. They can be induced to use correct information, even in the context of a single-shot survey, but it takes an extraordinarily obtrusive presentation of that information. People hold inaccurate factual beliefs, and do so confidently. The problem, then, at least with respect to attitudes about public policy, is not that people simply lack information, but that they firmly hold the wrong information—and use it to form preferences. Not only does this misinformation function as a barrier to factually educating citizens, it can lead to collective preferences that differ significantly from those that would exist if people were adequately informed.

The Psychology of Misinformation

To understand why people should hold any factual beliefs at all and why these beliefs often will be systematically skewed in the direction of their preferences, we need only to consider three mental processes that social and cognitive psychologists have documented as inherent in human thinking. The first is the drawing of social inferences, the second the strong drive toward belief and attitude consistency, and the third a tendency to become overconfident in one's beliefs and judgments.

People are constantly trying to make sense of the world. They seek to understand why situations exist, why events occur, and why others and they themselves act the way they do. To achieve this understanding, people do not act simply as passive receivers of stimuli from their environments. To the contrary, their minds actively (although often unconsciously) decide which information to attend to and how to interpret that information. When all the information is not available, which is most of the time, people make inferences. Metaphorically, they "fill in the blanks." Governing this process is what Abelson and Reich call the completion principle: inferring unknowns from what is stored in memory.

This implies that people do not necessarily make the most objective inferences they could. Rather, they strive for consistency in their beliefs and attitudes. When they already hold salient attitudes relevant to the subject at hand, they will be inclined to make biased and reinforcing inferences rather than accurate ones. Often this can be accomplished easily, either through searching out consistent and ignoring inconsistent information or by interpreting new information to be consistent with existing beliefs and attitudes.

Once people store their factual inferences in memory, these inferences are indistinguishable from hard data. And the more they then use this stored information, the more central it becomes to future inferences and judgments. Thus, many people quickly become overconfident about their factual beliefs. People constantly overrate the accuracy and reliability of their beliefs.

Data and Methodology

Our expectations are as follows. Not only will people hold factual beliefs about public policy, many will hold inaccurate ones and hold them confidently. Moreover, beliefs and preferences will be tightly intertwined. This combination—confidently held beliefs and a strong connection between those beliefs and existing preferences—will serve as a barrier to informing the American citizenry.

To test these propositions, we draw primarily on a telephone survey of a representative sample of Illinois residents. Half-hour interviews were completed with 1,160 respondents. The survey includes a series of questions on citizens' attitudes toward and perceptions of welfare policy. It also contains a number of question batteries and experimental manipulations designed to explore the psychology of mass opinion about public policy.

We used the following procedure. First, we created three randomly assigned groups, each containing about 300 respondents. Respondents in the first group received a set of six factual items that were designed to give them relevant contextual information about welfare. In selecting the facts to present, we consulted with welfare experts who identified a reasonably representative group of facts they deemed as fundamental to policy debates on welfare. In the guise of asking people whether they had heard the information, the interviewers told respondents the following: the percentage of families who are on welfare, the proportion of the federal budget that welfare absorbs, the average annual benefit amount for a welfare family, the percentage of welfare mothers who are on welfare for more than eight years, the percentage of welfare families who are African-American, and the percentage of welfare mothers who have less than a high school education. The items were presented in random order. Obviously, only a subset of all possible facts could be presented. Since there is no formula for choosing one set of facts over another, we claim only that the six items represent the kind of facts that someone intimately familiar with welfare would know and deem important.

A second group of respondents was given a multiple choice quiz on the same items of information for the purpose of getting them to retrieve and explicate their beliefs. The items had five options and were also presented in random order. After each of the quiz items, respondents were asked how confident they were of their answer, with the four options ranging from "very confident" to "not at all confident." A third group of respondents received no treatment at all. Individuals in this control group represent citizens as they actually evaluate policy under ordinary circumstances in the real world.

All three groups received the same questions about their policy preferences on welfare, the first two after they had dealt with the factual items. Specifically, respondents were asked to indicate their attitudes toward cutting welfare and toward imposing a two-year limit on welfare payments. Response options are on a five-point scale ranging from strongly support to strongly oppose.

The Prevalence of Misinformation

Responses to the survey questions reveal widespread mistaken beliefs about the realities of welfare. The proportion getting an individual fact wrong ranges from two-thirds on the percentage of all welfare families who are African-American to a striking 90% on the percentage of the federal budget that goes to welfare. On none of the individual items did a majority, or close to it, get the fact right. Moreover, although some individuals were more accurate across the six items than others, only 3% got more than half the facts right.

Most significant, those holding the least accurate beliefs perversely expressed the highest confidence in them. For example, 47% of those who estimated the proportion of American families on welfare correctly (at 7%) said they were very or fairly confident, while 74% of those who grossly overestimated the figure (at 25%) did. Similarly, 54% of those who estimated the average welfare payment correctly (at $6,000) were confident, while 77% of those who grossly overestimated it (at $18,000) were confident.

In sum, although factual inaccuracy is troublesome, it is the "I know I'm right" syndrome that poses the potentially formidable problem. It implies not only that most people will resist correcting their factual beliefs, but also that the very people who most need to correct them will be the least likely to do so.

Presentation of the Facts

What happens, then, if a champion of political education gives citizens correct facts? Do they use the new information to adjust their policy preferences appropriately?

In fact, this coefficient does not approach statistical significance, indicating that the preferences of the two groups do not differ. Those who were told the facts either did not absorb them or did but failed to change their preferences accordingly.

Conclusion

Judging from our findings on factual beliefs about welfare, many people are likely to be misinformed, not only inaccurate in their factual beliefs, but confident that they are right. Their errors can be skewed in a particular direction—for example, pro- or anti-welfare—and may cause or at least reinforce preferences about policy. To a degree that we cannot specify with much precision, people also resist correct information. We do not pretend to know how widespread misinformation is, how much it skews policy preferences or behavior, or whether any feasible changes in media practices or political debate could significantly reduce it. It will take a good deal of further research before we can answer these and related questions. Nevertheless, the notion of misinformation raises some implications for public opinion research.

The principal implication is that students of public opinion should take seriously the distinction between misinformation—confidently held false beliefs— and a mere lack of information. It is one thing not to know and be aware of one's ignorance. It is quite another to be dead certain about factual beliefs that are far off the mark.

Rather than respond willy-nilly to whatever cues the environment provides, people resist change. Unless they are "hit between the eyes" with the right facts, they continue to judge policy on the basis of their mistaken beliefs. In fact, it is likely that even those "hit between the eyes" with facts will eventually return to their original beliefs and preferences. In their work on deliberative polls, for example, Luskin, Fishkin, and Jowell found that people frequently changed their issue positions after participating in intense deliberations with fellow citizens and listening to testimony from politicians and policy experts. However, a follow-up survey found these changes to be largely temporary.

But returning to the problem of the quality of information available to citizens, how hard does government work to educate its citizens? Maybe not very hard at all, suggest Matthew Crenson and Benjamin Ginsberg. Governments increasingly treat citizens, not as participants in the task of governance, but as consumers to be managed and satisfied. Governments no longer need citizen participation to continue operating, except for the occasional visit to the voting booth, and even in those cases, the number of "safe" electoral districts is growing because politicians control districting. So it should not be surprising that well-funded lobbyists have more influence in determining policy than do ordinary citizens.

DOES ANYONE NEED CITIZENS?
MATTHEW A. CRENSON AND BENJAMIN GINSBERG

AMERICANS ARE entering a political world in which citizens have ceased to compose a public. Americans continue to participate in politics (at reduced levels and with diminished influence), but they do so increasingly on their own. America is becoming a nation of emphatically *private* citizens—customers and clients who find it difficult to express coherent, common interests through collective political action. In fact, Americans have sacrificed something of citizenship itself. Proper citizens have a collective identity. That is precisely what has been lost in the era of personal democracy.

So far, citizens have done little to reassert their collective status, though the profound alienation from politics that surfaces in public opinion polls and political commentary suggests that they are hardly satisfied with their current standing. Unless apathy and withdrawal are regarded as forms of political participation, however, citizens have made no concerted effort to change their standing. Personal democracy creates a Catch-22 for the collective mobilization of citizens. If citizens are to be roused from apathy to action, someone in a position to arouse them must have an interest in doing so, but one of the essential features of today's personal democracy is that hardly anyone in power fits that description.

Historians can point to some instances of spontaneous popular mobilization—urban mobs or peasant uprisings—that erupted without elite sponsorship. The protests of ordinary people, often driven by deprivation and injustice, have overthrown dynasties. Ordinary people swept away the old order in eighteenth-century France and prepared the way for the collapse of the Romanovs and the rise of Bolshevism in Russia. More recently, they assembled for nightly vigils in the city squares of East Germany until the rulers lost confidence in their own capacity to govern.

But spontaneous popular action, though sometimes decisive, is usually ephemeral. It takes place in what political scientist Aristide Zolberg calls a "moment of madness," a short burst of intense, sometimes violent political agitation that soon subsides. Ordinary citizens, after all, have to reconcile their political roles with their responsibilities as parents and breadwinners. If they are to play a continuing role in collective politics, their participation must be structured or subsidized by others who can reduce the costs of political activism or intensify the motives that stimulate it. Students and practitioners of mass politics have long recognized that spontaneous citizen movements seldom amount to much and last only briefly. Lenin, for example, argued that the working class on its own was capable of only very fitful and limited forms of political action. They needed a vanguard drawn from the bourgeois intelligentsia to develop their political consciousness and revolutionary ardor. Like proletarians, organized interest groups also require elite stimulation. The origins of modern interest groups have been traced to the activities of "organizational entrepreneurs" who had resources to invest in gathering together a membership.

Historically, the "assistance" needed to sustain popular political involvement has come from two sources. First, there was government, which sought to promote the political engagement of citizens in order to solidify the state. During the eighteenth and nineteenth centuries, Western governments learned that popular participation helped give the state access to a stabilizing base of taxpayers, soldiers, and citizen administrators. The expansion of suffrage, political representation, and civil rights from the time of the American Revolution to the early decades of the twentieth century signified that popular support was the principal source of political power and state legitimacy.

Competition for that citizen-based power produced the second stimulus to grassroots political participation. Political elites tried to mobilize popular support for their struggles against their political antagonists. When Western democracies expanded the electorate, they created a new realm of political possibilities in which the active support of ordinary citizens could be put to political use by leaders competing for power or struggling to achieve their policy objectives. In the

United States, from the time of the Jeffersonians and Federalists, competing elites appealed for popular support through political party organizations and their programs. Parties won control of government offices by bringing voters to the polls. Control of government gave the parties access to the patronage that brought activists into party organizations and enhanced the capacity to mobilize the electorate, which in turn enabled the party to win more offices. As long as elites needed the support of common citizens, they encouraged collective activism and fashioned their policies to attract wide support.

But the old patterns of leadership competition and state building have faded, and the elite encouragement of mass participation has weakened along with those patterns. To begin with, governments are no longer so dependent as they once were upon mobilized citizens. State construction eventually gives way to state conservation. Public administration, revenue collection, and the waging of war do not rely so heavily as they once did on popular activism and enthusiasm. Government today cultivates satisfied customers rather than mobilized citizens. This change is reflected in new forms of civic education that stress individual participation in non-controversial public service activities rather than public demands, debate, and collective engagement. In government bureaucracies, public service has been transformed into customer relations. The military today recruits volunteers by promising to make each soldier an "army of one." Instead of national health insurance, Congress produces a "patient's bill of rights." In one public setting after another, government disaggregates the public into a mass of individual clients, consumers, and contributors.

Not only has government found new and nonparticipatory ways of doing business, but the competing political elites that once activated and organized popular constituencies to influence or run the government have found other ways to achieve their ends. They rely on litigation, privileged access to bureaucratic regulatory processes, official recognition as "stakeholders," access to "insider" interest-group politics, and membership in the "political-donor class." Contemporary elites have found that they need not engage in the arduous task of building popular constituencies. Public interest groups and environmental groups have large mailing lists but few active members; civil rights groups field more attorneys than protestors; and national political parties activate a familiar few rather than risk mobilizing anonymous millions.

The rightward drift of American politics since the 1970s is, at least in part, a by-product of leftward demobilization. Today's progressives, unlike their Jeffersonian forebears, seldom seek to advance the interests of the disfavored by enlisting them in grassroots political movements. Today's conservatives, therefore, unlike their Federalist predecessors, are not so driven to compete for popular support as a means of political self-preservation. Though they sometimes strike a populist and patriotic stance on morally symbolic issues, there is little to deter them from public advocacy of tax and economic policies sharply slanted toward the royalists of wealth. It would be difficult for conservatives to mobilize broad popular support for a repeal of inheritance taxes, a reduction of capital gains levies, or a repeal of the alternative minimum tax for business corporations. Conservatives are spared the inconvenience, in part, because postmaterial progressives abstain from popular mobilization themselves.

Solutions Are the Problem

How can we make rulers take us seriously as citizens? The question itself assumes that the remedy lies with the citizens themselves. It suggests that we have not taken citizenship seriously enough—because we spend too much time watching television instead of attending to public affairs, because we have allowed the country's vital civic institutions to deteriorate, because we are insufficiently attentive to understand complex policy issues. In fact, the role of citizens has contracted not so much because citizens themselves have neglected their responsibilities but because the country's leaders have less use for citizens than they once did. If the ties that bind citizens to one another have weakened, one reason may be that today's political elites create few occasions to bring Americans together through the collective mobilization of grassroots support.

Any measures designed to encourage the vigorous exercise of American citizenship must be aimed at least as much at political leaders as at the citizens themselves. But because the target is so diffuse, the aim cannot be precise. Personal democracy is a political culture that reflects systemic changes in American politics. It will not give way to institutional tinkering alone. Our fondness for institutional remedies, in fact, may actually contribute to citizen disengagement. It draws us toward mechanical solutions, like term limits, that promise to provide for the general welfare without the intervention of public-spirited citizens. In fabricating their government, Americans aspired to create a "machine that would run of itself"—a government of laws resistant to human failings. It was designed to get by with leaders who were less than Washingtonian. It could hardly demand much of its citizens. This convenient fiction concealed the essential character of citizenship. It is hard work.

Americans have willingly undertaken the unglamorous work of citizenship in response to the incentives or inspiration offered by their political leaders. For a small minority, the work is its own reward. But for most, political activism is a chore undertaken only when vital interests are threatened and their leaders summon them compellingly to serve. Today the leaders seldom call, and they ask little when they do. Citizenship has withered as a result.

Leaders can motivate citizens, but they are unlikely to do so when they have few political incentives to mobilize popular constituencies. Too often, they find that they can achieve their aims more easily through lawsuits than by appeals to the public. Reducing leaders' opportunities to make public policy by litigation could reenergize citizens by encouraging leaders to address the public rather than the judiciary. Campaign finance reform could also help—but not the kind recently enacted by Congress. Reforms adopted in 2002 seek to restrict the soft money contributed to the national parties. These reforms will probably hasten the final stages of organizational decomposition that have made political parties incoherent congregations whose members adhere to no faith in particular.

Rather than destroy parties, America should adopt reforms that would make the parties the principal institutions for campaign finance. Such reforms might bolster the possibilities for collective political action and refill the nation's empty voting booths. But would the parties risk mobilizing voters whose political inclinations may not be fully known and tested? Perhaps the parties could be induced to take the risk by electoral regulations that invalidated the results of any contest in which a majority of the eligible public did not participate.

These remedies hardly add up to a comprehensive program of reform. They are simply examples of the kinds of measures that might help to reconstitute American citizens as an American public. What is at stake in this effort is not merely the distribution of the nation's power and wealth but also its identity. Imagine a society whose members no longer look for connections between their own interests and those of their neighbors, or become insensitive to the resonance between their own aspirations and those of their fellow citizens. Imagine a country whose inhabitants see no reason to explain their hopes to one another, or to justify their anxieties. That country may not remain imaginary much longer. Under the regime of personal democracy, citizens have scarcely any reason to explain themselves to one another or to justify their wants. The experience of collective mobilization encourages citizens to form their own interests within a framework of common goods. Without collective mobilization we become a nation of occupants. We will no doubt remain on speaking terms, and we may even argue with one another less frequently, but there will be fewer reasons for us to be interested in one another or to engage one another politically.

End of an Era

We are approaching the end of a political epoch, one in which citizens jointly inhabited a public sphere. They were gathered there because they mattered. Because the people were essential to the development and functioning of the state, elites could not govern without them. In the era of popular democracy, the support of this public was also essential to political leaders who wanted to win control of the state. Today the competition for power and the operation of government no longer depend so vitally upon the mass public.

Both the public and the citizens who make it up have become obsolete. They could hardly have been expected to go on forever. The public sphere was an artifact of modernity. It provided a place in which mere political subjects evolved into political actors and full citizens. The public sphere enabled them to become a public. Since these developments had a starting point in history, it is only reasonable to suppose that they may also come to an end. That end is now in sight. What will come after it is not yet visible, but we can imagine two futures for democracy—one dark and one somewhat brighter.

What lies ahead, perhaps, is a dissonant echo of the past. For the better part of its first two centuries, the American Republic experienced cycles of mobilization as competing elites vied with one another to expand their popular support. But the nation's new elites have discovered a succession of arrangements to achieve their aims without popular support. That process of discovery may not yet be over. The progressive demobilization of the public may continue as leaders find new ways to insulate themselves from the uncertainties of popular participation or to reduce the resources that must be devoted to popular mobilization. In other words, recurrent cycles of demobilization may go on unraveling popular democracy—a replay in reverse of the processes that once knit together the American public and integrated it into American politics.

The new terms of political combat may accelerate this downward spiral of demobilization. Political candidates already wage campaigns of attack designed not so much to mobilize supporters as to keep their opponents' partisans away from the polls. Another battle tactic in national politics is to disable the institutional support base of one's antagonists. Parties and politicians sustain themselves by colonizing institutions in and around government. They live off the "new patronage"—the grants, contracts, tax benefits, and programs that employ or finance their allies—and they seek victory by paralyzing or dismantling the institutional infrastructure that sustains their opponents. Budget cuts, devolution, privatization, and the launching of independent prosecutors on open-ended investigations are all employed to disable opponents. Among the institutions disabled may be some that still function to rouse citizens to action. Wrecking them will further reduce the scope of the politically active public.

The members of that public may not go quietly into political retirement. Inducing them to accept their new status depends on their ability to get what they want from government without resorting to collective mobilization. Personal democracy "empowers" citizens to get what they want on their own. It disaggregates the public into a collection of private customers, clients, cases, or consumers whose personal interests seldom grow into collective demands because government provides channels for satisfying those interests through market mechanisms, litigation, or administrative adjudication.

This does not mean that political elites are engaged in a conscious conspiracy to atomize the public. Some of the measures that moved us in this direction promised increases in institutional effectiveness or responsiveness. Others were popular. The government's support of home mortgages, highway construction, and low gasoline taxes combined to create a nation of suburbanites who pursued happiness and the good life not by pressing demands on local governments but by moving from one political jurisdiction to another. Instead of joining with their neighbors to voice demands for better public services or amenities, they exercise the quiet, private "exit" option.

There is nothing new about private solutions for public problems. The open frontier of the nineteenth century is sometimes invoked to explain why working-class insurgency played such a small role in American political history. Malcontents, the argument goes, moved west. Suburban commuters, however, have much less distance to travel, and private solutions in general have become more plentiful and easily accessible than they were in the past. The technology of governing now includes many mechanisms for translating public policy into private choices. In fact, the public use of private interest is consciously promoted as a technique of effective governance. It is a convenience not just for government but for citizens too. Collective action is complicated and time consuming. But convenience, as we have seen, comes at a cost.

Pluralists as long ago as Arthur Bentley have argued that the public was an empty abstraction; the public interest, non-existent. But the terms "public" and "public interest" continued to carry weight in political debate, and they have proven solid enough to curb some of the excesses of special interest and political self-dealing. Special prosecutors still depend upon some conception of a public interest. The public, however, is eroding. In time, it may become just as insubstantial as Bentley imagined it.

Politics without a public could be an Orwellian nightmare, but with multiple Big Brothers locked in political conflict high above the people that they presumably represent. Elites would not be completely free of democratic constraint. Government would still have to assure that its "customers" remained satisfied. If it failed to do so, the processes of demobilization outlined here could be interrupted as a result. Political leaders, after all, are not politically infallible. Because they are leaders, their mistakes often originate in hubris. Sometimes entire institutions are infected by it. In this case, hubris might lead them to believe that they could dispense with citizens or institutions still indispensable—and capable of retaliation. Even more likely is the possibility that combat among political elites may so damage public institutions that they are no longer able to deliver services that citizens regard as essential. Popular backlash might then halt the drift toward personal democracy, especially if popular leaders stood ready to take advantage of the backlash by mobilizing a popular constituency of angry citizens.

Personal democracy may therefore suffer from an internal contradiction that makes it inherently unstable. The institutional casualties of elite combat could impair the programs and organizations necessary for maintaining popular quiescence. Public reaction to the 1995 shutdown of the federal government may be an early sign of future possibilities. The Republican-controlled 104th Congress refused to grant funds for continuing government operations while it worked out a budget compromise with President Clinton. The maneuver backfired. Instead of demonstrating that the country could do without its government, Congress lost public support for paralyzing public authority in the cause of ideological correctness.

Finding hope for a reanimation of the public in government gridlock is not a happy prospect, but a functioning government with a disabled public is unlikely to serve the public good. Today, however, the vitality of the public as a force in American politics is crumbling, and the time may soon arrive when the most pressing and yet disturbing question in American politics is "Who cares?"

Discussion Questions

- Does Young's approach run the risk of perpetuating differences that should, with time, begin to fade into obscurity?

- Could paying special attention to minority groups and making spaces for their voices tend to create a sense of entitlement in victims of past oppression? Would this be a good thing or not?

- With education, could people overcome their tendency to stick to ill-founded opinions? What would this education entail?

- Perhaps the military draft should be re-established, shifting away from the current trend toward all-volunteer armies. Would that help reverse the trend toward citizen irrelevance? If the draft were re-established, should women be included? What duties should be required of draftees? Should public service to promote peace be an option?

Globalization, Sustainability, and Economic Justice

The world is shrinking, even as you read these words. The implications for justice are enormous. Everything discussed in the previous chapters should be viewed with the enormous changes that are occurring in mind. Identities and communities, for example, are affected by the widening and quickening scope of communication of people and ideas across national boundaries. Globalization is a fact of modern life. Indeed, the clothes we wear, the food we eat, the way we communicate with one another—all are shaped by the processes and practices of globalization. We are, as Immanuel Kant wrote, "unavoidably side by side."[1] Yet while penetrating nearly all aspects of our daily lives, globalization remains both ill defined and increasingly contentious. It is old in a way, but also new in its acceleration and reach.

There are both positive and negative aspects to this accelerated flow of goods and people that we call globalization. Those who argue that globalization is largely positive believe it brings greater wealth to the world's citizens by minimizing barriers to trade and commerce. The opening up of trade leads not only to increased economic activity, but also to political freedom through the free flow of goods and services and ideas. The skeptics argue that globalization increases inequality by eroding traditional relationships, limiting national sovereignty, and endangering the environment. Globalization increases the already awesome power of corporate capitalism. Therefore, as a dynamic

---

[1]David Held, "Globalization: The Dangers and the Answers," in *Debating Globalization*, edited by Anthony Barnett, David Held, and Casper Henderson (Malden, MA: Polity Press, 2005), p. 1.

process and set of practices that continue to integrate people throughout the world, globalization—for better or worse—has an impact on our ideas about distributive justice, or who should get what under a system of distribution that is fair and just.

Philosopher and neuroscientist Nayef Al-Rodhan offers a compelling description of globalization as it affects our contemporary existence: "Globalization is a process that encompasses the causes, course, and consequences of transnational and trans-cultural integration of human and non-human activities."[2] Globalization is not solely a matter of economics, political scientist David Held reminds us, it is also "cultural as well as commercial . . . it is about power as much as about prosperity."[3]

Issues of globalization, sustainability, and economic justice—the foci of this chapter— are intimately related to the nature of our relationship with our system of governance. Consider trade, a key component of contemporary globalization, which for centuries has created links across national borders, mountains, and oceans. Questions about how trade should be regulated, and if it should be regulated at all, are essentially issues of governance. Who will determine the nature of these exchanges? Who has a right to participate in these decisions? Will all who are affected be represented in decisions about the rules of global trade? Democracies champion self-determination, yet the reach of globalization often tests the limits of this commitment.

The task of the initial readings in this chapter is to help you characterize globalization in the context of current issues and controversies. We then explore the creative approaches that organizations and individuals have adopted in response to globalized relations. In the final section the focus shifts toward the impact of the global practices that we have learned about in this chapter. At issue are the problems of economic justice in a globalized world, and a critical assessment of our own role in that world. The goal of this chapter is not to uncover a clear winner from globalization debates, but rather to encourage careful and reflective thinking about the relationship between globalization and justice.

Globalization

Globalization can be understood from a variety of perspectives. The following article introduces us to current issues and controversies around globalization and several theoretical vantage points from which to critique its processes. The most pressing issues raised by globalization cannot be adequately understood without considering larger, historical contexts. Author Barbara Thomas-Slayter argues, for example, that many of the current inequalities and injustices experienced in developing nations have their roots in colonialism and long periods of exploitation of peoples and land. Centuries

---

[2]Geneva Center for Security Policy, *Definitions of Globalization: A Comprehensive Overview and a Proposed Definition*, by Nayef Al-Rodhan. (Programs on the Geopolitical Implications and Transnational Security, June 19, 2006). Retrieved May 12, 2010, from http://pdfcast.org/pdf/definitions-of-globalization.

[3]Held, "Globalization," p. 13.

of colonialism throughout the global south have left many developing nations structurally disadvantaged vis à vis countries from the global north, including the United States and many in Western Europe. This relative weakness makes it difficult for countries to survive in a competitive global capitalist economy.

WHAT IS DEVELOPMENT?
BARBARA P. THOMAS-SLAYTER

Traditional measures of development have been largely economic. People have looked at the capacity of a national economy to generate and sustain increases in gross national income that exceed population growth rates. Economists have also regarded development in terms of changes in the structures of production and employment. As agriculture's share of production and employment has declined and that of industry, manufacturing, and services increased, development is said to be taking place. This is, of course, a narrow definition; it has become clear over time that nations could achieve growth targets in GNI gross national income without the quality of life for the majority of people improving at all. Many scholars, philosophers, policymakers, and development practitioners—not to mention ordinary citizens around the world—are aware that reductions of poverty, inequality, and unemployment, among other things, are essential ingredients in a "development process."

So what does development include? Denis Goulet, an economist-cum-philosopher, offers a thoughtful definition based on three core values: life sustenance, self-esteem, and freedom. For him, life sustenance includes adequate food, shelter, health, and security and can be measured in the form of calories consumed, literacy rates, school enrollments, life expectancy, or infant mortality. These constitute a necessary but not sufficient condition for development.

Self-esteem entails a sense of self-worth and respect. The nature and form of self-esteem vary from one society and culture to another, but it entails maintaining confidence in one's own way of life and viewpoints. Freedom, Goulet's last core value, involves freedom from harmful material conditions of life, such as physical violence or intimidation, and freedom for increased choices of behavior and lifestyle. In that sense, "development" is composed of physical, ethical, and philosophical elements. Development is not value free, and it evolves within a sociopolitical context that varies with each society and culture.

From *Southern Exposure: International Development and the Global South in the Twenty-First Century* by Barbara P. Thomas-Slayter. (Bloomfield, CT: Kumarian Press, 2003). Reprinted by permission.

It is easy but incorrect to assume that the lifestyle assuring a TV in every living room, a sports utility vehicle in the garage, and a dishwasher in the kitchen is the lifestyle to which everyone around the world aspires. While material wealth is no doubt increasingly associated with self-esteem, it does not follow that "to be richer is to be better" is a universally held value. For the Masai in Kenya and Tanzania, for example, a treasured way of life involves keeping large numbers of cattle and the freedom to move about in wide open spaces. Masai perceptions of material need differ greatly from those of small-town, or even rural, America.

So what definition of development can encompass the perspectives of the Masai in Kenya, the landless laborer in Bangladesh, the garment worker in Nicaragua, and the packer of takeout food orders in the United States? To return to Goulet, if "development" is taking place, the availability and distribution of basic life-sustaining goods—food, health, and shelter—should be increasing. For levels of living to improve, there is a concomitant need for employment and educational opportunities, and for economic and social choices to open up.

Development, to expand upon Goulet's ideas, also entails an increasing capacity of people to influence their future both individually and collectively. This concept includes economic productivity and the capacity to develop political and social institutions, as well as addressing equity issues. When people are broadly empowered to achieve influence and leverage over decisions shaping their lives, "development" is taking place. Development also needs to be sustainable and to take the future into account; otherwise the process is one of pillaging the future to accommodate the present, which is hardly "development."

Amartya Sen, an economist who won the 1998 Nobel Prize in Economics, helps us address fundamental questions about the meaning of development. He observes a world of unprecedented opulence along with remarkable deprivation, widespread hunger, extensive damage to the environment, and violation of human dignity. Two concepts that Sen analyzes are important for our discussion here: the meaning of inequality and an interpretation of the meaning of development. In examining economic inequality and poverty, Sen criticizes approaches that concentrate on achievements (such as income) rather than focusing on the capacity or freedom to achieve. He wants to move attention from commodities and income to functionings and capabilities. Sen argues that development is a process of expanding freedoms. He uses the term "unfreedom" to describe such conditions as poverty, tyranny, poor economic opportunities, systematic social deprivation, neglect of public facilities, or repressive states, and he suggests that development requires the removal of the major sources of these "unfreedoms." In exploring the meaning of development and in assessing the causes of inequality, Sen shies away from a focus on economic wealth. While economic growth may be valued, it is important for what it permits an individual to do, primarily to lead a more enriched, unfettered life. The expansion of freedom is both a primary end and the principal means of development. Freedom, therefore, has intrinsic value as well as instrumental value. The ends and means of development, argues Sen, call for placing the perspective of freedom at center stage.

What kind of development is, then, most desirable? Although each society must determine that for itself, the task may be increasingly difficult given the processes of globalization currently under way. How can the nations of the South best achieve their economic and social objectives, either individually or in cooperation with one another and with the countries of the North? This question remains critical. We must learn to listen to other voices, the voice of the Masai herder, the Bengali farmer, the seamstress in Nicaragua, and the young man from Iran delivering pizza in New York City.

Using Theory to Explain Processes of Economic and Social Change

The challenge of understanding processes of economic and social change has engaged theorists and activists of all descriptions from time immemorial. Scholars of ancient Greece reflected on these concerns, as did scholars, philosophers, and social reformers in England and Europe in the seventeenth, eighteenth, and nineteenth centuries. Here we focus briefly on the period of time since World War II when theorists, citizens, and policymakers, in many corners of the world, have searched for the keys to economic growth and broadly improving livelihoods, with increased equity, justice, and well-being for all peoples. These keys have been hard to find. Not only are they elusive, but the explanations about where to find them often seem diametrically opposed. Moreover, there are many explanations, confusing in their complexity and their differing assumptions, strategies, and analyses.

These theories reside in three broad categories: a neoclassical approach, the political economy school, and alternative perspectives on development, the latter including postmodernists, feminists, and those concerned about globalization and global ethics. The term "paradigm" is frequently used when discussing various theories of development and underdevelopment. A paradigm in this context is a worldview, a perspective broadly shared by a group of people on a specific topic. Paradigms focusing on development and underdevelopment have several characteristics: value assumptions about human nature and about what the good life should be, operational criteria for achieving that life, and a strategy or guide for getting there. Almost all textbooks written in the past forty years on the topic of development deal with the first two theoretical categories in some detail. Critiques of the development paradigm have arisen among the postmodernist scholars. Feminist perspectives have cut across these viewpoints and are rarely included in the "development literature" despite their relevance. Finally post–Cold War theories pertinent to ethics, development, and globalization are just now emerging and do not yet constitute a definable school of thought.

A Neoclassical Approach

The neoclassical approach is the one most closely aligned with capitalism, market economies, and the economic successes of the Western world. It has other names and is sometimes called the orthodox, conventional, or traditional economic approach, or modernization theory. Its focus or *unit of analysis* is the nation-state. It regards the state as an independent actor that can make policy decisions that will guide a nation and its citizens through the processes of economic growth and development. According to this view, traditional agrarian societies are stagnant and unchanging; life is based on the seasons and has a circular rhythm. There is no notion of progress, improvement, or change. Human beings are rational, know their own interests, and can act upon them. This approach regards economic interests as paramount and views people largely as economic beings with needs to consume. The critical issue—and the one around which economics as a discipline focuses—is scarcity. Resources are scarce; there are competing needs and objectives, and the resources must be allocated among competing goals. According to this paradigm, the problems of resource allocation can be dealt with most efficiently through the marketplace which will enable the economy to operate efficiently with the greatest production given the resources available.

What is required for development to take place according to the neoclassical argument? The task at hand is to build capital by saving, reinvesting, and producing more profits leading to increased savings and investment.

A Political Economy Approach

A political economy approach to understanding development and under development focuses on systems and structures, rather than individual behavior and nations. Over time this perspective has come to regard capitalism as a means for perpetuating underdevelopment. According to this viewpoint, increasing integration of the world capitalist system intensifies the economic, political, and cultural subordination of the poor countries to the rich. Capitalist institutions within the poor countries likely aggravate, rather than diminish, inequalities in the distribution of wealth and power. The consequences of the perpetuation of underdevelopment are increasing conflict and violence.

Within this broad framework is the Dependency School, originating with a group of Latin American scholars in the mid-1960s. Dependency theorists reject the neoclassical paradigm completely. They observe patterns of dominance and dependence in which the political structures and traditional economies of poor and colonized countries are reshaped to serve the needs of the dominant, imperial power rather than those of local peoples. Dependency theorists also observe the establishment of a domestic elite that works in collusion with foreign powers. Such elites, with their interest in luxury consumption or in stashing their financial gains in a safe place, do not often lead poor nations to economic growth with improved capital infrastructure and the adoption of modernizing methods of economic organization and production.

Postmodernist Challenges to the Development Discourse

Postmodernists assert that Third World countries need alternatives to industrial, growth-oriented economies. Effort on the part of poor countries to catch up simply creates an illusion. Catching up is not possible because the industrialized nations are oriented toward transforming advanced technology and toward competitive obsolescence. Despite an effort to catch up, the gap between rich and poor countries is not only maintained but continues to widen at an accelerating pace. It is, says one scholar, a "fraud to hold up the image of the world's rich as a condition available to all. Yet this is what the economic development mythology of catching up does."

In sum, postmodernists claim that the modern conceptualization of development is bankrupt. They argue that the whole paradigm of development should be abandoned and that there should be a search for alternatives to development. These alternatives should be defined by local histories, contexts, and knowledge and based upon self-defined goals that emphasize and celebrate difference, fragmentation, and otherness. Alternatives to development should cherish the uncertainty and individuality of life.

Feminist Critiques of Development Processes

From feminist scholars and practitioners in the South comes a focus on the linkages between gender and other forms of inequities and subordination. This perspective endorses the postmodern emphasis on the local, but looks for certain universal forms of experience. Some call themselves postcolonial feminists and focus on the experiences of women of color throughout a long history of colonization, neocolonialism, and the current impacts of globalization. They use the term "recolonization" to refer to an intensifying colonization in the South and the extension of colonizing practices to the North, occurring through processes of globalization. Many feminists of the Global South define their feminism as a struggle against all forms of oppression, whether it occurs because of gender, race, ethnicity, religion, caste, or some other attribute. For them there is a global vision of freedom for all peoples from systems of domination or exploitation. They are activists; they work at the grassroots in their own communities; but they are conscious of the larger arenas in which human beings must also strive for justice and dignity.

Who Cares about Development Issues?

Since the last decade of the twentieth century, the United States has been, on the one hand, increasingly dominant—the only remaining superpower—and clearly the strongest economic and political power. On the other hand, the United States has also been mysteriously unable to impose its authority as a host of international actors crowd the economic and political scene, making power elusive. Our security depends on ensuring that other countries have a stake in the international system, which is extremely complicated as globalized market forces increase inequalities within a traditional nation-state system.

The nation-state seems less powerful than in times past. This fact is, in and of itself, an interesting phenomenon because new nations burst onto the international scene in the post-World War II period. From India's dramatic celebration of independence in August 1947, to celebrations of Zimbabwe's independence in 1980 and to Eritrea's in 1993—both after long struggles—this half-century has constituted an era of expansion of the nation-state system. In 1946 there were 74 independent countries; in 1950, 89, and by 1995, the number was 192.

At the same time, after World War II, the United States was catapulted into a position of world prominence and power. Europe was in a state of collapse after the war, and power was polarized between the United States and the Soviet Union. Now, however, the Cold War is over. The moral and ethical concerns remain. The range of problems—malnutrition, illiteracy, starvation—may be diminishing in some places, but they remain critical problems in many parts of the world. For perhaps a dozen countries the North-South economic gap is narrowing, but it continues to widen for more than 100 others. Moreover, widening income disparities are occurring within most nations as the wealthier gain through restructuring and globalization and the poorer lose as they are marginalized or left behind. The borderless world means that advantage and disadvantage do not adhere to strict boundaries. Strengths and vulnerabilities are increasingly shared. Those may be economic; they may relate to terrorism, violence, or other insecurities. They are not going away, and we serve ourselves, our communities, our nation, and our global community best if we address them.

What Issues Confront Both South and North at the Beginning of the Twenty-First Century?

The issues to be addressed by peoples of North and South are numerous. We identify twelve within the overall framework of the need to conceptualize a new North-South agenda.

A Global System

Transforming the face of the world is a globalization process cutting across all sectors of activity. BankBoston, merely a medium-size bank recently purchased by Fleet Bank, nevertheless obtained approximately 20 percent of its revenues from Brazil and Argentina, an indication of the spread and strength of Northern-based financial houses around the world. Wal-Mart is represented in fifty U.S. states, and nine countries, even China, and has over five hundred stores in Mexico. In 1998, Home Depot, a chain of do-it-yourself hardware and construction supply warehouses, opened its doors in Latin America and has since expanded to eight stores—four in Chile and four in Argentina. In October 2000, Starbucks opened a shop, complete with glazed donuts and banana walnut muffins, in Beijing's Forbidden City, just opposite the Palace of Heavenly Purity. Oxfam, the British non-governmental relief and development organization, started in Oxford as a relief agency during World War II. There are now eleven different Oxfams around the world, and Oxfam International is a growing entity. The environmental movement, from Greenpeace to the Women, Environment, and Development office in New York, to the activists protesting large-scale dam construction by the World Bank in India, knows no national boundaries. Immigrants crisscross the globe seeking employment in many parts of the world: Senegalese in New York, Sri Lankans in Rome, Iranians in Tokyo, Somalis in Stockholm. Surely the evidence is strong that globalization is well under way. If globalization is the dominant force in the world today, it also has its underside, a crossroads where globalization meets terrorism. "All the wondrous developments of the new economy—falling costs, fewer borders, easy communications—help international terrorists and criminals as much as they do businessmen." This global system is a beast of many parts.

The Nation-State

While globalization is an ongoing process, the nation-state seems to be under attack from two directions. First, many are dwarfed by large-scale economic actors such as

Goldman Sachs, investment bankers whose year 2000 annual earnings were $3.25 billion contributing to total assets of $290 billion. Goldman Sachs alone maintains a financial value greater than the GNI of approximately 118 nations. The banks and investment houses are joined in scale by the multinationals, including oil companies, such as Shell or British Petroleum, Dow Chemical, and a wide variety of transnational corporations operating across a range of sectors. Reebok shoes, Liz Claiborne clothes, Pepsi-Cola, or Procter and Gamble all have round-the-world production and sales. It is difficult for governments—either the home government or the receiving government—to monitor and control their activities.

The nation-state is also under siege from another direction. Many countries face the centrifugal tendencies generated by powerful regions; ethnic, religious, or other subgroups; and weak central governments. Since the last decade of the twentieth century, widespread breakdown of national loyalties has characterized Eastern Europe, Central Asia (formerly part of the Soviet Union), and many parts of Africa. The levels of animosity between the Hutu and the Tutsi in Rwanda, between factions fighting in southern Sudan or in Angola, or between the Serbs and the Albanians in Kosovo are grim reminders that only tenuous threads hold some nations together. So, at a time when strong governmental activities would be valuable to address a variety of problems, the state's resources and energies are sapped in new ways.

A Poverty Curtain

The "iron curtain" separating the Soviet Union from the capitalist world has disappeared, but a new curtain is rapidly gaining visibility. This one is a "poverty curtain" dividing an affluent North from an impoverished South. The buying power of many Third World countries is declining. Jobs and working conditions become bargaining chips for firms in a world economy that has few regulations. Nike can pick up its sneaker-making operations and move them from Indonesia to Bangladesh when it finds it can pay Bangladeshis a wage that is a fraction of that of the Indonesians. Laborers on sugar plantations in the Philippines find their wages dropping as the powerful lobby of sugar beet farmers in America moves into action. Young men from China, or Honduras or Mexico or many other places, pay large sums to escape hopelessness in their home countries only to discover the despair of poverty elsewhere. The gaps between the very few rich and the very many poor are deepening the world over.

The Debt Crisis

One cannot consider the "poverty curtain" without also identifying the debt crisis as a critical issue in need of a fresh approach. The debt crisis continues to plague many nations. Between 1980 and 1995, the total external debt of low income countries rose from $55 billion to $215 billion, more than twice their export earnings. The debt crisis has drained financial resources from poor countries to rich banks. It has threatened to overwhelm a number of countries that pay a high percentage of their gross national income in servicing their debt. It is a causal factor in the deepening drug trade in several parts of the world including Colombia and Bolivia.

It was deeply implicated in the Asian and Latin American economic crises of 1998 and 1999. The World Bank, under pressure from non-governmental organizations, has established the Heavily Indebted Poor Countries Initiative (HIPC) in order to bring about early implementation of better terms for the indebted countries, including significant debt relief.

The Information Age

Cliches abound about the information age. Information is knowledge and knowledge is power, we are told. The comments may seem trite, but in truth transformation in communication and the capacity to control and exchange information underlie the changes in our global system. Forty years ago an international telephone call was an accomplishment usually accompanied by a long wait and a lot of static. It was rarely an edifying experience and hardly ever conducive either to enjoyment or to conducting business. Today's telephone conversations from just about anywhere in the world are sparklingly clear; faxes are in widespread use; and e-mail is often nearly simultaneous. If it is a pleasure and a luxury to be able to communicate with colleagues, friends, and family around the world, it is also a facilitator of business and financial arrangements. Acknowledging that these new levels of communication have both positive and negative repercussions, the capacity to engage in them is critical to entry into the global system. Access of countries of the South to these modern technologies varies widely, and this access is another item for the South-North agenda.

Social Polarization and Regional Imbalances

Inequities seem to be increasing everywhere. Within many nations class distinctions are growing aided and abetted by a global economic system whose restructuring seems only to aggravate social difference. Income disparities are widening, not only in well-known cases—the United States or Brazil, for example—but in many others as well. Some of the southern African countries have extreme forms of social inequities. Namibia, for example, has been described as "one country, two worlds" with a small affluent white population, a large black population living in abject poverty, and prosperous foreign-owned mining companies. Others also have deep-rooted social and economic structures that reproduce poverty and perpetuate inequality. In Indonesia, Malaysia, and Thailand, which had achieved some breakthroughs in moving people out of poverty in the 1980s and early 1990s, some lower income groups are plummeting into poverty as a consequence of the Asian economic crisis of the late 1990s.

Corruption and Crime

Perhaps corruption and crime should not be lumped together. Crime is certainly a broader category than corruption; presumably corruption is always a crime, even if it is one that is tolerated or even encouraged in some situations. The mysterious disappearance of government funds, international aid that makes its way into private ministerial bank accounts, or the bloated bureaucracies mismanaging public sector business—all are a focus of any effort to address international debt and to begin to build public accountability into systems of governance. Then, too, there is the drug trade and the crime associated with trafficking, a topic that is closely linked to the debt and international trade issues noted above. Indeed, the underbelly of globalization is the underground economy and a range of activities that include smuggling, illicit logging, trading of conserved species of plants and animals, trade in contraband arms, or trafficking in people. Sometimes these illegal economic activities are linked to powerful figures in bureaucracies, the military, the police, or politics, a reminder of the dark side of our political and economic systems.

Environmental Degradation

Around the world peoples of North and South are becoming conscious of their deteriorating environments. In the North Atlantic the collapse of the Atlantic cod fishery has been declared "the ecological disaster of the century." Forest fires that swept through Indonesia in late 1997 not only destroyed vast timber reserves, but polluted the atmosphere for hundreds of miles around. The collapse of irrigation schemes from salinization, the destruction of topsoils from illicit timbering, the erosion caused by farming on steep slopes, the continuing rise of CO_2 emissions, and many more flagrant abuses of the environment suggest that in the twenty-first century both South and North need to think much more deeply about our custodial responsibilities in relation to the environment.

Statistics provide overwhelming evidence that a typical North American adult consumes far more resources than a typical Bangladeshi or Malian. For most Americans, this is a distant topic, one that somebody else is concerned about and which does not affect them very much. To many others around the world, it is yet another indication of U.S. insensitivity and disregard for global justice.

Urbanization

Perhaps the twentieth century will be remembered particularly for its incredible rates of urbanization. In 1900, approximately 150 million people, or 10 percent of the world's population, lived in cities. Toward the end of the century this figure had grown to over 2 billion. Of the ten largest cities in 2002, seven are located in the developing world. Cities serve as magnets for the rural unemployed and landless who seek new opportunities in the cities of their homeland or elsewhere in the world. Urban problems of housing, sanitation, education, transport, infrastructure, security, care for the impoverished, and cultural amenities are extraordinary.

Agrarian Reform

Although land tenure systems vary widely from country to country, it would not be inaccurate to state that many systems favor the large landholder over small-scale farmers, favor men over women, favor owners over renters or landless laborers, and favor inherited land/wealth over open access on an egalitarian basis. In many countries good agricultural land is a scarce and coveted commodity, particularly given rapidly growing populations and inadequate alternatives for employment in manufacturing, industry, or services. Women rarely have ownership rights in land; rather, their rights come through marriage and family, and they can easily be deprived of those rights—no matter how much work they have put into the land—should those relationships change. International agribusiness, too, is a factor with which many nations must contend, whether it is the Philippines and Del Monte, Kenya and Brooke Bond, or Honduras and Dole. Such corporations control vast amounts of land and are a major influence, not only in the communities in which they operate, but also in policy at the national level.

HIV/AIDS

At the UN Special Session in June 2001 the international community adopted a plan of action to fight the global epidemic of HIV/AIDS. The mood was somber. Twenty years into the worst epidemic in modern times, 36 million people around the world were infected with HIV, and some 20 million had died. The UN Secretary-General Kofi Annan has called the UN's Declaration of Commitment on HIV/AIDS a blueprint from which the whole of humanity can work in building a global response to a truly global challenge. While Africa has been most severely affected by the HIV/AIDS epidemic, new regions in which HIV/AIDS is making significant inroads are Eastern Europe and China. Clearly, a massive and focused response to the AIDS pandemic is a priority for the coming decades.

Armaments

Military expenditures grew worldwide from $400 billion in 1960 to $798 billion in 2000. Nowhere is the harm caused by the devotion of vast sums to armaments greater than in the developing countries. In the face of extreme poverty, famine, expanding debt, poor health, and inadequate livelihood opportunities, many nations are spending more than ever on military activities and the arms that permit them. In the 1980s the five largest recipients of U.S. weapons in sub-Saharan Africa were Liberia, Angola, Somalia, Sudan, and Zaire, all of which disintegrated into civil war. According to Demilitarization for Democracy, a Washington anti-proliferation watchdog group, by the late 1990s the United States had given military assistance to nearly every African country, training over three thousand military officers, most of whom came from nations with dictatorships or on the brink of collapse. Preventing conflict and bringing about peace and security are far more complex problems than simply looking at issues of armaments, but clearly this arena needs transparency, accountability, and attention from the public. In the new century's riveting and growing concerns about widespread terrorism, wisdom in this realm is critical.

Looking back for a moment at what you learned in studying aspirations for human rights for all in Chapter 4, it is obvious that much remains to be done. It is also obvious why so many people have decided to leave the places where they were born and grew up in hopes of finding a more secure future elsewhere. The harsh impact of globalization on the poor of the Earth is often overlooked. While considerable attention has focused on the upper end of the globalized workforce—the "high-tech" sector—the groups most acutely affected are those whose skills rarely command large wages in highly industrialized countries. Many of these people leave towns with few job opportunities in order to earn money to send home to support families. Many also leave to escape violent regimes and ordinary criminal violence, some of which has arisen out of "dirty wars" that the United States has supported, particularly in Latin America. Businesses and governments have responded to this tendency for people to migrate to seek better opportunities. Workforces increasingly include immigrant labor. International banking policies have created incentives for immigration and many governments have come to rely on the money sent home to feed families. In 2008, for example, migrants sent over 25 billion dollars to Mexico as remittances, and remittances comprised between 15–20 percent of El Salvador's gross domestic product (GDP). Even greater sums are sent to China (40 billion) and India (45 billion).[4]

Globalization has made immigrants all over the world. While in many nations men and women emigrate in roughly the same percentages, they tend to experience the process of immigration differently. Indeed, globalization itself is a gendered phenomenon. In the following reading, Cynthia Enloe explains how the international market policies of the late 1940s that introduced the humble banana to global consumption also reproduced a highly gendered workforce, with compensation and status largely divided along gender lines. This cheap fruit we often take for granted is actually a huge international business. The United States is the largest consumer of bananas, virtually all of which are grown in other countries. In 2006, Americans consumed 26 percent of the world's bananas. India was the top banana producing nation in 2007.[5] Other leading exporting countries are Ecuador, Costa Rica, the Philippines, and Colombia, which together accounted for about two-thirds of exports.[6]

Given the considerable profits made from bananas, it is unsurprising that cultivation and processing of this fruit take on the highly stratified characteristics of many global businesses. Like working women everywhere, female banana producers have had to manage not just their paid jobs, but also the day-to-day responsibilities of sustaining their families. These duties are often called "women's work," a designation that is political in its purpose and effect. Cynthia Enloe argues that global markets tend to marginalize or simply ignore women's contributions to sustaining their households.

---

[4]Dilip Rathia, *Migration and Remittances Factbook, 2008* (Washington, DC: World Bank Publications, March 2008). Retrieved May 12, 2010, from http://econ.worldbank.org/WBSITE/ EXTERNAL/EXTDEC/EXTDECPROSPECTS/0,,contentMDK:21352016~pagePK:64165401~piP K:64165026~theSitePK:476883,00.html.

[5]Food and Agricultural Organization of the United Nations. Market Information in the Commodities Area. Retrieved May 12, 2010, from http://www.unctad.org/infocomm/anglais/ banana/market.htm#prod.

[6]Ibid.

'I'M CHIQUITA BANANA AND I'VE COME TO SAY'
CYNTHIA ENLOE

The banana has a history, a gendered history. The fruit has its origins in Southeast Asia and was carried westward by traders. By the fifteenth century it had become a basic food for Africans living on the Guinean coast. When Portuguese and Spanish slave-traders began raiding the coast for Africans to serve as forced labor on colonial estates, they chose bananas as the food to ship with them; it was local and cheap. These were red bananas, a variety still popular in the West Indies and Africa. The yellow banana so familiar today to consumers in Europe, Japan, the Persian Gulf and North America wasn't developed as a distinct variety until the nineteenth century. Then it was imagined to be food fit not for slaves, but for the palates of the wealthy. The first record of bunches of bananas being brought to New York from Havana was in 1804. But it was when the yellow banana was served as an exotic delicacy in the homes of affluent Bostonians in 1875 that it took off as an international commodity. In 1876 the banana was featured at the United States Centennial Exhibition in Philadelphia. The yellow banana symbolized America's new global reach.

Notions of masculinity and femininity have been used to shape the international political economy of the banana. Banana plantations were developed in Central America, Latin America, the Caribbean, Africa and the Philippines as a result of alliances between men of different but complementary interests: businessmen and male officials of the importing countries on the one hand, and male landowners and government officials of the exporting countries on the other. To clear the land and harvest the bananas they decided they needed a male workforce, sustained at a distance by women as prostitutes, mothers and wives. However company executives' manly pride was invested not so much in their extensive plantations as in the sophisticated equipment and technology they developed to transport the fragile tropical fruit to far-away markets: railroads, wire services and fleets of refrigerator ships. Even today company officials take special satisfaction in describing their giant cold-storage ships circling the globe, directed by a sophisticated international communications network, all to ensure that bananas that leave Costa Rica or the Philippines by the green tonnage will arrive in New York or Liverpool undamaged and unspoiled, ready for the ripening factory. The companies envisaged their customers to be women: mothers and housewives concerned about their families' nutrition and looking for a reliable product. The most successful way of bonding housewives' loyalty to a particular company was to create a fantasized market woman.

The United Fruit Company, the largest grower and marketer of bananas, made its contribution to America's 'Good Neighbor' culture. In 1943 the company opened a Middle American Information Bureau to encourage 'mutual knowledge and mutual understanding'. The bureau wrote and distributed materials which emphasized the value of Central American products such as hardwoods, coffee, spices and fruits to the US war effort. It targeted school children and housewives: those who ate bananas and those who bought them. *Nicaragua in Story and Pictures* was a company-designed school text celebrating the progress brought to Nicaragua by foreign-financed railroads and imported tractors. 'Fifty Questions on Middle America for North American Women' and 'Middle America and a Woman's World' explained to the North American housewife, United Fruit's chief customer, how the Japanese invasion of Malaysia made imported foods from Nicaragua and Costa Rica all the more important to her wartime security.

United Fruit's biggest contribution to American culture, however, was 'Chiquita Banana'. In 1944, when Carmen Miranda was packing movie houses and American troops were landing on Europe's beaches, United Fruit advertising executives created a half-banana, half-woman cartoon character destined to rival Donald Duck. Dressed as a Miranda-esque market woman, this feminized banana sang her calypso song from coast to coast. Chiquita Banana helped to establish a twentieth-century art form, the singing commercial. One could hear her singing the praises of the banana on the radio 376 times daily.

United Fruit sales strategists set out to do the impossible—to create in housewives a brand-name loyalty for a generic fruit. They wanted women to think 'Chiquita' when they went to the grocery store to buy bananas. Roosevelt's 'Good Neighbor' policy and Carmen Miranda's Hollywood success had set the stage; animated cartoons and the commercial jingle did the rest. Between the woman consumer and the fruit there now was only a corporation with the friendly face of a bouncy Latin American market woman. Forty years later United Fruit Company has become United Brands; its principal subsidiary is Chiquita Brands, bringing us not only bananas, but melons, grapefruits and tropical juices.

Today virtually every affluent, industrialized country imports bananas from mainly poor, still agrarian countries. Each consumer society gets its bananas from two or three large agribusiness corporations which either have large plantations of their own or monopolize the marketing system through which small growers sell their fruit. Since United Fruit's advertising coup in 1944, its competitors have followed suit, designing stickers for their own bananas. This allows a shopper to go into any grocery store in Europe, North America or Japan and check at a glance the state of international banana politics: just look for the sticker with its corporate logo and the country of origin. In London one might peel off a Geest sticker that says 'WIN-BAN' (the Windward Island nations of St Lucia, St Vincent or Dominica) or look for the Fyffes sticker (Fyffes is United Brands' European subsidiary) that gives the country of origin as Surinam. In Detroit or Toronto a shopper would be more likely to find a Chiquita, Del Monte or Dole sticker, with Costa Rica, Ecuador or Colombia written below the logo in small print, while in Tokyo Sumitomo's Banambo sticker would identify bananas produced in the Philippines.

After a century of banana big business, Americans remain the largest consumers of bananas, eating some 2 million tons of the fruit each year. But with the opening of the Philippines to banana companies, especially under the debt-ridden Marcos regime, hungry for foreign investment, consumers in Japan and the Persian Gulf have become the latest targets for advertising campaigns.

Women Weed, Women Clean

The banana plantation has never been as exclusively male as popular imagery suggests. It takes women's paid and unpaid labor to bring the golden fruit to the world's breakfast tables.

A banana plantation is closest to a male enclave at the beginning, when the principal task is bulldozing and clearing the land for planting. But even at this stage women are depended upon by the companies—and their male employees—to play their roles. As in the male-dominated mining industry from Chile to South Africa and Indonesia, companies can recruit men to live away from home only if someone back home takes care of their families and maintains their land. The 'feminization of agriculture'—that is, leaving small-scale farming to women, typically without giving them training, equipment or extra finance—has always been part and parcel of the masculinization of mining and banana plantations. The male labor force has to make private arrangements with wives, mothers or sisters to assure them of a place to return to when their contracts expire, when they get fed up with supervisors' contemptuous treatment or when they are laid off because world prices have plummeted. Behind every all male banana plantation stand scores of women performing unpaid domestic and productive labor. Company executives, union spokesmen and export-driven government officials have all preferred not to take this into account when working out their bargaining positions. International agencies such as the International Monetary Fund scarcely give a thought in women as wives and subsistence farmers when they press indebted governments to open up more land to plantation companies in order to correct their trade imbalances and pay off foreign bankers.

Once the banana trees have been planted, women are likely to become residents and workers on the plantations. Plantation managers, like their diplomatic and military counterparts, have found marriage both a political asset and a liability. On the one hand, having young male workers without wives and children has advantages: the men are in their physical prime, they are likely to view life as an adventure and be willing to tolerate harsh working and living conditions. On the other hand, young unattached men are more volatile and are willing to take risks if angered precisely because they will not jeopardize anyone's security aside from their own. This makes the married male worker seem more stable to a calculating plantation manager. He may demand more from the company in the form of rudimentary amenities for his wife and children, but he is more likely to toe the company line for their sake.

Women are most likely to be employed by the banana companies if the plantation cannot recruit men from a low-status ethnic group, like Amerindians in Central America, to do the least prestigious and lowest-paid jobs. In all sorts of agribusiness, women tend to be given the most tedious, least 'skilled' jobs, those that are most seasonal, the least likely to offer year-round employment and those company benefits awarded to full-time employees. Weeding and cleaning are the quintessential 'women's' jobs in agriculture, both in socialist and capitalist countries.

Bananas today are washed, weighed and packed in factories on the plantations before being transported to the docks for shipment overseas. Inside these packing houses one finds the women on the modern banana plantation. They remove the bunches of fruit from the thick stems, an operation that has to be done carefully (one might say skillfully) so that the bananas are not damaged. They wash the bananas in a chemical solution, a hazardous job. They select the rejects, which can amounts to up to half the bananas picked in the fields. Companies often dump-rejected bananas in nearby streams, causing pollution which kills local fish. Women weigh the fruit and finally attach the company's tell-tale sticker on each bunch. They are paid piece-rates and foremen expect them to work at high speed. In between harvests they may have little work to do and not receive any pay. At harvest time they are expected to be available for long stretches, sometimes around the clock, to meet the company's tight shipping schedule.

Tess is a Filipino woman who works for TADECO, a subsidiary of United Brands, Philippines. She works on a plantation on the country's southern island, Mindanao. A decade-long war has been fought in the area between government troops and indigenous Muslim groups protesting against the leasing of large tracts of land either to multinational pineapple and banana companies or to wealthy Filipino landowners, who then work out lucrative contracts with those corporations. Tess herself is a Christian Filipina. She, like thousands of other women and men, migrated, with government encouragement, to Mindanao from other islands in search of work once the bottom fell out of the once-dominant sugar industry. She works with other young women in the plantation's packing plant, preparing bananas to be shipped to Japan by Japanese and American import companies. She is paid approximately $1 a day. With an additional living allowance, Tess can make about $45 a month; she sends a third of this home to her family in the Visayas.

Tess uses a chemical solution to wash the company's bananas. There is a large, reddish splotch on her leg where some of the chemical spilled accidentally. At the end of a day spent standing for hours at a time, Tess goes 'home' to a bunkhouse she shares with 100 other women, twenty-four to a room, sleeping in eight sets of three-tiered bunks.

Many women working on banana plantations are young and single, and, in the Philippines, often have secondary-school or even college educations. They may be the daughters of male employees, or they may be recruited from outside. They are subjected to sexual harassment in the packing plants and can be fired if found to be pregnant. The life of a banana washer is dull and isolated: 'We have no choice than to stay here. First, the company is quite far from the highway and if we. . . spend our fare what else would be left for our food?'

Large banana companies—Geest in Britain, United Brands, Del Monte and Dole in the United States and Japan's Sumitomo—also require workers at the other end of the food chain, in the countries where they market their bananas. The docks, the trucks and the ripening plants reveal how company managers shape the sexual division of labor. Stevedors in every country are thought of as doing a classic 'man's' job, though again ethnic politics may determine which men will unload the bananas from the company's ships. Today in Japan, where immigrant labor is being increasingly relied upon to do the low-status, low-paid jobs, Filipino men do the heavy work of transferring bananas from ships to trucks. The job has become so closely associated with the fruit that to be a longshoreman in Japan is to be a 'banana'. Women are hired in all the consumer countries to weigh and sort at the ripening plant before the fruit heads for the supermarket. Food processing is as feminized—as dependent on ideas about femininity—as nursing, secretarial work and sewing.

Women are hired by the banana companies to do low-paid, often seasonal jobs that offer little chance of training and promotion; some involve the hazards of chemical pollution and sexual harassment. But many women still seek these jobs because they seem better than the alternatives: dependence on fathers or husbands (if they are employed), life on the dole (if work is not available), work in the entertainment industry around a military base, subsistence farming with few resources, emigration.

Many women are heads of households and take exploitative jobs in order to support their children; other women see their employment as part of being dutiful daughters, sending part of their meager earnings back to parents, who may be losing farm land to agribusinesses. Neither women nor men working on any plantation—banana, tea, rubber, sugar, pineapple, palm oil, coffee—are simply 'workers'. They are wives, husbands, daughters, sons, mothers, fathers, lovers; and each role has its own politics. The politics of being a daughter, a mother or a wife allows First World and Third World governments to rely on international plantation companies, which in turn are able to recruit and control women workers and win the consumer loyalty of women buyers. 'Daughter', 'mother', and 'wife' are ideas on which the international political system today depends.

'The farmer and his wife' disguises the reality of the world's food production. Most technical agencies agree that women produce at least half of the world's food. In Africa they produce between 60 per cent and 80 per cent. It is the politics of land *ownership* that obscures this reality. If one is talking about food production, not land ownership, it might be more accurate to refer to 'the farmer and her husband.'

More seriously, 'the farmer and his wife' not only obscures the gendered politics of land ownership; it also makes invisible the ways in which women organize their daily lives to sustain families and still produce bananas on their small holdings. The use of 'the household' as the unit for measuring the success or failure of any project or policy is radically flawed. It presumes—without testing that presumption against reality—that the relationships within any house are equal, that emotional, sexual and economic relationships between men and women and sons and daughters are naturally harmonious, without tension, without intimidation or coercion.

This was the presumption used in Britain, France, Canada and the United States to deny women the right to vote: why would a woman need a vote of her own when her father, husband or brother would 'naturally' cast his ballot with her best interest in mind? What was a naïve assumption in the suffrage debate is an unfounded argument in the politics of the banana.

Feminists in Third World countries who have made land reform a political cause have insisted that dismantling large plantations—whether locally or foreign-owned— must not be seen as sufficient to ensure that women gain the power and resources they need to shape rural development so that women as well as men benefit. If land reform is implemented without a critical examination of *which* small farmers will receive the precious land title, land reform can serve to perpetuate patriarchal inequities in the countryside.

It may be tempting to imagine plantations as part of an 'old-fashioned' way of life. They seem to symbolize the bad old days of slavery and colonialism. They conjure up the American ante-bellum South or the British empire according to Somerset Maugham. In reality plantations are as modern (or 'post-modern') as the home computer or toxic waste. Large plantation companies such as Castle and Cook (owner of Dole and Standard Fruit), Unilever (owner of both Liptons and Brooke Bond), Del Monte (recently purchased by R. J. Reynolds as part of its buyout of RJR Nabisco) and United Brands, are some of the largest multinational companies in the world today, wielding influence over their own as well as foreign governments.

These plantation companies and the importing and exporting governments that rely on them for tax revenues and political support each make gendered calculations. They appeal to women as food purchasers and as food preparers. If Carmen Miranda helped smooth the way for a more subtle form of American regional influence, 'Chiquita Banana' helped create consumer loyalty for a product that yielded huge profits for an American corporation; the real market women of Latin America were marginalized by a potent combination of 'Good Neighbor' diplomacy and agribusiness advertising. On the other hand, while women consumers often have a difficult time acquiring accurate nutritional information, acting together they have helped open up the files of food corporations. Women who today buy more fresh broccoli than canned peas are not merely passive creatures in an advertising agency's scenario.

All too often the international politics of bananas (and sugar, rubber and broccoli) are discussed as if they were formulated only in bankers' board rooms or union leaders' meetings. Because both of these settings have been so male-dominated, the dependence of food politics on women and on ideas about masculinity and femininity has been ignored. This in turn has meant that even genuine non-feminist attempts to reform agrarian politics—in the name of nationalism or development— have failed to change patriarchal relationships. The politics of bananas and broccoli cannot be fully transformed until both women and men are made visible, as consumers, producers, managers and policy-makers.

What are some of the challenges to justice that emerge from globalization? An important concern for developing nations has been the policies of the International Monetary Fund (IMF), the World Bank, and various UN organizations. International banking institutions sometimes encourage or allow the governments of developing countries to take out loans that the people must then repay. In agreeing to these loans, the borrower nations often must accept loan conditions that reduce state spending on social programs and promote exports. Increasing exports increases the borrower nation's integration into the world economy, but at the same time erodes its ability to control its economic destiny.

Faced with annually mounting debt, countries can become trapped in a cycle of borrowing to pay off interest. They find themselves unable to meet the basic needs of their people. Economist Alison Jaggar argues that much of the debt accrued by borrowing nations should not be viewed as morally binding because the debt represents a no-win situation for borrowers: "The obligation to service the debt traps citizens within an economic order that severely disadvantages them."[7] Additionally, the global accounting systems that the International Monetary Fund uses to calculate debt largely ignore the damage that global capitalism has done poor countries in the form of environmental degradation, massive workforce migration, and harm to land and waterways. Jaggar states that "when the supposed debt is seen in this light, it becomes much less clear who owes what to whom" (p. 134).[8]

In the following reading, LaDawn Haglund observes that developing countries have been encouraged by "free market" policies of the IMF and the World Bank to sell off basic public services to the private sector. During the past three decades, some nations have allowed for-profit firms to take over basic services, such as utilities. The theory is that increased competition, brought about by the privatization of these previously public goods, will increase efficiency and bring down prices. However, many countries lack sufficient infrastructure to adequately supervise and regulate this process. Development lending often supports large private companies who bid to deliver services at a handsome profit. But, with little true competition among providers at the local scale, services deteriorate while simultaneously becoming more expensive. In the process, debt increases, making poor countries more prone to control by rich nations than ever. Privatization of basic services like water and electricity can also have corrosive effects on social human rights.

---

[7]Alison Jaggar, "A Feminist Critique of the Alleged Southern Debt," *Hypatia*, vol. 17 (4): pp. 119–42 (2002).

[8]Ibid.

LIMITING RESOURCES: MARKET-LED REFORM AND THE TRANSFORMATION OF PUBLIC GOODS

LaDawn Haglund

Introduction

Public Utility Reform: Problems and Perspectives

Over the last 25 years, extensive programs designed to encourage private participation in the provision of public utilities have been implemented globally. In Latin America, where fiscal austerity and divestiture in state-run firms became a condition for access to development loans, privatization was particularly widespread. Citing problems of corruption and inefficiency in state-owned enterprises, economists and advisors in the region promoted market solutions, even in sensitive utility sectors:

> In 1993, the World Bank approved policies that stressed the need for sound commercial practices, independent regulation, and extensive private sector participation in the energy sector. These policies extended to the power sector a process that had first begun with the oil and gas sector in 1983. . .

El Salvador was one country that took World Bank prescriptions to heart. The Salvadoran government, "realized early on that without significantly changing the way the public sector operates; providing a credible framework; and involving increasingly the private sector in service provision, it [would] be difficult to maintain the high levels of growth needed to reduce wide spread poverty, particularly in the rural areas." A massive transfer of assets and activities from the state to the private sector, non-governmental organizations, and local government occurred during the 1990s. The international rating agency for private investment, Fitch New York, was so impressed by these structural reforms that they granted El Salvador high investment ratings, but warned that "further privatization and prudent liability management [would] also be necessary to limit the deterioration of the government's balance sheet."

But despite the praise and guidance of international investors and economists, the promise of privatization and other forms of marketization fell short for ordinary Salvadorans. In rural sectors, rate increases following electricity privatization took a serious toll, with the additional burden of rising costs for energy-dependent services such as deep-well water pumps. Poor sectors that consumed less electricity saw rate increases of up to 47%, while high-usage customers paid 24% more. Meanwhile, few improvements in service quality or coverage were evident in the years following privatization.

A similar set of privatization policies—accompanied by similar shifts in social relations and patterns of resistance—were seen in other countries of the region. In May 2008, for example, over a dozen people were injured in Sardinal, Costa Rica by flying stones, sticks, and teargas in clashes over the construction of a privately financed and publicly built aqueduct. Representatives for the water company held that, though the government should have explained the project better to the community, the degree of unrest was not due to any genuine threat posed by the project, but to special interest groups such as free trade opponents. Protestors disagreed, complaining that the government had granted the concession to assist a group of private hotel developers without considering the impact such a project could have on their community. They cited drought conditions, as well as contamination in other areas from tourism and plantations to justify their resistance. There was a strong sense of urgency to the protest, and anger at being excluded from discussions: "Nobody said anything to us about the aqueduct. We realized what was happening only after it was already partly completed." Some government officials also expressed concern about the project. Municipal president Claudio Rivas suspended its permit, charging that the project—initially approved because it promised improvements to the existing aqueduct—was being designed to carry water to tourism projects outside the area. The national Public Interest Office criticized the project as well, arguing that the public water company would be obliged, in the design of the system, to cater to private interests rather than public welfare.

In the narratives presented above, and myriad others like them throughout the developing world, we see the contentious and unpredictable nature of market transformations in public goods sectors. These transformations bring to the fore latent conflicts between public and private sectors; among competing industries such as tourism, agribusiness, and industry; and among different stakeholders such as citizens, investors, and the natural environment. Given the proliferation of privatization and marketization policies since 1980, as well as conflicting evidence regarding their costs and benefits, there is a pressing need to examine these policies more closely. It is not simply a matter of economics: the principles underlying different models of service provision—public, private, or mixed—circumscribe and define available public goods policy alternatives at a time when states and communities need more, not fewer, options for addressing urgent public health, social justice, and sustainability issues.

Markets and Justice

The efficiency argument regarding the superiority of markets as allocation mechanisms rests on deeper assumptions about human nature, social justice, and the meaning of freedom. Three philosophical traditions in particular—utilitarianism, classical liberalism, and libertarianism—see market organization as positively linked to social justice. Utilitarianism measures justice according to welfare gains or losses that accompany social arrangements. It uses current and potential distribution as the justice metric: whether anyone can be made better off without others being made worse off. If changes would not improve the situation, it is said to be "Pareto optimal." Just policies are those that promote *subsistence* (people are assured access to resources created through their labor), *security* (property and tenure are protected), *abundance* (policies promote the productive use of resources), and *equality* (distribution promotes the greatest happiness for greatest number). The first two factors possess an inherent priority, being "objects of life itself," while the latter are mere "ornaments of life." These criteria indicate that utilitarians value market processes, property rights, and hard work as routes to general prosperity, while leaving open the possibility of government intervention to promote human welfare. However, though redistribution might be justified and certain rights—to personal security, to property, and to "receiving aid in case of need"—may be granted, state action should not interfere with private ownership or destroy incentives for individual productivity, for "if the lot of the industrious was not better than the lot of the idle, there would be no longer any motives for industry" (Bentham 1864, p. 99)

Classical liberalism also has a clear preference for market mechanisms, despite the fact that the term "liberal" encompasses a variety of economic and political viewpoints. In this, it has a great deal in common with (right) libertarianism, a less widely held but still influential theory. Classical liberals and libertarians share with utilitarians a concern for the security of property rights, yet both are much less willing to allow states to act beyond providing "pure" public goods, believing instead that a society ordered by the "invisible hand" of market forces, driven by the self-interested transactions among market participants, is the essence of freedom. They are deeply concerned about what is termed "procedural justice," especially the establishment of individual rights against arbitrary coercion or encroachments by the state. Redistribution, for example through progressive taxation, is distasteful to classical liberals and out of the question for libertarians, as the pattern of rewards and benefits that arises from the free play of market forces is considered already to be just. If inequality arises from a historically just (i.e., "free" market) process, there is no injustice, for it is market processes and security of property that propel productivity, capital accumulation, and growth in society. Classical liberalism encompasses a slightly broader range of options for state intervention than libertarianism, but still places emphasis on limiting state action as much as possible.

There is no question that the "minimal state" and a focus on individual property rights and capital accumulation envisioned by libertarians and classical liberals reduce the policy options available for the provision of public goods. This orientation places constraints on the ability of state actors to raise funds for public aims, to limit private prerogative for the purpose of planning or conservation, and to redirect resources toward creating universal access to essential goods. It also fails to deal effectively with issues prevalent in many developing countries, such as communal or other forms of property ownership, severe inequality in initial resource distribution, and extreme deprivation that limits the capacity of individuals to participate meaningfully in a market society. These theories also tend to ignore historical injustices wrought by colonialism, imperial domination, and the overwhelming power of multi-national corporations over local communities and even nation-states. More importantly, the institutional mechanisms created to put these ideas into practice increase the constraints on states and further limit alternatives. The "freedom" arising from these ideas is not freedom for the weak to "live lives they have reason to value", or freedom for state actors comprehensively to redress social or economic injustices.

Utilitarianism permits more leeway in dealing with the issues mentioned above, but still suffers from some debilitating features. Though "welfare" is the metric used to measure justice, the fairness of the initial distribution from which Pareto optimality is calculated is not challenged. Like libertarianism and classical liberalism, utilitarianism cannot deal adequately with inequality, much less the colonial, exploitative history of most developing countries. Though ostensibly egalitarian, when the security of those who hold property is threatened by measures to promote equality (which is almost always the case), utilitarians prioritize security. There are few options for improving the lot of the most vulnerable members of society under such constraints. This focus on efficiency without an attendant commitment to fairness leaves us with a situation considered just, "even when some people are rolling in luxury and others are near starvation, as long as the starvers cannot be made better off without cutting into the pleasures of the rich". The overriding concern with security of property also debilitates state and community capacity to address ecological problems. This is exacerbated by the focus on "abundance," which prioritizes productive uses of land and resources over conservation, thus undermining the sustainability that has become a central concern in public resource management.

In their ten year examination of compliance with environmental rules and pro-environmental behaviors, Syme et al. (2006) found that though the influence of self-interest increased as decisions became more central to the personal life and livelihood of citizens, they were unwilling to allow self-interest to prevail at the expense of the common good. Moreover, they saw intergenerational and intragenerational fairness as complementary, not in competition. In a component study of perceptions of fairness in water-allocation decisions, the authors concluded that, "self-interest is tempered by pro-social motivations" (Syme, Nancarrow, and McCreddin 1999, p. 51), and that the public was capable of participating in decision-making that involved relatively complicated judgments on multiple dimensions.

By way of summary, I have discussed a range of *market-based organizing principles* that have been increasingly influential over the last few decades in framing public goods policy. These include "laws of the market" such as pricing, supply, and demand; efficiency through competition and incentives; profit maximization; individualistic pursuit of self-interest; property rights; and capital accumulation. This delineation of principles can be used to clarify the moral basis upon which policy decisions are based. In the sections to come, I expand this conceptual pool to include a wider range of organizing principles that encompass both equality and environmental protection. In public goods sectors, especially, this sort of broad theoretical framing is crucial to ensure the development and implementation of strategies that address the full implications of public goods provision, including social justice, human rights, and ecological sustainability.

The "Most Likely" Case of El Salvador: An Appraisal

El Salvador provides a good context for testing theoretical claims that privatization will improve public services where states have failed, as it is a case in which such arguments are "most likely" to be true. But the gains from the liberal transformation were mixed.

Public monopolies in electricity that were supposed to improve with unbundling and private competition were transformed instead into private monopolies. Service improvements were questionable at best, while externalities that were already serious continued or worsened, due in part to the incentive of profit-oriented firms to externalize costs. Privatization not only led to a loss of income in the case of profitable companies, but also opened up tempting opportunities for corruption.

Private investors were supposed to save the public from the inadequacies of state provision, but the arrival of neoliberalism instead reinforced official neglect of social and economic rights by shifting responsibility to the private sector, taking the spotlight off of state actors, and allowing state capacity-building for provision and regulation to fall by the wayside. Reforms, especially privatization, allowed elites to regroup under insecure post-war conditions and colonize new spaces of power, thereby reproducing the inequalities at the base of Salvadoran social conflict. Though the structure of the economy changed, the level of economic injustice did not. If anything, it intensified with the concentration of wealth in five, rather than the notorious "14 families".

Reforms also weakened state autonomy and altered state-society ties. Central government control over financial decisions left state-owned "autonomous" institutions with little independence. Responsiveness on the part of the state to social needs was seen as a distortion of the market. Once privatization occurred, state actors found themselves with less control over resources and the means of production of public goods, as well as fewer policy options for addressing negative externalities. Private firms were oriented, by law, toward securing profits for stockholders rather than ensuring the satisfaction of economic and social rights (profits were privatized). Deregulation, meanwhile, allowed private firms greater leeway in determining how to cut costs and organize production in order to maximize profits (costs were socialized). Regulatory activities focused more on fostering competition than meeting any particular planning goals or holistic objectives such as river basin management. Information deficiencies complicated the role of the regulator, especially in countries with limited bureaucratic capacity and in which powerful multinational firms operated. Strapped regulators were forced to rely on information provided by firms and/or self-monitoring to judge whether private sector decisions were in the public interest. Thus the ties between economy and society, moderated by the state, shifted to favor the private sector.

The effect of organizing public goods according to market principles was the marginalization of other ideals: social, political, and environmental. But as privatization experiences around the world have shown, markets are hazardous mechanisms by which to allocate essential resources. For one, structural discrimination is virtually inevitable when access is granted to those with better market positions. Women are often hardest hit by fees and shortfalls in social goods, as in general they are ultimately responsible for family welfare and must compensate with their own resources and labor. This has also adversely affected ethnic minorities, whose communal resources have slowly been privatized, as on the Atlantic Coast of Nicaragua. Targeting to address inequality in privatized sectors had direct costs in terms of personnel training, capacity building, and monitoring, as well as indirect transaction costs, yet states received no monetary return on these inputs. In some cases, it created "a vicious cycle whereby cuts in benefit entitlements leads to demands for lower taxes . . . which in turn leads to pressure to cut entitlements still further and so on" (Tsakalotos 2004, p. 422). In already polarized countries like El Salvador, this approach naturalized inequality and legitimized the status quo. In social democratic countries like in Costa Rica, it undermined the bedrock of that system: solidarity.

The shift to exclusionary economic regimes not only undermined social solidarity and exacerbated existing inequalities, but also concretely threatened the health of populations. For example, in places where water was subjected to "full cost recovery," people were forced either to pay a large proportion of their income for water or to seek other sources that were unfit for human consumption. In South Africa, thousands of people were cut off from potable water supplies because they could not pay tariff increases that amounted to up to 50% of their income. Residents began retrieving water from nearby rivers that were severely polluted, and weeks later South Africa plunged into the worst cholera outbreak in modern history. Market realities also undermined environment and labor protections: private firms resisted such protections, as compliance could be costly. Further, capitalist competition reduced incentives by forcing cost-cuts that did not improve the bottom line. Regulation of sensitive sectors placed burdens on the state that were sometimes greater than public ownership itself, especially where firms set rates and artificially restricted supply under oligopoly conditions. For less-developed countries and small local governments, where power relations and regulation favored the private sector, the problem was even more acute.

The commodification of public goods thus pitted different interests against each other. This is true of most economic policy that, while not always zero-sum, by definition distributes rewards and sacrifices in politically-determined ways. But for essential goods, the conflict can be quite significant. An example is the tourist industry in Costa Rica, which relies on the protection and preservation of land, water, and biodiversity to attract "buyers" (i.e., visitors) seeking an authentic natural experience. Agricultural, urban, and profit-making interests, on the other hand, rely on exploiting land and water for other ends. This can and has led to usage conflicts. But beyond this "public" problem, there is a deeper issue of the commodification of land itself: even "green" tourism does not protect land and water in ways that answer to their own reproductive needs. It answers to the needs of tourism by building hotels in ecologically sensitive areas and redirecting water to toilets and swimming pools and away from the ecosystem. Attempts to commodify water rights and access highlight these conflicts, as well as the conflict between commodification and preservation, and underscore the importance of state intervention in moderating or preventing these conflicts.

Proponents of contracting, privatization, and deregulation may admit that reform can be complicated and requires a strong and capable state, but fail to mention why, then, marketization policies should be implemented at all. If the state can be strengthened and reorganized adequately to supervise difficult market arrangements, why should it hopelessly and forever be incompetent at carrying out the provision of key public services? Incentives can be built into state operations, and internal reorganization and external coordination prior to and even without privatization is not only possible but in many cases highly successful. The case for privatization is unconvincing unless the private sector possesses skills, innovation, expertise, or technology that public providers do not and cannot possess, and unless those contributions can be effectively utilized in the receiving context. The devastating reality is that places most in need the kinds of outcomes reformers promise seem least likely to benefit because of contextual deficits. Privatization, contracting, and concessions require a degree of state capacity and commitment to social and environmental values that is not prevalent in countries like El Salvador, but which must be built. Yet if privatization is most likely to work in the places where it is least needed, the whole approach deserves greater scrutiny.

The real problem hindering global democracy, Benjamin Barber argues, is the continuation of "outdated" notions of state sovereignty, that is, the belief that nations have supreme authority over their territory. Barber calls for an account of political change rooted in the realities of global interdependence. Barber advocates an end to the idea of independent sovereign states with weak ties to each other. He would strengthen international organizations, including the United Nations, World Bank, and the International Monetary Fund. Others tend to agree, at least with respect to some international institutions. The former head of the United Nations, Kofi Annan, for example, suggests that global justice can be achieved through international cooperation: "The United Nations offers the best hope of a stable world and a broadly equitable global order, based on generally accepted rules."[9] Yet, Barber and Annan acknowledge that this centralized approach to global governance is not without challenges. Given the range of goals and definitions of the good life that exist in the world's countries, how do we determine the principles that can unify people around the globe? How do we ensure that all nations are fairly represented? What about the voices of citizens of countries that do not share these collective beliefs? What about the voices of over 300 million indigenous peoples and others without official state membership?

Readings from this section have shown that the fruits of globalization are not distributed evenly. However, as philosopher John Rawls points out, a just system of distributing goods does not necessarily require an absolutely equal distribution. What is needed, Rawls suggests, is equality of opportunity. He argues, in essence, for meritocracy; that is, the distribution of positions and privileges based on individual merit. Yet basing decisions on merit alone may also be unjust because it fails to consider life histories and the hardships some bear. The difficult dilemma—one that societies expounding meritocratic principles must constantly wrestle with—is when and how these individual histories should be taken into account in allocating scarce social goods. The same questions about starting points can be asked at the level of individual people, groups, or nations, as this and previous chapters suggest.

---

[9]Kofi Annan, "Three Crises and the Need for American Leadership," in *Debating Globalization*, edited by Anthony Barnett, David Held, and Casper Henderson (Malden, MA: Polity Press, 2005), p. 134.

Discussion Questions

- In what ways does globalization challenge state sovereignty?

- Is sovereignty the same for every country, or do some nations enjoy a lot more of it than others?

- How can the theories discussed in this chapter (neoclassical economics, political economy, and feminist theories) help us understand globalization?

- What does it mean to say that the globalized labor force is gendered?

Sustainability and Economic Justice

As globalization marches onward, we should pause to consider if more attractive alternatives might exist. Are there other ways to organize our interactions within a global community? Could other approaches bring about a more just life for the world's citizens? Is there perhaps a middle ground that blunts the most egregious inequalities of globalization, while recognizing the reality of an increasingly connected world? Muhammad Yunus, a former college professor and a Nobel Peace Prize recipient, thinks we could do much better by helping the world's poor achieve economic success. With a small loan to a poor woman in Bangladeshi over 25 years ago, Yunus began combating world poverty. Since then, the microloans provided by his Grameen banks have lifted millions out of poverty, particularly in developing countries, including his native Bangladesh. More recently, Yunus developed the concept of a "social business," which is devoted to solving social and environmental problems using capitalist principals. "A social business," Yunus describes, "is cause-driven, rather than profit-driven, with the potential to act as a change agent for the world."[10] In this reading, Yunus, a strong proponent of the free market, details the workings of his microcredit loan program and the social business model that he designed to harness the capacity of international trade to help reduce poverty.

A New Kind of Business
Muhammad Yunus

Since the fall of the Soviet Union in 1991, free markets have swept the globe. Free-market economics has taken root in China, Southeast Asia, much of South America, Eastern Europe, and even the former Soviet Union. There are many things that free markets do extraordinarily well. When we look at countries with long histories under capitalist systems—in Western Europe and North America—we see evidence of great wealth. We also see remarkable technological innovation, scientific discovery, and educational and social progress. The emergence of modern capitalism three hundred years ago made possible material progress of a kind never before seen. Today, however—almost a generation after the Soviet Union fell—a sense of disillusionment is setting in.

To be sure, capitalism is thriving. Businesses continue to grow, global trade is booming, multinational corporations are spreading into markets in the developing world

---

[10]Muhammad Yunus, *Creating a World Without Poverty: Small Business and the Future of Capitalism* (New York: PublicAffairs, 2007), p. 22.

---

and the former Soviet bloc, and technological advancements continue to multiply. But not everyone is benefiting. Global income distribution tells the story: Ninety-four percent of world income goes to 40 percent of the people, while the other 60 percent must live on only 6 percent of world income. Half of the world lives on two dollars a day or less, while almost a billion people live on less than one dollar a day.

Poverty is not distributed evenly around the world; specific regions suffer its worst effects. In sub-Saharan Africa, South Asia, and Latin America, hundreds of millions of poor people struggle for survival Periodic disasters, such as the 2004 tsunami that devastated regions of the Indian Ocean, continue to kill hundreds of thousands of poor and vulnerable people. The divide between the global North and South—between the world's richest and the rest—has widened.

Some of the countries that have enjoyed economic success over the past three decades have paid a heavy price, however. Since China introduced economic reforms in the late 1970s, it has experienced rapid economic growth, and, according to the World Bank, over 400 million Chinese have escaped poverty. (As a result, India has now become the nation with the largest population of poor people, even though China has a bigger overall population.)

But all of this progress has brought with it a worsening of social problems. In their rush to grow, Chinese officials have looked the other way when companies polluted the water and air. And despite the improved lot of many poor, the divide between the haves and have-nots is widening. As measured by technical indicators such as the Gini coefficient, income inequality is worse in China than in India.

Even in the United States, with its reputation as the richest country on earth, social progress has been disappointing. After two decades of slow progress, the number of people living in poverty has increased in recent years. Some forty-seven million people, nearly a sixth of the population, have no health insurance and have trouble getting basic medical care. After the end of the Cold War, many hoped for a "peace dividend"—defense spending could decline, and social programs for education and medical care would increase. But especially since September 11, 2001, the U.S. government has focused on military action and security measures, ignoring the poor.

These global problems have not gone unnoticed. At the outset of the new millennium, the entire world mobilized to address them. In 2000, world leaders gathered at the United Nations and pledged, among other goals, to reduce poverty by half by 2015. But after half the time has elapsed, the results are disappointing, and most observers think the Millennium Goals will not be met. (My own country of Bangladesh, I'm happy to say, is an exception. It is moving steadily to meet the goals and is clearly on track to reduce poverty by half by 2015.)

What is wrong? In a world where the ideology of free enterprise has no real challenger, why have free markets failed so many people? As some nations march toward ever greater prosperity, why has so much of the world been left behind?

The reason is simple. Unfettered markets in their current form are not meant to solve social problems and instead may actually exacerbate poverty, disease, pollution, corruption, crime, and inequality.

I support the idea of globalization—that free markets should expand beyond national borders, allowing trade among nations and a continuing flow of capital, and with governments wooing international companies by offering them business facilities, operating conveniences, and tax and regulatory advantages. Globalization, as a general business principle, can bring more benefits to the poor than any alternative. But without proper oversight and guidelines, globalization has the potential to be highly destructive.

Global trade is like a hundred-lane highway criss-crossing the world. If it is a free-for-all highway, with no stoplights, speed limits, size restrictions, or even lane markers, its surface will be taken over by the giant trucks from the world's most powerful economies. Small vehicles—a farmer's pickup truck or Bangladesh's bullock carts and human-powered rickshaws—will be forced off the highway.

In order to have win-win globalization, we must have fair traffic laws, traffic signals, and traffic police. The rule of "the strongest takes all" must be replaced by rules that ensure that the poorest have a place on the highway. Otherwise the global free market falls under the control of financial imperialism.

In the same way, local, regional, and national markets need reasonable rules and controls to protect the interests of the poor. Without such controls, the rich can easily bend conditions to their own benefit. The negative impact of unlimited single-track capitalism is visible every day—in global corporations that locate factories in the world's poorest countries, where cheap labor (including children) can be freely exploited to increase profits; in companies that pollute the air, water, and soil to save money on equipment and processes that protect the environment; in deceptive marketing and advertising campaigns that promote harmful or unnecessary products.

Above all, we see it in entire sectors of the economy that ignore the poor, writing off half the world's population. Instead, businesses in these sectors focus on selling luxury items to people who don't need them, because that is where the biggest profits are.

I believe in free markets as sources of inspiration and freedom for all, not as architects of decadence for a small elite. The world's richest countries, in North America, Europe, and parts of Asia, have benefited enormously from the creative energies, efficiencies, and dynamism that free markets produce. I have devoted my life to bringing those same benefits to the world's most neglected people—the very poor, who are not factored in when economists and business people speak about the market. My experience has shown me that the free market—powerful and useful as it is—could address problems like global poverty and environmental degradation, but not if it must cater solely and relentlessly to the financial goals of its richest shareholders.

Is Government the Answer?

Many people assume that if free markets can't solve social problems, government can. Just as private businesses are devoted to individual profit, government is supposed to represent the interests of society as a whole. Therefore, it seems logical to believe that large-scale social problems should be the province of government.

Government can help create the kind of world we all want to live in. There are certain social functions that can't be organized by private individuals or private organizations—national defense, a central bank to regulate the money supply and the banking business, a public school system, and a national health service to ensure medical care for all and minimize the effects of epidemics. Equally important, government establishes and enforces the rules that control and limit capitalism—the traffic laws. In the world economy, rules and regulations concerning globalization are still being debated. An international economic regulatory regime has yet to fully emerge. But on the national and local levels, many governments do a good job of policing free markets. This is especially true in the industrialized world, where capitalism has a long history and where democratic governments have gradually implemented reasonable regulatory systems.

The traffic laws for free markets oversee inspection of food and medicine and include prohibitions against consumer fraud, against selling dangerous or defective products, against false advertising and violation of contracts, and against polluting the environment. These laws also create and regulate the information framework within which business is conducted—the operation of stock markets, disclosure of company financial information, and standardized accounting and auditing practices. These rules ensure that business is conducted on a level playing field.

The traffic laws for business are not perfect, and they are not always enforced well. Thus some companies still deceive consumers, foul the environment, or defraud investors. These problems are especially serious in the developing world, with its often weak or corrupt governments. In the developed world, governments usually perform their regulatory tasks reasonably well, although starting in the 1980s, conservative politicians have taken every opportunity to undermine government regulations.

However, even an excellent government regulatory regime for business is not enough to ensure that serious social problems will be confronted, much less solved. It can affect the way business is done, but it cannot address the areas that business neglects. Business cannot be mandated to fix problems; it needs an incentive to want to do so. Traffic rules can make a place for small cars and trucks and even rickshaws on the global economic highway. But what about the millions of people who don't own even a modest vehicle? What about the millions of women and children whose basic human needs go unmet? How can the bottom half of the world's population be brought into the mainstream world economy and given the capability to compete in the free market? Economic stop signs and traffic police can't make this happen.

Governments have long tried to address these problems. During the late Middle Ages, England had Poor Laws to help those who might otherwise starve. Modern governments have programs that address social problems and employ doctors, nurses, teachers, scientists, social workers, and researchers to try to alleviate them.

In some countries, government agencies have made headway in the battle against poverty, disease, and other social ills. Such is the case with overpopulation in Bangladesh, which is one of the world's most densely populated countries, with 145 million people in a land area the size of Wisconsin. Or, to put it another way, if the *entire population of the world* were squeezed into the area of the United States of America, the resulting population density would be *slightly less* than exists in Bangladesh today! However, Bangladesh has made genuine progress in alleviating population pressure. In the last three decades, the average number of children per mother has fallen from 6.3 in 1975 to 3.3 in 1999, and the decline continues. This remarkable improvement is largely due to government efforts, including the provision of family planning products, information, and services through clinics around the country. Development and poverty-alleviation efforts by nongovernmental organizations, or NGOs, as well as Grameen Bank have also played an important role.

Governments can do much to address social problems. They are large and powerful, with access to almost every corner of society, and through taxes they can mobilize vast resources. Even the governments of poor countries, where tax revenues are modest, can get international funds in the form of grants and low-interest loans. So it is tempting to simply dump our world's social problems into the lap of government and say, "Here, fix this."

But if this approach were effective, the problems would have been solved long ago. Their persistence makes it clear that government alone does not provide the answer. Why not?

There are a number of reasons. One is that governments can be inefficient, slow, prone to corruption, bureaucratic, and self-perpetuating. These are all side effects of the advantages governments possess: Their vast size, power, and reach almost inevitably make them unwieldy as well as attractive to those who want to use them to amass power and wealth for themselves.

Government is often good at creating things but not so good at shutting them down when they are no longer needed or become burdens. Vested interests—especially jobs—are created with any new institution. In Bangladesh, for example, workers whose sole job was to wind the clocks on the mantelpieces of government administrators retained their positions, and their salaries, for many years after wind-up clocks were superseded by electrical timepieces.

Politics also stands in the way of efficiency in government. Of course, "politics" can mean "accountability." The fact that groups of people demand that government serve their interests and put pressure on their representatives to uphold those interests is an essential feature of democracy.

But this same aspect of government sometimes means that progress is thwarted in favor of the interests of one or more powerful groups. For example, look at the illogical, jerry-rigged, and inefficient health-care system in the United States, which leaves tens of millions of people with no health insurance. Reform of this system has so far been impossible because of powerful insurance and pharmaceutical companies.

These inherent weaknesses of government help to explain why the state-controlled economies of the Soviet era ultimately collapsed. They also explain why people around the world are dissatisfied with state-sponsored solutions to social problems.

Government must do its part to help alleviate our worst problems, but government alone cannot solve them.

The Contribution of Nonprofit Organizations

Frustrated with government, many people who care about the problems of the world have started nonprofit organizations. Nonprofits may take various forms and go under many names: not-for-profits, nongovernmental organizations, charitable organizations, benevolent societies, philanthropic foundations, and so on.

Charity is rooted in basic human concern for other humans. Every major religion requires its followers to give to the needy. Especially in times of emergency, nonprofit groups help get aid to desperate people. Generous assistance from people within the country and around the world has saved tens of thousands of lives in Bangladesh after floods and tidal waves.

Yet nonprofits alone have proven to be an inadequate response to social problems. The persistence and even worsening of global poverty, endemic disease, homelessness, famine, and pollution are sufficient evidence that charity by itself cannot do the job. Charity too has a significant built-in weakness: It relies on a steady stream of donations by generous individuals, organizations, or government agencies. When these funds fall short, the good works stop. And as almost any director of a nonprofit organization will tell you, there is never enough money to take care of all the needs. Even when the economy is strong and people have full purses, there is a limit to the portion of their income they will donate to charity. And in hard times, when the needs of the unfortunate are greatest, giving slows down. Charity is a form of trickle-down economics; if the trickle stops, so does help for the needy.

Relying on donations creates other problems. In countries where the social needs are greatest—Bangladesh, elsewhere in South Asia, and in large parts of Latin America and sub-Saharan Africa—the resources available for charity are usually very small. And it is often difficult to get donors from the richest countries to take a sustained interest in giving to distant countries they may never have visited, to benefit people they will never know. This is understandable, but it leaves serious social problems in those countries unaddressed.

The problems become even greater in times of crisis—when a natural disaster strikes, when war causes population upheavals and suffering, when an epidemic strikes, or when environmental collapse makes whole districts unlivable. The demand for charity quickly outpaces the supply. And today, with news and information constantly coming in from around the world, the demands for our attention and concern have never been greater. Dramatic disasters reported on television absorb the lion's share of charitable giving, while less publicized calamities that may be equally destructive are ignored. And eventually, "compassion fatigue" sets in, and people simply stop giving.

As a result, there is a built-in ceiling to the reach and effectiveness of nonprofit organizations. The need to constantly raise funds from donors uses up the time and energy of nonprofit leaders, when they should be planning the growth and expansion of their programs. No wonder they don't make much progress in their battles against social problems.

For all the good work that nonprofits, NGOs, and foundations do, they cannot be expected to solve the world's social ills. The very nature of these organizations as defined by society makes that virtually impossible.

Multilateral Institutions—The Development Elite

There is another category of organizations known as *multilateral institutions*. These are sponsored and funded by governments. Their mission is to eliminate poverty by promoting economic development in countries and regions that are lagging behind the prosperous nations of the northern hemisphere. Among the multilateral institutions, the World Bank leads the way. The World Bank has a private sector window called the International Finance Corporation. There are also four regional development banks, which closely follow the lead of the World Bank.

Unfortunately, in practice, the multilaterals have not achieved much in attaining their professed social goals either. Like governments, they are bureaucratic, conservative, slow-moving, and often self-serving. Like nonprofits, they are chronically underfunded, difficult to rely upon, and often inconsistent in their policies. As a result, the hundreds of billions of dollars they have invested over the past several decades have been largely ineffective—especially when measured against the goal of alleviating problems like global poverty.

Multilateral institutions like the World Bank name elimination of poverty as their overarching goal. But they focus exclusively on pursuing this goal through large-scale economic growth. This means that, as long as gross domestic product (GDP) is increasing in a country or a region, the World Bank feels that it is achieving its mission. This growth may be excruciatingly slow; it may be occurring without any benefits to the poor; it may even be occurring at the expense of the poor—but none of this persuades the World Bank to change its policies.

Growth is extremely important in bringing down poverty—there is no doubt about it. But to think that the only way to reduce poverty is to promote growth drives the policymaker to a straight theoretical path of building infrastructure to promote industrialization and mechanization.

There is a debate about the type of growth we should pursue based on serious concerns about the hazards of the World Bank's approach. "Pro-poor growth" and "anti-poor growth" are often treated as separate policy options. But my concern is different. Even if the policymaker identifies and works only for pro-poor growth, he is still missing the real issue. The objective of the policymaker is obviously to generate a spin in the economy so that the poor people are drawn into the spin. But in this conceptualization, the poor people are looked at as objects. In this frame of mind, policymakers miss the tremendous potential of the poor, particularly poor women and the children of poor families. They cannot see the poor as independent actors. They worry about the health, the education, and the jobs of the poor. They cannot see that the poor people can be actors themselves. The poor can be self-employed entrepreneurs and create jobs for others.

Furthermore, in their pursuit of growth, policymakers are focusing on efforts to energize well-established institutions. It never occurs to them that these institutions themselves may be contributing to creating or sustaining poverty. Institutions and policies that created poverty cannot be entrusted with the task of eliminating it. Instead, new institutions designed to solve the problems of the poor need to be created.

Another problem arises from the channel that donors use for the selection and implementation of projects. Both bilateral and multilateral donors work almost exclusively through the government machine. To make a real impact, they should be open to all segments of society and be prepared to utilize the creative capacity that is lying outside the government. I am sure that once donors begin to reach beyond the government, they'll come up with many exciting innovations. They can start with small projects and then let them grow if they see positive results.

Over the years, I have been watching the difference between the business styles of the World Bank and Grameen Bank. Theoretically, we are in the same business—helping people get out of poverty. But the ways in which we pursue this goal are very different.

Grameen Bank has always believed that if a borrower gets into trouble and cannot pay back her loan, it is our responsibility to help her. If we have a problem with our borrower, we tell ourselves that she is right—that we must have made some mistake in our policies or in our implementation of those policies. So we go back and fix ourselves. We make our rules very flexible so that they can be adjusted to the requirements of the borrower.

We also encourage our borrowers to make their own decisions about how to use the loans. If a borrower asks a Grameen staff member, "Please tell me what would be a good business idea for me," the staff member is trained to respond this way:

"I am sorry, but I am not smart enough to give you a good business idea. Grameen has lots of money, but no business ideas. That's why Grameen has come to you. You have the idea, we have the money. If Grameen had good business ideas, instead of giving the money to you, it would use the money itself and make more money."

We want our borrowers to feel important. When a borrower tries to shy away from a loan offer, saying that she has no business experience and does not want to take money, we work to convince her that she can come up with an idea for a business of her own. Will this be her very first experience of business? That is not a problem. Everything has to have a beginning somewhere, we tell her.

It is quite different with the World Bank. If you are lucky enough to be funded by them, they give you money. But they also give you ideas, expertise, training, plans, principles, and procedures. Your job is to follow the yellow lines, the green lines, and the red lines—to read the instructions at each step and obey them precisely. Yet, despite all this supervision, the projects don't always work out as planned. And when this happens, it is the recipient country that usually seems to bear the blame and to suffer the consequences.

There are also big differences in the incentive systems in the two organizations. In Grameen Bank, we have a five-star evaluation and incentive system for our staff and our branches. If a staff member maintains a 100 percent repayment record for all his borrowers (usually 600), he gets a green star. If he generates profit through his work, he gets another star—a blue star. If he mobilizes more in deposits than the amount of his outstanding loans, he gets a third star—a violet star. If he makes sure all the children of all his borrowers are in school, he gets a brown star. Finally, if all his borrowers move out of poverty, he gets a red star. The staff member can display the stars on his chest. He takes tremendous pride in this accomplishment.

By contrast, in the World Bank, a staff member's success is linked to the amount of the loans he has successfully negotiated, not the impact his work has made. We don't even consider the amount of loans made by a staff member in our reward system.

There have been campaigns to close down the World Bank and the International Monetary Fund. I have always opposed such campaigns. These are important global institutions created for very good causes. Rather than close them down, we should overhaul them completely. The world has changed so much since the time they were created, it is time to revisit them. It is obvious that the present architecture and work procedures are not adequate to do the job. If I were asked about my ideas, I'd emphasize the following:

- A new World Bank should be open to both government and private investors, with private investment following the social business model I will describe.

- It should work through governments, NGOs, and the new type of organization I am proposing in this book—social businesses.

- Instead of the International Finance Corporation, the World Bank should have another window—a social business window.

- The president of the World Bank should be selected by a search committee that will consider qualified candidates from anywhere in the world.

- The World Bank should work through semi-autonomous national branches, each with its own board of advisors, rather than powerless country offices.

- Evaluation of the staff should be related to the quality of their work and the impact it has made, not the volume of loans negotiated. If a project fails or performs poorly, the staff member involved in designing and promoting it should be held responsible.

- The World Bank should grade all projects each year on the basis of their impact on poverty reduction, and each country office should be graded on the same basis.

Corporate Social Responsibility

Still another response to the persistence of global poverty and other social ills has been a call for social responsibility on the part of business. NGOs, social activists, and politicians have put pressure on corporations to modify their policies in regard to labor, the environment, product quality, pricing, and fair trade.

To their credit, many businesses have responded. Not so long ago, many executives managed corporations with a "public be damned" attitude. They exploited their workers, polluted the environment, adulterated their products, and committed fraud—all in the name of profit. In most of the developed world, those days are long gone. Government regulation is one reason for this, and another is the movement for corporate social responsibility (CSR).

Millions of people are now better informed than ever about both the good and the bad things that corporations can do. Newspapers, magazines, television, radio, and the Internet investigate and publicize episodes of business wrongdoing. Many customers will avoid patronizing companies that harm society. As a result, most corporations are eager to create a positive image. And this has given a strong push to CSR.

CSR takes two basic forms. One, which might be called "weak CSR," has the credo: *Do no harm to people or the planet (unless that means sacrificing profit).* Companies that practice weak CSR are supposed to avoid selling defective goods, dumping factory wastes into rivers or landfills, or bribing government officials.

The second form, "strong CSR," says: *Do good for people and the planet (as long as you can do so without sacrificing profit).* Companies that practice strong CSR actively seek out opportunities to benefit others as they do business. For example, they may work to develop green products and practices, provide educational opportunities and health plans for their employees, and support initiatives to bring transparency and fairness to government regulation of business.

Is CSR a force that is leading to positive change among business leaders? Could it be that CSR is the mechanism we have been searching for, the tool with which at least some of the problems of society can be fixed?

Unfortunately, the answer is no. There are several reasons why.

The concept of socially responsible business is built on good intentions. But some corporate leaders misuse the concept to produce selfish benefits for their companies. Their philosophy seems to be: Make as much money as you can, even if you exploit the poor to do so—but then donate a tiny portion of the profits for social causes or create a foundation to do things that will promote your business interest. And then be sure to publicize how generous you are!

For companies like these, CSR will always be mere window dressing. In some cases, the same company that devotes a penny to CSR spends 99 cents on moneymaking projects that make social problems *worse*. This is not a formula for improving society!

There are a few companies whose leaders are sincerely interested in social change. Their numbers are growing, as a younger generation of managers rises to the top. Today's young executives, raised on television and the Internet, are more aware of social problems and more attuned to global concerns than any previous generation. They care about issues like climate change, child labor, the spread of AIDS, the rights of women, and world poverty. As these young people become corporate vice presidents, presidents, and CEOs, they bring these concerns into the boardroom. These new leaders are trying to make CSR into a core part of their business philosophy.

This is a well-intended effort. But it runs up against a basic problem. Corporate managers are responsible to those who own the businesses they run—either private owners or shareholders who invest through the stock market. In either case, those owners have only one objective: *To see the monetary value of their investment grow*. Thus, the managers who report to them must strive for one result: *To increase the value of the company*. And the only way to achieve this is by increasing the company's profits. In fact, maximizing profit is their legal obligation to their shareholders unless the shareholders mandate otherwise.

Companies that profess a belief in CSR always do so with this proviso, spoken or unspoken. In effect, they are saying, "We will do the socially responsible thing—so long as it doesn't prevent us from making the largest possible profit." Some proponents of CSR say that pursuit of profit and social responsibility need not be in conflict Sometimes this is true. Occasionally, through a happy accident, the needs of society and opportunities for high profits happen to coincide.

But what happens when profit and CSR do *not* go together? What about when the demands of the marketplace and the long term interests of society conflict? What will companies do? Experience shows that profit always wins out. Since the managers of business are responsible to the owners or shareholders, they *must* give profit the highest priority. If they were to accept reduced profit to promote social welfare, the owners would have reason to feel cheated and consider corporate social responsibility as corporate financial *irresponsibility.*

Thus, although advocates of CSR like to talk about the "triple bottom line" of financial, social, and environmental benefits by which companies should be measured, ultimately only one bottom line call the shots: financial profit.

Throughout the 1990s and into the new century, American auto companies have produced gas-guzzling, super-sized SUVs, which demand enormous resources to manufacture, use huge amounts of fuel and create terrible pollution. But they are very popular—and very profitable—and car makers continue to build and sell them by the millions. SUVs are bad for society, for the environment, and for the world, but the big auto companies' primary goal is to make profits, so they keep on doing something very socially irresponsible.

This example illustrates the most fundamental problem with CSR. By their nature, corporations are not equipped to deal with social problems. It's not because business executives are selfish, greedy, or bad. The problem lies with the very nature of business. Even more profoundly, it lies with the concept of business that is at the center of capitalism.

Capitalism Is a Half-Developed Structure

Capitalism takes a narrow view of human nature, assuming that people are one-dimensional beings concerned only with the pursuit of maximum profit. The concept of the free market, as generally understood, is based on this one-dimensional human being.

Mainstream free-market theory postulates that you are contributing to the society and the world in the best possible manner if you just concentrate on getting the most for yourself. When believers in this theory see gloomy news on television, they should begin to wonder whether the pursuit of profit is a cure-all, but they usually dismiss their doubts, blaming all the bad things in the world on "market failures." They have trained their minds to believe that well-functioning markets simply cannot produce unpleasant results.

I think things are going wrong not because of "market failures." The problem is much deeper than that. Mainstream free-market theory suffers from a "conceptualization failure," a failure to capture the essence of what it is to be human.

In the conventional theory of business, we've created a one-dimensional human being to play the role of business leader, the so-called entrepreneur. We've insulated him from the rest of life, the religious, emotional, political, and social. He is dedicated to one mission only—maximize profit. He is supported by other one-dimensional human beings who give him their investment money to achieve that mission. To quote Oscar Wilde, they know the price of everything and the value of nothing.

Our economic theory has created a one-dimensional world peopled by those who devote themselves to the game of free-market competition, in which victory is measured purely by profit. And since we are persuaded by the theory that the pursuit of profit is the best way to bring happiness to humankind, we enthusiastically imitate the theory, striving to transform ourselves into one-dimensional human beings. Instead of theory imitating reality, we force reality to imitate theory.

And today's world is so mesmerized by the success of capitalism it does not dare doubt that system's underlying economic theory.

Yet the reality is very different from the theory. People are not one-dimensional entities; they are excitingly multi-dimensional. Their emotions, beliefs, priorities, and behavior patterns can best be compared to the millions of shades we can produce from the three primary colors. Even the most famous capitalists share a wide range of interests and drives, which is why tycoons from Andrew Carnegie and the Rockefellers to Bill Gates have ultimately turned away from the game of profit to focus on higher objectives.

The presence of our multi-dimensional personalities means that not every business should be bound to serve the single objective of profit maximization.

While Yunus sees vast potential in the free market opened by globalization, others challenge his optimistic assessment of microcredit. In her study of microenterprise, Nancy Jurik argues that the use of free-market principals and for-profit management models offer limited success in lifting people out of poverty, as most fail to account for larger structural and institutional barriers, including inadequate housing, child care, and gender and racial discrimination faced by many poor people. Jurik suggests that "the impetus to define poor and marginalized individuals as entrepreneurs emerges from increased global insecurity and the decline of state responsibility for social welfare."[11] Robin Isserles views this matter similarly, arguing that many microfinance programs act as a cover for the rollback of state services that is occurring worldwide under the banner of neoliberalism. Microcredit may be best understood as "the policy version of bootstrap theory"—the idea that anyone can make it in the marketplace if he or she works hard enough. The same theory underlies the welfare-to-work legislation that Congress passed in 1996 (the Personal Responsibility and Work Opportunity Reconciliation Act). Advocates often tout these "bootstrap" programs on the basis of the number of loans repaid or the number of people taken off the welfare rolls. This is a mistake, Isserles contends. One must also consider whether people are indeed "making it" under current policies.[12] These critiques of microlending and other market-based approaches to solving social problems encourage us to think critically about the role of government in providing services and opportunities for its citizens.

---

[11]Nancy Jurik, *Bootstrap Dreams* (London Cornell University Press, 2005), p. 201.

[12]Robin G. Isserles, "Microcredit: The Rhetoric of Empowerment, the Reality of "Development as Usual," *Women's Studies Quarterly*, vol. 31 (3, 4): pp. 38–57 (Fall 2003). Retrieved May 12, 2010, from http://politicaleconomy.ca/courses/3365F/week_5_S_microcredit_rhetoric.pdf.

Economic arrangements can either aid or hinder the opportunity of people to lead healthy and meaningful lives. Globalization has fundamentally altered the economic arrangements that nations have devised, sometimes in unplanned ways. What follow is a classic reading that considers the connection between economic arrangements and social justice. Living amid the sharp social upheaval that occurred during European industrialization, Karl Marx (1818–1883) and Friedrich Engels were well-situated to comment on the social and economic effects of industrialization. Industrialization drew people from the rural, mostly agricultural areas into the city to work for a wage. The prevailing economic theory of the time was that increasing trade and opening avenues for exchange would benefit everyone. Trade would make goods cheaper and more plentiful while drawing the world together into one harmonic, inter-connected whole. But that was the theory. Marx and Engels were interested in the realities of industrial production and global commerce. They observed that industrialization increased poverty and disparities among wealthy and poor. In the following excerpt from the "Manifesto of the Communist Party"—a deliberately polemical piece—Marx and Engels predict many of the problems that contemporary critics of the global economy have described. This reading reminds us that the fundamental issues involving globalization have deep historical roots.

MANIFESTO OF THE COMMUNIST PARTY

KARL MARX AND FRIEDRICH ENGELS

A spectre is haunting Europe—the spectre of Communism. All the Powers of old Europe have entered into a holy alliance to exorcise this spectre: Pope and Czar, Metternich and Guizot, French Radicals and German police-spies.

Two things result from this fact.

I. Communism is already acknowledged by all European Powers to be itself a Power.

II. It is high time that Communists should openly, in the face of the whole world, publish their views, their aims, their tendencies, and meet this nursery tale of the Spectre of Communism with a Manifesto of the party itself.

To this end, Communists of various nationalities have assembled in London, and sketched the following Manifesto, to be published in the English, French, German, Italian, Flemish and Danish languages.

Bourgeois and Proletarians

The history of all hitherto existing societies is the history of class struggles.

Freeman and slave, patrician and plebeian, lord and serf, guild-master and journey-man, in a word, oppressor and oppressed, stood in constant opposition to one another, carried on an uninterrupted, now hidden, now open fight, a fight that each time ended, either in a revolutionary re-constitution of society at large, or in the common ruin of the contending classes.

In the earlier epochs of history, we find almost everywhere a complicated arrange-ment of society into various orders, a manifold gradation of social rank. In ancient Rome we have patricians, knights, plebeians, slaves; in the Middle Ages, feudal lords, vassals, guild-masters, journeymen, apprentices, serfs; in almost all of these classes, again, subordinate gradations.

The modern bourgeois society that has sprouted from the ruins of feudal society has not done away with class antagonisms. It has but established new classes, new conditions of oppression, new forms of struggle in place of the old ones. Our epoch, the epoch of the bourgeoisie, possesses, however, this distinctive feature: it has simplified the class antagonisms. Society as a whole is more and more splitting up into two great hostile camps, into two great classes, directly facing each other: Bourgeoisie and Proletariat.

From the serfs of the Middle Ages sprang the chartered burghers of the earliest towns. From these burgesses the first elements of the bourgeoisie were developed.

The discovery of America, the rounding of the Cape, opened up fresh ground for the rising bourgeoisie. The East-Indian and Chinese markets, the colonisation of America, trade with the colonies, the increase in the means of exchange and in com-modities generally, gave to commerce, to navigation, to industry, an impulse never before known, and thereby, to the revolutionary element in the tottering feudal soci-ety, a rapid development.

The feudal system of industry, under which industrial production was monopolised by closed guilds, now no longer sufficed for the growing wants of the new markets. The manufacturing system took its place. The guild-masters were pushed on one side by the manufacturing middle class; division of labour between the different corpo-rate guilds vanished in the face of division of labour in each single workshop.

Meantime the markets kept ever growing, the demand ever rising. Even manufacture no longer sufficed. Thereupon, steam and machinery revolutionised industrial pro-duction. The place of manufacture was taken by the giant, Modern Industry, the place of the industrial middle class, by industrial millionaires, the leaders of whole industrial armies, the modern bourgeois.

Modern industry has established the world-market, for which the discovery of America paved the way. This market has given an immense development to commerce, to navi-gation, to communication by land. This development has, in its time, reacted on the extension of industry; and in proportion as industry, commerce, navigation, railways extended, in the same proportion the bourgeoisie developed, increased its capital, and pushed into the background every class handed down from the Middle Ages.

Each step in the development of the bourgeoisie was accompanied by a corresponding political advance of that class. An oppressed class under the sway of the feudal nobility, an armed and self-governing association in the mediaeval commune; here independent urban republic (as in Italy and Germany), there taxable "third estate" of the monarchy (as in France), afterwards, in the period of manufacture proper, serving either the semi-feudal or the absolute monarchy as a counterpoise against the nobility, and, in fact, corner-stone of the great monarchies in general, the bourgeoisie has at last, since the establishment of Modern Industry and of the world-market, conquered for itself, in the modern representative State, exclusive political sway. The executive of the modern State is but a committee for managing the common affairs of the whole bourgeoisie.

The bourgeoisie, wherever it has got the upper hand, has put an end to all feudal, patriarchal, idyllic relations. It has pitilessly torn asunder the motley feudal ties that bound man to his "natural superiors," and has left remaining no other nexus between man and man than naked self-interest, than callous "cash payment." It has drowned the most heavenly ecstasies of religious fervour, of chivalrous enthusiasm, of philistine sentimentalism, in the icy water of egotistical calculation. It has resolved personal worth into exchange value, and in place of the numberless and indefeasible chartered freedoms, has set up that single, unconscionable freedom—Free Trade. In one word, for exploitation, veiled by religious and political illusions, naked, shameless, direct, brutal exploitation.

The bourgeoisie has stripped of its halo every occupation hitherto honoured and looked up to with reverent awe. It has converted the physician, the lawyer, the priest, the poet, the man of science, into its paid wage labourers.

The bourgeoisie has torn away from the family its sentimental veil, and has reduced the family relation to a mere money relation.

The need of a constantly expanding market for its products chases the bourgeoisie over the whole surface of the globe. It must nestle everywhere, settle everywhere, establish connexions everywhere.

The bourgeoisie has through its exploitation of the world-market given a cosmopolitan character to production and consumption in every country. To the great chagrin of Reactionists, it has drawn from under the feet of industry the national ground on which it stood. All old-established national industries have been destroyed or are daily being destroyed. They are dislodged by new industries, whose introduction becomes a life and death question for all civilised nations, by industries that no longer work up indigenous raw material, but raw material drawn from the remotest zones; industries whose products are consumed, not only at home, but in every quarter of the globe. In place of the old wants, satisfied by the productions of the country, we find new wants, requiring for their satisfaction the products of distant lands and climes. In place of the old local and national seclusion and self-sufficiency, we have intercourse in every direction, universal inter-dependence of nations. And as in material, so also in intellectual production. The intellectual creations of individual nations become common property.

National one-sidedness and narrow-mindedness become more and more impossible, and from the numerous national and local literatures, there arises a world literature.

The bourgeoisie, by the rapid improvement of all instruments of production, by the immensely facilitated means of communication, draws all, even the most barbarian, nations into civilisation. The cheap prices of its commodities are the heavy artillery with which it batters down all Chinese walls, with which it forces the barbarians' intensely obstinate hatred of foreigners to capitulate. It compels all nations, on pain of extinction, to adopt the bourgeois mode of production; it compels them to introduce what it calls civilisation into their midst, i.e., to become bourgeois themselves. In one word, it creates a world after its own image.

The bourgeoisie, during its rule of scarce one hundred years, has created more massive and more colossal productive forces than have all preceding generations together. Subjection of Nature's forces to man, machinery, application of chemistry to industry and agriculture, steam-navigation, railways, electric telegraphs, clearing of whole continents for cultivation, canalisation of rivers, whole populations conjured out of the ground—what earlier century had even a presentiment that such productive forces slumbered in the lap of social labour?

We see then: the means of production and of exchange, on whose foundation the bourgeoisie built itself up, were generated in feudal society. At a certain stage in the development of these means of production and of exchange, the conditions under which feudal society produced and exchanged, the feudal organisation of agriculture and manufacturing industry, in one word, the feudal relations of property became no longer compatible with the already developed productive forces; they became so many fetters. They had to be burst asunder; they were burst asunder.

Into their place stepped free competition, accompanied by a social and political constitution adapted to it, and by the economical and political sway of the bourgeois class.

A similar movement is going on before our own eyes. Modern bourgeois society with its relations of production, of exchange and of property, a society that has conjured up such gigantic means of production and of exchange, is like the sorcerer, who is no longer able to control the powers of the nether world whom he has called up by his spells. For many a decade past the history of industry and commerce is but the history of the revolt of modern productive forces against modern conditions of production, against the property relations that are the conditions for the existence of the bourgeoisie and of its rule. It is enough to mention the commercial crises that by their periodical return put on its trial, each time more threateningly, the existence of the entire bourgeois society. In these crises a great part not only of the existing products, but also of the previously created productive forces, are periodically destroyed. In these crises there breaks out an epidemic that, in all earlier epochs, would have seemed an absurdity—the epidemic of over-production. Society suddenly finds itself put back into a state of momentary barbarism; it appears as if a famine, a universal war of devastation had cut off the supply of every means of subsistence; industry and commerce seem to be destroyed; and why?

Because there is too much civilisation, too much means of subsistence, too much industry, too much commerce. The productive forces at the disposal of society no longer tend to further the development of the conditions of bourgeois property; on the contrary, they have become too powerful for these conditions, by which they are fettered, and so soon as they overcome these fetters, they bring disorder into the whole of bourgeois society, endanger the existence of bourgeois property. The conditions of bourgeois society are too narrow to comprise the wealth created by them. And how does the bourgeoisie get over these crises? On the one hand inforced destruction of a mass of productive forces; on the other, by the conquest of new markets, and by the more thorough exploitation of the old ones. That is to say, by paving the way for more extensive and more destructive crises, and by diminishing the means whereby crises are prevented.

The weapons with which the bourgeoisie felled feudalism to the ground are now turned against the bourgeoisie itself.

But not only has the bourgeoisie forged the weapons that bring death to itself; it has also called into existence the men who are to wield those weapons—the modern working class—the proletarians.

In proportion as the bourgeoisie, i.e., capital, is developed, in the same proportion is the proletariat, the modern working class, developed—a class of labourers, who live only so long as they find work, and who find work only so long as their labour increases capital. These labourers, who must sell themselves piece-meal, are a commodity, like every other article of commerce, and are consequently exposed to all the vicissitudes of competition, to all the fluctuations of the market.

Owing to the extensive use of machinery and to division of labour, the work of the proletarians has lost all individual character, and consequently, all charm for the workman. He becomes an appendage of the machine, and it is only the most simple, most monotonous, and most easily acquired knack, that is required of him. Hence, the cost of production of a workman is restricted, almost entirely, to the means of subsistence that he requires for his maintenance, and for the propagation of his race.

No sooner is the exploitation of the labourers by the manufacturer, so far at an end, that he receives his wages in cash, than he is set upon by the other portions of the bourgeoisie, the landlord, the shopkeeper, the pawnbroker, etc.

The lower strata of the middle class—the small tradespeople, shopkeepers, retired tradesmen generally, the handicraftsmen and peasants—all these sink gradually into the proletariat, partly because their diminutive capital does not suffice for the scale on which Modern Industry is carried on, and is swamped in the competition with the large capitalists, partly because their specialized skill is rendered worthless by the new methods of production. Thus the proletariat is recruited from all classes of the population.

The proletariat goes through various stages of development. With its birth begins its struggle with the bourgeoisie. At first the contest is carried on by individual labourers, then by the workpeople of a factory, then by the operatives of one trade, in one locality, against the individual bourgeois who directly exploits them. They direct their attacks not against the bourgeois conditions of production, but against the instruments of production themselves; they destroy imported wares that compete with their labour, they smash to pieces machinery, they set factories ablaze, they seek to restore by force the vanished status of the workman of the Middle Ages.

At this stage the labourers still form an incoherent mass scattered over the whole country, and broken up by their mutual competition. If anywhere they unite to form more compact bodies, this is not yet the consequence of their own active union, but of the union of the bourgeoisie, which class, in order to attain its own political ends, is compelled to set the whole proletariat in motion, and is moreover yet, for a time, able to do so. At this stage, therefore, the proletarians do not fight their enemies, but the enemies of their enemies, the remnants of absolute monarchy, the landowners, the non-industrial bourgeois, the petty bourgeoisie. Thus the whole historical movement is concentrated in the hands of the bourgeoisie; every victory so obtained is a victory for the bourgeoisie.

But with the development of industry the proletariat not only increases in number; it becomes concentrated in greater masses, its strength grows, and it feels that strength more. The various interests and conditions of life within the ranks of the proletariat are more and more equalised, in proportion as machinery obliterates all distinctions of labour, and nearly everywhere reduces wages to the same low level. The growing competition among the bourgeois, and the resulting commercial crises, make the wages of the workers ever more fluctuating. The unceasing improvement of machinery, ever more rapidly developing, makes their livelihood more and more precarious; the collisions between individual workmen and individual bourgeois take more and more the character of collisions between two classes. Thereupon the workers begin to form combinations (Trades Unions) against the bourgeois; they club together in order to keep up the rate of wages; they found permanent associations in order to make provision beforehand for these occasional revolts. Here and there the contest breaks out into riots.

Now and then the workers are victorious, but only for a time. The real fruit of their battles lies, not in the immediate result, but in the ever-expanding union of the workers. This union is helped on by the improved means of communication that are created by modern industry and that place the workers of different localities in contact with one another.

Finally, in times when the class struggle nears the decisive hour, the process of dissolution going on within the ruling class, in fact within the whole range of society, assumes such a violent, glaring character, that a small section of the ruling class cuts itself adrift, and joins the revolutionary class, the class that holds the future in its hands. Just as, therefore, at an earlier period, a section of the nobility went over to the bourgeoisie, so now a portion of the bourgeoisie goes over to the proletariat, and in particular, a portion of the bourgeois ideologists, who have raised themselves to the level of comprehending theoretically the historical movement as a whole.

Of all the classes that stand face to face with the bourgeoisie today, the proletariat alone is a really revolutionary class. The other classes decay and finally disappear in the face of Modern Industry; the proletariat is its special and essential product. The lower middle class, the small manufacturer, the shopkeeper, the artisan, the peasant, all these fight against the bourgeoisie, to save from extinction their existence as fractions of the middle class. They are therefore not revolutionary, but conservative. Nay more, they are reactionary, for they try to roll back the wheel of history. If by chance they are revolutionary, they are so only in view of their impending transfer into the proletariat, they thus defend not their present, but their future interests, they desert their own standpoint to place themselves at that of the proletariat.

The "dangerous class," the social scum, that passively rotting mass thrown-off by the lowest layers of old society; may, here and there, be swept into the movement by a proletarian revolution; its conditions of life, however, prepare it far more for the part of a bribed tool of reactionary intrigue.

In depicting the most general phases of the development of the proletariat, we traced the more or less veiled civil war, raging within existing society, up to the point where that war breaks out into open revolution, and where the violent overthrow of the bourgeoisie lays the foundation for the sway of the proletariat.

Hitherto, every form of society has been based, as we have already seen, on the antagonism of oppressing and oppressed classes. But in order to oppress a class, certain conditions must be assured to it under which it can, at least, continue its slavish existence. The serf, in the period of serfdom, raised himself to membership in the commune, just as the petty bourgeois, under the yoke of feudal absolutism, managed to develop into a bourgeois. The modern laborer, on the contrary, instead of rising with the progress of industry, sinks deeper and deeper below the conditions of existence of his own class. He becomes a pauper, and pauperism develops more rapidly than population and wealth. And here it becomes evident, that the bourgeoisie is unfit any longer to be the ruling class in society, and to impose its conditions of existence upon society as an over-riding law. It is unfit to rule because it is incompetent to assure an existence to its slave within his slavery, because it cannot help letting him sink into such a state, that it has to feed him, instead of being fed by him. Society can no longer live under this bourgeoisie, in other words, its existence is no longer compatible with society.

The immediate aim of the Communist is the same as that of all the other proletarian parties: formation of the proletariat into a class, overthrow of the bourgeois supremacy, conquest of political power by the proletariat.

Communism deprives no man of the power to appropriate the products of society; all that it does is to deprive him of the power to subjugate the labour of others by means of such appropriation.

It has been objected that upon the abolition of private property all work will cease, and universal laziness will overtake us.

According to this, bourgeois society ought long ago to have gone to the dogs through sheer idleness; for those of its members who work, acquire nothing, and those who acquire anything, do not work. The whole of this objection is but another expression of the tautology: that there can no longer be any wage-labour when there is no longer any capital. But don't wrangle with us so long as you apply, to our intended abolition of bourgeois property, the standard of your bourgeois notions of freedom, culture, law, etc. Your very ideas are but the outgrowth of the conditions of your bourgeois production and bourgeois property, just as your jurisprudence is but the will of your class made into a law for all, a will, whose essential character and direction are determined by the economical conditions of existence of your class.

The selfish misconception that induces you to transform into eternal laws of nature and of reason, the social forms springing from your present mode of production and form of property—historical relations that rise and disappear in the progress of production—this misconception you share with every ruling class that has preceded you. What you see clearly in the case of ancient property, what you admit in the case of feudal property, you are of course forbidden to admit in the case of your own bourgeois form of property.

We have seen above, that the first step in the revolution by the working class, is to raise the proletariat to the position of ruling as to win the battle of democracy.

The proletariat will use its political supremacy to wrest, by degrees, all capital from the bourgeoisie, to centralise all instruments of production in the hands of the State, i.e., of the proletariat organised as the ruling class; and to increase the total of productive forces as rapidly as possible.

Of course, in the beginning, this cannot be effected except by means of despotic inroads on the rights of property, and on the conditions of bourgeois production; by means of measures, therefore, which appear economically insufficient and untenable, but which, in the course of the movement, outstrip themselves, necessitate further inroads upon the old social order, and are unavoidable as a means of entirely revolutionising the mode of production.

These measures will of course be different in different countries.

Nevertheless in the most advanced countries, the following will be pretty generally applicable.

1. Abolition of property in land and application of all rents of land to public purposes.
2. A heavy progressive or graduated income tax.
3. Abolition of all right of inheritance.
4. Confiscation of the property of all emigrants and rebels.
5. Centralisation of credit in the hands of the State, by means of a national bank with State capital and an exclusive monopoly.
6. Centralisation of the means of communication and transport in the hands of the State.

7. Extension of factories and instruments of production owned by the State; the bringing into cultivation of waste-lands, and the improvement of the soil generally in accordance with a common plan.

8. Equal liability of all to labour. Establishment of industrial armies, especially for agriculture.

9. Combination of agriculture with manufacturing industries; gradual abolition of the distinction between town and country, by a more equable distribution of the population over the country.

10. Free education for all children in public schools. Abolition of children's factory labour in its present form.

When, in the course of development, class distinctions have disappeared, and all production has been concentrated in the hands of a vast association of the whole nation, the public power will lose its political character. Political power, properly so called, is merely the organised power of one class for oppressing another. If the proletariat during its contest with the bourgeoisie is compelled, by the force of circumstances, to organise itself as a class, if, by means of a revolution, it makes itself the ruling class, and, as such, sweeps away by force the old conditions of production, then it will, along with these conditions, have swept away the conditions for the existence of class antagonisms and of classes generally, and will thereby have abolished its own supremacy as a class.

In place of the old bourgeois society, with its classes and class antagonisms, we shall have an association, in which the free development of each is the condition for the free development of all.

WORKING MEN OF ALL COUNTRIES, UNITE!

Marx and Engels argues that economic justice is an artifact of prevailing economic arrangements. Once capitalism is introduced, it will tend to expand until it dominates all other forms of exchange. Can economic justice be achieved under capitalism? For Marx & Engels, the answer is no. Proponents of capitalism would, of course, disagree. The debate over the potential for achieving justice in a system organized around capitalism is an old one. A key question is whether government can actually control or regulate the excesses of capitalism. Can culture and civil society soften its harsh effects on those who lose the race for wealth in a market system?

Note the fundamental difference between calls to improve society by expanding opportunities for the market to operate, which tend to emphasize the considerable assets and competitive strengths of the private sector, and calls for greater social responsibility, which tend to emphasize more "social investment" in people by government. How should this social investment occur? Ideas under discussion include cooperatives, community organizations, and alternative forms of not-for-profit organizations. Vanna Gonzales has been studying this issue to determine how and to what extent specific types of social-welfare delivery systems work to improve the quality of social life. When do they foster greater social inclusion among marginalized groups? When do they contribute to the ability of social-welfare recipients to function effectively in civic life? Her work on Italian social cooperatives suggests that they can mitigate, and in some instances counteract, the social and civic isolation that economically marginalized people would otherwise suffer.[13]

Is a meritocratic system really possible, and even if it is, is a system of rewards based on merit a just system? The final reading in this chapter challenges the widely held belief in meritocracy in North America. Meritocracy assumes that jobs and other desirable positions in society should be distributed based on individual talent. This idea has deep cultural roots in our society; we often are reminded that employers seek to hire "the best person for the job." Yet as the following section details, a far more complex process actually takes place in the United States when someone is chosen for a job or granted admission into exclusive universities. Stephen McNamee and Robert K. Miller Jr. highlight the role that ideology plays in the myth that individuals get ahead in schooling and at work through their own merits. Why, then, is rugged individualism such an integral part of the American Dream?

THE MERITOCRACY MYTH
STEPHEN J. MCNAMEE

In the image of the American Dream, America is the land of opportunity. If you work hard enough and are talented enough, you can overcome any obstacle and achieve success. No matter where you start out in life, the sky is the limit. You can go as far as your talents and abilities can take you.

Although most Americans enthusiastically endorse this image in abstract terms, their lived experiences often tell them that factors other than individual merit play a role in getting ahead: "It takes money to make money" (inheritance); "It's not what you know but who you know" (connections); "What matters is being in the right place at the right time" (luck); "There is not an even playing field" (discrimination); and "He or she married into money" (marriage).

---

[13]Vanna Gonzales "A Different Kind of Social Enterprise: Social Cooperatives and the Development of Civic Capital," *Italy Community Development*, vol. 41 (1): p. 50 (2010).

Americans have great ambivalence about economic inequality. Indeed, Americans often simultaneously hold contradictory principles about how income and wealth should be distributed. While most Americans, for instance, proudly proclaim the virtues of "getting out of the system what you put into it" (meritocracy), they also steadfastly defend the right of individuals to dispose of their property when they die "as they personally see fit" (inheritance). These beliefs, however, pose a fundamental contradiction between freedom of choice at the individual level and equality of opportunity at the societal level. Simply put, to the extent that income and wealth are distributed on the basis of inheritance, they are not distributed on the basis of merit.

The principle of meritocracy is closely tied to the idea of the "American Dream." The latter term was first popularized by historian James Truslow Adams in his 1931 best-selling book, *The Epic of America*. Adams defined it as "that dream of a land in which life should be better and richer and fuller for every man, with opportunity for each according to his ability or achievement" (1931, 404). In a general way, people understand the idea of the American Dream as the fulfillment of the promise of meritocracy. The American Dream is fundamentally rooted in the historical experience of the United States as a new nation of immigrants. Unlike European societies historically dominated by hereditary aristocracies, the ideal in America was that its citizens were "free" to achieve on their own merits. The American Dream was the hope of fulfillment of individual freedom and the chance to succeed in the "New World."

These meritocratic tenets are deeply ingrained in the American consciousness. Survey research repeatedly confirms that most Americans enthusiastically subscribe to them. But the endorsement of meritocracy is not evenly distributed among Americans. Reflecting the reality of their life circumstances, nonwhites and those with less income are more likely to identify "family background," "who you know," and "discrimination" as relevant factors in where people end up in the system. Nevertheless, the overall pattern is clear: Most Americans not only believe that meritocracy is the way the system *should* work; they also believe that meritocracy is the way the system does work.

In industrial societies such as the United States, inequality is justified by an ideology of meritocracy. America is seen as the land of opportunity where people get out of the system what they put into it. Ostensibly, the most talented, hardest working, and most virtuous get ahead. The lazy, shiftless, and indolent fall behind. You may not be held responsible for where you start out in life, but you are responsible for where you end up. If you are truly meritorious, you will overcome any obstacle and succeed.

The acceptance of meritocracy in America is predicated not on what "is" but on the *belief* that the system of inequality is "fair" and it "works." According to the ideology of meritocracy, inequality is seen to be "fair" because everyone presumably has an equal (or at least an adequate) chance to succeed, and success is determined by *individual* merit. The system ostensibly "works" because it is seen as providing an individual incentive to achieve that is good for society as a whole; that is, those who are most talented, the hardest working, and the most virtuous *get* and *should get* the most rewards.

Individualism and The Origins of The American Dream

One source of American individualism is the religious backgrounds of the European colonists in America, who were mostly members of various Protestant religious sects. These sects were part of the many splinter groups that formed in the aftermath of the Protestant Reformation, which began in Europe in the sixteenth century. The conquering English population, as part of the spoils of victory, established the rules of the game. Those who followed had to adopt those rules or risk isolation or exclusion. In this way, the cultural ideals of the conquering white Anglo-Saxon Protestants (WASPs) became the dominant cultural force in America.

The constellation of cultural values that became known as the "Protestant ethic" found its greatest expression among the various Puritan sects that formed the dominant religious backgrounds of the early American colonists. The principles of the Protestant ethic were analyzed by the German sociologist Max Weber in his classic work, *The Protestant Ethic and the Spirit of Capitalism* (1905). The core of Weber's argument is that the twin ethics of diligence and asceticism were associated with the early development of capitalism. Diligence stimulated productivity, and asceticism encouraged savings. Capitalism—particularly early capitalism—needed both a highly motivated labor force and investment "capital." Because people worked hard, they became productive, while the self-denial of asceticism encouraged saving by discouraging self-indulgence.

As part of the break with Catholicism, Protestantism emphasized an individual rather than communal relationship with God. Puritans in particular eschewed Catholicism's communalism and the elaborate ritual system associated with it. Instead, the emphasis was on a direct relationship with God through individual prayer and reading of the Bible. The Protestant Reformation also shifted the traditional Catholic view of work as "punishment" for "original sin" to the idea of work as a sacred calling, a mission from God to subdue nature and gain control over it. People should become instruments of God's will on earth and were called upon to transform the world and remake it in God's image, what Weber called "world mastery."

These Puritan values of individual "industry, frugality, and prudence" were reflected in early American moralistic novels (Wiess 1969) and were integrated into the core of an emerging national culture. The best known of these was a popular series of 107 "rags to riches" novels by Horatio Alger (1832–1899). Alger was the son of a Unitarian minister and a Harvard graduate who for a short time also served in the ministry. Puritan themes were reinforced as well in a series of widely used early American primary school "readers," written by William McGuffey, who was also a minister turned writer.

Making the Grade: Education and Mobility

According to the American Dream, education identifies and selects intelligent, talented, and motivated individuals and provides educational training in direct proportion to individual merit. The amounts and kinds of education attained are taken as measures of merit and are used as criteria of eligibility for occupations and the material awards attached to them. In the American Dream, education is the "engine" of meritocracy. Most Americans believe that education is the key to success: to get ahead in life you need a "good education."

A radically different view of the role of education sees education not as a cause but as an effect of social class. Working-class children get working-class educations, middle-class children get middle-class educations, and upper-class children get upper-class educations. In each case, children from these different class backgrounds are groomed for different roles that they will likely fill as adults. In this way, education largely reproduces existing inequalities across generations.

In America, as in all contemporary industrial societies, education has come to play an important role in selecting people for positions in the occupational structure. The overall relationship between education and future income is clear—the more education, the greater the chances of higher income (see table 5.1).

The close connection between "getting ahead" and education, however, is relatively recent. At first education seemed an unlikely avenue. Businessmen, many of whom were "self-made men" with little formal schooling, graduates of the "school of hard knocks"—typically thought that schooling made young people unfit for the "real world" or at least didn't prepare them very well for it. Gradually, however, education increasingly came to be viewed as a replacement for the faltering promise of the family farm or business entrepreneurship. Andrew Carnegie, for example, believed that schools and colleges should be made into "ladders upon which the aspiring can rise" (1899, 663). But at the end of the nineteenth century, America's schools hardly constituted a well-organized ladder to success. It was during the first few decades of the twentieth century that the patchwork of American schooling was reorganized into the ladder structure that people like Andrew Carnegie advocated, thereby providing

Table 5.1. Median Annual Income for All Workers Eighteen Years and Over by Educational Attainment, 2001

Education Level	Median Income ($)
Professional degree	71,606
Doctorate degree	63,952
Master's degree	49,324
Bachelor's degree	37,203
Associate degree	28,563
Some college, no degree	21,658
High school graduate, including GED	19,900
Not high school graduate	11,864

Source: Adapted from U.S. Census Bureau, *Current Population Survey, Detailed Tables PPL-169,* Table 8 (Washington, D.C.: U.S. Government Printing Office, 2002).

a mechanism to keep the American promise of opportunity at the very time when fundamental changes in the economy were threatening to destroy it.

Since World War II, growth in corporate size and concentration have continued, and opportunities for upward mobility through various forms of entrepreneurship have continued to decline. As this occurred, young people began to see diplomas and degrees as an alternate and less risky means to upward mobility as tickets to the newer white-collar jobs that had proliferated. This view was reflected in public support for the building of secondary means of providing training and skills needed to fill occupations in America's modern and changing industrial economy. The educational requirements of jobs in industrial society constantly increase as a result of technological change. The proportion of jobs that require low skill declines while the proportion that requires high skill increases. What is more, the same jobs are continually upgraded in their skill requirements. The result is educational expansion: educational requirements for employment continually rise and more and more people are required to spend longer and longer periods in school. The most obvious meritocratic aspect of this theory is its clear claim that the opportunity to acquire training and skills is directly proportional to individual merit: talent and ability. By implication, educational expansion should reduce socioeconomic inequality, since educational opportunity is apportioned on the basis of individual merit, which is distributed equally among the social classes.

In economics, human capital theory (Schultz 1961) suggests that human resources are a form of capital. Humans can invest in themselves to increase their capital, thereby increasing their productivity and their earnings. In modern society, the education system is the most important means through which individuals can invest in their "human capital" (skills and knowledge). In short, education increases productive capacities and thus earnings. The argument has considerable appeal: The worker is no mere "wage-earner" who holds no property and controls neither the work process nor the product of his labor, but instead is transformed into a capitalist. In this view, the worker is a holder of capital—human capital—and has the capacity to invest in himself through education.

Social Class and Education

Meritocracy requires equality of educational opportunity. The schooling system, however, provides the most privileged in society with greater opportunities to succeed and fewer chances to fail than it does for those from less privileged backgrounds. This is so because it frequently fails to identify and reward the potential and achievements of those who do not inherit the social, cultural, and economic capital of the privileged classes.

French sociologist Pierre Bourdieu emphasized that schools are instruments of social and cultural reproduction, which are means of social class reproduction. According to Bourdieu, schools do not produce cultural capital or even the means to appropriate it. Instead, they recognize it, reward the possession of it, and certify its possession by differentially awarding educational credentials in proportion to the amount of cultural capital possessed. Children from lower classes with less cultural capital are eliminated from the system because of their cultural capital deficits, or self-eliminate as they come to recognize their low objective chances of success within the system. Thus, school tends to reinforce the cultural capital inequalities based on differences in family socioeconomic status.

The Social Construction of "Individual" Merit

Education certifies individual skills, knowledge, and other competencies in the form of diplomas, certificates, and degrees. These certifications are not merely purchased or assigned; individuals must demonstrate competencies through examination and other forms of assessment. Such certifications therefore are widely regarded as evidence of personal achievement and individual merit. The opportunity to acquire such competencies, however, is socially constructed. In this way, education performs a dual role in both certifying individual achievement and reproducing existing inequalities.

There are several ways in which the social construction of individual merit occurs. Children from privileged families, for instance, are more likely to be the beneficiaries of home environments that promote cognitive development and provide the social and cultural capital needed to do well in school. Therefore, privileged children are already ahead of the less privileged in cognitive ability, social skills, and cultural capital when they enter school. They are also more likely to attend "good" schools that are staffed by competent and experienced teachers, provide an academic college preparatory curriculum, and are populated by other privileged students. Once in school, teacher expectations build on these initial advantages: Teachers expect more of children from higher class backgrounds, and differential treatment based on these expectations leads to better performance among these children.

Another practice that jeopardizes equality of educational opportunity is tracking. Approximately five out of six U.S. public schools use some form of tracking in which children are placed in different groups or tracks that prepare some for college and others for vocational skills that do not lead to college. There has been much research on the factors that influence track placement and the outcomes of such placement, but conclusions are complex because of the variety of tracking systems in use. One early study showed that all factors that could conceivably be taken to measure cognitive ability and academic performance *together explain less than half of the variation in track placement*. So much for the argument that individual "merit" measured by cognitive ability and academic performance is the primary determinant of track placement. While many studies do show that measured intellectual skills are factors most directly responsible for track placement, recall that cognitive skills and academic performance are influenced by family SES. In short, tracking has tended to separate children by class background and race.

The outcomes of tracking are also fairly clear. First, track mobility is typically low: Once placed in a low track, it is difficult to "move up," and for those placed in a high track, it is difficult to do poorly enough to "move down." In short, tracking affects teacher expectations, access to quality teachers, and access to courses needed for college eligibility. Tracking produces self-fulfilling prophecies. Children in higher college preparatory tracks tend to improve in academic achievement over the years, while those in lower tracks tend to perform at levels that make them ineligible for higher education. Children in higher tracks are less likely to drop out of school, have higher educational aspirations, and are more likely to attend college. In short, tracking works to reinforce class differences and has an independent effect of further differentiating children in terms of family background.

Has Educational Expansion Led to Greater Social Mobility?

By now it should be clear that some Americans do "get ahead." However, we have also shown that the extent of such mobility has been exaggerated and that the forces that reproduce inequalities across generations are strong.

Have advantages of the privileged been reduced by the expansion of education? If we examine the correlation between family background and educational attainments over time, we see that differences among socioeconomic groups have not narrowed despite the vast expansion of schooling. This is because high-status parents continue to have greater economic, social, and cultural resources to provide better educational opportunities for their children than do lower-status parents.

What is more, school systems have responded to increased demand for credentials in ways that have not reduced class advantages. Educational expansion has been accompanied by the development of an elaborately differentiated structure of tiers and quality levels. Lower-status children tend to be limited to the lower tiers of the system and channeled into the lower quality sectors within tiers, while upper-status children are more likely to make it into the higher tiers and enjoy the advantages of the higher quality sectors within each tier. In short, educational expansion has simply led to segregation within tier and the transfer of class differences to higher levels of the system. For example, when working-class children became better represented in high school, college became the key to higher social status. When working- and lower-middle-class children began to enter college in larger numbers, the system shifted again to a higher point, and graduate or professional school has become the key to higher social status. Thus, increases in educational attainment are completely compatible with stable levels of social inequality and class reproduction.

If college admissions and attendance were based mostly on cognitive ability or intelligence, there would be much less class reproduction. But as we have noted, socioeconomic inequality operates to weaken the relationship between cognitive ability and college attendance. Family background differences in college completion are also striking. Even at the height of the equal opportunity era in the United States—roughly from the end of World War II until 1980—bright children whose fathers had blue-collar occupations were less likely than other children to obtain a college degree. Using General Social Survey data, sociologists Hout, Raftery, and Bell (1993, 46) found that unskilled blue-collar workers' children who had high IQs (top 14% on a word recognition test) who reached college age in the 1950s and early

1960s had slightly more than a 50% chance of completing college. This was significantly lower than the 80% chance of graduating enjoyed by high IQ children who had professional or managerial fathers. And it was not even as good a chance as the 70% completion rate enjoyed by children of all IQ levels who were lucky enough to have been born into families in the top tenth of the occupational hierarchy. In short, controlling for cognitive ability, children from privileged backgrounds are more likely to attend college, to start college right out of high school, to go to a four-year institution, to go to a "quality" college or university, and to graduate on time.

Interestingly, college attendance seems to provide significant occupational and income rewards only for those who graduate. On average, those who have completed "some college" (one to three years) do not earn much more than those who have only completed high school (see table 5.1). This strongly suggests that it is the *credential*, and not the increments of information or skill provided by each additional year, that counts.

We conclude that education in America, including higher education, is not governed by strict principles of meritocracy, but instead reflects, legitimizes, and reproduces class inequalities. Those from privileged families (top quarter of an index of socioeconomic status composed of parents' education, income and occupation) are three times as likely as those from less privileged families to be admitted to elite highly selective colleges and universities. This is because all the advantages of class that we have already discussed—inherited familial economic resources (which translate into "quality education" and high educational aspirations), social capital (which include parental "connections" and positive peer influences), and cultural capital—collectively produce K–12 educational outcomes, including high grade point averages, standardized and AP test scores, and SAT scores, that are the primary selection criteria for America's "best" colleges and universities. Thus, the advantages of high class produce the credentials sought by America's elite universities. But there are additional advantages that accrue to class privilege, ranging from the simple ability to *pay* for an elite private college or university education, to the financial ability to take advantage of "early acceptance" programs at such institutions, to elaborate, back-channel "slotting" operations in which highly connected and expert high school and prep counselors work closely with admissions officials to virtually place high SES students at these institutions. Finally, "the increasing concentration of wealth and power among [these select elite institutions] . . . sets them apart from the public colleges and universities in terms of their respective roles in the nurturing of young talent for positions of leadership and lives of intellectual creativity". In short, America's system of higher education is clearly not an "engine of meritocracy" but rather a basic component in a system that reproduces unequal starting points from one generation to the next.

Summary

Being bright, working hard, and getting more education do help people get ahead. But there is more to it than that. First, the competition for success is structured by an educational system that does not provide equality of opportunity. Second, quite independent of individual ability, the demands of a complex and changing corporate economy condition opportunities and the likelihood for success.

Equality of educational opportunity is a crucial component of the American Dream, but it has never come close to existing in America. Family socioeconomic status and other ascribed characteristics directly and indirectly affect educational attainment. Schools both reflect and re-create existing inequalities in society. Schools reward children of the privileged by certifying and enhancing their social and cultural capital. On the other hand, schools punish children of lower socioeconomic status for their lack of such capital, consigning them to teachers, curricula, tracks, and the self-fulfilling prophecies of low expectations that these produce. The results are that less privileged children are awarded fewer and lower-valued credentials, and inequality is largely reproduced across generations.

The inequalities reproduced across generations are substantial but far from perfect. In part this is because some parents, regardless of class position, are more successful in promoting the futures of their children. And some children, regardless of class position, are more capable than others. As a result, some rich kids fail and some poor kids succeed. These exceptions, however infrequently they do occur, help to sustain at least the outward appearance of meritocracy and the American Dream.

Discussion Questions

- What are some of the limitations of charities and NGOs in reducing world poverty?

- What would be the fairest and most useful way to evaluate a policy idea like micro-credit for poor women?

- Despite unprecedented crop yields, starvation continues to be widespread globally. How can we explain this seeming paradox?